Canada's Residential Schools

Volume 6

MCGILL-QUEEN'S INDIGENOUS AND NORTHERN STUDIES
(In memory of Bruce G. Trigger)
Sarah Carter and Arthur J. Ray, Editors

For a complete Series list please visit
www.mqup.ca

Canada's Residential Schools:
Reconciliation

The Final Report of the
Truth and Reconciliation
Commission of Canada

Volume 6

Published for the
Truth and Reconciliation Commission

by

McGill-Queen's University Press
Montreal & Kingston • London • Chicago

2015

Truth and Reconciliation Commission of Canada

Website: www.trc.ca

ISBN 978-0-7735-4661-5 (v. 6 : bound).   ISBN 978-0-7735-4662-2 (v. 6 : paperback).

Reprinted 2016, 2021

Printed in Canada on acid-free paper

Funded by the Financé par le
Government gouvernement
of Canada du Canada

Canada

Canada Council Conseil des arts
for the Arts   du Canada

We acknowledge the support of the Canada Council for the Arts.
Nous remercions le Conseil des arts du Canada de son soutien.

Library and Archives Canada Cataloguing in Publication
Truth and Reconciliation Commission of Canada
[Canada's residential schools]
    Canada's residential schools : the final report of the Truth and Reconciliation Commission of Canada.

(McGill–Queen's Indigenous and northern studies ; 80–86)
Includes bibliographical references and index.
Contents: v. 1. The history. Part 1, origins to 1939 — The history. Part 2, 1939 to 2000 — v. 2. The Inuit and
    northern experience — v. 3. The Métis experience — v. 4. The missing children and unmarked burials
    report — v. 5. The legacy — v. 6. Reconciliation

Issued in print and electronic formats.
ISBN 978-0-7735-4649-3 (v. 1, pt. 1 : bound).   ISBN 978-0-7735-4650-9 (v. 1, pt. 1 : paperback).
ISBN 978-0-7735-4651-6 (v. 1, pt. 2 : bound).   ISBN 978-0-7735-4652-3 (v. 1, pt. 2 : paperback).
ISBN 978-0-7735-4653-0 (v. 2 : bound).   ISBN 978-0-7735-4654-7 (v. 2 : paperback).
ISBN 978-0-7735-4655-4 (v. 3 : bound).   ISBN 978-0-7735-4656-1 (v. 3 : paperback).
ISBN 978-0-7735-4657-8 (v. 4 : bound).   ISBN 978-0-7735-4658-5 (v. 4 : paperback).
ISBN 978-0-7735-4659-2 (v. 5 : bound).   ISBN 978-0-7735-4660-8 (v. 5 : paperback).
ISBN 978-0-7735-4661-5 (v. 6 : bound).   ISBN 978-0-7735-4662-2 (v. 6 : paperback).
ISBN 978-0-7735-9817-1 (v. 1, pt. 1 : ePDF).   ISBN 978-0-7735-9818-8 (v.1, pt. 1 : ePUB).
ISBN 978-0-7735-9819-5 (v. 1, pt. 2 : ePDF).   ISBN 978-0-7735-9820-1 (v. 1, pt. 2 : ePUB).
ISBN 978-0-7735-9821-8 (v. 2 : ePDF).   ISBN 978-0-7735-9822-5 (v. 2 : ePUB).
ISBN 978-0-7735-9823-2 (v. 3 : ePDF).   ISBN 978-0-7735-9824-9 (v. 3 : ePUB).
ISBN 978-0-7735-9825-6 (v. 4 : ePDF).   ISBN 978-0-7735-9826-3 (v. 4 : ePUB).
ISBN 978-0-7735-9827-0 (v. 5 : ePDF).   ISBN 978-0-7735-9828-7 (v. 5 : ePUB).
ISBN 978-0-7735-9829-4 (v. 6 : ePDF).   ISBN 978-0-7735-9830-0 (v. 6 : ePUB)

1. Native peoples—Canada—Residential schools. 2. Native peoples—Education—Canada.
3. Native peoples—Canada—Government relations. 4. Native peoples—Canada—Social conditions.
5. Native peoples—Canada—History. I. Title. II. Series: McGill–Queen's Indigenous and northern studies ; 80–86

E96.5.T78 2016   971.004'97   C2015-905971-2
                                            C2015-905972-0

Contents

2

Canada's Residential Schools

Volume 6

Introduction

To some people, "reconciliation" is the re-establishment of a conciliatory state. However, this is a state that many Aboriginal people assert has never existed between Aboriginal and non-Aboriginal people. To others, "reconciliation," in the context of Indian residential schools, is similar to dealing with a situation of family violence. It is about coming to terms with events of the past in a manner that overcomes conflict and establishes a respectful and healthy relationship among people going forward. It is in the latter context that the Truth and Reconciliation Commission of Canada (TRC) has approached the question of reconciliation.

To the Commission, "reconciliation" is about establishing and maintaining a mutually respectful relationship between Aboriginal and non-Aboriginal peoples in this country. For that to happen, there has to be awareness of the past, acknowledgement of the harm that has been inflicted, atonement for the causes, and action to change behaviour.

We are not there yet. The relationship between Aboriginal and non-Aboriginal peoples is not a mutually respectful one. But we believe we can get there, and we believe we can maintain it. Our ambition is to show how we can do that.

In 1996, the *Report of the Royal Commission on Aboriginal Peoples* urged Canadians to begin a national process of reconciliation that would have set the country on a bold new path, fundamentally changing the very foundations of Canada's relationship with Aboriginal peoples. Much of what the Royal Commission had to say has been ignored by government; a majority of its recommendations were never implemented. But the report and its findings opened people's eyes and changed the conversation about the reality for Aboriginal people in this country.

In 2015, as the Truth and Reconciliation Commission of Canada wraps up its work, the country has a rare second chance to seize a lost opportunity for reconciliation. We live in a twenty-first-century global world. At stake is Canada's place as a prosperous, just, and inclusive democracy within that global world. At the TRC's first National Event in Winnipeg, Manitoba, in 2010, residential school Survivor Alma Mann Scott said,

> The healing is happening—the reconciliation.... I feel that there's some hope for us not just as Canadians, but for the world, because I know I'm not the only one. I know that Anishinaabe people across Canada, First Nations, are not the only

ones. My brothers and sisters in New Zealand, Australia, Ireland—there's different areas of the world where this type of stuff happened.... I don't see it happening in a year, but we can start making changes to laws and to education systems
... so that we can move forward.[1]

Reconciliation must support Aboriginal peoples as they heal from the destructive
legacies of colonization that have wreaked such havoc in their lives. But it must do
even more. Reconciliation must inspire Aboriginal and non-Aboriginal peoples to
transform Canadian society so that our children and grandchildren can live together
in dignity, peace, and prosperity on these lands we now share.

The urgent need for reconciliation runs deep in Canada. Expanding public dialogue and action on reconciliation beyond residential schools will be critical in the
coming years. Although some progress has been made, significant barriers to reconciliation remain. The relationship between the federal government and Aboriginal
peoples is deteriorating. Instead of moving towards reconciliation, there have been
divisive conflicts over Aboriginal education, child welfare, and justice. The daily news
has been filled with reports of controversial issues ranging from the call for a national
inquiry on violence towards Aboriginal women and girls to the impact of the economic
development of lands and resources on Treaties and Aboriginal title and rights.[2] The
courts continue to hear Aboriginal rights cases, and new litigation has been filed by
Survivors of day schools not covered under the Indian Residential Schools Settlement
Agreement, as well as by victims of the "Sixties Scoop."[3] The promise of reconciliation,
which seemed so imminent back in 2008 when the prime minister, on behalf of all
Canadians, apologized to Survivors, has faded.

Too many Canadians know little or nothing about the deep historical roots of
these conflicts. This lack of historical knowledge has serious consequences for First
Nations, Inuit, and Métis peoples, and for Canada as a whole. In government circles,
it makes for poor public policy decisions. In the public realm, it reinforces racist attitudes and fuels civic distrust between Aboriginal peoples and other Canadians.[4] Too
many Canadians still do not know the history of Aboriginal peoples' contributions to
Canada, or understand that by virtue of the historical and modern Treaties negotiated
by our government, we are all Treaty people. History plays an important role in reconciliation; to build for the future, Canadians must look to, and learn from, the past.

As Commissioners, we understood from the start that although reconciliation could
not be achieved during the TRC's lifetime, the country could and must take ongoing
positive and concrete steps forward. Although the Commission has been a catalyst
for deepening our national awareness of the meaning and potential of reconciliation,
it will take many heads, hands, and hearts, working together, at all levels of society to
maintain momentum in the years ahead. It will also take sustained political will at all
levels of government and concerted material resources.

The thousands of Survivors who publicly shared their residential school experiences at TRC events in every region of this country have launched a much-needed dialogue about what is necessary to heal themselves, their families, their communities, and the nation. Canadians have much to gain from listening to the voices, experiences, and wisdom of Survivors, Elders, and Traditional Knowledge Keepers—and much more to learn about reconciliation. Aboriginal peoples have an important contribution to make to reconciliation. Their knowledge systems, oral histories, laws, and connections to the land have vitally informed the reconciliation process to date, and are essential to its ongoing progress.

At a Traditional Knowledge Keepers Forum sponsored by the TRC, Anishinaabe Elder Mary Deleary spoke about the responsibility for reconciliation that both Aboriginal and non-Aboriginal people carry. She emphasized that the work of reconciliation must continue in ways that honour the ancestors, respect the land, and rebalance relationships.

> I'm so filled with belief and hope because when I hear your voices at the table, I hear and know that the responsibilities that our ancestors carried ... are still being carried ... [E]ven through all of the struggles, even through all of what has been disrupted ... we can still hear the voice of the land. We can hear the care and love for the children. We can hear about our law. We can hear about our stories, our governance, our feasts, [and] our medicines.... We have work to do. That work we are [already] doing as [Aboriginal] peoples. Our relatives who have come from across the water [non-Aboriginal people], you still have work to do on your road.... The land is made up of the dust of our ancestors' bones. And so to reconcile with this land and everything that has happened, there is much work to be done ... in order to create balance.[5]

At the Victoria Regional Event in 2012, Survivor Archie Little said,

> [For] me reconciliation is righting a wrong. And how do we do that? All these people in this room, a lot of non-Aboriginals, a lot of Aboriginals that probably didn't go to residential school; we need to work together.... My mother had a high standing in our cultural ways. We lost that. It was taken away.... And I think it's time for you non-Aboriginals ... to go to your politicians and tell them that we have to take responsibility for what happened. We have to work together.[6]

The Reverend Stan McKay of the United Church, who is also a Survivor, believes that reconciliation can happen only when everyone accepts responsibility for healing in ways that foster respect.

> [There must be] a change in perspective about the way in which Aboriginal peoples would be engaged with Canadian society in the quest for reconciliation.... [We cannot] perpetuate the paternalistic concept that only Aboriginal peoples are in need of healing.... The perpetrators are wounded and marked by history in

ways that are different from the victims, but both groups require healing.... How can a conversation about reconciliation take place if all involved do not adopt an attitude of humility and respect? ... We all have stories to tell and in order to grow in tolerance and understanding we must listen to the stories of others.[7]

Over the past five years, the Truth and Reconciliation Commission of Canada has urged Canadians not to wait until its final report was issued before contributing to the reconciliation process. We have been encouraged to see that across the country, many people have been answering that call.

The youth of this country are taking up the challenge of reconciliation. Aboriginal and non-Aboriginal youth who attended TRC National Events made powerful statements about why reconciliation matters to them. At the Alberta National Event in Edmonton in March 2014, an Indigenous youth spoke on behalf of a national Indigenous and non-Indigenous collaboration called the 4Rs Youth Movement. Jessica Bolduc said,

We have re-examined our thoughts and beliefs around colonialism, and have made a commitment to unpack our own baggage, and to enter into a new relationship with each other, using this momentum, to move our country forward, in light of the 150th anniversary of the Confederation of Canada in 2017.

At this point in time, we ask ourselves, "What does that anniversary mean for us, as Indigenous youth and non-Indigenous youth, and how do we arrive at that day with something we can celebrate together?" ... Our hope is that, one day, we will live together, as recognized nations, within a country we can all be proud of.[8]

In 2013, at the British Columbia National Event in Vancouver, where over 5,000 elementary and secondary school students attended Education Day, several non-Aboriginal youth talked about what they had learned. Matthew Meneses said, "I'll never forget this day. This is the first day they ever told us about residential schools. If I were to see someone who's Aboriginal, I'd ask them if they can speak their language because I think speaking their language is a pretty cool thing." Antonio Jordao said, "It makes me sad for those kids. They took them away from their homes—it was torture, it's not fair. They took them away from their homes. I don't agree with that. It's really wrong. That's one of the worst things that Canada did." Cassidy Morris said, "It's good that we're finally learning about what happened." Jacqulyn Byers told us, "I hope that events like this are able to bring closure to the horrible things that happened, and that a whole lot of people now recognize that the crime happened and that we need to make amends for it."[9]

At the same National Event, TRC Honorary Witness Patsy George paid tribute to the strength of Aboriginal women and their contributions to the reconciliation process despite the oppression and violence they have experienced.

Women have always been a beacon of hope for me. Mothers and grandmothers in the lives of our children, and in the survival of our communities, must be recognized and supported. The justified rage we all feel and share today must be turned into instruments of transformation of our hearts and our souls, clearing the ground for respect, love, honesty, humility, wisdom, and truth. We owe it to all those who suffered, and we owe it to the children of today and tomorrow. May this day and the days ahead bring us peace and justice.[10]

Aboriginal and non-Aboriginal Canadians from all walks of life spoke to us about the importance of reaching out to one another in ways that create hope for a better future. Whether one is First Nations, Inuit, Métis, a descendant of European settlers, a member of a minority group that suffered historical discrimination in Canada, or a new Canadian, we all inherit both the benefits and obligations of Canada. We are all Treaty people who share responsibility for taking action on reconciliation.

Without truth, justice, and healing, there can be no genuine reconciliation. Reconciliation is not about 'closing a sad chapter of Canada's past' but about opening new healing pathways of reconciliation that are forged in truth and justice. We are mindful that knowing the truth about what happened in residential schools in and of itself does not necessarily lead to reconciliation. Yet the importance of truth telling in its own right should not be underestimated; it restores the human dignity of victims of violence and calls governments and citizens to account. Without truth, justice is not served, healing cannot happen, and there can be no genuine reconciliation between Aboriginal and non-Aboriginal peoples in Canada. Speaking to us at the Traditional Knowledge Keepers Forum in June 2014, Elder Dave Courchene posed a critical question: "When you talk about truth, whose truth are you talking about?"[11]

The Commission's answer to Elder Courchene's question is that by *truth* we mean not only the truth revealed in government and church residential school documents but also the truth of lived experiences as told to us by Survivors and others in their statements to this Commission. Together, these public testimonies constitute a new oral history record, one based on Indigenous legal traditions and the practice of witnessing.[12] As people gathered at various TRC National Events and Community Hearings, they shared experiences of truth telling and offered expressions of reconciliation.

Over the course of its work, the Commission inducted a growing circle of TRC Honorary Witnesses. Their role has been to bear official witness to the testimonies of Survivors and their families, former school staff and their descendants, government and church officials, and any others whose lives have been affected by the residential schools. Beyond the work of the TRC, the Honorary Witnesses have pledged their commitment to the ongoing work of reconciliation between Aboriginal and non-Aboriginal peoples. We also encouraged everyone who attended TRC National Events or Community Hearings to see themselves as witnesses, with an obligation to find ways of making reconciliation a concrete reality in their own lives, communities, schools, and workplaces.

As Elder Jim Dumont explained at the Traditional Knowledge Keepers Forum in June 2014, "in Ojibwe thinking, to speak the truth is to actually speak from the heart."[13] At the Community Hearing in Key First Nation, Saskatchewan, in 2012, Survivor Wilfred Whitehawk told us he was glad that he had disclosed his abuse.

> I don't regret it because it taught me something. It taught me to talk about truth, about me, to be honest about who I am.... I am very proud of who I am today. It took me a long time, but I'm there. And what I have, my values and belief systems are mine and no one is going to impose theirs on me. And no one today is going to take advantage of me, man or woman, the government or the RCMP [Royal Canadian Mounted Police], because I have a voice today. I can speak for me and no one can take that away.[14]

Survivor and the child of Survivors Vitaline Elsie Jenner said, "I'm quite happy to be able to share my story.... I want the people of Canada to hear, to listen, for it is the truth.... I also want my grandchildren to learn, to learn from me that, yes, it did happen."[15]

Another descendant of Survivors, Daniel Elliot, told the Commission,

> I think all Canadians need to stop and take a look and not look away. Yeah, it's embarrassing, yeah, it's an ugly part of our history. We don't want to know about it. What I want to see from the Commission is to rewrite the history books so that other generations will understand and not go through the same thing that we're going through now, like it never happened.[16]

At the Saskatchewan National Event, president of the Métis National Council Clement Chartier spoke to the Commission about the importance of truth to justice and reconciliation.

> The truth is important. So I'll try to address the truth and a bit of reconciliation as well. The truth is that the Métis Nation, represented by the Métis National Council, is not a party to the Indian Residential Schools Settlement Agreement.... And the truth is that the exclusion of the Métis Nation or the Métis as a people is reflected throughout this whole period not only in the Indian Residential Schools Settlement Agreement but in the apology made by Canada as well....
>
> We are, however, the products ... of the same assimilationist policy that the federal government foisted upon the Treaty Indian kids. So there ought to be some solution.... The Métis boarding schools, residential schools, are excluded. And we need to ensure that everyone was aware of that and hopefully [at] some point down the road, you will help advocate and get, you know, the governments or whoever is responsible to accept responsibility and to move forward on a path to

reconciliation, because reconciliation should be for all Aboriginal peoples and not only some Aboriginal peoples.[17]

At the British Columbia National Event, former lieutenant-governor of British Columbia the Honourable Steven Point said,

> And so many of you have said today, so many of the witnesses that came forward said, "I cannot forgive. I'm not ready to forgive." And I wondered why. Reconciliation is about hearing the truth, that's for sure. It's also about acknowledging that truth. Acknowledging that what you've said is true. Accepting responsibility for your pain and putting those children back in the place they would have been, had they not been taken from their homes....
>
> What are the blockages to reconciliation? The continuing poverty in our communities and the failure of our government to recognize that "yes, we own the land." Stop the destruction of our territories and for God's sake, stop the deaths of so many of our women on highways across this country.... I'm going to continue to talk about reconciliation, but just as important, I'm going to foster healing in our own people, so that our children can avoid this pain, can avoid this destruction and finally take our rightful place in this "Our Canada."[18]

When former residential school staff attended public TRC events, some thought it was most important to hear directly from Survivors, even if their own perspectives and memories of the schools might differ from those of the Survivors. At a Community Hearing in Thunder Bay, Ontario, Merle Nisley, who worked at the Poplar Hill Residential School in the early 1970s, said,

> I think it would be valuable for people who have been involved in the schools to hear stories personally. And I also think it would be valuable, when it's appropriate ... [for] former students who are on the healing path to ... hear some of our stories, or to hear some of our perspectives. But I know that's a very difficult thing to do.... Certainly this is not the time to try to ask all those former students to sit and listen to the rationale of the former staff because there's just too much emotion there ... and there's too little trust ... [Y]ou can't do things like that when there's low levels of trust. So I think really a very important thing is for former staff to hear the stories and to be courageous enough just to hear them.... Where wrongs were done, where abuses happened, where punishment was over the top, and wherever sexual abuse happened, somehow we need to courageously sit and talk about that, and apologize. I don't know how that will happen.[19]

Nisley's reflections highlight one of the difficulties the Commission faced in trying to create a space for respectful dialogue between former residential school students and staff. Although, in most cases, this was possible, in other instances, Survivors and their family members found it very difficult to listen to former staff, particularly if they perceived the speaker to be an apologist for the schools.

At the TRC Victoria Regional Event, Brother Tom Cavanaugh, the district superior of the Oblates of Mary Immaculate for British Columbia and the Yukon, spoke about his time as a supervisor at the Christie Residential School.

> What I experienced over the six years I was at Christie Residential School was a staff, Native and non-Native alike, working together to provide, as much as possible, a safe, loving environment for the children attending Christie School. Was it a perfect situation? No, it wasn't a perfect situation ... but again, there didn't seem to be, at that time, any other viable alternative in providing a good education for so many children who lived in relatively small and isolated communities.

Survivors and family members who were present in the audience spoke out, saying, "Truth, tell the truth." Brother Cavanaugh replied, "If you give me a chance, I will tell you the truth." When TRC chair Justice Murray Sinclair intervened to ask the audience to allow Brother Cavanaugh to finish his statement, he was able to do so without further interruption. Visibly shaken, Cavanaugh then went on to acknowledge that children had also been abused in the schools, and he condemned such actions, expressing his sorrow and regret for this breach of trust.

> I can honestly say that our men are hurting too because of the abuse scandal and the rift that this has created between First Nations and church representatives. Many of our men who are still working with First Nations have attended various truth and reconciliation sessions as well as Returning to Spirit sessions, hoping to bring about healing for all concerned. The Oblates desire healing for the abused and for all touched by the past breach of trust. It is our hope that together we can continue to build a better society.[20]

Later that same day, Ina Seitcher, who attended the Christie Residential School, painted a very different picture of the school from what Brother Cavanaugh had described.

> I went to Christie Residential School. This morning I heard a priest talking about his Christie Residential School. I want to tell him [about] my Christie Residential School. I went there for ten months. Ten months that impacted my life for fifty years. I am just now on my healing journey.... I need to do this, I need to speak out. I need to speak for my mom and dad who went to residential school, for my aunts, my uncles, all that are beyond now.... All the pain of our people, the hurt, the anger.... That priest that talked about how loving that Christie Residential School was—it was not. That priest was most likely in his office not knowing what was going on down in the dorms or in the lunchroom.... There were things that happened at Christie Residential School, and like I said, I'm just starting my healing journey. There are doors that I don't even want to open. I don't even want to open those doors because I don't know what it would do to me.[21]

These two seemingly irreconcilable truths are a stark reminder that there are no easy shortcuts to reconciliation. That there were few direct exchanges at TRC events between Survivors and former school staff indicates that for many the time for reconciliation had not yet arrived. Indeed, for some, it may never arrive. At the Manitoba National Event in 2010, Survivor Evelyn Brockwood talked about why it is important to ensure that there is adequate time for healing to occur in the truth and reconciliation process.

> When this came out at the beginning, I believe it was 1990, about residential schools, people coming out with their stories, and ... I thought the term, the words they were using, were *truth*, *healing* and *reconciliation*. But somehow it seems like we are going from truth telling to reconciliation, to reconcile with our white brothers and sisters. My brothers and sisters, we have a lot of work to do in the middle. We should really lift up the word *healing*.... Go slow, we are going too fast, too fast.... We have many tears to shed before we even get to the word *reconciliation*.[22]

To determine the truth and to tell the full story of residential schools in this country, the TRC needed to hear from Survivors and their families, former staff, government and church officials, and all those affected by residential schools. Canada's national history in the future must be based on the truth about what happened in the residential schools. One hundred years from now, our children's children and their children must know and still remember this history, because they will inherit from us the responsibility to ensure that it never happens again.

What is reconciliation?

During the course of the Commission's work, it has become clear that the concept of reconciliation means different things to different people, communities, institutions, and organizations. The TRC mandate describes "reconciliation" as

> an ongoing individual and collective process, and will require commitment from all those affected including First Nations, Inuit and Métis former Indian Residential School (IRS) students, their families, communities, religious entities, former school employees, government and the people of Canada. Reconciliation may occur between any of the above groups.[23]

The Commission defines *reconciliation* as an ongoing process of establishing and maintaining respectful relationships. A critical part of this process involves repairing damaged trust by making apologies, providing individual and collective reparations, and following through with concrete actions that demonstrate real societal change. Establishing respectful relationships also requires the revitalization of Indigenous law and legal traditions. It is important that all Canadians understand how traditional First Nations, Inuit, and Métis approaches to resolving conflict, repairing harm, and restoring relationships can inform the reconciliation process.

Traditional Knowledge Keepers and Elders have long dealt with conflicts and harms by using spiritual ceremonies and peacemaking practices, and by retelling oral history stories that reveal how their ancestors restored harmony to families and communities. These traditions and practices are the foundation of Indigenous law; they contain wisdom and practical guidance for moving towards reconciliation across this land.[24]

As First Nations, Inuit, and Métis communities access and revitalize their spirituality, cultures, languages, laws, and governance systems, and as non-Aboriginal Canadians increasingly come to understand Indigenous history within Canada, and to recognize and respect Indigenous approaches to establishing and maintaining respectful relationships, Canadians can work together to forge a new covenant of reconciliation.

Despite the ravages of colonialism, every Indigenous nation across the country, each with its own distinctive culture and language, has kept its legal traditions and peacemaking practices alive in its communities. Although Elders and Knowledge Keepers across the land have told us that there is no specific word for *reconciliation* in their own languages, there are many words, stories, and songs, as well as sacred objects such as wampum belts, peace pipes, eagle down, cedar boughs, drums, and regalia, that are used to establish relationships, repair conflicts, restore harmony, and make peace. The ceremonies and protocols of Indigenous law are still remembered and practised in many Aboriginal communities.

At the TRC Traditional Knowledge Keepers Forum in June 2014, TRC Survivor Committee member and Elder Barney Williams told us that

> from sea to sea, we hear words that allude to ... what is reconciliation? What does healing or forgiveness mean? And how there's parallels to all those words that the Creator gave to all the nations.... When I listen and reflect on the voices of the ancestors, your ancestors, I hear my ancestor alluding to the same thing with a different dialect.... My understanding [of reconciliation] comes from a place and time when there was no English spoken ... from my grandmother who was born in the 1800s.... I really feel privileged to have been chosen by my grandmother to be the keeper of our knowledge.... What do we need to do? ... We need to go back to ceremony and embrace ceremony as part of moving forward. We need to understand the laws of our people.[25]

At the same forum, Elder Stephen Augustine explained the roles of silence and negotiation in Mi'kmaq law. He said that silence is a concept that can be used to respond to a wrong action or to teach a lesson. Silence is employed according to proper procedures, and it ends at a particular time too. Elder Augustine suggested that there is both a place for talking about reconciliation and a need for quiet reflection. Reconciliation cannot occur without listening, contemplation, meditation, and deeper internal deliberation. Silence in the face of residential school harms is an appropriate response for many Indigenous peoples. We must enlarge the space for respectful silence in journeying towards reconciliation, particularly for Survivors who regard this as key to healing. There is also a place for discussion and negotiation for those who want to move beyond silence. Dialogue and mutual adjustment are significant components of Mi'kmaq law. Elder Augustine suggested that other dimensions of human experience—our relationships with the earth and all living beings—are also relevant in working towards reconciliation. This profound insight is an Indigenous law that could be applied more generally.[26]

Elder Reg Crowshoe told the Commission that Indigenous peoples' worldviews, oral history traditions, and practices have much to teach us about how to establish respectful relationships among peoples and with the land and all living things. Learning how to live together in a good way happens through sharing stories and practising reconciliation in our everyday lives.

> When we talk about the concept of reconciliation, I think about some of the stories that I've heard in our culture, and stories are important.... These stories are so important as theories but at the same time stories are important to oral cultures. So when we talk about stories, we talk about defining our environment and how we look at authorities that come from the land and how that land, when we talk about our relationship with the land, how we look at forgiveness and reconciliation is so important when we look at it historically.
>
> We have stories in our culture about our superheroes, how we treat each other, stories about how animals and plants give us authorities and privileges to use plants as healing, but we also have stories about practices. How would we practise reconciliation? How would we practise getting together to talk about reconciliation in an oral perspective? And those practices are so important.[27]

As Elder Crowshoe explained further, reconciliation requires talking, but our conversations must be broader than Canada's conventional approaches. Reconciliation between Aboriginal and non-Aboriginal Canadians, from an Aboriginal perspective, also requires reconciliation with the natural world. If human beings resolve problems between themselves but continue to destroy the natural world, then reconciliation remains incomplete. This is a perspective that we as Commissioners have repeatedly heard: that reconciliation will never occur unless we are also reconciled with the earth. Mi'kmaq and other Indigenous laws stress that humans must journey through life in conversation and negotiation with all creation. Reciprocity and mutual respect help sustain our survival. It is this kind of healing and survival that is needed in moving forward from the residential school experience.

Over the course of its work, the Commission created space for exploring the meanings and concepts of reconciliation. In public Sharing Circles at National Events and Community Hearings, we bore witness to powerful moments of truth sharing and humbling acts of reconciliation. Many Survivors had never been able to tell their own families the whole truth of what had happened to them in the schools. At hearings in Regina, Saskatchewan, Elder Kirby Littletent said, "I never told. I just told my children, my grandchildren I went to boarding school, that's all. I never shared my experiences."[28]

Many spoke to honour the memory of relatives who have passed on. Simone, an Inuk Survivor from Chesterfield Inlet, Nunavut, said,

> I'm here for my parents—'Did you miss me when I went away?' 'Did you cry for me?'—and I'm here for my brother, who was a victim, and my niece at the age of five who suffered a head injury and never came home, and her parents never had closure. To this day, they have not found the grave in Winnipeg. And I'm here for them first, and that's why I'm making a public statement.[29]

Others talked about the importance of reconciling with family members, and cautioned that this process is just beginning. Patrick Etherington, a Survivor from the St. Anne's Residential School in Fort Albany, Ontario, walked with his son and others from Cochrane, Ontario, to the National Event in Winnipeg. He said that the walk helped him to reconnect with his son, and that he "just wanted to be here because I feel this process that we are starting, we got a long ways to go."[30]

We saw the children and grandchildren of Survivors who, once they heard about and began to understand the experiences of their relatives who went to the schools, found compassion and gained new respect for them. At the Northern National Event in Inuvik, Northwest Territories, Maxine Lacorne said,

> As a youth, a young lady, I talk with people my age because I have a good understanding. I talk to people who are residential school Survivors because I like to hear their stories, you know, and it gives me more understanding of my parents.... It is an honour to be here, to sit here among you guys, Survivors. Wow. You guys are strong people, you guys survived everything. And we're still going to be here. They tried to take us away. They tried to take our language away. You guys are still here, we're still here. I'm still here.[31]

We heard about children whose small acts of everyday resistance in the face of rampant abuse, neglect, and bullying in the schools were quite simply heroic. At the TRC British Columbia National Event, Elder Barney Williams said that "many of us, through our pain and suffering, managed to hold our heads up ... We were brave children."[32] We saw old bonds of childhood friendship renewed as people gathered and found each other at TRC-sponsored events. Together, they remembered the horrors they had endured even as they recalled with pride long-forgotten accomplishments in various school sports, music, or art activities. We heard from resilient, courageous Survivors who, despite their traumatic childhood experiences, had gone on to become influential leaders in their communities and in all walks of Canadian life, including politics, government, law, education, medicine, the corporate world, and the arts.

We heard from officials representing the federal government that had administered the schools. In a Sharing Circle at the Manitoba National Event, the Honourable Chuck Strahl (then minister of Indian affairs and northern development) said,

> Governments like to write ... policy, and they like to write legislation, and they like to codify things and so on. And Aboriginal people want to talk about restoration, reconciliation, forgiveness, about healing ... about truth. And those things are all things of the heart and of relationship, and not of government policy. Governments do a bad job of that.[33]

Church representatives spoke about their struggles to right the relationship with Aboriginal peoples. In Inuvik, Anglican Archbishop Fred Hiltz told us that

> as a church, we are renewing our commitment to work with the Assembly of First Nations in addressing long-standing, Indigenous justice issues. As a church we are requiring anyone who serves the church at a national level to go through anti-racism training ... We have a lot to do in our church to make sure that racism is eliminated.[34]

Educators told us about their growing awareness of the inadequate role that post-secondary institutions played in training the teachers who taught in the schools. They have pledged to make educational practices and curriculum more inclusive of Aboriginal knowledge and history. Artists shared their ideas and feelings about truth and reconciliation through songs, paintings, dance, film, and other media. Corporations provided resources to bring Survivors to events and, in some cases, some of their own staff and managers.

For non-Aboriginal Canadians who came to bear witness to Survivors' life stories, the experience was powerful. One woman said simply, "By listening to your story, my story can change. By listening to your story, I can change."[35]

Reconciliation as relationship

In its 2012 Interim Report, the TRC recommended that federal, provincial, and territorial governments, and all parties to the Settlement Agreement, undertake to meet and explore the *United Nations Declaration on the Rights of Indigenous Peoples* as a framework for reconciliation in Canada. We remain convinced that the *United Nations Declaration* provides the necessary principles, norms, and standards for reconciliation to flourish in twenty-first-century Canada.

A reconciliation framework is one in which Canada's political and legal systems, educational and religious institutions, corporate sector, and civil society function in ways that are consistent with the *United Nations Declaration on the Rights of Indigenous Peoples*, which Canada has endorsed. The Commission believes that the following guiding principles of truth and reconciliation will assist Canadians moving forward:

1. The *United Nations Declaration on the Rights of Indigenous Peoples* is the framework for reconciliation at all levels and across all sectors of Canadian society.

2. First Nations, Inuit, and Métis peoples, as the original peoples of this country and as self-determining peoples, have Treaty, constitutional, and human rights that must be recognized and respected.

3. Reconciliation is a process of healing relationships that requires public truth sharing, apology, and commemoration that acknowledge and redress past harms.

4. Reconciliation requires constructive action on addressing the ongoing legacies of colonialism that have had destructive impacts on Aboriginal peoples' education, cultures and languages, health, child welfare, administration of justice, and economic opportunities and prosperity.

5. Reconciliation must create a more equitable and inclusive society by closing the gaps in social, health, and economic outcomes that exist between Aboriginal and non-Aboriginal Canadians.

6. All Canadians, as Treaty peoples, share responsibility for establishing and maintaining mutually respectful relationships.

7. The perspectives and understandings of Aboriginal Elders and Traditional Knowledge Keepers of the ethics, concepts, and practices of reconciliation are vital to long-term reconciliation.

8. Supporting Aboriginal peoples' cultural revitalization and integrating Indigenous knowledge systems, oral histories, laws, protocols, and connections to the land into the reconciliation process are essential.

9. Reconciliation requires political will, joint leadership, trust building, accountability, and transparency, as well as a substantial investment of resources.

10. Reconciliation requires sustained public education and dialogue, including youth engagement, about the history and legacy of residential schools, Treaties, and Aboriginal rights, as well as the historical and contemporary contributions of Aboriginal peoples to Canadian society.

Together, Canadians must do more than just *talk* about reconciliation; we must learn how to *practise* reconciliation in our everyday lives—within ourselves and our families, and in our communities, governments, places of worship, schools, and work-places. To do so constructively, Canadians must remain committed to the ongoing work of establishing and maintaining respectful relationships.

For many Survivors and their families, this commitment is foremost about healing themselves, their communities, and their nations in ways that revitalize individuals as well as Indigenous cultures, languages, spirituality, laws, and governance systems. For governments, building a respectful relationship involves dismantling a centuries-old political and bureaucratic culture in which, all too often, policies and programs are still based on failed notions of assimilation. For churches, demonstrating long-term commitment requires atoning for actions within the residential schools, respecting Indigenous spirituality, and supporting Indigenous peoples' struggles for justice and equity. Schools must teach history in ways that foster mutual respect, empathy, and engagement. All Canadian children and youth deserve to know Canada's honest his-tory, including what happened in the residential schools, and to appreciate the rich history and knowledge of Indigenous nations, which continue to make such a strong contribution to Canada, including our very name and collective identity as a country. For Canadians from all walks of life, reconciliation offers a new way of living together.

CHAPTER 1

The challenge of reconciliation

Canada has a long history of colonialism in relation to Aboriginal peoples. This history and its policies of cultural genocide and assimilation have left deep scars on the lives of many Aboriginal people, on Aboriginal communities, as well as on Canadian society, and have deeply damaged the relationship between Aboriginal and non-Aboriginal peoples. It took a long time for that damage to be done and for the relationship we see to be created, and it will take us a long time to fix it. But the process has already begun.

An important process of healing and reconciling this relationship began in the 1980s with churches' apologies for their treatment of Aboriginal peoples and disrespect of their cultures. It continued with the findings of the Royal Commission on Aboriginal Peoples, along with court recognition of the validity of the Survivors' stories. It culminated in the Indian Residential Schools Settlement Agreement and the prime minister of Canada's apology in Parliament in June 2008, along with the apologies of all other parliamentary leaders. This process of healing and reconciliation must continue. The ultimate objective must be to transform our country and restore mutual respect between peoples and nations.

Reconciliation is in the best interests of all of Canada. It is needed not only to resolve the ongoing conflicts between Aboriginal peoples and institutions of the country but also to remove a stain from Canada's past so that it can maintain its claim to be a leader in the protection of human rights among the nations of the world. Canada's historical development, as well as the view held strongly by some that the history of this development is accurately portrayed as beneficent raises significant barriers to reconciliation in the twenty-first century.

No Canadian can take pride in this country's treatment of Aboriginal peoples, and for this reason, all Canadians have a critical role to play in advancing reconciliation in ways that honour and revitalize the nation-to-nation Treaty relationship.

At the Truth and Reconciliation Commission of Canada's (TRC) Traditional Knowledge Keepers Forum held in June 2014, Chief Ian Campbell said, "Our history is your history as Canada ... Until Canada accepts that, ... this society will never flourish to its full potential."[1]

The history and destructive legacy of the residential school system is a powerful reminder that Canada disregarded its own historical roots. Canada's determination to assimilate Aboriginal peoples, in spite of the early relationship established at first contact and formalized and maintained in Treaties, attests to this fact. As Gerry St. Germain (Métis), then a Canadian senator, said,

> There can be no doubt that the founders of Canada somehow lost their moral compass in their relations with the people who occupied and possessed the land.... While we cannot change history, we can learn from it and we can use it to shape our common future.... This effort is crucial in realizing the vision of creating a compassionate and humanitarian society, the society that our ancestors, the Aboriginal, the French and the English peoples, envisioned so many years ago—our home, Canada.[2]

Aboriginal peoples have always remembered the original relationship they had with early Canadians. This relationship of mutual support, respect, and assistance was confirmed by the Royal Proclamation of 1763 and the Treaties with the Crown that were negotiated in good faith by their leaders. This memory, confirmed by historical analysis and passed down through Indigenous oral histories, has sustained Aboriginal peoples in their long political struggle to live with dignity as self-determining peoples with their own cultures, laws, and connections to the land.

The destructive impacts of residential schools, the *Indian Act*, and the Crown's failure to keep its Treaty promises have damaged the relationship between Aboriginal and non-Aboriginal peoples. The most significant damage is to the trust that has been broken between the Crown and Aboriginal peoples. This broken trust must be repaired. The vision that led to this breach in trust must be replaced with a new vision for Canada—one that fully embraces Aboriginal peoples' right to self-determination within, and in partnership with, a viable Canadian sovereignty. If Canadians fail to find this vision, Canada will not resolve long-standing conflicts between the Crown and Aboriginal peoples over Treaty and Aboriginal rights, lands, and resources, or the education, health, and well-being of Aboriginal peoples. Reconciliation will not be achieved, and neither will the hope for reconciliation be sustainable over time. It is not inconceivable that the unrest we see today among young Aboriginal people could grow to become a challenge to the country's own sense of well-being and its very security.

Reconciliation must become a way of life. It will take many years to repair damaged trust and relationships in Aboriginal communities and between Aboriginal and non-Aboriginal peoples. Not only does reconciliation require apologies, reparations, the relearning of Canada's national history, and public commemoration, but it also needs real social, political, and economic change. Ongoing public education and dialogue are essential to reconciliation. Governments, churches, educational institutions, and Canadians from all walks of life are responsible for taking action on reconciliation in concrete ways, working collaboratively with Aboriginal peoples. Reconciliation begins with each and every one of us.

The Aboriginal and non-Aboriginal youth of our country have told the Commission that they want to know the truth about the history and legacy of residential schools. They want to understand their responsibilities as parties to the same Treaties—in other words, as Treaty people. They want to learn about the rich contributions that Aboriginal peoples have made to this country. They understand that reconciliation involves a conversation not only about residential schools but also about all other aspects of the relationship between Aboriginal and non-Aboriginal peoples.

As Commissioners, we believe that reconciliation is about respect. This includes both self-respect for Aboriginal people and mutual respect among all Canadians. All young people need to know who they are and from where they come. Aboriginal children and youth, searching for their own identities and places of belonging, need to know and take pride in their Indigenous roots. They need to know the answers to some very basic questions. Who are my people? What is our history? How are we unique? Where do I belong? Where is my homeland? What is my language and how does it connect me to my nation's spiritual beliefs, cultural practices, and ways of being in the world? They also need to know why things are the way they are today. This requires an understanding of the history of colonization, including the residential school system and how it has affected their families, their communities, their people, and themselves.

Of equal importance, non-Aboriginal children and youth need to comprehend how their own identities and family histories have been shaped by a version of Canadian history that has marginalized Aboriginal peoples' history and experience. They need to know how notions of European superiority and Aboriginal inferiority have tainted mainstream society's ideas about, and attitudes towards, Aboriginal peoples in ways that have been profoundly disrespectful and damaging. They too need to understand Canada's history as a settler society and how assimilation policies have affected Aboriginal peoples. This knowledge and understanding will lay the groundwork for establishing mutually respectful relationships.

The Royal Commission on Aboriginal Peoples

In the summer of 1990, at Oka, Québec, the Mohawks of Kanesatake, the Government of Québec, the Québec provincial police, and the Canadian military became embroiled in a violent confrontation over the town's plan to develop a golf course on Mohawk burial grounds located in a forested area known as "The Pines." The Mohawks' claim to that land and demands for the recognition of their traditional territory had gone unheeded for years by the federal government. The resulting confrontation, according to historian J. R. Miller, was "proof of Canada's failed Indian [land] claims policy."[3] What had begun as a peaceful act of resistance by Mohawk people defending their lands took a violent turn.[4] The "Oka crisis," as it became widely known in the media, led to a seventy-eight-day standoff and involved armed resistance led by militarily trained Mohawk warriors.[5] It was an event that shook Canada's complacency about Aboriginal demands to the core. Shortly after an end to the siege had been negotiated, Prime Minister Brian Mulroney wrote,

> The summer's events must not be allowed to over-shadow the commitment that my government has made to addressing the concerns of aboriginal people.... These grievances raise issues that deeply affect all Canadians and therefore must be resolved by all Canadians working together.... The government's agenda responds to the demands of aboriginal peoples and has four parts: resolving land claims; improving the economic and social conditions on reserves; defining a new relationship between aboriginal peoples and governments; and addressing the concerns of Canada's aboriginal peoples in contemporary Canadian life. Consultation with aboriginal peoples and respect for the fiduciary responsibilities of the Crown are integral parts of the process. The federal government is determined to create a new relationship among aboriginal and non-aboriginal Canadians based on dignity, trust and respect.[6]

The Government of Canada subsequently created a royal commission to look into the state of affairs of Aboriginal peoples in Canada. In 1996, the *Report of the Royal Commission on Aboriginal Peoples* provided a glimpse into just how bad things had become, made hundreds of recommendations, and tabled a twenty-year renewal plan that would have rebalanced the political and economic power between Aboriginal peoples and governments. The report's recommendations focused on five key themes:

> *First, Aboriginal nations have to be reconstituted.*

> *Second, a process must be established for the assumption of powers by Aboriginal nations.*

> *Third, there must be a fundamental reallocation of lands and resources.*

> *Fourth, Aboriginal people need education and crucial skills for governance and self-reliance.*

> *Finally, economic development must be addressed if the poverty and despondency of lives defined by unemployment and welfare are to change.*[7]

The Royal Commission on Aboriginal Peoples (RCAP) put forward a bold and comprehensive vision of reconciliation. The RCAP report observed that if Canada was to thrive in the future, the relationship between Aboriginal peoples and the Crown must be transformed. The report concluded that the policy of assimilation was a complete failure and that Canada must look to the historical Treaty relationship to establish a new relationship between Aboriginal and non-Aboriginal peoples, based on the principles of mutual recognition, mutual respect, sharing, and mutual responsibility.[8]

The Royal Commission emphasized that Aboriginal peoples' right to self-determination is essential to a robust upholding of Canada's constitutional obligations to Aboriginal peoples and compliance with international human rights law.

> It is the hope of Indigenous peoples everywhere, including Aboriginal people in Canada, that international pressure will force countries with Aboriginal populations to assure their cultural survival and recognize their right to have their own land and their own systems of government.... We now have an unprecedented opportunity to learn from the mistakes of the past and to set out, both as governments and as peoples, in totally new directions. If Canada has a meaningful role to play on the world stage (and we would like to think that it has) then it must first set its domestic house in order and devise, with the full participation of the federal government, the provinces and the Aboriginal peoples, a national policy of reconciliation and regeneration of which we can all be proud.[9]

In other words, the RCAP report saw reconciliation as placing a heavy onus on the Government of Canada to change its conduct and to see the validity of the Aboriginal perspective on how the relationship should be in the future.

In the years following the release of the RCAP report, developing a national vision of reconciliation has proved to be challenging. In principle, Aboriginal peoples, governments, and the courts agree that reconciliation is needed. In practice, it has been difficult to create the conditions for reconciliation to flourish.

In 1998, the federal government released "Gathering Strength: Canada's Aboriginal Action Plan" in response to the RCAP. The action plan focused on four priority areas: renewing the partnership, strengthening Aboriginal governance, developing a new fiscal relationship, and supporting strong communities, people, and economies. The action plan acknowledged the importance of affirming the Treaty relationship (both historic and modern), recognizing the inherent right of self-government, and improving the land claims process. A northern agenda was to guide the development of new constitutional arrangements and governance structures in the new Nunavut government and through land claims and self-government agreements in the Northwest and Yukon Territories.[10] "Gathering Strength" included a "Statement of Reconciliation" in which the federal government formally acknowledged and expressed "profound regret" for the historical injustices that Aboriginal peoples had experienced. The statement made particular mention of the sexual and physical abuse at residential schools, for which the government was "deeply sorry." The action plan also included $350 million to support community-based healing initiatives.[11]

In 2006, on the tenth anniversary of the release of the RCAP report, the Assembly of First Nations (AFN) issued a detailed ten-year report card assessing the action plan's results. The report card noted that the "Statement of Reconciliation," the successful negotiation of an agreement-in-principle of the Indian Residential Schools Settlement Agreement in 2005, and the establishment of the Aboriginal Healing Foundation indicated that some progress had been made on residential schools issues. However, the AFN concluded that in terms of key socio-economic indicators, the action plan had done little to change the unacceptable status quo. Rather, "any major improvements in individual communities or regions have been led by those communities for those communities."[12]

The Indian Residential Schools Settlement Agreement, including the creation of the Truth and Reconciliation Commission of Canada, was an attempt to resolve the thousands of lawsuits brought against the government for cases of historical abuse. Its implementation has also been challenging. Canada and the churches have made apologies to Survivors, their families, and their communities. The courts have produced a body of law on reconciliation in relation to Aboriginal rights, which has established some parameters for discussion and negotiations, but there remains no ongoing national process or entity to guide that discussion. Canadian government actions continue to be unilateral and divisive, and Aboriginal peoples continue to resist such actions. Negotiations on Treaties and land claims agreements continue with a view to reconciling Aboriginal title and rights with Crown sovereignty. However, many cases remain unresolved and progress has been slow.

Under the federal government's comprehensive land claims policy, 122 claims have been accepted for negotiation, but only 26 land claims agreements or modern-day Treaties have been finalized in the forty-two years since the policy was first introduced in 1973.[13] In September 2014, Aboriginal Affairs and Northern Development Canada (AANDC) issued an interim comprehensive claims policy for discussion as the federal government prepared to once again update its policy.[14]

In April 2015, Ministerial Special Representative Douglas R. Eyford, who was appointed by the minister of Aboriginal affairs and northern development, the Honourable Bernard Valcourt, to engage in policy discussions with Aboriginal groups, released his report, "A New Direction: Advancing Aboriginal and Treaty Rights." He found that

> [d]espite the Court's preference that reconciliation be pursued through good faith negotiations, litigation continues to dominate Aboriginal-Crown relations. Several federal departments or agencies are involved in Aboriginal rights litigation. AANDC alone is a party in 452 proceedings involving section 35(1) rights.... The cost of Aboriginal rights litigation is significant. AANDC spent in excess of $100 million for litigation legal services over the past five years ... Aboriginal rights claims highlight the tremendous inefficiencies of litigation as a dispute resolution tool.[15]

Eyford observed a general consensus among Aboriginal groups that "reconciliation will become a meaningless concept if the Crown fails to address Aboriginal interests in a generous and timely manner."[16] He concluded that "Over the past six decades, various approaches to reconciliation have been proposed. Many initiatives have been implemented but they have produced uneven results. It has been challenging for the parties to get it right."[17]

What is clear to this Commission is that Aboriginal peoples and the Crown have very different and conflicting views on what reconciliation is and how it is best achieved. The Government of Canada appears to believe that reconciliation entails Aboriginal peoples' accepting the reality and validity of Crown sovereignty and parliamentary supremacy in order to allow the government to get on with business. Aboriginal people, on the other hand, see reconciliation as an opportunity to affirm their own sovereignty and return to the 'partnership' ambitions they held after Confederation.

The *United Nations Declaration on the Rights of Indigenous Peoples* as a framework for reconciliation

Aboriginal peoples in Canada were not alone in the world when it came to being treated harshly by colonial authorities and settler governments. Historical abuses of Aboriginal peoples and the taking of Indigenous lands and resources throughout the world have been the subject of United Nations (UN) attention for many years. On September 13, 2007, after almost twenty-five years of debate and study, the United Nations adopted the *Declaration on the Rights of Indigenous Peoples*. As a declaration, it calls upon member states to adopt and maintain its provisions as a set of "minimum standards for the survival, dignity and well-being of the indigenous peoples of the world."[18]

The Commission concurs with the view of S. James Anaya, UN Special Rapporteur on the Rights of Indigenous Peoples, who observes,

> It is perhaps best to understand the Declaration and the right of self-determination it affirms as instruments of reconciliation. Properly understood, self-determination is an animating force for efforts toward reconciliation—or, perhaps, more accurately, conciliation—with peoples that have suffered oppression at the hands of others. Self-determination requires confronting and reversing the legacies of empire, discrimination, and cultural suffocation. It does not do so to condone vengefulness or spite for past evils, or to foster divisiveness but rather to build a social and political order based on relations of mutual understanding and respect. That is what the right of self-determination of indigenous peoples, and all other peoples, is about.[19]

Canada, as a member of the United Nations, initially refused to adopt the *Declaration*. It joined the United States, Australia, and New Zealand in doing so. It is not a coincidence that all these nations have a common history as part of the British Empire. The historical treatment of Aboriginal peoples in these other countries has strong parallels to what happened to Aboriginal peoples in Canada. Specifically, Canada objected to the *Declaration*'s

> provisions dealing with lands, territories and resources; free, prior and in-formed consent when used as a veto; self-government without recognition of the importance of negotiations; intellectual property; military issues; and the need to achieve an appropriate balance between the rights and obligations of Indige-nous peoples, member States and third parties.[20]

Although these four countries eventually endorsed the *Declaration*, they have all done so conditionally. In 2010, Canada endorsed the *Declaration* as a "non-legally binding aspirational document."[21] Despite this endorsement, we believe that the pro-visions and the vision of the *Declaration* do not currently enjoy government accep-tance. However, because Canada has accepted the *Declaration*, we hold the federal government to its word that it will genuinely aspire to achieve its provisions.

In 2011, Canadian churches and social justice advocacy groups that had cam-paigned for Canada's adoption of the *Declaration* urged the federal government to implement it. However, Canada's interpretation of the *Declaration* remained unchanged. On September 22, 2014, at the World Conference on Indigenous Peoples (wcip) in New York, the United Nations General Assembly adopted an action-oriented "Outcome Document" to guide the implementation of the *Declaration*. Member states from around the world committed, among other things, to the following:

> Taking, in consultation and cooperation with indigenous peoples, appropriate measures at the national level, including legislative, policy, and administrative measures, to achieve the ends of the *Declaration*, and to promote awareness of it among all sectors of society, including members of legislatures, the judiciary and the civil service.... [para. 7]. We commit ourselves to cooperating with indigenous peoples, through their own representative institutions, to develop and imple-ment national action plans, strategies or other measures, where relevant, to achieve the ends of the Declaration [para. 8] ... [and also] encourage the private sector, civil society and academic institutions to take an active role in promoting and protecting the rights of indigenous peoples [para. 30].[22]

The "Outcome Document" represented an important step forward with regard to implementing the *Declaration* in practical terms. The development of national action plans, strategies, and other concrete measures will provide the necessary structural and institutional frameworks for ensuring that Indigenous peoples' right to self-deter-mination is realized across the globe.

Canada issued a formal statement at the WCIP, objecting to certain paragraphs of the document related to the principle of obtaining the "free, prior and informed consent" (FPIC) of Indigenous peoples when states are making decisions that will affect their rights or interests, including economic development on their lands.

> Free, prior and informed consent, as it is considered in paragraphs 3 and 20 of the WCIP Outcome Document, could be interpreted as providing a veto to Aboriginal groups and in that regard, cannot be reconciled with Canadian law, as it exists.... Canada cannot support paragraph 4, in particular, given that Canadian law, recently reaffirmed in a Supreme Court of Canada decision, states the Crown may justify the infringement of an Aboriginal or Treaty right if it meets a stringent test to reconcile Aboriginal rights with a broader public interest.[23]

In a public statement, Indigenous leaders and their supporters said that Canada's concerns were unfounded, noting that

> the notion that the *Declaration* could be interpreted as conferring an absolute and unilateral veto power has been repeatedly raised by Canada as a justification for its continued opposition to the *Declaration*. This claim, however, has no basis either in the *UN Declaration* or in the wider body of international law. Like standards of accommodation and consent set out by the Supreme Court of Canada, FPIC in international law is applied in proportion to the potential for harm to the rights of Indigenous peoples and to the strength of these rights. The word "veto" does not appear in the *UN Declaration*.... Canada keeps insisting that Indigenous peoples don't have a say in development on their lands. This position is not consistent with the *UN Declaration on the Rights of Indigenous Peoples*, decisions by its own courts, or the goal of reconciliation.[24]

Reflecting on the importance of the *Declaration* to First Nations, Inuit, and Métis peoples in Canada, Grand Chief Edward John, Hereditary Chief of the Tl'azt'en Nation in northern British Columbia, explained,

> We have struggled for generations for recognition of our rights. We have fought for our survival, dignity and well-being, and the struggle continues. Canada's denial of First Nations' land rights falls well short of the minimum standards affirmed by the *Declaration* and demonstrates a clear failure by Canada to implement its human rights obligations. Prime Minister Harper's apology for Canada's role in the Indian Residential Schools acknowledged that the policy of assimilation was wrong and has no place in our country. Yet Canada's policy of denying Aboriginal title and rights is premised on the same attitude of assimilation. It is time for this attitude and the policies that flow from it to be cast aside. The *Declaration* calls for the development of new relationships based on recognition and respect for the inherent human rights of Indigenous peoples.[25]

The TRC considers reconciliation to be an ongoing process of establishing and maintaining respectful relationships at all levels of Canadian society. The Commission therefore believes that the *United Nations Declaration on the Rights of Indigenous Peoples* is the appropriate framework for reconciliation in twenty-first-century Canada. Studying the *Declaration* with a view to identifying its impacts on current government laws, policy, and behaviour would enable Canada to develop a holistic vision of reconciliation that embraces all aspects of the relationship between Aboriginal and non-Aboriginal Canadians, and to set the standard for international achievement in its circle of hesitating nations.

Aboriginal peoples' right to self-determination must be integrated into Canada's constitutional and legal framework and into its civic institutions in a manner consistent with the principles, norms, and standards of the *Declaration*. Aboriginal peoples in Canada have Aboriginal and Treaty rights. They have the right to access and revitalize their own laws and governance systems within their own communities and in their dealings with governments. They have a right to protect and revitalize their cultures, languages, and ways of life. They have the right to reparations for historical harms.

In 2014, the Supreme Court of Canada ruled that the Tsilhqot'in peoples have Aboriginal title to their lands in northern British Columbia, and "ownership rights similar to those associated with fee simple, including: the right to decide how the land will be used; the right of enjoyment and occupancy of the land; the right to possess the land; the right to the economic benefits of the land; and the right to pro-actively use and manage the land."[26] The court said, "Governments and individuals proposing to use or exploit land, whether before or after a declaration of Aboriginal title, can avoid a charge of infringement or failure to adequately consult by obtaining the consent of the interested Aboriginal group."[27]

In the face of growing conflicts over lands, resources, and economic development, the scope of reconciliation must extend beyond residential schools to encompass all aspects of Aboriginal and non-Aboriginal relations and connections to the land. Therefore, in our view, it is essential that all levels of government endorse and implement the *Declaration*. The Commission urges the federal government to reverse its position and fully endorse the "Outcome Document." We believe that the federal government must develop a national action plan to implement the *Declaration*. This would be consistent with the direction provided by the Supreme Court of Canada. More importantly, it would be consistent with the achievement of reconciliation.

Calls to action:

43) We call upon federal, provincial, territorial, and municipal governments to fully adopt and implement the *United Nations Declaration on the Rights of Indigenous Peoples* as the framework for reconciliation.

44) We call upon the Government of Canada to develop a national action plan, strategies, and other concrete measures to achieve the goals of the *United Nations Declaration on the Rights of Indigenous Peoples*.

Doctrine of Discovery

European states relied on the Doctrine of Discovery and the concept of *terra nullius* (lands belonging to no one) to justify empire building and the colonization of Aboriginal peoples and their lands in North America and across the globe. Far from being ancient history with no relevance for reconciliation today, the Doctrine of Discovery underlies the legal basis on which British Crown officials claimed sovereignty over Indigenous peoples and justified the extinguishment of their inherent rights to their territories, lands, and resources.

The Commission concurs with the findings and recommendation of the Royal Commission on Aboriginal Peoples with regard to the Doctrine of Discovery and *terra nullius*. The RCAP concluded that these concepts "have no legitimate place in characterizing the foundations of this country, or in contemporary policy making, legislation or jurisprudence,"[28] and it recommended that Canada acknowledge that such concepts "are factually, legally and morally wrong," and must no longer form the basis of federal lawmaking, policy development, or the Crown's legal arguments in court.[29]

Speaking at the Manitoba National Event in 2010, former day school student, political leader, and educator Sol Sanderson explained the importance of making the connection between the policies and practices of imperialism and colonization and the need for transformative change in Canadian society.

> What were the objectives of those empire policies? Assimilation, integration, civilization, Christianization, and liquidation. Who did those policies target? They targeted the destruction of our Indigenous families worldwide. Why? Because that was the foundation of our governing systems. They were the foundations of our institutions, and of our societies of our nations. Now those policies still form the basis of Canadian law today, not just in the *Indian Act*, [which] outlawed our traditions, our customs, our practices, our values, our language, our culture, our forms of government, our jurisdiction.... They say we have constitutionally protected rights in the form of inherent rights, Aboriginal rights, and Treaty rights, but we find ourselves in courts daily defending those rights against the colonial laws of the provinces and the federal government. Now, we can't allow that to continue.[30]

From 2010 to 2014, the United Nations Permanent Forum on Indigenous Issues undertook a number of studies and reports on the Doctrine of Discovery. During this same period, the Settlement Agreement churches also began to examine the

Christian thinking that had justified taking Indigenous lands and removing children from their families and communities. Writing about the Roman Catholic foundations of Aboriginal land claims in Canada, historian Jennifer Reid explains why the doctrine remains relevant today.

> Most non-Aboriginal Canadians are aware of the fact that Indigenous peoples commonly regard land rights as culturally and religiously significant. Fewer non-natives, I suspect, would consider their own connection with property in the same light, and fewer still would regard the legal foundation of all land rights in Canada as conspicuously theological. In fact, however, it is. The relationship between law and land in Canada can be traced to a set of fifteenth-century theological assumptions that have found their way into Canadian law.... The Doctrine of Discovery was the legal means by which Europeans claimed rights of sovereignty, property, and trade in regions they allegedly discovered during the age of expansion. These claims were made without consultation or engagement of any sort with the resident populations in these territories—the people to whom, by any sensible account, the land actually belonged. The Doctrine of Discovery has been a critical component of historical relationships between Europeans, their descendants, and Indigenous peoples, and it underlies their legal relationships to this day, having smoothly and relatively uncritically transitioned from Roman Catholic to international law.[31]

In April 2010, the Permanent Observer Mission of the Holy See (the UN representative from the Roman Catholic Vatican) issued a statement regarding the Doctrine of Discovery at the ninth session of the UN Permanent Forum on Indigenous Issues.[32] The statement noted that earlier papal bulls regarding territorial expansion and the forced conversion of Indigenous peoples had subsequently been abrogated or annulled by the Roman Catholic Church.

> Regarding the question of the doctrine of discovery and the role of the Papal Bull *Inter Coetera*, the Holy See notes that *Inter Coetera*, as a source of international law ... was first of all abrogated by the Treaty of Tordesilles in 1494, and that circumstances have changed so much that to attribute any juridical value to such a document seems completely out of place.... In addition, it was also abrogated by other Papal Bulls, for example, *Sublimis Deus* in 1537, which states, *"Indians and all other people who may later be discovered by Christians, are by no means to be deprived of their liberty or the possession of their property ... [S]hould the contrary happen, it shall be null and have no effect."* This view was expanded upon and reinforced in *Immensa Pastorum* of [Pope] Benedict XIV of 20 December 1741 and a number of other Papal Encyclicals, statements and decrees. If any doubt remains, it is abrogated by Canon 6 of the Code of Canon Law of 1983 which abrogates in general all preceding penal and disciplinary laws.... Therefore, for International Law and for the Catholic Church Law, the Bull *Inter Coetera* is a historic remnant with no juridical, moral or doctrinal value.... The fact that juridical systems may

employ the "Doctrine of Discovery" as a juridical precedent is now therefore a characteristic of the laws of those states and is independent of the fact that for the Church the document has had no value for centuries. The refutation of this doctrine is therefore now under the competence of national authorities, legislators, lawyers and legal historians.[33]

For many, this Catholic statement was inadequate. The doctrine's influence in Western law and its destructive consequences for Indigenous peoples have been well documented by scholars and other experts.[34]

In 2014, the North American representative to the UN Permanent Forum on Indigenous Issues, Grand Chief Edward John, tabled "A Study on the Impacts of the Doctrine of Discovery on Indigenous Peoples, Including Mechanisms, Processes, and Instruments of Redress." The study concluded,

> With regard to land dispossessions, forced conversions of non-Christians, the deprivation of liberty and the enslavement of indigenous peoples, the Holy See reported that an "abrogation process took place over the centuries" to invalidate such nefarious actions. Such papal renunciations do not go far enough. There is a pressing need to decolonize from the debilitating impacts and ongoing legacy of denial by States of indigenous peoples' inherent sovereignty, laws, and title to the lands, territories, and resources. At the same time, there is a growing movement among faith-based bodies to repudiate the doctrine of discovery.[35]

In 2010, the Anglican Church of Canada was the first of the Settlement Agreement churches in Canada to reject the Doctrine of Discovery and to "review the Church's policies and programs with a view to exposing the historical reality and impact of the Doctrine of Discovery and eliminating its presence in its contemporary policies, program, and structures."[36] In 2013, the Anglican Church established a Commission on Discovery, Reconciliation, and Justice, which had three goals:

1. to examine the Anglican Church of Canada's policies and practices, and revise them as necessary to be consistent with its repudiation of the Doctrine of Discovery;

2. to look into the question "what is reconciliation?"; and

3. to review the church's commitment to addressing long-standing injustices borne by Indigenous peoples in Canada.

The Commission on Discovery, Reconciliation, and Justice will table a final report to the Anglican General Synod in 2016.[37]

In February 2012, the Executive Committee of the World Council of Churches (WCC) also repudiated the Doctrine of Discovery. The WCC represents over 500 million Christians in more than 110 countries in 345 member churches, including three of the Settlement Agreement churches.[38] The WCC statement denounced the Doctrine of Discovery and urged governments to "dismantle the legal structures and policies based on the Doctrine of Discovery ... [and to] ensure that they conform to the *United Nations Declaration on the Rights of Indigenous Peoples*." The statement expressed solidarity with Indigenous peoples and affirmed their rights of self-determination and self-governance. The WCC also asked its member churches to support Indigenous self-determination in spiritual matters and education of all members of their churches.[39]

The United Church of Canada responded to this call. At its meeting in March 2012, the Executive of the General Council of the United Church "agreed unanimously to disown the Doctrine of Discovery, a historical concept which has been used to rationalize the enslavement and colonization of Indigenous peoples around the world."[40]

At the eleventh session of the UN Permanent Forum in May 2012, KAIROS, an inter-church social justice advocacy organization, made a joint statement with the Assembly of First Nations, Chiefs of Ontario, Grand Council of the Crees (Eeyou Istchee), Amnesty International, and the Canadian Friends Service Committee (Quakers) on the Doctrine of Discovery. The statement said that "while churches have begun to repudiate this racist doctrine, States around the world have not." It recommended that states, in conjunction with Indigenous peoples, undertake legal and policy reform to remove "any remnants of doctrines of superiority, including 'discovery,' as a basis for the assumed sovereignty over Indigenous peoples and their lands and resources."[41]

In his report to the UN Permanent Forum, Grand Chief Edward John focused on how Canadian courts have dealt with sovereignty issues.

> The highest court of Canada has recognized the need for reconciliation of "pre-existing aboriginal sovereignty with assumed Crown sovereignty." The Supreme Court has taken judicial notice of "such matters as colonialism, displacement and residential schools," which demonstrate how "assumed" sovereign powers were abused throughout history. The root cause of such abuse leads back to the Doctrine of Discovery and other related fictitious constructs which must therefore be addressed.[42]

At the thirteenth session of the UN Permanent Forum in May 2014, Haudenosaunee Faith Keeper Oren Lyons spoke about the principles of good governance as they relate to the *United Nations Declaration*.

> We recognize the Doctrine of Discovery and its long-term effects on our peoples led to the atrocities we faced in residential and boarding schools, both in Canada and the U.S. ... the Doctrine of Discovery has been invoked as a justification for the ongoing exploitation of our lands, territories, and resources and directly violates Article 7 paragraph 2 of the UNDRIP [the *Declaration*].[43]

The Doctrine of Discovery and the related concept of *terra nullius* underpin the requirement for Aboriginal peoples to prove their pre-existing occupation of the land in court cases in order to avoid having their land and resource rights extinguished in contemporary Treaty and land claims processes. Such a requirement does not conform to international law or contribute to reconciliation. Such concepts are a current manifestation of historical wrongs and should be formally repudiated by all levels of Canadian government.

Our intention in so concluding is to highlight that there is an important distinction to be drawn between the Doctrine of Discovery and its related concepts and the several inherently unjust policies, laws, and principles to which they have given rise over the years. It would not be enough to repudiate the Doctrine of Discovery, for example, while still maintaining the requirement for Aboriginal people to prove the validity of their existence and territoriality. We are not suggesting that the repudiation of the Doctrine of Discovery necessarily gives rise to the invalidation of Crown sovereignty. The Commission accepts that there are other means to establish the validity of Crown sovereignty without undermining the important principle established in the Royal Proclamation of 1763, which is that the sovereignty of the Crown requires that it recognize and deal with Aboriginal title in order to become perfected. It must not be forgotten that the terms of the Royal Proclamation were explained to, and accepted by, Indigenous leaders during the negotiation of the Treaty of Niagara of 1764.

Treaties: Honouring the past and negotiating the future

It is important for all Canadians to understand that without Treaties, Canada would have no legitimacy as a nation. Treaties between Indigenous nations and the Crown established the legal and constitutional foundation of this country. Historian J. R. Miller has concluded,

> Treaties were, are, and always will be an important part of Canadian life. Binding agreements between the Crown and Aboriginal peoples have played a central role in Native-newcomer relations since contact, and are still a significant public policy issue now. Non-Native Canadians might not universally recognize their significance, but treaties will continue to play an important role in Canada for the foreseeable future....

> The longer narrative of treaty-making is useful as a means to understand how the Native-newcomer relationship has changed since the early seventeenth century. It also permits an appreciation of how indigenous populations have responded to the challenges treaty-making created. Moreover, in the early twenty-first century, this shifting, multi-faceted treaty-making process continues. Treaty-making in Canada has a future as well as a past and present.[44]

Elder Fred Kelly has emphasized that Treaty making and Aboriginal peoples' ways of resolving conflict must be central to reconciliation.

> There are those who believe that a generic reconciliation process is a Western-based concept to be imposed on the Aboriginal peoples without regard to their own traditional practices of restoring personal and collective peace and harmony. We must therefore insist that the Aboriginal peoples have meaningful participation in the design, administration, and evaluation of the reconciliation process so that it is based on their local culture and language. If reconciliation is to be real and meaningful in Canada, it must embrace the inherent right of self-determination through self-government envisioned in the treaties....
>
> Where government refuses to implement Aboriginal rights and the original spirit and intent of the treaties, the citizens of Canada must take direct action to forcefully persuade its leadership. Treaties and memoranda of agreement are simply the stage-setting mechanisms for reconciliation. There must be action ... [A]ll Canadians have treaty rights.... It is upon these rights and obligations that our relationship is founded.[45]

If Canada's past is a cautionary tale about what not to do, it also holds a more constructive history lesson for the future. The Treaties are a model for how Canadians, as diverse peoples, can live respectfully and peacefully together on these lands we now share.

The Royal Proclamation of 1763 and the Treaty of Niagara of 1764

The history of Treaty making in Canada is contentious. Aboriginal peoples and the Crown have interpreted the spirit and intent of the Treaties quite differently. Generally, government officials have viewed the Treaties as legal mechanisms by which Aboriginal peoples ceded and surrendered their lands to the Crown. In contrast, First Nations, Inuit, and Métis peoples understand Treaties as a sacred obligation that commits both parties to maintaining respectful relationships and sharing lands and resources equitably.

Indigenous peoples have kept the history and ongoing relevance of the Treaties alive in their own oral histories and legal traditions. Without their perspectives on the history of Treaty making, Canadians know only one side of this country's history. This story cannot simply be told as the story of how Crown officials unilaterally imposed Treaties on Aboriginal peoples; they were also active participants in Treaty negotiations.[46] The history and interpretation of Treaties and the Aboriginal–Crown relationship as told by Indigenous peoples enrich and inform our understanding of why we are all Treaty people.[47] This is evident, for example, in the story of the Royal

Proclamation of 1763 and its relationship to the Treaty of Niagara of 1764. The Royal Proclamation, which was issued by colonial officials, tells only half this story.

On October 7, 1763, King George III issued this Royal Proclamation by which the British Crown first recognized the legal and constitutional rights of Aboriginal peoples in Canada. In the Royal Proclamation of 1763, the British declared that all lands west of the established colonies belonged to Aboriginal peoples and that the Crown could legally acquire these lands only by negotiating Treaties.

At a time when Aboriginal peoples still held considerable power and conflicts with settlers were increasing, British officials sought to establish a distinct geographical area that would remain under the jurisdiction of Indigenous nations until Treaties were negotiated.

Anishinaabe legal scholar John Borrows notes that the Royal Proclamation can be fully understood only in relation to the Treaty of Niagara, in which the terms of the proclamation were ratified by Indigenous nations in 1764. As Borrows explains, the Indigenous leaders who negotiated the Treaty of Niagara with the Crown did so with the understanding that they would remain free and self-determining peoples.

> The Proclamation uncomfortably straddled the contradictory aspirations of the Crown and First Nations when its wording recognized Aboriginal rights to land by outlining a policy that was designed to extinguish these rights.... The different objectives that First Nations and the Crown had in the formulation of the principles surrounding the Proclamation is the reason for the different visions embedded within its text. Britain was attempting to secure territory and jurisdiction through the Proclamation, while the First Nations were concerned with preserving their lands and sovereignty.[48]

The Royal Proclamation was ratified by over 2,000 Indigenous leaders who had gathered at Niagara in the summer of 1764 to make a Treaty with the Crown.[49] The Treaty negotiations, like earlier Treaties of trade and those of peace and friendship, were conducted in accordance with Indigenous law and diplomatic protocol. John Borrows presents evidence that Aboriginal peoples, some fifty-four years after the Treaty of Niagara was negotiated and ratified, still remembered the promises that were made by the Crown. In 1818, a Crown representative, Captain Thomas G. Anderson, gave the following account of a meeting between Anishinaabe peoples and the Crown at Drummond Island in Lake Huron.

> The Chiefs did decamp, laying down a broad Wampum Belt, made in 1764.... Orcata [an Anishinaabe] speaker ... holding the Belt of 1764 in his hand ... said: Father, this my ancestors received from our Father, Sir. W. Johnson. You sent word to all your red children to assemble at the crooked place (Niagara). They heard your voice—obeyed the message—and the next summer met you at the place. You then laid this belt on a mat, and said—'Children, you must all touch this Belt of Peace. I touch it myself, that we may all be brethren united, and hope

our friendship will never cease. I will call you my children; will send warmth (presents) to your country; and your families shall never be in want. Look towards the rising sun. My Nation is as brilliant as it is, and its word cannot be violated.' Father, your words were true—all you promised came to pass. On giving us a Belt of Peace, you said—'If you should ever require my assistance, send this Belt, and my hand will be immediately stretched forth to assist you.' Here the speaker laid down the Belt.[50]

Over the years, Indigenous leaders involved in Treaty negotiations not only used wampum belts to recount the Treaty of Niagara but also presented original copies of the Royal Proclamation to government officials. In 1847, a colonial official reported,

> The subsequent proclamation of His Majesty George Third, issued in 1763, furnished them with a fresh guarantee for the possession of their hunting grounds and the protection of the crown. This document the Indians look upon as their charter. They have preserved a copy of it to the present time, and have referred to it on several occasions in the representations to government.[51]

On October 7, 2013, Canada marked the 250th anniversary of the Royal Proclamation of 1763. The governor general of Canada, His Excellency the Right Honourable David Johnston, spoke about the proclamation's importance.

> This extraordinary document is part of the legal foundation of Canada. It is enshrined in the Constitution Act of 1982, and it sets out a framework of values or principles that have given us a navigational map over the course of the past two-and-a-half centuries.... Its guiding principles—of peace, fairness and respect—established the tradition of treaty-making, laid the basis for the recognition of First Nations rights, and defined the relationship between First Nations peoples and the Crown.... All history reverberates through the ages, but the Royal Proclamation is uniquely alive in the present-day. Not only is it a living constitutional document, its principles are of great relevance to our situation today, in 2013, and to our shared future.... Without a doubt, we have faced, and are facing challenges, and we have much hard work to do on the road to reconciliation, but it is a road we must travel together. In modern time, the successful conclusion of comprehensive land claims agreements are an example of the principles of the Royal Proclamation in action.[52]

Across the country, Indigenous peoples also commemorated the anniversary, calling on Canadians to honour the spirit and intent of the Royal Proclamation. In British Columbia, where very few Treaties were signed, the First Nations Summit leaders issued a statement reminding Canadians that the principles set out in the proclamation were still relevant in present-day Canada. They said,

> With Confederation, the First Nations–Crown relationship has regrettably been guided by federal control under the constraints of the *Indian Act*, not by the principles articulated in the Proclamation.... The time has arrived for all Canadians

to move into an era of recognition and reconciliation between First Nations and the Crown. Although there is general recognition of Aboriginal title and rights, far too often these rights exist without an effective remedy. There are many solutions that have the potential of moving us to where we need to be. Such solutions include the negotiation of modern-day treaties, agreements and other constructive arrangements, consistent with the principles of the Proclamation.[53]

Across the river from the Parliament Buildings in Ottawa that October, Idle No More supporters gathered in Gatineau, Québec, at the Canadian Museum of Civilization to commemorate the Royal Proclamation as part of a national and international day of action. One of the organizers, Clayton Thomas-Muller, said, "We are using this founding document of this country and its anniversary to usher in a new era of reconciliation of Canada's shameful colonial history, to turn around centuries of neglect and abuse of our sacred and diverse nations."[54]

In Toronto, the focus was on the Gus-Wen-Tah, or Two-Row Wampum Treaty belt, used by the Mohawk in Treaty negotiations with colonial European officials.[55] As Aboriginal and non-Aboriginal people gathered to mark the historic day, speaker Davyn Calfchild said, "Everyone needs to learn about the Two-Row and the nation-to-nation relationships it represents. It's not just for Native people; it's for non-Native people too." The gathering ended with a march as people carried a replica of the Two-Row Wampum through the streets of the city.[56] Those who commemorated the Royal Proclamation and the Two-Row Wampum emphasized that the principles and practices that cemented the Treaty relationship remain applicable today.

The Royal Proclamation of 1763, in conjunction with the Treaty of Niagara of 1764, established the legal and political foundation of Canada and the principles of Treaty making based on mutual recognition and respect. A royal proclamation is also an important symbol. Issued at the highest level, it sends a message to all citizens about the values and principles that define the country. There is a need for a new proclamation that reaffirms the long-standing, but often disregarded, commitments between Canada and Aboriginal peoples. The proclamation would include an official disavowal of the Doctrine of Discovery and commitment to the full implementation of the *United Nations Declaration*.

Call to action:

45) We call upon the Government of Canada, on behalf of all Canadians, to jointly develop with Aboriginal peoples a Royal Proclamation of Reconciliation to be issued by the Crown. The proclamation would build on the Royal Proclamation of 1763 and the Treaty of Niagara of 1764, and reaffirm the nation-to-nation

relationship between Aboriginal peoples and the Crown. The proclamation would include, but not be limited to, the following commitments:

i. Repudiate concepts used to justify European sovereignty over Indigenous lands and peoples such as the Doctrine of Discovery and *terra nullius.*

ii. Adopt and implement the *United Nations Declaration on the Rights of Indigenous Peoples* as the framework for reconciliation.

iii. Renew or establish Treaty relationships based on principles of mutual recognition, mutual respect, and shared responsibility for maintaining those relationships into the future.

iv. Reconcile Aboriginal and Crown constitutional and legal orders to ensure that Aboriginal peoples are full partners in Confederation, including the recognition and integration of Indigenous laws and legal traditions in negotiation and implementation processes involving Treaties, land claims, and other constructive agreements.

Covenant of Reconciliation

The principles enunciated in the Royal Proclamation of Reconciliation will serve as the foundation for an action-oriented Covenant of Reconciliation that points the way toward an era of mutual respect and equal opportunity.

A covenant is a pledge or promise made by Treaty partners that establishes how they will conduct themselves as they fulfill their respective Treaty obligations and responsibilities. The historical roots of Indigenous diplomacy and covenant making can be traced back to the Haudenosaunee (Iroquois Confederacy), the Silver Covenant Chain, and the Two-Row Wampum. This complex Treaty system bound the Haudenosaunee nations together in peace and established the original foundations of the Aboriginal-Crown relationship in eastern North America in the early seventeenth century. Legal scholar Robert A. Williams Jr. notes,

> For the Iroquois, the story of the Covenant Chain extended back in time to the period of their first encounters and ensuing treaty relationships with the strange and alien European newcomers to their lands. As a matter of constitutional principle, both the Iroquois and the English were obligated to sustain this story of multicultural unity that had proven to be of such great value to both parties in their struggles for survival in North America. This, of course, accorded precisely with Iroquois constitutional tradition, for as the story of the founding of their own ancient confederacy has told, human solidarity can only be achieved if different peoples imagine the possibilities of linking arms together.[57]

The Haudenosaunee Constitution, the Great Law of Peace, is the authority for establishing and maintaining Treaty alliances, which are recorded on various wampum belts, including the Gus-Wen-Tah, or Two Row Wampum. Legal scholar John Borrows observes that the Gus-Wen-Tah and the Silver Covenant Chain are integral to the constitutional record of the Haudenosaunee nations.

> The belt consists of two rows of purple wampum beads on a white background. Three rows of white beads symbolizing peace, friendship, and respect separate the two purple rows. The two purple rows symbolize two paths or two vessels travelling down the same river. One row symbolizes the Haudenosaunee people with their laws and customs, while the other row symbolizes European law and customs. As nations move together side by side on the river of life, they are to avoid overlapping or interfering with one another. These legal precepts are said to be embedded in subsequent agreements. Another symbol related to the *Gus Wen Tah* that communicates Haudenosaunee independence is the Silver Covenant Chain. It is to be pure, strong, and untarnished, and bind nations together without causing them to lose their individual characteristics or their independence. Those holding the Covenant Chain are responsible for keeping their relationships bright and preventing them from breaking.[58]

Metaphorically, the shared responsibility for repairing a damaged relationship is known as 'polishing the chain' in order to keep the silver from tarnishing.

The ongoing relevance of the Silver Covenant Chain to the Haudenosaunee and to all Indigenous peoples in Canada was made clear on January 24, 2012, at the Crown–First Nations Gathering. To signify the importance of the long-standing relationship between First Nations and the Crown, then AFN National Chief Shawn A-in-chut Atleo presented a Silver Covenant Chain of Peace and a Friendship Belt to Prime Minister Harper and the governor general of Canada, the Right Honourable David Johnston. He explained,

> The Covenant Chain belt represents one of the earliest treaties between the Crown and First Nations peoples and established the foundation for First Nations–Crown relationships for generations thereafter. The belt shows that the Crown is linked by a chain to the First Nations peoples of this land. The three links of the chain represent a covenant of friendship, good minds, and the peace that shall always remain between us. The covenant chain is made of silver symbolizing that the relationship will be polished from time to time to keep it from tarnishing. This was the basis of the Nation to Nation relationship between the British Crown and the First Nations who became their allies in the formation of Canada.[59]

The long, rich history of Indigenous diplomacy and covenant making has been largely forgotten or misunderstood by Canadians. Williams reminds us that the

Indigenous visions of law and peace that prevailed in the seventeenth and eighteenth centuries across North America have great relevance for today.

> [T]here was a time when the West had to listen seriously to these indigenous tribal visions of how different peoples might live together in relationships of trust, solidarity, and respect.... In countless treaties, councils, and negotiations, [North] American Indians insisted upon the relevance of the principles contained in tribal traditions such as the *Gus-Wen-Tah* for ordering the unique and fractious kind of multicultural society that was emerging on the continent. Throughout this period, Europeans secured Indian trade, alliances, and goodwill by adapting themselves to tribal approaches to the problems of achieving law and peace in a multicultural world.
>
> The treaties, councils, and negotiations between Europeans and Indians during the Encounter era reveal a truly unique North American indigenous perspective on the principles and governing paradigms for achieving justice between different peoples.... Given the fragmenting nature of our present societal and world order, there are a number of important reasons for trying to develop a better understanding of these ... tribal visions of law, peace, and justice between different peoples.[60]

In the Commission's view, the spiritual, legal, and moral foundations of reconciliation can be found in these early Treaties and covenants. Canada and the world have much to gain by once again listening seriously—that is, with respect—to Indigenous peoples' teachings about how to resolve conflicts constructively and make peace among diverse groups and nations.[61]

Churches and covenant making

Along with governments, the churches have a role to play in covenant making. At the TRC's Manitoba National Event, the church parties to the Settlement Agreement hosted an Interfaith Tent. During the panel "We Are All Treaty People," leaders from various faiths pointed out that many spiritual traditions—Indigenous, Christian, Muslim, and Jewish—share a belief in sacred covenants between peoples and the Creator God, which for Indigenous peoples is manifested in Treaty covenants.

In the 1980s, several church institutions established the Aboriginal Rights Coalition to support Aboriginal peoples in their efforts to entrench their right to self-determination in the Canadian Constitution.[62] Following the repatriation of Canada's Constitution in 1982, church representatives attended each of the First Ministers' Conferences held during the mid-1980s as observers under the auspices of the various national Aboriginal organizations. They participated in consultation sessions and met with federal and provincial politicians to support Aboriginal issues.

In February 1987, nine national leaders of denominations and major church organizations issued *A New Covenant: Towards the Constitutional Recognition and Protection of Aboriginal Self-Government in Canada, A Pastoral Statement by the Leaders of the Christian Churches on Aboriginal Rights and the Canadian Constitution.* The *New Covenant* declared, in part,

> As pastoral leaders, we believe that this is an historic movement in the life of this country. This round of constitutional negotiations will affect the lives of some two million Indian, Inuit and Métis people and their descendants for the generations to come. Many of these Aboriginal peoples, whose ancestors have inhabited this country since time immemorial, are members of our churches.... It is a time to establish a new covenant with the first peoples and nations of Canada....
>
> The idea of covenant-making has deep spiritual roots, which, in turn, can teach us a great deal about the true purpose and meaning of covenant-making and covenant-keeping among peoples today....
>
> Thus there are moral and spiritual dimensions to making and keeping covenants ... A new covenant would recognize the rights and responsibilities of Indian, Inuit and Métis to be distinct peoples and cultures. A new covenant should affirm their rights and responsibilities as self-determining nations and societies within Canada....
>
> Today, after the experience of cultural oppression and economic dependency in recent centuries, Aboriginal peoples are struggling to decolonize themselves and regain recognition of their historic rights in Canada. These Aboriginal rights are recognized in both international law and the historic documents of this country. We maintain, however, that the rights of Aboriginal peoples are not simply a legal or political issue, but first and foremost, a moral issue touching the very soul and heart of Canada....
>
> Self-government is the means by which Aboriginal peoples could give concrete expression of themselves as distinct peoples, develop the economic potential of their own lands, and design their own cultural, social and religious institutions to meet the needs of their own people....
>
> Canada could become a living example, before the rest of the world, of a society that is coming to terms with the historic demands for justice affecting the descendants of its original inhabitants. In doing so, we might be able to recover some of the deeper spiritual meaning of covenant-making.[63]

In 1993, during the proceedings of the Royal Commission on Aboriginal Peoples, Christian churches, as well as the Aboriginal Rights Coalition, made submissions to the RCAP. Separately and together through the coalition, their presentations reiterated the three key messages contained in the earlier *New Covenant* pastoral statement: Aboriginal peoples' right to be distinct peoples, their right to an adequate land base, and their right to self-determination.[64] In a ceremony in Winnipeg in 2007, the churches marked the twenty-year anniversary of the *New Covenant* by renewing and reaffirming their commitment to the covenant made in 1987.[65]

Together all of the parties to the Settlement Agreement must demonstrate leadership by establishing and implementing a Covenant of Reconciliation. Coupled with a Royal Proclamation of Reconciliation, implementation of the *UN Declaration*, and repudiation of the Doctrine of Discovery and *terra nullius*, the covenant would reaffirm past undertakings and establish inclusive principles for action on reconciliation.

Call to action:

46) We call upon the parties to the Indian Residential Schools Settlement Agreement to develop and sign a Covenant of Reconciliation that would identify principles for working collaboratively to advance reconciliation in Canadian society, and that would include, but not be limited to:

    i. Reaffirmation of the parties' commitment to reconciliation.

    ii. Repudiation of concepts used to justify European sovereignty over Indigenous lands and peoples, such as the Doctrine of Discovery and *terra nullius*, and the reformation of laws, governance structures, and policies within their respective institutions that continue to rely on such concepts.

    iii. Full adoption and implementation of the *United Nations Declaration on the Rights of Indigenous Peoples* as the framework for reconciliation.

    iv. Support for the renewal or establishment of Treaty relationships based on principles of mutual recognition, mutual respect, and shared responsibility for maintaining those relationships into the future.

    v. Enabling those excluded from the Settlement Agreement to sign onto the Covenant of Reconciliation.

    vi. Enabling additional parties to sign onto the Covenant of Reconciliation.

Governments at all levels of Canadian society must also commit to a new framework for reconciliation to guide their relations with Aboriginal peoples.

Call to action:

47) We call upon federal, provincial, territorial, and municipal governments to repudiate concepts used to justify European sovereignty over Indigenous peoples and lands, such as the Doctrine of Discovery and *terra nullius*, and to reform those laws, government policies, and litigation strategies that continue to rely on such concepts.

Churches and faith groups also have an important role to play in fostering reconciliation through support for the *United Nations Declaration* and repudiation of the Doctrine of Discovery.

Calls to action:

48) We call upon the church parties to the Settlement Agreement, and all other faith groups and interfaith social justice groups in Canada who have not already done so, to formally adopt and comply with the principles, norms, and standards of the *United Nations Declaration on the Rights of Indigenous Peoples* as a framework for reconciliation. This would include, but not be limited to, the following commitments:

   i. Ensuring that their institutions, policies, programs, and practices comply with the *United Nations Declaration on the Rights of Indigenous Peoples*.

   ii. Respecting Indigenous peoples' right to self-determination in spiritual matters, including the right to practise, develop, and teach their own spiritual and religious traditions, customs, and ceremonies, consistent with Article 12:1 of the *United Nations Declaration on the Rights of Indigenous Peoples*.

   iii. Engaging in ongoing public dialogue and actions to support the *United Nations Declaration on the Rights of Indigenous Peoples*.

   iv. Issuing a statement no later than March 31, 2016, from all religious denominations and faith groups, as to how they will implement the *United Nations Declaration on the Rights of Indigenous Peoples*.

49) We call upon all religious denominations and faith groups who have not already done so to repudiate concepts used to justify European sovereignty over Indigenous lands and peoples, such as the Doctrine of Discovery and *terra nullius*.

CHAPTER 2

Indigenous law: Truth, reconciliation, and access to justice

All Canadians need to understand the difference between Indigenous law and Aboriginal law. Long before Europeans came to North America, Indigenous peoples, like all societies, had political systems and laws that governed behaviour within their own communities and their relationships with other nations. Indigenous law is diverse; each Indigenous nation across the country has its own laws and legal traditions. Aboriginal law is the body of law that exists within the Canadian legal system. The Supreme Court of Canada has recognized the pre-existence and ongoing validity of Indigenous law.[1] Legal scholar John Borrows explains that,

> The recognition of Indigenous legal traditions alongside other legal orders has historic precedent in this land. Prior to the arrival of Europeans and explorers from other continents, a vibrant legal pluralism sometimes developed amongst First Nations. Treaties, intermarriages, contracts of trade and commerce, and mutual recognition were legal arrangements that contributed to long periods of peace and helped to restrain recourse to war when conflict broke out. When Europeans came to North America, they found themselves in this complex socio-legal landscape....
>
> There were wider systems of diplomacy in use to maintain peace through councils and elaborate protocols. For example, First Nations and powerful individuals would participate in such activities as smoking the peace pipe, feasting, holding a Potlatch, exchanging ceremonial objects, and engaging in long orations, discussions and negotiations. Diplomatic traditions among Indigenous peoples were designed to prevent more direct confrontation....
>
> Treaties are a form of agreement that can be very productive as a method for securing peace....
>
> Peace was also pursued through intersocietal activities between First Nations to bridge division and discord. These less formalized paths to peace should not be underestimated; they contain lessons about how to effectively overcome problems today.[2]

If Canada is to transform its relationship with Aboriginal peoples, Canadians must understand and respect First Nations, Inuit, and Métis peoples own concepts of reconciliation. Many of these concepts are found in Indigenous law.

In undertaking this journey, it must be recognized that understanding and applying these concepts can be hard work. As with the common law and civil law systems, Indigenous law is learned through a lifetime of work. Applying Indigenous law also requires an acknowledgement that it exists in the real world and has relevance today. It is most helpful when applied to humankind's most troubling behaviours.

One of the most damaging consequences of residential schools has been that so many Survivors, their families, and whole communities have lost the connection to their own cultures, languages, and laws. The opportunity to learn, understand, and practise the laws of their ancestors as part of their heritage and birthright was taken away. Yet despite years of oppression, this knowledge did not disappear; many Elders and Knowledge Keepers have continued to carry and protect the laws of their peoples to the present day.

At the Truth and Reconciliation Commission's (TRC) Traditional Knowledge Keepers Forum, Blackfoot Elder Reg Crowshoe said,

> When I was younger, in my community my grandmother brought me to the societies ... I believed [that] everything was equal—plants, animals, the air, the moon, the sun, everything was equal. That was the belief system that we had in our culture. Out of that belief system, we developed practices, practices where we sat in circles in a learning society ... And once you join the society, you become part of that learning society and your responsibility [was] to be a part of [the] practices that allowed you to survive, which includes reconciliation and forgiveness ...
>
> When we look at our oral cultures and we look at who we are and the environment, the geographic territory we've come from, we are given all kinds of challenges every day. How do we access our theories? How do we access our stories? How do we access our Elders? Where do we pay our fees and what are our protocols? So we are looking at finding those true meanings of reconciliation and forgiveness. We need to be aware or re-taught how to access those stories of our Elders, not only stories but songs, practices that give us those rights and privileges to access those stories ... So when we are looking at [the] concept of reconciliation, there's a lot to learn ...
>
> The Elders say that we live in a geographic location in Southern Alberta as Blackfoot. Our authorities come from our ties to that land, the songs that come from that land, that's where our authorities come. Other First Nations have their geographic location, their ties to that land. So when I go into some other territory, I honour and respect that territory and use their songs. I have songs for rocks that allow me the rights and privileges to use rocks for a sweat, for example, but when I go into another territory, I have to depend on that territory's songs that allows

them to use their rocks for healing, I have to respect that, and for hundreds of years we respected each other and we visited each other. I encourage all the First Nations to go back to their theories, go back to their stories, go back to their Elders, go back to your protocols, and find the solutions because we need them today.[3]

There are many sources of Indigenous law that hold great insight for reconciliation. The further understanding and development of Indigenous law promise to reveal treasured resources for decision making, regulation, and dispute resolution. Legal scholar Val Napoleon explains,

> Indigenous law is a crucial resource for Indigenous peoples. It is integrally connected with how we imagine and manage ourselves both collectively and individually. In other words, law and all it entails is a fundamental aspect of being collectively and individually self-determining as peoples. Indigenous law is about building citizenship, responsibility and governance, challenging internal and external oppressions, safety and protection, lands and resources, and external political relations with other Indigenous peoples and the state.[4]

First Nations, Inuit, and Métis communities across the country are making concerted efforts to recover and revitalize their laws and legal traditions. They must be supported in these efforts.

Canadian law and Aboriginal peoples: Uncovering truth

Law is essential to finding truth. It is a necessary part of realizing reconciliation. This is because law liberates the flow of information that might otherwise be blocked. Without this transparency, truth can fall victim to manipulation, suppression, and concealment. Without healthy legal processes, facts can be hidden from public view when people are charged with wrongdoing. Law provides public spaces for testing truth. It does so through oath-bound testimonies and disclosures concerning contested events. Law is also a tool for pursuing reconciliation. Whenever disputes arise, law facilitates dialogue through the hearing, consideration, incorporation, rejection, or adoption of different points of view. Law encourages listening and deliberation. It is designed to accomplish these goals while judging issues by broader standards aimed at societal peace.

Until recently, Canadian law was used by Canada to suppress truth and deter reconciliation. Parliament's creation of assimilative laws and regulations facilitated the oppression of Aboriginal cultures and enabled the Indian residential school system. In addition, Canada's laws and associated legal principles fostered an atmosphere of secrecy and concealment. When children were abused in residential schools, the law, and the ways that it was enforced (or not), became a shield behind which churches, governments, and individuals could hide to avoid the consequences of horrific truths. Decisions not to charge or prosecute abusers allowed people to escape the harmful consequences of their actions. In addition, the right of Aboriginal communities and leaders to function in accordance with their own customs, traditions, laws, and cultures was taken away by law. Those who continued to act in accordance with those cultures could be, and were, prosecuted. Aboriginal people came to see law as a tool of government oppression.

To this point, the country's civil laws continued to overlook the truth that the extinguishment of peoples' languages and cultures is a personal and social injury of the deepest kind. It is difficult to understand why the forced assimilation of children through removal from their families and communities—to be placed with people of another race for the purpose of destroying the race and culture from which the children come—is not a civil wrong even though it can be deemed an act of genocide under Article 2(e) of the *United Nations Convention on Genocide.*

Failure to recognize such truths hinders reconciliation. Many Aboriginal people have a deep and abiding distrust of Canada's political and legal systems because of the damage these systems have caused. They often see Canada's legal system as being an arm of a Canadian governing structure that has been diametrically opposed to their interests. Despite court judgments, not only has Canadian law generally not protected Aboriginal land rights, resources, and governmental authority, but it has also allowed, and continues to allow, the removal of Aboriginal children through a child-welfare system that cuts them off from their culture. As a result, law has been, and continues to be, a significant obstacle to reconciliation. This is the case despite the recognition that courts have begun to show that justice has historically been denied and that such denial should not continue. Given these circumstances, it should come as no surprise that formal Canadian law and Canada's legal institutions are still viewed with suspicion within many Aboriginal communities.

Yet that is changing. Court decisions since the repatriation of Canada's Constitution in 1982 have given hope to Aboriginal people that the recognition and affirmation of their existing Treaty and Aboriginal rights in Section 35 of the *Constitution Act, 1982* may be an important vehicle for change. However, the view of many Aboriginal people is that the utilization of Canada's courts is fraught with danger. Aboriginal leaders and communities turn to the courts literally because there is no other legal mechanism. When they do so, it is with the knowledge that the courts are still reluctant to recognize their own traditional means of dispute resolution and law.

Reconciliation will be difficult to achieve until Indigenous peoples' own traditions for uncovering truth and enhancing reconciliation are embraced as an essential part of the ongoing process of truth determination, dispute resolution, and reconciliation. No dialogue about reconciliation can be undertaken without mutual respect as shown through protocols and ceremony. Just as the mace, for example, is essential to a session of Parliament, the presence of the pipe for some tribes would be necessary to a formal process of reconciliation.

The road to reconciliation also includes a large, liberal, and generous application of the concepts underlying Section 35(1) of Canada's Constitution so that Aboriginal rights are implemented in a way that facilitates Aboriginal peoples' collective and individual aspirations. The reconciliation vision that lies behind Section 35 should not be seen as a means to subjugate Aboriginal peoples to an absolutely sovereign Crown but as a means to establish the kind of relationship that should have flourished since Confederation, as was envisioned in the Royal Proclamation of 1763 and the post-Confederation Treaties. That relationship did not flourish because of Canada's failure to live up to that vision and its promises. So long as the vision of reconciliation in Section 35(1) is not being implemented with sufficient strength and vigour, Canadian law will continue to be regarded as deeply adverse to realizing truth and reconciliation for many First Nations, Inuit, and Métis people. To improve Aboriginal peoples' access to justice, changes must occur on at least two fronts: at a national level and within each Aboriginal community.

The *United Nations Declaration on the Rights of Indigenous Peoples* and access to justice

The *United Nations Declaration on the Rights of Indigenous Peoples* and the UN "Outcome Document" provide a framework and a mechanism to support and improve access to justice for Indigenous peoples in Canada. Under Article 40 of the *Declaration,*

> Indigenous peoples have the right to access to and prompt decision through just and fair procedures for the resolution of conflicts and disputes with States or other parties, as well as to effective remedies for all infringements of their individual and collective rights. Such a decision shall give due consideration to the customs, traditions, rules and legal systems of the indigenous peoples concerned and international human rights.[5]

In 2013, the UN Expert Mechanism on the Rights of Indigenous Peoples issued the study "Access to Justice in the Promotion and Protection of the Rights of Indigenous Peoples." It made several key findings that are relevant to Canada. The international study noted that states and Indigenous peoples themselves have a critical role to play in implementing Indigenous peoples' access to justice. Substantive changes are required within the criminal legal system and in relation to political self-determination, community well-being, and Indigenous peoples' rights to their lands, territories, and natural resources.[6] The study made several key findings and recommendations, including the following:

> The right to self-determination is a central right for indigenous peoples from which all other rights flow. In relation to access to justice, self-determination affirms their right to maintain and strengthen indigenous legal institutions, and to apply their own customs and laws.
>
> The cultural rights of indigenous peoples include recognition and practice of their justice systems ... as well as recognition of their traditional customs, values and languages by courts and legal procedures.
>
> Consistent with indigenous peoples' right to self-determination and self-government, States should recognize and provide support for indigenous peoples' own justice systems and should consult with indigenous peoples on the best means for dialogue and cooperation between indigenous and State systems.
>
> States should recognize indigenous peoples' rights to their lands, territories and resources in laws and should harmonize laws in accordance with indigenous peoples' customs on possession and use of lands. Where indigenous peoples have won land rights and other cases in courts, States must implement these decisions. The private sector and government must not collude to deprive indigenous peoples of access to justice.
>
> Indigenous peoples should strengthen advocacy for the recognition of their justice systems.
>
> Indigenous peoples' justice systems should ensure that indigenous women and children are free from all forms of discrimination and should ensure accessibility to indigenous persons with disabilities.
>
> Indigenous peoples should explore the organization and running of their own truth-seeking processes.[7]

These conclusions are consistent with this Commission's own views. We also concur with the 2014 report issued by S. James Anaya, the United Nations Special Rapporteur on the Rights of Indigenous Peoples, about the state of Canada's relationship with Indigenous peoples. He concluded that the

> Government of Canada has a stated goal of reconciliation, which the Special Rapporteur heard repeated by numerous government representatives with whom he met. Yet even in this context, in recent years, indigenous leaders have expressed concern that progress towards this goal has been undermined by actions of the Government that limit or ignore the input of indigenous governments and representatives in various decisions that concern them....

[D]espite positive steps, daunting challenges remain. Canada faces a continuing crisis when it comes to the situation of indigenous peoples of the country. The well-being gap between aboriginal and non-aboriginal people in Canada has not narrowed over the last several years, treaty and aboriginal claims remain persistently unresolved, indigenous women and girls remain vulnerable to abuse, and overall there appear to be high levels of distrust among indigenous peoples towards government at both the federal and provincial levels.[8]

In Canada, law must cease to be a tool for the dispossession and dismantling of Aboriginal societies. It must dramatically change if it is going to have any legitimacy within First Nations, Inuit, and Métis communities. Until Canadian law becomes an instrument supporting Aboriginal peoples' empowerment, many Aboriginal people will continue to regard it as a morally and politically malignant force. A commitment to truth and reconciliation demands that Canada's legal system be transformed. It must ensure that Aboriginal peoples have greater ownership of, participation in, and access to its central driving forces.

Canada's Constitution must become truly a constitution for all of Canada.[9] Aboriginal peoples need to become the law's architects and interpreters where it applies to their collective rights and interests. Aboriginal peoples need to have more formal influence on national legal matters in order to advance and realize their diverse goals. At the same time, First Nations, Inuit, and Métis peoples need greater control of their own regulatory laws and dispute-resolution mechanisms.

Recovering and revitalizing Indigenous law

Aboriginal peoples must be recognized as possessing the responsibility, authority, and capability to address their disagreements by making laws within their communities. This undertaking is necessary to facilitate truth and reconciliation within Aboriginal societies.

Law is necessary to protect communities and individuals from the harmful actions of others. When such harm occurs within Aboriginal communities, Indigenous law is needed to censure and correct citizens when they depart from what the community defines as being acceptable. Any failure to recognize First Nations, Inuit, and Métis law would be a failure to affirm that Aboriginal peoples, like all other peoples, need the power of law to effectively deal with the challenges they face.

The Commission believes that the revitalization and application of Indigenous law will benefit First Nations, Inuit, and Métis communities, Aboriginal–Crown relations, and the nation as a whole. For this to happen, Aboriginal peoples must be able to recover, learn, and practise their own, distinct legal traditions. That is not to say that the development of self-government institutions and laws must occur at the band or village level. In its report, the Royal Commission on Aboriginal Peoples spoke about the development of self-government by Aboriginal nations:

> We have concluded that the right of self-government cannot reasonably be exercised by small, separate communities, whether First Nations, Inuit or Métis. It should be exercised by groups of a certain size—groups with a claim to the term 'nation.'

> The problem is that the historical Aboriginal nations were undermined by disease, relocations and the full array of assimilationist government policies. They were fragmented into bands, reserves and small settlements. Only some operate as collectivities now. They will have to reconstruct themselves as nations.[10]

We endorse the approach recommended by the Royal Commission.

Indigenous law, like so many other aspects of Aboriginal peoples' lives, has been impacted by colonization. At the TRC's Knowledge Keepers Forum in 2014, Mi'kmaq Elder Stephen Augustine spoke about the Mi'kmaq concept for "making things right." He shared a story about an overturned canoe in the river. He said, "We'll make the canoe right and ... keep it in water so it does not bump on rocks or hit the shore.... [When we tip a canoe] we may lose some of our possessions.... Eventually we will regain our possessions [but] they will not be the same as the old ones."[11]

We can consider this concept in relation to the great and obvious loss caused by the residential schools. The Mi'kmaq idea for "making things right" implies that sometimes, in certain contexts, things can be made right—but the remedy might not allow us to recapture what was lost. Making things right might involve creating something new as we journey forward. Just as the Canadian legal system has evolved over time, Indigenous law is not frozen in time. Indigenous legal orders adapt with changing circumstances. The development and application of Indigenous law should be regarded as one element of a broader holistic strategy to deal with the residential schools' negative effects.

Gender, power, and Indigenous law

The high levels of discrimination and violence against Aboriginal women and girls that exist in their own communities and in broader Canadian society have been well documented. Volumes of research and reports produced over the years, including that of the Royal Commission on Aboriginal Peoples, attest to the fact that the *Indian Act* has had very specific and devastating impacts on the lives of Aboriginal women and their children.[12] Despite the equality guarantees in the *Constitution Act, 1982* and the Charter of Rights and Freedoms, scholar Joyce Green observes that "this has not translated into equitable treatment or representation as *Aboriginal* women in either

Aboriginal or settler political institutions or policies."[13] Violence against Aboriginal women and girls has reached epidemic proportions. The Commission has called for a public inquiry into the causes of, and remedies for, the disproportionate victimization of Aboriginal women and girls, including an investigation into missing and murdered Aboriginal women and girls, and the links to the intergenerational legacy of residential schools (see Call to Action 41).

Aboriginal women themselves have been at the forefront of advocating for, and in some cases achieving, legal and social change with regard to their rights in their own communities, in the Canadian courts, and on the international front in negotiating the *UN Declaration on the Rights of Indigenous Peoples*.[14] The *Declaration* includes specific articles affirming Indigenous women's collective and individual right to live free of gender discrimination and violence.[15] Article 44 of the *Declaration* states, "All the rights and freedoms recognized herein are equally guaranteed to male and female indigenous individuals."

The Commission rejects any use of Indigenous or other laws that fundamentally treat women or men in ways that communicate or create subordination. Any law that creates or reproduces gendered hierarchies that subordinate women or men must be contested and overturned. Fortunately, tools exist within Indigenous legal traditions, international law, and Canadian constitutional law to strongly address these challenges without undermining Indigenous legal systems.[16] In fact, Indigenous law is significantly strengthened as it empowers Indigenous women and men to interrogate and overturn damaging gender assumptions and activities.

Yet law is a living system of social order. When any legal tradition is applied, it must be remembered that it never produces a final work. The need for constant monitoring of these questions will always be relevant (as is the case with any set of legal traditions, including the common law or civil legal tradition). As Indigenous studies scholar Emma LaRocque writes,

> as women we must be circumspect in our recall of tradition. We must ask ourselves whether and to what extent tradition is liberating to us as women. We must ask ourselves wherein lies (lie) our source(s) of empowerment. We know enough about human history that we cannot assume that all Aboriginal traditions universally respected and honoured women. (And is 'respect' and 'honour' all that we can ask for?) ... [W]e are challenged to change, create, and embrace 'traditions' consistent with contemporary and international human rights standards.[17]

Likewise, historian Kim Anderson cautions,

> As we fervently recover our spiritual traditions, we must also bear in mind that regulating the role of women is one of the hallmarks of fundamentalism. This regulation is accomplished through prescriptive teachings related to how

women should behave, how they should dress and, of course, how well they symbolize and uphold the moral order.[18]

It is crucial to ask critical and constructive questions about tradition and power wherever they are deployed. As noted, this goes as much for Canadian laws more generally as it does for Indigenous peoples' own law. No one in any legal system is safe from the reach of oppressive traditions. Contemporary issues concerning gender and other inequalities must necessarily be part of these laws for them to be persuasively applicable in the present day.

As sociologist Emily Snyder has argued, working with Indigenous law must involve discussion about how gender, power relations, and ideas about Indigenous women's traditional role in society can inform the interpretation and application of Indigenous law in ways that combat colonialism, sexism, and oppression in Aboriginal communities.[19] In reflecting on present applications of Indigenous law, she identifies questions that should be asked, such as:

> Who is included in discussions about Indigenous law? Are women present? ...
> Who is leading these discussions? ... Are there specific contexts in which men are
> considered the authoritative speakers and decision-makers? Specific contexts in
> which women are? How are men and women involved in the legal process simi-
> larly and/or differently? ... Is gender talked about? ... If legal decisions are made,
> are men and women impacted differently by them? ... How are legal principles
> (for example, respect and reciprocity) talked about? ... What is missing? Does
> gendered conflict need to be acknowledged? If it were, how might it change the
> discussion? ... Are the legal processes, interpretations, and decisions empower-
> ing for Indigenous women? ... Is there space for women to challenge the process
> if need be?[20]

These questions must be centrally alive in the application of any law, including those that arise from Indigenous peoples' own legal traditions. The Commission is resolute in proclaiming that the application of Indigenous law must comply with all international and constitutional laws related to gender and other inequalities for it to have a productive role related to reconciliation in Canada. We believe Indigenous legal systems exist in this realm and are capable of facilitating reconciliation while ensuring that power is appropriately exercised and checked when applying Indigenous law.

Practising Indigenous law

As Commissioners, we recognize that every Indigenous nation across North America has its own culturally specific laws that are enacted, validated, and enforced through protocols and ceremonies that are uniquely their own. With limited time and resources, it was not possible for the Commission to highlight them all in this report.

We do believe however that it is essential to provide some representative examples that will give all Canadians, Aboriginal and non-Aboriginal alike, a better understanding of the breadth, scope, and richness of Indigenous law and its potential for justice, healing, and reconciliation.

We must emphasize that these examples are by no means exhaustive accounts; they provide the merest of glimpses into how these complex and diverse legal systems addressed conflict and restored peaceful relationships in the past and how such laws and practices are being restored and applied today. The expertise and authority to explain and use these laws and traditions rest with the Indigenous nations to whom they belong. This highlights the urgent need to ensure that First Nations, Inuit, and Métis peoples have the necessary support and resources to undertake this important work themselves.

We also wish to be clear that the decision to use Indigenous laws, protocols, and ceremonies to pursue reconciliation *must* rest with each Indigenous nation as self-determining peoples. Neither the Commission, nor the federal government, nor any other body has authority to initiate these proceedings.

Haudenosaunee peoples

The Haudenosaunee peoples (Iroquois Confederacy or Six Nations)[21] of the eastern woodlands have legal traditions for establishing and repairing relationships—a vital component of reconciliation. These laws also contain practices that could be adopted more generally to facilitate healing. A significant Haudenosaunee tradition, designed to alleviate grief and restore balance, is the Condolence ceremony.[22]

The Haudenosaunee peoples, joined together in a Confederacy under the Great Law of Peace, have used the Condolence ceremony for thousands of years in protocols for peacemaking and in Treaty diplomacy. Wampum belts record this history, depicting the process of "clearing obstructions from the path, polishing the covenant chain, building up the council fire and the procedures at the Wood's Edge. The metaphors of the fire, the path and the chain reveal ... the Iroquoian view [that] the alliance was naturally in a state of constant deterioration and in need of attention."[23]

The Condolence ceremony allows people who have been through traumatic experiences together—those who are healthy, those who are in mourning, and those who have caused harm—to work together to address losses.[24] Through this ceremony, apologies and restitution are embodied in expressive performances as people are called upon to tell stories and acknowledge losses related to the harms they have suffered.[25] The ceremony occurs in a precise sequence, employing vivid imagery, and can be used in many circumstances where trust and understanding have been broken because of a party's harmful actions.[26]

Legal scholar Robert A. Williams Jr. has described historical accounts of the Condolence ceremony and its significance for Treaty making within the Iroquois Confederacy and with colonial officials.

> Following the greeting at the wood's edge, the Clear-Minded, together with the Mourners, perform the Condolence Council ritual ... A speaker for the Mourners "wipes the eyes" of the weary travelers from the Clear-Minded side with buckskin cloth, so that they will be able to see normally again. He then "clears their ears" of all they have heard that might cause them to alter their messages of peace and condolence. Then, offering a beverage, he "clears the obstructions from their throats" coated with dust from the forest paths so that they will be able to speak normally once again....
>
> [T]he Mourners [then] lead the Clear-Minded "by the arm" to the village council house, where the condolence ceremony continues. At the village, the Clear-Minded initiate a sequenced exchange of gifts of wampum strings and belts ... with the Mourners....
>
> A speaker for the Clear-Minded side offers the wampum gifts to the Mourners, telling the stories spoken by the wampum: stories of rekindling the fire "to bind us close"; of grave sorrow for the dead chief; of wiping away any bad blood between the two sides; of sharing the same bowl to eat together; of dispelling the clouds and restoring the sun that shines truth on all peoples. More songs follow this ritualized exchange of wampum to condole the loss of the deceased chief. After the Clear-Minded finish with their side of the ceremony, the Mourners reciprocate by presenting their own gifts of wampum, stories, condolences, and songs to the Clear-Minded.
>
> With completion of these condoling ceremonies, the new Iroquois chief, selected by the clan women of the Mourning village who own the chief's name and title, is installed. This ceremony is followed by a great dance and terminal feast. The society is restored ...
>
> Throughout the treaty literature, Iroquois diplomats can be witnessed conducting virtually all of their treaty negotiations according to ritual structures adapted from the Condolence Council. The exigencies of forest diplomacy often required certain modifications to the traditional mourning ceremony ... [For example,] Condolence Council rituals were performed by Iroquois diplomats to mourn the deaths of non-Iroquois allies.[27]

Denis Foley, curator at the Lewis Henry Morgan Institute in Utica, New York, has written about how the Condolence ceremony has been adapted to meet changing circumstances.

In the late twentieth century, *Hatahts'ikrehtha'* ("he makes the clouds descend"), Cayuga Chief Jacob ("Jake") Thomas, became a condolence ritualist for the Confederate chiefs at the Six Nations Reserve, Ontario. The hereditary chiefs here were [supposedly] ousted from formal governing power in 1923 by Canadian authorities in a bloodless coup. An elective council [supposedly] replaced the chiefs. After this event the Alliance Condolence evolved into a version that stresses discontent at the white man's suppression of Iroquois rights. In this ceremony Thomas used the traditional purple wampum strings, which he symbolically passed over the fire to his white allies. Chief Thomas, however, changed the accompanying metaphors of wiping tears from the eyes, unplugging the ears, and removing blood from the mat to metaphors reflecting the theft of Iroquois lands and broken promises and treaties. Recriminations intended for the non-Iroquois participants were added through new metaphors: removing the fog that prevents one from seeing the truth, removing dirt from one's ears so the story of the Iroquois people can be heard, and washing the blood of the Iroquois people from the white man's hands so that they may know the clasp of true friendship.[28]

Mohawk scholar Taiaiake Alfred explains the ongoing relevance of the Condolence ceremony today for the Rotinoshonni[29] as they seek to honour and revitalize their traditional teachings and laws.

> Only by heeding the voices of our ancestors can we restore our nations and put peace, power, and righteousness back into the hearts and minds of our people. The Condolence ritual pacifies the mind and emboldens the hearts of mourners by transforming loss into strength. In Rotinoshonni culture, it is the essential means of recovering the wisdom seemingly lost with the passing of a respected leader. Condolence is the mourning of a family's loss by those who remain strong-minded. It is a gift promising comfort, recovery of balance, and revival of spirit to those who are suffering. By strengthening family ties, sharing knowledge, and celebrating the power of traditional teachings, the Condolence ritual heals. It fends off destruction of the soul and restores hearts and minds. It revives the spirit of the people and brings forward new leaders embodying ancient wisdom and new hope.[30]

The Condolence ceremony is a living tradition and can be adapted according to current leaders' ideas, protocol, and needs. The requirements for a Condolence ceremony are certainly met by the residential school experience. The living nature of this legal, diplomatic, and spiritual tradition means that it could be adapted to fit these circumstances. The Condolence ceremony has been used, for example, by Mohawk women to address intergenerational abuse, trauma, and grief.[31]

The physical nature of the ceremony could help the government, churches, and those who are harmed recognize that everything that happened at the residential schools had physical, spiritual, emotional, and metaphysical dimensions. A

Condolence ceremony would highlight the harmful consequences suffered by all Survivors, regardless of their individual experiences at residential school. At the same time, the ceremony would help to create recognition among the wider population of the spiritual, emotional, and metaphysical nature of what was lost through the residential schools.

Any use of the ceremony would have to adhere to what was required of the Haudenosaunee Confederacy under the Great Law of Peace.[32] However, if a decision was ever made by the Haudenosaunee peoples to apply these practices and principles, they would demonstrate more fully the nature of the harms flowing from residential school experiences. Such ceremonies would also point the way to future actions in regard to building better relationships. They would help to restore the well-being of all those who participate and would enable government and church officials to make apologies and provide restitution in accordance with the principles and protocols of Haudenosaunee law.

Cree peoples

The Cree peoples of the Prairies and the Hudson Bay watershed use the circle as a symbol of and vehicle for reconciliation. The circle reminds people of the broader motions of life, which must eventually be reconciled in relation to Mother Earth. The earth's shape is a circle, her seasons move through a circle, and all peoples' journeys through life are part of this circle. People are born as infants, before growing into small children, who then become adults, parents, and possibly even Elders, before they return to their mother, who gave them life. When actions must be taken to facilitate reconciliation, Cree people often gather in circles to conduct such business. These circles exist to remind participants of these sacred teachings and of the impact that their deliberations will have on a person's and community's progression through life. By using circles, the Cree reaffirm their unity under the Creator's laws and their understanding of the larger wheel of life.[33] Black Elk, a well-known and highly respected nineteenth-century spiritual leader from the Plains, expressed the importance of the circle.

> Everything the power of the world does is always done in a circle. The sky is round and I have heard that the earth is round like a ball and so are all the stars. The wind, in its greatest power, whirls. Birds make their nests in circles, for theirs is the same religion as ours. The sun comes forth and goes down again in a circle. The moon does the same and both are round. Even the seasons form a great circle in their changing and always come back again to where they were. The life of a man is a circle from childhood to childhood, and so it is in everything where power moves. Our teepees were round like the nests of birds, and these were

always set in a circle, the nation's hoop, a nest of many nests, where the Great Spirit meant for us to hatch our children.[34]

Although other traditions and approaches to reconciliation are apparent within Cree society, circles are critically important in working towards reconciliation within Cree law. In fact, there are many types of circles that can be convened in a Cree context, including prayer circles, talking circles, and healing circles.[35] Such circles can be activated when someone is unbalanced and does something harmful. These circles provide a place where such people can discuss the causes and consequences of their actions with family members, Cree Elders, leaders, and medicine people in an attempt to restore proper balance in their lives and within their communities.[36]

These laws were discussed at a gathering of Cree Knowledge Keepers and Treaty 6 territory Elders on March 22 and 23, 2011. At this meeting, *nêhiyaw wiyasowêwina* (Cree law) was identified as residing within an intricate matrix of complex principles. The Elders identified eight principles within their laws that helped to balance their communities. These principles are *pimâtisiwin* (life), *pimâcihowin* (livelihood), *pâstâhowin* (breaking laws against humans), *ohcinêwin* (breaking laws against anything other than a human), *manâtisiwin* (respect), *miyo-ohpikinâwasowin* (good childrearing), *wahkôtowin* (kinship), and *tâpowakêyihtamowin* (faith, spirituality). All were recognized as being an essential part of Cree life.[37] These legal principles have obvious value for reconciliation since each concept is directed towards healthier relationships.

Legal scholar Val Napoleon has likewise discussed aspects of Cree law that can help to reveal truth and facilitate reconciliation. In her graphic novel *Mikomosis and the Wetiko*, she explains the importance of seeing Cree law as a mechanism for ensuring that people are accountable to one another.[38] She does this by demonstrating how Cree law must be principled and collaborative. She says that "Cree Law, like any other law[,] is about contestation, collective problem solving and collaborative management of large groups."[39] This partly occurs through the recognition that there are four groups of decision makers in the Cree legal order: medicine people, Elders, family members, and the larger group. She says that each group is important because 'unquestioned truths' might be privileged without broader practical engagements. In this respect, she particularly cautions against having single Elders as sole legal authorities because of gender, culture, or other biases that might be reproduced in the absence of a more holistic approach. Her work also suggests that Cree law must incorporate community safety and respect for people affected by the search for reconciliation.[40]

Inuit peoples

Inuit of the Circumpolar North have legal traditions aimed at restitution and reconciliation. These modes of conduct were formed through experiences living on the land
in close-knit territorial camps for thousands of years. The extremely cold weather of
these regions often made life precarious. Food could be scarce, and people depended
on every single person to be a productive member of the community. Inuit could not
afford to let harm fester for too long because such conflict could endanger all who
lived together.[41]

Therefore, historically, when strangers arrived in Inuit territory they were careful
to follow the customs of the people they visited. Deference in such cases was a sign of
respect that acknowledged the force of the northern land and the laws of the people
they visited.[42]

Of course, like all peoples, Inuit did not always live by their highest values.[43] When
proper deference and acknowledgement were not forthcoming, harm could result.
When such harm was experienced, Inuit legal traditions provided options for dealing
with the problem (just as they do today). As human communities, they applied both
reason and custom to the challenges they faced. This process allows tradition to be
calibrated and updated as necessary.[44]

When harm occurred within Inuit society, one possibility for working towards
reconciliation involved designating a person within a community who would gather
people together for the purpose of addressing the harm.[45] During such gatherings,
"everyone would talk about what was wrong and what was expected to resolve their
problems. Everyone had a chance to express his or her side of the story (aniaslu-
tik)."[46] This allowed people to characterize and/or address a problem at issue from
many different perspectives. Other forms of address could take place; for instance,
song-duels sometimes occurred to facilitate communication when it was not clear
who had done wrong.[47]

These gatherings were often accompanied by a feast where people could also discuss problems on a more informal basis. Checks and balances in the development
and application of tradition are present when facts and standards for judgment draw
from multiple procedures, making it less likely for one person or method to dominate
when problems are addressed.[48]

When a wrongdoing became evident during these gatherings, it was intended to be
an embarrassing affair for the wrongdoer.[49] In fact, wrongdoers were to be brought to
tears as they understood the criticisms of everyone present.[50] Acknowledgement and
remorse are important steps in this strand of Inuit tradition. People cannot apologize,
nor can a community move towards reconciliation, until wrongdoers have both fully
heard about and honestly confronted and acknowledged the harm they caused to others. Although such events were embarrassing for the wrongdoers, such catharsis was

said to be less humiliating than the future consequences that could flow from hiding or denying the harm.[51]

Inuit society governed the behaviour of its members with clearly defined expectations, and "these rules of behavior, and ways to deal with infractions, were passed on to younger generations through the oral traditions of the group and by following examples set by older members."[52]

There were, of course, other legal traditions that helped the Inuit to deal with harm, apology, and reconciliation. Inuit law and custom are a complex set of ideas and practices that draw on past experiences and present concerns to resolve disputes and regulate behaviour. Legal traditions exist as resources and standards for present action; they should not be regarded as an inflexible set of models frozen in a distant past.

If Inuit traditions were applied to assist Canada in working through issues of harm, apology, and reconciliation, such attention would bring into focus the necessity of deference to Indigenous peoples' knowledge as it relates to law. This could become a significant sign of respect and an acknowledgement that, within Canada, we all live in precarious circumstances. All Canadians need Indigenous law to help us cope with the devastating colonial legacy we continue to experience as a nation, of which the residential schools are but one prominent part.

Inuit law also emphasizes the significance of widespread participation in characterizing and addressing harm, as well as the importance of embarrassment and remorse being expressed by the perpetrators of harm. There is also an important place for feasting, singing, and recounting past harms, which can help parties learn how to address past and present harms and avoid future wrongdoing. Inuit tradition also highlights the importance of reason *and* custom in identifying and addressing harms. This way of approaching conflict deploys customary cultural values as living legal traditions. In this light, Inuit law can serve as a significant resource in meeting present needs, particularly in relation to apologies, restitution, and reconciliation.

Mi'kmaq peoples

The Mi'kmaq of the Atlantic region possess legal traditions that are relevant for considering apologies and reconciliation in a broader light. For example, Mi'kmaq leader Andrew Denny, who holds the title of Kji Keptin (Grand Captain) in the Mi'kmaq governance body called the Grand Council, has commented on the reciprocal role of church, government, and Mi'kmaq laws, values, and concepts in facilitating reconciliation.

> The apologies [by the government and churches] have cleared the path for the Mawio'mi's renewal of our alliance with the Church and an opportunity to continue a path of reconciliation and peace in this sacred journey. It will not be an

easy journey. A continuing dialogue needs to be developed among the leadership of the Mawio'mi and Mi'kmaq organizations and the Bishops and priests to work together so that Mi'kmaq can become whole and complete once again. We need to return to the spiritual teachings that our Creator gave to our Elders....

Mi'kmaq and non-Mi'kmaq each needs to recognize the shared spirituality with the ecology and our shared spirit of humanity that generates the responsibility to repair the failed relationship in the next hundred years.[53]

This call for a continuing dialogue to clear a path for reconciliation has a profound source within Mi'kmaq law and practice. Mi'kmaq law is built upon deep connections between ecologies and peoples,[54] which encourage mutuality and respect.[55] It is concerned with *netukulimk*, among other things, which is a sophisticated legal concept that guides community action across the generations when people interact with the world around them.[56]

The application of Mi'kmaq law related to reconciliation is demonstrated throughout Mi'kma'ki (Mi'kmaq territory) in various ways during the year.[57] One example occurs every summer at Potlotek (Chapel Island). During this celebration, thousands of members of the Mi'kmaq Nation gather at St. Anne's Mission to feast, socialize, conduct ceremonies, and listen to the teachings of the Elders and the Grand Council. Wampum belts are read, baptisms are conducted, and the Sakamaw (Grand Chief) and Kji Keptin (Grand Captain) speak about important issues within Mi'kma'ki. In such settings, community safety and individual responsibility are promoted.[58]

In Mi'kmaq communities, harm is addressed as it arises because it is widely known through family and community networks. If harm occurs, facts are gathered by people closest to those who have caused harm, and actions are taken to address and remedy misdeeds. If wrongs are confirmed, apologies might be forthcoming from the person who committed them, or from the immediate family of that person. In more serious cases, an older family member might guide the reconciliation process.

The most serious cases of harm are dealt with by the Kji Keptin and/or Grand Council members because they might be required to facilitate reconciliation between *sakamowati* (districts) of the Mi'kmaq Nation or between Mi'kmaq and other peoples. Before the terms of a formal apology can be developed, extensive discussions must take place with respected leaders and Elders to reach decisions about how to best respond to a harm that has occurred.[59]

These living Mi'kmaq legal traditions hold great wisdom for guiding us towards reconciliation in the present day. Although remedial actions have to take place at a national level between governments, institutions, and Aboriginal peoples, reconciliation must also move through communities and families for it be to most effective.

Métis peoples

Métis peoples also have legal traditions that could be applied to facilitate reconciliation. Métis laws are both oral and written. The historic laws of St. Laurent, for example, were very extensive. Although the laws of the buffalo hunt were less explicit, they still provide great detail about the consequences of violating law.[60] Métis laws are also contemporary and likewise concern themselves with reconciliation.

Writing about the origins of Métis customary law, scholars Lawrence J. Barkwell and Amanda Rozyk and Métis Elder Anne Carriere Acco say that historically "Metis government was based in consensus democracy ... Everyone had a part in making the laws ... [Today] an objective of Metis justice is the revival and recognition of traditional non-adversarial dispute resolution. This includes the use of Elders as advisors and mediators."[61]

Explaining the teachings of the Métis-Cree community of Cumberland House in Saskatchewan, Elder Carriere Acco says,

> The law is to be understood by means of education at the community level. This is the means by which all community members stay within the circle of well-being. Minoh nani mohwin.
>
> The law must have the human resources and materials to maintain the state of well-being. A community cannot just speak about what it can do to maintain order; it must have the will, the means and the support of the human resources within the community. Ekota pohko ka isi ka pohieyan....
>
> A forum must have the protocols in place to call on the learned, the keepers of wisdom concerning every aspect of life. This provides the civil order that has to be maintained. The knowledgeable people, "Ahneegay-kaashigakick" come to give of their expertise. Then within the community forum the people agree by consensus what the advice means in terms of community and family action. Kawaskimohn is followed by Kawaskimohin.[62]

Storytelling is an important aspect of Métis legal traditions.

> Social control begins at the family level, and is then transferred to the community or national level.... Metis children are taught about the consequences of behaviour through the teachings of their Grandmothers and traditional stories.... These stories are instructive as to accepted community standards as well as the natural, supernatural and cultural sanctions that flow from breaches of the standards and principles.[63]

To illustrate, renowned Métis lawyer Jean Teillet tells a story of a young girl who was bitten by a dog in a Métis community.[64] After the young girl was injured, the dog was picked up by a nurse and a representative of the Ministry of Natural Resources.

Thinking they were doing the right thing, but violating community customs, the two bagged the dog after it was killed and put him in the community freezer. These actions violated Métis law, which required the application of Métis principles to restore balance.

First, the Elders had many questions that they asked those involved. They wondered why the little girl was out by herself, why the dog was loose, why the nurse or Natural Resources officer killed the dog, and why they put the dog in the freezer (which was filled with caribou and other meat).

In deciding what should happen to reconcile people in these circumstances and restore harmony after this event, the Elders in this case were not interested in taking any punitive measures. They made sure that the little girl was okay. They required compensation be made to the person whose dog was killed. They also asked those responsible for putting the dog in the community freezer to restock it because the caribou and other meat had been contaminated by the dead dog as a result of their actions.

This process demonstrates that Métis law is relevant for working towards reconciliation in a community context. The principles they followed could also be applied on a broader basis to address issues arising from harms caused by the residential schools.

Métis legal principles were evident in various national dialogues that brought Métis Survivors, Elders, and political leaders together to share their truths about their residential and day school experiences. It was clear from their stories and comments that for the many Métis Survivors who attended schools that were excluded from the Indian Residential Schools Settlement Agreement, reconciliation remained elusive.[65] They emphasized the importance of Métis community support for Survivors and their families.

At the Métis Nation Residential School Dialogue in Saskatoon, Saskatchewan, in March 2012, John Morrisseau, a member of the TRC Survivors Committee, said,

> There [is] so much that could be told about what took place in the Métis communities. This dialogue was the opening of things to come for Métis people.
> In order to tell our stories properly, we will need to learn to trust ourselves as family. Right now everyone wants to hear, and everyone is afraid to say. But there is a need to get beyond that in order to share and feel trust and kindness from one another. That [will] come after we have had a chance to be together a few more times ... Métis have been excluded ... [I]t has been the story of our lives. The issue we are dealing with is ... a moral issue ... I do not want money for healing because I do not think money will solve things; however, if people could look at me and respect me for who I am, that would be a big step in the right direction.[66]

Survivor Angie Crerar said,

I talk with Elders who have been my strength. But that horror lives in our soul. It's not a pretty story. How could it be? ... I have scars on my body, my heart and my soul that will never be erased. Some of them are scars of honour because no matter what they did, they did not break my spirit.... This journey we will walk together. This Dialogue has started the support, being there for each other, sharing what we learned and also our pain. That is who we are. We help each other and will never stand alone.... Our work will never be done but together with our children and grandchildren, we will take a step forward. It is not up to our elected officials to do it all, it is up to each one of us. How proud are we of our heritage? How proud are we of our identity? ... We are Métis, and we always will be.[67]

For those who attended the national dialogues, the opportunity for Survivors and intergenerational Survivors to share their stories, their truths, was essential to their own healing and that of the Métis Nation. Jaime Koebel, of the Métis National Council, said, "Not everyone is ready to talk, but in time, somewhere, the stories need to get out and be heard to help further justice in this area."[68] The principles and practices of Métis law and legal traditions will be critical to such a reconciliation process.

In the broader context of reconciliation, Métis law, like other Indigenous legal traditions, can also inform a wide range of Aboriginal-Crown alternative dispute-resolution and negotiation processes involving Treaty and Aboriginal rights, land claims, and resource-use conflicts. Elmer Ghostkeeper, a Métis Elder and past president of the Federation of Métis Settlements in Alberta, points out that Indigenous approaches to resolving conflicts and establishing mutually respectful relationships are frequently ignored by government representatives. He explains that for him the concept of "traditional knowledge" is problematic "because it suggests [something] old and aging. As [Métis] people we are just as contemporary and creative as others. We do have old traditions, but we also have current practices that form part of our wisdom." He says that the term "Aboriginal wisdom" more accurately describes "the body of information, rules, beliefs, values, behavioural and learning experiences which made existence possible and meaningful for the Métis."[69] Elder Ghostkeeper explains that "our [Métis] wisdom sits in our personal experience and the experience of others. It is both old and current knowledge primarily passed on through oral histories and stories that contain many teachings and lessons in many forms."[70]

Tlingit peoples

The Teslin Tlingit peoples of the Yukon have recently established a Peacemaker Court under the authority of their land claims agreement that draws on traditional and modern laws to facilitate peace, order, and good government.[71] This court has similarities to many American tribal courts that deploy Indigenous peoples' codes, customs, and traditions to resolve disputes.

The Tlingit peoples' Peacemaker Court has jurisdiction over disputes that occur within their communities. This is guided by the *Peacemaker Court and Justice Council Act*, which has codified some of the important procedures, obligations, and principles related to reconciliation.[72] For example, there are five clans within the community: the Raven (Kùkhhittàn), Frog (Ishkìtàn), Wolf (Yanyèdí), Beaver (Dèshitàn), and Eagle (Dakhl'awèdí).[73] Based on traditional practices, each of these clans has different roles and responsibilities in attaining justice and reconciliation.

In the Peacemaker Court, five representatives from each of the five clans form the decision circle. Section 9(2) of the *Peacemaker Court and Justice Council Act* enumerates some important guiding principles of the court. These principles govern how peace and reconciliation should be pursued:

> 9(2) The following principles will guide the Court when it carries out its authority:
>
> (a) The values of respect, integrity, honesty and responsibility;
>
> (b) The collective nature of Teslin Tlingit society;
>
> (c) The obligation to preserve the land, environment and all resources within the Teslin Tlingit Traditional Territory for the well-being of both present and future Teslin Tlingit generations; and
>
> (d) The Teslin Tlingit culture which is based on traditional knowledge, customs, language, oral history and spiritual beliefs and practices which is important for the well being of present and future generations.[74]

It is possible to imagine the principles identified in this section of the *Peacemaker Court and Justice Council Act* being applied by Canada to guide its attempts to reconcile with the Tlingit and other Aboriginal peoples. This activity would be most effective if governments were sensitive to the cultural nuances of Indigenous peoples and applied their legal principles as required by the Act in its context.

An example of how the Act could be interpreted in the context of an apology for residential schools might occur in the following way. The Act as a whole suggests that the best forums for reconciliation are Indigenous-based. Thus the Canadian government might follow up on its formal apology by working with various Aboriginal groups to apologize in an Indigenous forum. Subsection (a) of the Act suggests that such apologies and other activities should "be guided by the values of respect, integrity, honesty and responsibility," as interpreted by Aboriginal people. Subsection (b) suggests that Teslin Tlingit as a whole should be considered in pursuing reconciliation.

Since all members of society—from Elders to adults, youth, and children—are valued, a harm that affects all of them should be rectified in a way that involves as many of them as possible. Subsections (c) and (d) suggest that Aboriginal histories, languages, traditions, customs, beliefs, and practices should guide reconciliation. References to the land, environment, and resources suggest that reconciliation should also consider the broader policies that the government pursues in relation to these matters as it works towards reconciliation. This list is not exhaustive but provides an idea of what the Canadian government might do in collaboration with the Teslin Tlingit and other Indigenous peoples as it continues to follow through on its apology for the harms caused by residential schools.

Anishinaabe peoples

The Anishinaabe peoples of central Canada have legal concepts related to apology, restitution, and reconciliation, and some of these principles are embedded in the very words of their language. Balance is central to understanding Indigenous law. The Anishinaabe peoples have many legal traditions and practices that encourage *mino-bimaadiziwin* (good living), and that are relevant to reconciliation.

Although many historic examples of these laws could be cited,[75] recent Anishinaabe practice has highlighted the Seven Grandfather and Grandmother Teachings.[76] These laws encourage Anishinaabe peoples to live in accordance with *nibwaakaawin* (wisdom), *zaagi'idiwin* (love), *mnaadendiwin* (respect), *aakwaadiziwin* (courage), *dbaadendiziwin* (humility), *gwekwaadiziwin* (honesty), and *debwewin* (truth). These guiding principles are enacted as living traditions in many people's lives within Anishinaabe-akiing (Anishinaabe territory), although many fall far short of them in their daily lives (as is the case with all other humans who try to live in accordance with their highest laws). Nevertheless, these traditions stand as a guide towards a better way of being in the world. They are found in daily living, and are also chronicled in numerous stories, songs, sayings, teachings, and ceremonies that exist to mediate relationships with the human and wider world.[77]

Powerful changes would flow into the reconciliation process if wisdom, love, respect, courage, humility, honesty, and truth were regarded as forming the country's guiding principles.[78] If the Seven Grandfather and Grandmother Teachings were applied, Canada would renew a foundational set of aspirations to guide its actions beyond the broad principles currently outlined in the Canadian Charter of Rights and Freedoms and other constitutional traditions. These teachings would help Canadians to build their country in accordance with its formative Treaty relationships, which flowed from Anishinaabe and other Indigenous perspectives, where peace, friendship, and respect stood at the heart of kin-based ties that encouraged the adoption of every newcomer to this land as a brother or sister.[79]

If we learn anything from Indigenous legal traditions in this report, it should be the need to live together using wisdom, love, respect, courage, humility, honesty, and truth as our strongest guides. That these principles also coincide with Canada's oldest Treaty commitments could help us to see a broader political underpinning in their development and application in a contemporary context through Section 35(1) of Canada's Constitution.

Of course, although these traditions can be reflected in a secular constitutional context, they can also transcend it. In an Anishinaabe context, the Seven Grandfather and Grandmother Teachings are highlighted when people gather in ceremonies to petition the spirit world and draw closer to creation and their brothers and sisters. *Asemaa* (tobacco) is a sacred plant offered at the beginning of such events as an expression of gratitude, modesty, humility, and meekness. The offering of asemaa acknowledges Anisihinaabe dependence on the spirits, rocks, plants, animals, and others for their very survival, even in contemporary urban settings. At the time of offering, a prayer is often given to further acknowledge human indebtedness and weakness. Such prayers confess that we all make mistakes and must ask for pity and *zhawenimaan* (blessings) in all we do.[80]

Elder Dr. Basil Johnston gives an example of this approach when discussing a father's prayer with his son while preparing for a vision quest: "On their arrival, Ogauh [who was the father] placed an offering of tobacco in the centre of the circle. 'Forgive us,' he said, 'Forgive my son, I bring him to you that he may receive a vision. We ask that you be generous and grant him dreams.'"[81] Although this is one small example, it represents the idea that many Anishinaabe people regard apologies as a necessary part of their preparations in working together to live well in *mino-bimaa-diziwin* (the world).

In light of our earlier discussion, it could be instructive to regard apologies as having a constitutional dimension—constituting who we are as human beings and who we are as a nation-state. Because tobacco and apologies are constitutional, at least in the former sense, they are an important part of Anishinaabe reconciliation in many settings. At the same time, the use of asemaa and apologies could also be regarded as constitutional in a more formal sense as well. When asemaa is used in a pipe ceremony, as was the case when most Treaties were agreed upon, more formality is required. When tobacco is offered and a pipe is used in its transmission, the tobacco becomes a vehicle for reconciliation between those who participate,[82] as occurred in Treaties. The use of the Seven Grandfather and Grandmother Teachings, tobacco, and apologies could have constitutional significance for Canadians more generally, who trace their rights to land and governance in this country to the Treaties.[83]

The need for Anishinaabe to apologize and work towards reconciliation is illustrated in the example of four respected Anishinaabe leaders who personally applied these laws and traditions to their residential school experiences. The four leaders were

Tobasonakwut Kinew (Anishinaabe Elder, pipe carrier, and Medewin medicine society member), Fred Kelly (Anishinaabe Elder, Medewin member, and team member who negotiated the Indian Residential School Agreement), Phil Fontaine (former Grand Chief of the Assembly of First Nations, who is regarded as being most responsible for the 2005 Indian Residential School Agreement and the 2008 formal apology by the Canadian government), and Bert Fontaine (brother of Phil and a leader in the Sagkeeng First Nation of Manitoba). On April 14, 2012, these men adopted as their brother the Catholic Archbishop James Weisgerber of Winnipeg.[84] They did so using the principles described above in a traditional Naabaagoondiwin ceremony at Thunderbird House in Winnipeg, Manitoba.

During the ceremony, Phil Fontaine offered a personal apology to the Catholic Church. He acknowledged that his public reaction to his personal residential school experience "overshadowed the goodness of many people."[85] He said, "My bitterness and anger hurt many good people dedicated to our well-being and I only focused on the people who hurt us.... I tarred everyone with the same brush and I was wrong. As you apologized to me on more than one occasion, I apologize to you."[86] The ceremony included singing and drumming, as well as the exchange of gifts and the sharing a ceremonial pipe. As part of the gesture of reconciliation, Tobasonakwut Kinew said,

> I have accepted James Weisgerber as part of my family, as my brother. We are now prepared to move ahead as brothers and sisters. I leave the past of the residential schools behind me.

> The ceremony is a public event so that more survivors, the generation following who are still impacted and leaders can witness the historic and unbreakable bond that will be made.[87]

The significance of this event as an example of personal reconciliation between Indigenous peoples and their neighbours should not be overlooked. It demonstrates the wisdom, love, respect, courage, humility, honesty, and truth of the men involved in this event. They recognized their weaknesses and apologized for them, despite having arguably lesser culpability because of the physical and other abuses they suffered in residential schools. If those who have suffered can apologize for their actions in relation to residential schools, this might serve as an example for other people throughout the country who have not suffered as gravely, and who want to improve their broader relationships.

We all have weaknesses as people. If we look at this issue from an Indigenous political perspective, we can see that each person's weakness, at some level, has contributed to our collective malaise in how we are dealing with reconciliation in Canada. We recognize that people who have philosophies that are not guided by these laws and traditions may reject such characterizations; however, in light of the Commission's study of these issues from many perspectives and having heard from people from coast to coast to coast, we affirm that apologies make a difference in the life of our nation and to the individuals within it.

Although we acknowledge the broader importance of apologies in Canada, we must stress that the apology offered by the four Anishinaabe leaders was not a formal political event; it was not sponsored by institutions such as governments, churches, or Aboriginal organizations. It shows that reconciliation can proceed in important ways even if broader institutions are not involved. The Naabaagoondiwin ceremony is focused on individuals and families, and it seeks to build relationships on a family basis—at least initially. In keeping with this example, much more could be done to extend bonds of kinship between Indigenous and non-Indigenous peoples in more decentralized ways. It is not necessary to wait for institutions to initiate and continue the work of reconciliation. At the same time, there is nothing to prevent broader institutional application of these legal traditions if supported by an institution's leaders.

Some might argue that the principles of wisdom, love, respect, courage, humility, honesty, and truth are much too vague to possess legal relevance. Those who make this argument could reflect on the broad framing of other central legal values in Canada. It is arguable that concepts like freedom of religion, conscience, speech, assembly, life, liberty, security, equality, and so on are equally vague as a starting point for protecting peoples' fundamental rights. Nevertheless, through continually extensive analysis and application, these concepts remain at the heart of Canada's constitutional regime despite their definitional challenges. Vagueness alone is not a reason for rejecting the Seven Grandfather and Grandmother Teachings as legal standards; in fact, like the concepts within the Canadian Charter, the very reason we should adopt them may be their broad aspirational nature, which allows them to have so many meanings to different people, and to motivate our actions at the highest levels.

Hul'q'umi'num peoples

Another example of how Indigenous peoples deploy their traditions to resolve disputes through apology, restitution, and reconciliation is found among the Coast Salish Hul'q'umi'num peoples on southern Vancouver Island and the Gulf Islands in the Salish Sea.[88] These practices are grounded in their *snuw'uyulh* (teaching), which contains the "fundamental rules of life, the truths of life that are based on the Hul'q'umi'num concept of Respect."[89] Coast Salish Elder Ellen White Rice describes this concept as "Respect for others and their differences and for the power of love. The teachings show that we are all different but the power of love and commitment transcends all differences."[90]

Respect is an essential component of reconciliation and must always be part of any meaningful apology and restitution. When the snuw'uyulh is applied to facilitate reconciliation, it is important to remember that there are degrees of depth and learning within this concept.[91] Furthermore, it is important to recognize that each Hul'q'umi'num community "may have slightly different Snuw'uyulh, based on their surroundings and environment."[92]

One of the understandings flowing from the snuw'uyulh is that apologies and restitution are necessary to restore balance within a community when someone is harmed. Usually, such actions are taken and offered by individuals and families most immediately affected by harm. Apologies and reconciliation are often localized within Hul'q'umi'num society because it is considered disgraceful to have somebody else resolve your problems.[93] Individuals' own families are most qualified to help people clear their heart and mind if they have harmed someone or been harmed themselves. In terms of administering this system, it is often Elders within a family who will teach wrongdoers how to apologize.[94]

Apologies and restitution frequently consist of offerings and verbal confessions by those who caused harm, including acknowledgement of the cause and consequences of the wrong.[95] In describing these practices, Hereditary Chief Frank Malloway has observed,

> If you did something wrong the family would take the responsibility and make an offering. They call it an offering. Some of the things in the old days were canoes, because they were like cars today, "Ah, I'll give you my car if you forget about this." But it was canoes in those days. I don't think it was really food because food was so plentiful that it wasn't expensive. Later on, my dad was saying, when it was settlement time, it was horses. They took the place of canoes. He talked about bringing horses right into the longhouse to distribute to somebody.[96]

If the apology and offerings are accepted, there might be some form of acknowledgement made to the wrongdoer by those who were harmed.

The advancement of offerings and apologies is said to "bring good feeling back."[97] This is part of the snuw'uyulh. As one Elder has said, an exchange of offerings means "we're not mad at you anymore."[98] Another Elder has explained,

> I think if they, the family, agree that this person is sorry and really trying to pay back by doing different things[,] they'll agree, 'okay, maybe you've done enough.' Maybe then they'll have a little ceremony to say, 'okay we'll agree with that family and this family,' do it publicly in a feast or potlatch or something.... Of course they agree to it first.[99]

Some harms may be more serious than others due to the scale of their impact. In these cases, reconciliation requires a broader approach; apologies are to be given publicly at a potlatch or other ceremonial gathering.[100] Gifts may be offered as compensation or other forms of restitution made to the injured party during feasts or other ceremonies.[101]

Canada could learn from the snuw'uyulh by following through with demonstrations of remorse, offerings, and ceremonies once it has apologized. If this does not occur, Hul'q'umi'num legal traditions teach us that ill feelings between the parties will certainly persist until the government gives up something very important to it and shows a serious commitment to changing its relationship with Aboriginal peoples.

Gitxsan peoples

In British Columbia, feasting and the potlatch system have been used for millennia as legal and political mechanisms for addressing harms in a way that enables people to achieve a measure of justice and that restores relationships. Legal scholar John Borrows explains the central role that feasting plays in the legal, political, and socio-economic lives of Aboriginal peoples in certain regions of British Columbia.

> For millennia, their histories have recorded their organization into Houses and Clans in which hereditary chiefs have been responsible for the allocation, administration and control of traditional lands. Within these Houses, chiefs pass on important histories, songs, crests, lands, ranks and property from one generation to the next. The transfer of these legal, political, social and economic entitlements is performed and witnessed through Feasts. Feasts substantiate the territories' relationships. A hosting House serves food, distributes gifts, announces the House's successors to the names of deceased chiefs, describes the territory, raises totem poles, and tells the oral history of the House. Chiefs from other Houses witness the actions of the Feast, and at the end of the proceedings, they validate the decisions and declarations of the Host House. The Feast is thus an important institution through which the people governed themselves.[102]

Writing about the *bah'lats* (potlatch) of the Ned'u'ten people (Lake Babine First Nation in British Columbia), legal scholar June McCue describes the shaming and cleansing ceremonies that Canada would have to undergo in order to clear its name. She explains that to restore the honour of the Crown, Canada must enter the feast hall. There, she says, "Canada's colonizing record would be heard ... Canada would acknowledge this wrongdoing, make apologies and be prepared to compensate or retribute the Ned'u'ten for such conduct with gifts. It may take a series of *bah'lats* for Canada to bring respect to its name."[103]

In a similar vein, while acknowledging that Indigenous legal systems have been damaged by colonization, legal scholar Val Napoleon observes that in spite of this lived reality, Gitxsan law is still viable today; it is still a living legal order.

> Many Gitxsan laws have been violated by both Gitxsan and non-Gitxsan, and this contributes to cultural paralysis.... Reconciliation here would mean either an explicit acknowledgment of, and agreement to, the changes to Gitxsan laws to fit

contemporary circumstances, or application of Gitxsan laws to deal with trans-
gressions ... It would be difficult to force the participation of the transgressor,
but nonetheless, the process of dealing with transgression through the Gitxsan
system even without the transgressing parties, would be healthy and constructive for the Gitxsan.[104]

This observation is demonstrated in one example of a welcome home and apology
feast held in 2004 for Gitxsan Survivors who had attended the Edmonton Residential
School. The apology feast was unique in that it was hosted by the Canadian government and the United Church. These institutions were held accountable in accordance
with Gitxsan law. This feast, which applied Gitxsan legal traditions, "connected the
cultural loss experienced by ... survivors to a powerful public reclaiming of history,
culture, family, community, and nation in a way that also brought Canada and the
United Church into the feast hall—as hosts with particular responsibilities to fulfill."[105]

That two non-Indigenous institutions served as hosts for this feast demonstrates
the applied and living nature of Indigenous law; the Gitxsan adapted their customary
feasting protocols creatively to allow these institutions to apologize for their actions
in running residential schools. These changes in protocol were carefully negotiated in
advance to ensure that Canada and the United Church operated in accordance with
Gitxsan law.[106]

This "living peacemaking process" shows how Indigenous legal orders are "capable
of adapting old diplomatic and legal principles in new ways to accommodate changing circumstances."[107] "In giving government and church responsibilities as hosts, the
Gitxsan used their legal system to respond constructively to the legacy of residential
schools. They sought a way to reintegrate into Gitxsan society those who had been
lost."[108] The ceremony itself allowed the Canadian government and the United Church
to apologize for their actions in residential schools; it also allowed the community to
publicly commemorate "the names of all the Gitxsan children—those still living and
those now lost to their families and nation," as their names were "read out in order to
remember and honour them."[109]

The apology became part of the oral history record of Gitxsan law. Those who
attended the ceremony witnessed how Gitxsan law provided an opportunity to begin
repairing the relationship between the Gitxsan peoples, the Crown, and the church.
Government and church representatives worked directly with Survivors, Elders, and
Hereditary Chiefs for many weeks to prepare for the feast and fulfill their responsibilities as hosts. Working together at the community level enabled all those involved to
begin to develop a different kind of relationship—one based on mutual respect and
empathy. The feast hall created a space where Survivors' experiences were acknowledged, and where they were honoured and welcomed back into the community.

One of the non-Indigenous hosts who participated in the feast described the powerful teachings that Indigenous law holds for all Canadians.

The feast taught me important lessons, compelling me to rethink my cultural assumptions about the meanings of history, truth, justice, and reconciliation. I learned that history resides not in dusty books but lives in the stories we carry in our hearts, minds, and spirits as we struggle to understand, acknowledge, and transform the past that is still present. I learned that truth is not only about facts but about the harsh realities of a shared colonial experience that is rooted in human relationships. I learned that justice is found not only in case law and courtrooms but in the exquisite beauty of sacred dances, symbols, and songs, in the strong words of elders, *simgigyat, sigid'm hanaak*, and families, and in the healing ceremonies and rituals of the feast hall that express the laws of the Gitxsan nation. I learned that reconciliation is not a goal but a place of transformative encounter where all participants gather the courage to face our troubled history without minimizing the damage that has been done, even as we find new decolonizing ways of working together that shift power and perceptions. I learned that Indigenous sacred places are powerful. They make space for us to connect with each other, exchanging testimony, making restitution and apology in ways that speak to our highest values as human beings.[110]

As Commissioners, we have participated in many community feasts and other ceremonial practices of Indigenous law and peacemaking. We are convinced that there are urgent and compelling reasons to learn from these legal traditions; they have great relevance for Aboriginal peoples and all Canadians today. They should be regarded as the laws of the land and applied to the broader reconciliation process.

Indigenous legal concepts related to apology, restitution, and reconciliation are embedded in First Nations, Inuit, and Métis languages. The words contain standards about how to regulate our actions and resolve our disputes in order to maintain or restore balance to individuals, communities, and the nation. The revitalization of Indigenous law and governance systems depends on the revitalization of Indigenous languages.

Whether codified in the Peacemaker Court, practised more informally at the community level, or used with governments, churches, and other institutions, Indigenous law is being recovered and revitalized by Aboriginal peoples across the land. This work is just beginning; much more must be done.

The way forward: The Accessing Justice and Reconciliation project

Both the *UN Declaration on the Rights of Indigenous Peoples* and the study by the UN Expert Mechanism on the Rights of Indigenous Peoples that we referred to earlier affirm that Indigenous peoples' right to self-determination is the centralizing principle from which all other rights flow, including the right to access and practise their own laws. The Commission believes that many Aboriginal communities want and need more opportunities to work with their Elders and Knowledge Keepers in order to learn about and use their own legal traditions. Developing collaborative community-based research and learning, sharing best practices, and producing educational resources on Indigenous law will ensure long-term support for communities in achieving this goal.

In 2012, the TRC partnered with the Indigenous Bar Association and the Indigenous Law Clinic of the University of Victoria's Faculty of Law to develop a national research initiative, the Accessing Justice and Reconciliation (AJR) project. Working with seven community partners, the AJR project examined six different legal traditions across the country: Coast Salish (Snuneymuxw First Nation, Tsleil-Waututh Nation), Tsilhqot'in (Tsilhqot'in National Government), Northern Secwepemc (T'exelc Williams Lake Indian Band), Cree (Aseniwuche Winewak Nation), Anishinabek (Chippewas of Nawash Unceded First Nation No. 27), and Mi'kmaq (Mi'kmaq Legal Services Network, Eskasoni).

The AJR project's final report describes its vision and goal.

> The overall vision for this project was to honour the internal strengths and resiliencies present in Indigenous societies, including the resources within these societies' own legal traditions. The goal of the AJR project was to better recognize how Indigenous societies used their own legal traditions to successfully deal with harms and conflicts between and within groups and to identify and articulate legal principles that could be accessed and applied today to work toward healthy and strong futures for communities.[111]

The project began with a nationwide call to Indigenous communities for expressions of interest in collaboratively developing the project. After communities responded and agreed to work with the project, student researchers received an intensive orientation in Indigenous legal theories, Indigenous laws, and community-based research skills. With the blessing of the seven participant communities, the researchers next analyzed publicly available stories related to how Indigenous peoples dealt with harm. The animating question the researchers asked in analyzing the stories was, "how are harms dealt with in [Indigenous] communities, and between communities?" After significant study, cross-referencing, and correlation, legal principles were drawn from each tradition.

Once this preliminary work was finished, the researchers approached the communities that had agreed to participate; they took what they learned to the communities they had studied. The principle of reciprocity required this background preparation. Principles of respect required serious preparation before engaging with the Indigenous law Knowledge Keepers; it was important not to 'lightly' ask people for their stories. Rather, the researchers approached the Knowledge Keepers with something to give. The stories provided an excellent starting point for discussion, as community members discussed their teachings and how they should or should not apply to harms today.

Reports were then produced and presented to the communities. By analyzing the legal processes, responses and resolutions, obligations, rights, and general underlying principles found in the stories and oral traditions of specific communities, the project provided insights into how Indigenous law in all its diversity and interconnectedness is applied in real-life situations. The AJR project also included a public education component designed to ensure that the project report, community reports, and other materials and resources are widely accessible.[112] The AJR website has links to the published reports, papers, a teaching guide, and a graphic novel on Cree law.[113]

The AJR final report presented the following findings and recommendations:

> There is no 'one size fits all' approach within or among Indigenous legal traditions. There are a wide variety of principled legal responses and resolutions to harm and conflict within each legal tradition.
>
> Recommendation 1.1. Further research is needed to identify and articulate the full breadth of principled legal response and resolutions within Indigenous legal traditions.
>
> Recommendation 1.2. Further research is needed (i) to more clearly identify or develop legal processes necessary for a decision to be accepted as legitimate by those impacted by it, and (ii) identify the guiding or underlying constitutive principles that form interpretive bounds within specific Indigenous legal orders.

Indigenous legal traditions reveal both consistency and continuity over time, and responsiveness and adaptability to changing contexts.

> Recommendation 2.1. Support community-based research and engagement processes to enable communities to identify and discuss legal principles so they become more explicit and accessible within communities themselves.
>
> Recommendation 2.2. Support community justice and wellness initiatives to identify and articulate guiding or supporting legal principles, as a basis for developing, grounding and evaluating current practices and programming addressing pressing social issues within their communities.[114]

The Commission concurs with these findings and recommendations. We conclude that Indigenous laws must receive heightened attention, encouragement, and support to ensure that First Nations, Inuit, and Métis communities benefit from their continued growth, development, and application.

The AJR project's final report concluded that many more Aboriginal communities across the country would benefit from recovering and revitalizing their laws. Doing so would enable First Nations, Inuit, and Métis communities to more effectively remedy community harms and resolve internal conflicts, as well as external conflicts with governments. Legal scholar Val Napoleon, the project's academic lead, and Hadley Friedland, the project coordinator, write,

> We believe there is much hope that even the process of intentionally and seri-ously continuing ... [this work] will contribute to a truly robust reconciliation in Canada.... This work is vital for the future health and strength of Indigenous societies and has much to offer Canada as a whole.... Legal traditions are not only prescriptive, they are descriptive. They ascribe meaning to human events, challenges and aspirations. They are intellectual resources that we use to frame and interpret information, to reason through and act upon current problems and projects, to work toward our greatest societal aspirations.
>
> Finding ways to support Indigenous communities to access, understand and apply their own legal principles today is not just about repairing the immense damages from colonialism. As Chief Doug S. White III (Kwulasultun) puts it ... "Indigenous law is the great project of Canada and it is the essential work of our time. It is not for the faint of heart, it is hard work. We need to create meaningful opportunities for Indigenous and non-Indigenous people to critically engage in this work because all our futures depend on it."[115]

Canada at the crossroads: Choosing our path

In his paper "The Duty to Learn: Taking Account of Indigenous Legal Orders in Practice," delivered at a conference on "Indigenous Legal Orders and the Common Law" held in Vancouver, British Columbia, in 2012, Chief Justice Lance Finch talked about how Canadians can be a part of reconciliation.

> As part of this process, I suggest the current Canadian legal system must recon-cile itself to coexistence with pre-existing Indigenous legal orders.... How can we make space within the legal landscape for Indigenous legal orders? The answer depends, at least in part, on an inversion of the question: a crucial part of this process must be to find space for ourselves, as strangers and newcomers, within the Indigenous legal orders themselves....
>
> For non-Indigenous lawyers, judges, and students, this awareness is not re-stricted to recognizing simply that there is much we don't know. It is that we don't know how much we don't know.[116]

Justice Finch's words evoke the need for the Seven Grandfather and Grandmother Teachings outlined earlier: wisdom, love, respect, courage, humility, honesty, and truth.

Indigenous peoples' knowledge systems are full of profound teachings, including legal teachings. If used in contemporary circumstances, they can help guide this country into better relationships among all beings inhabiting Turtle Island (North America). Chief Justice Finch described it best. We all have a "duty to learn" about Indigenous law. There is a duty to listen to the voices of those who lived on this land for thousands of years. Ignorance will take us down the wrong road. Honest efforts are needed to learn and apply Indigenous principles of apology, restitution, and reconciliation.

In applying Indigenous law and diplomacy to facilitate reconciliation, we must remember that legal traditions are never static.[117] Traditions become irrelevant, even dangerous and discriminatory, if they do not address each generation's shifting needs. Canadian common law and civil law traditions have grown and developed through time. For example, the common laws of tort, contract, and property have been changed since the Industrial Revolution. They were transformed to provide remedies for new harms that developed when society became increasingly complex. Likewise, the civil code of Quebec was adapted to address new social realities. This led to new provisions to deal with inequality between spouses, privacy, and personal rights. Additionally, Canadian constitutional law and other public laws have evolved to implement international law related to human rights and freedoms.

Indigenous legal traditions also continue to grow and develop. They change through time to adapt to new complexities. Indigenous law practitioners creatively strive to retain order as their communities move through time, as is the case with practitioners of Canadian law more generally. Unfortunately, Canadian law has discriminatorily constrained the healthy growth of Indigenous law contrary to its highest principles.[118] Nevertheless, many Indigenous people continue to shape their lives by reference to their customs and legal principles.[119]

These legal traditions are important in their own right. They can also be applied towards reconciliation for Canada, particularly when considering apologies, restitution, and reconciliation. Ensuring that Indigenous peoples can access and apply their own laws both within their communities and to resolve conflicts and negotiate Treaties and other agreements with the Crown is essential to reconciliation.

Without Indigenous law and protocol establishing the common ground on which the parties meet—reconciliation will always be incomplete. At the same time, we recognize that Indigenous forms of reconciliation will not be available to the Canadian state until First Nations, Inuit, and Métis peoples decide to offer them, leaving significant power in the hands of Indigenous peoples. Canada is not the only party necessary to activate national healing and justice. This is as it should be. Indigenous nations are self-determining communities. They have the ability to decide whether they will receive or act on Canada's overtures towards reconciliation.

Practically speaking, Indigenous peoples will genuinely respond to Canada's offerings of apology or initiate their own overtures only when they are satisfied that Canada has sincerely created conditions that will allow Indigenous law and protocol to be meaningfully received and acted upon.[120] Until this happens, Indigenous peoples will likely not offer Canada the conditions necessary for reconciliation.

In the meantime, our country will continue to suffer in relation to its unity, reputation, and productivity. This will be a tremendous loss for every Canadian. Yet, when people are gravely harmed, it is unfair to expect them to act otherwise. Indigenous nations retain the ability to reject what Canada does in the name of reconciliation until they judge Canada as acting in good faith in relation to creating a meaningful set of better relationships. It will therefore be vital to set the tone and express the principles for establishing respectful relationships with an official public declaration—a Royal Proclamation of Reconciliation (see Call to Action 45)—that commits all Canadians to reconciliation.

The Commission emphasizes that the teaching and application of First Nations, Inuit, and Métis peoples' laws and legal traditions hold great promise for taking the country towards reconciliation by guiding it further along pathways of truth, healing, and justice. Only then will Canada finally live up to the true spirit and intent of the Treaties that were, and still are, envisioned by Indigenous nations. Only then will all Canadians truly be Treaty people; the work of reconciliation is up to all of us.

Call to action:

50) In keeping with the *United Nations Declaration on the Rights of Indigenous Peoples,* we call upon the federal government, in collaboration with Aboriginal organizations, to fund the establishment of Indigenous law institutes for the development, use, and understanding of Indigenous laws and access to justice in accordance with the unique cultures of Aboriginal peoples in Canada.

CHAPTER 3

From apology to action:
Canada and the churches

From the outset, this Commission has emphasized that reconciliation is not a one-time event; it is a multi-generational journey that involves all Canadians. The public apologies and compensation to residential school Survivors, their families, and their communities by Canada and the churches that ran the residential schools marked the beginning, not the end, of this journey. Survivors needed to hear government and church officials admit that the cultural, spiritual, emotional, physical, and sexual abuse that they suffered in the schools was wrong and should never have happened, but they needed more.

The children and grandchildren of Survivors needed to hear the truth about what happened to their parents and grandparents in the residential schools. At the Commission's public events, many Survivors spoke in the presence of their children and grandchildren for the first time about the abuses they had suffered as children, and about the destructive ways of behaving they had learned at residential school. Many offered their own heartfelt apologies to their families for having been abusive or unable to parent, or simply to say, "I love you."

Apologies are important to victims of violence and abuse. Apologies have the potential to restore human dignity and empower victims to decide whether they will accept an apology or forgive a perpetrator. Where there has been no apology, or one that victims believe tries to justify the behaviour of perpetrators and evade responsibility, reconciliation is difficult, if not impossible, to achieve. The official apologies from Canada and the churches sent an important message to all Canadians that Aboriginal peoples had suffered grievous harms at the hands of the state and church institutions in the schools, and that, as the parties responsible for those harms, the state and the churches accepted their measure of responsibility. The apologies were a necessary first step in the process of reconciliation.

The history and destructive legacy of the residential schools is a sober reminder that taking action does not necessarily lead to positive results. Attempts to assimilate First Nations, Inuit, and Métis peoples into mainstream Canadian society were a dismal failure. Despite the devastating impacts of colonization, Indigenous peoples have always resisted (although in some places not always successfully) attacks on their cultures, languages, and ways of life.

If Canadians are to keep the promise of the apologies made on their behalf—the promise of "never again!"—then we must guard against simply replicating the assimilation policies of the past in new forms today. As Truth and Reconciliation Commission (TRC) Honorary Witness Wab Kinew writes, "The truth about reconciliation is this: It is not a second chance at assimilation. It should not be a kinder, gentler evangelism, free from the horrors of the residential school era. Rather, true reconciliation is a second chance at building a mutually respectful relationship."[1]

The words of the apologies will ring hollow if Canada's actions fail to produce social, cultural, political, and economic change that benefits Aboriginal peoples and all Canadians.

A just reconciliation requires more than simply talking about the need to heal the deep wounds of history. Words of apology alone are insufficient; concrete actions on both symbolic and material fronts are required. Reparations for historical injustices must include not only apology, financial redress, legal reform, and policy change but also the rewriting of national history and public commemoration.

In every region of the country, Survivors and others have sent a strong message, as received by this Commission: for reconciliation to thrive in the coming years, Canada must move from apology to action.

Why are official apologies important to reconciliation?

Official apologies can play a significant role in national reconciliation. Although victims may demand an apology, the state ultimately has the power to decide whether it will comply. Legal scholar Martha Minow points out that "official apologies can correct a public record, afford public acknowledgment of a violation, assign responsibility, and reassert the moral baseline to define violations of basic norms."[2]

An official apology constitutes a public admission that acceptable societal norms and values have been violated and that, as a result, civic trust has been broken.[3]

Unlike a personal apology made by an individual to a specific individual or group of individuals that he or she has harmed directly, an official apology is made by a high-ranking government or institutional official with authority to speak on behalf of his or her constituents. Official apologies can help to change public attitudes about historical matters and verify the credibility of victims whose claims have been disbelieved.

A sincere apology should explain to the general public why a particular government policy or institutional action was wrong and demonstrate that the wrongdoer accepts responsibility for the individual and collective harms that resulted. This public accountability provides the necessary rationale and justification for making other forms of reparations to victims, such as financial compensation and commemoration.[4] But official apologies are not just about the past: they also have implications for the future.[5]

Global context: Indigenous peoples and government apologies

In the final years of the twentieth century and into the new millennium, victims of violence and human rights violations throughout the world have sought truth and demanded justice from the state. This has given rise, particularly in Western countries, to what some have described as an "age of apology."[6]

When a historical injustice involves Indigenous peoples, an official apology raises questions concerning its authenticity, purpose, and function because colonialism and oppression still define their relationship with the state. Governments in Australia, the United States, New Zealand, and Canada have all, at various times and for various reasons, issued apologies to Indigenous peoples as a way to deal with their unsavory colonial pasts. Indigenous studies scholar Jeff Corntassel and philosopher Cindy Holder argue that

> decolonization and restitution are necessary elements of reconciliation because these are necessary to transform relations with indigenous communities in the way justice requires. Whether the mechanism attempting to address injustice to indigenous peoples and remedy wrongs is an apology or a truth and reconciliation commission, it must begin by acknowledging indigenous peoples' inherent right to self-determination.[7]

Their observations aptly sum up the controversies and tensions surrounding Canada's apology. The many references to the apology heard by this Commission showed that some saw it as an important step towards individual, community, and national healing, whereas others viewed it as nothing more than some well-crafted words designed to make the government look good. It is important to assess whether an apology is genuine because, as historian Michael Marrus points out, "even beautifully crafted apologies can fail."[8] A failed apology may make matters even worse than no apology at all; victims may feel that they have been revictimized.

Political scientist Matt James, drawing on the work of various scholars of political apologies, concludes that a genuine apology

(1) is recorded officially in writing;

(2) names the wrongs in question;

(3) accepts responsibility;

(4) states regret;

(5) promises nonrepetition;

(6) does not demand forgiveness;

(7) is not hypocritical or arbitrary; and

(8) undertakes—through measures of publicity, ceremony, and concrete reparation—both to engage morally those in whose name the apology is made and to assure the wronged group that the apology is sincere.[9]

Official apologies offered to Aboriginal peoples by the state and its institutions must not only meet the criteria of Western-based political and legal cultures but must be measured by Indigenous criteria as well. Indigenous peoples document their histories through oral-based tradition, including the official recording of apologies and restitution made in order to rectify harms. In doing so, they rely on their own culturally specific laws, ceremonies, and protocols.[10]

Canada's apology

June 11, 2008, was an important day for the Aboriginal peoples of Canada, and for the country as a whole. It has come to be known as the "Day of the Apology," the day when Prime Minister Stephen Harper, and the leaders of all other federal political parties, formally apologized in the House of Commons for the harms caused by the residential school system. In their presentations to the TRC, many Survivors clearly recalled the day of the apology. They recalled where they were, who they were with, and most importantly, how they felt. Many spoke of the intense emotions they had when they heard the prime minister acknowledge that it had been wrong for the government to take them away from their families for the purpose of "killing the Indian" in them. They talked of the tears that fell when they heard the words "we are sorry."

Survivors and their families needed to hear those words. They had lived with pain, fear, and anger for most of their lives, resulting from the abrupt separation from their families and their experiences at residential schools, and they wanted desperately to begin their healing. They needed validation of their sense that what had been done to them was wrong. They wanted to believe that things would begin to change—not the schools, which had long been closed, but the attitude and behaviours that lay behind the existence of the schools. They wanted to believe that the government that had so long controlled their lives and abused its relationship with them now 'saw the light.' They wanted to believe that the future for their children and their grandchildren would be different from their own experiences—that their lives would be better. The apology gave them cause to think that their patience and perseverance through the trauma and negativity of their experiences in and beyond the residential schools had been worth the struggle. It gave them hope.

At the TRC's Saskatchewan National Event, National Chief of the Assembly of First Nations Shawn A-in-chut Atleo said,

> I think as was heard here, what I'm so grateful for is that there's a growing experience ... about the work of reconciliation.... How do communities reconcile? Well, it begins with each and every one of us. How fortunate I am as a young man to have spent time with my late grandmother. I held her hand. She was eighty-seven years old, still here. During that apology, she said, "Grandson, they're just starting to see us, they're just beginning to see us." That's what she said. And she found that encouraging, because it's the first step, actually seeing one another, having the silence broken and the stories starting to be told.... I think that's where it begins, isn't it? Between us as individuals sharing the stories from so many different perspectives so that we can understand.[11]

Honour of the Crown: Repairing trust and ensuring accountability

Survivors are more than just victims of violence. They are also holders of Treaty, constitutional, and human rights.[12] They are women and men who have resilience, courage, and vision. Many have become Elders, community leaders, educators, lawyers, and political activists who are dedicated to revitalizing their cultures, languages, Treaties, laws, and governance systems. Through lived experience, they have gained deep insights into what victims of violence require to heal. Equally important, they have provided wise counsel to political leaders, legislators, policymakers, and all citizens about how to prevent such violence from happening again.

The Commission agrees with Anishinaabe scholar and activist Leanne Simpson, who has urged Canadians not to think about reconciliation in narrow terms or to view Survivors only as victims.

> If reconciliation is focused only on residential schools rather than the broader set of relationships that generated policies, legislation, and practices aimed at assimilation and political genocide, then there is a risk that reconciliation will "level the playing field" in the eyes of Canadians.... I also worry that institutionalization of a narrowly defined "reconciliation" subjugates treaty and nation-based participation by locking our Elders—the ones that suffered the most directly at the hands of the residential school system—into a position of victimhood. Of course, they are anything but victims. They are our strongest visionaries and they inspire us to vision alternative futures.[13]

Speaking at the British Columbia National Event, Honorary Witness and former lieutenant-governor of British Columbia the Honourable Steven Point said,

> We got here to this place, to this time, because Aboriginal Survivors brought this [litigation on residential schools] to the Supreme Court of Canada. The churches and the governments didn't come one day and say, "Hey, you know, we did something wrong and we're sorry. Can you forgive us?" Elders had to bring this matter to the Supreme Court of Canada. It's very like the situation we have with Aboriginal rights, where nation after nation continues to seek the recognition of their Aboriginal title to their own homelands.[14]

The Commission believes that Survivors, who took action to bring the history and legacy of the residential schools to light, who went to court to confront their abusers, and who ratified the Settlement Agreement, have made a significant contribution to reconciliation. The Truth and Reconciliation Commission of Canada was not established because of any widespread public outcry demanding justice for residential school Survivors.[15] Neither did the Settlement Agreement, including the TRC, come about only because government and church defendants, faced with huge class-action lawsuits, decided it was preferable to litigation. Focusing only on the motivations of the defendants does not tell the whole story. It is important not to lose sight of the many ways that Aboriginal peoples have succeeded in pushing the boundaries of reconciliation in Canada.

From the early 1990s onward, Aboriginal people and their supporters had been calling for a public inquiry into the residential school system. The Royal Commission on Aboriginal Peoples made this same recommendation in 1996. A majority of Survivors ratified the Indian Residential Schools Settlement Agreement, partly because they were dissatisfied with the litigation process. Survivors wanted a public forum such as a truth and reconciliation commission so that Canada could hear their unvarnished truths about the residential schools. Survivors also wanted a formal apology from Canada that acknowledged the country's wrongdoing.[16] Due in large part to their efforts, the prime minister delivered an official apology to Survivors on behalf of Canada.

Although societal empathy for Aboriginal victims of abuse in residential schools is important, this sentiment alone will not prevent similar acts of violence from recurring in new institutional forms. There is a need for a clear and public recognition that Aboriginal peoples must be seen and treated as much more than just the beneficiaries of public goodwill. As holders of Treaty, constitutional, and human rights, they are entitled to justice and accountability from Canada to ensure that their rights are not violated.

In his initial report, tabled in August 2012, Pablo de Greiff, the first UN Special Rapporteur on the Promotion of Truth, Justice, Reparation and Guarantees of Non-Recurrence, points out that in countries where prosecuting individual perpetrators of criminal acts involving human rights violations has been difficult, other measures such as truth-seeking forums, reparations, and institutional reforms are especially critical. Such measures enable victims of state violence to develop some confidence in the legitimacy and credibility of the state's justice system. But de Greiff cautions that implementing these measures alone does not guarantee that reconciliation will follow. Apologies, commemoration, public memorials, and educational reform are also required in order to transform social attitudes and foster long-term reconciliation.[17]

The Treaty, constitutional, and human rights violations that occurred in and around the residential school system confirm the dangers that exist for Aboriginal peoples when their right to self-determination is ignored or limited by the state, which purports to act 'in their best interests.' Historically, whenever Aboriginal peoples have been targeted as a specific group that is deemed by government to be in need of protective legislation and policies, the results have been culturally and ethnically destructive.

For Aboriginal peoples in Canada, the protection and exercise of their right to self-determination are the strongest antidote to further violation of their rights. In the coming years, governments must remain accountable for ensuring that Aboriginal peoples' rights are protected and that government actions do in fact repair trust and foster reconciliation. Repairing trust begins with an apology, but it involves far more than that.

The report of the Royal Commission on Aboriginal Peoples noted that for some time after settler contact, the relationship between Aboriginal and non-Aboriginal peoples had been one of mutual support, co-operation, and respect. Despite incidents of conflict, Aboriginal peoples' acceptance of the arrival of Europeans, and their willingness to participate with the newcomers in their economic pursuits, to form alliances with them in their wars, and to enter into Treaties with them for a variety of purposes, showed a wish to coexist in a relationship of mutual trust and respect.[18] This aspect of the relationship was confirmed on the non-Aboriginal side by evidence such as the Royal Proclamation of 1763 and the Treaty of Niagara of 1764, as discussed earlier.

The trust and respect initially established were ultimately betrayed. Since Confederation in 1867, the approach of successive Canadian federal governments to the Crown's fiduciary obligation to provide education for Aboriginal peoples has been deeply flawed. Equally important, the consequences of this broken trust have serious implications well beyond residential schools. The trust relationship and Canada's particular obligation to uphold the honour of the Crown with regard to Aboriginal peoples go to the very heart of the relationship itself.

As the original occupants for thousands of years of the lands and territories that became Canada, Aboriginal peoples have unique legal and constitutional rights. These rights arose from their initial occupation and ownership of the land, and were affirmed in the Royal Proclamation of 1763, which also decreed that the Crown had a special duty to deal fairly with, and protect, Aboriginal peoples and their lands. Subsequently, the Dominion of Canada assumed this fiduciary obligation under Section 91(24) of the *Constitution Act, 1867*, which gave Parliament legislative authority over "Indians, and lands reserved for Indians." Section 35 of the *Constitution Act, 1982* also recognized and affirmed existing Aboriginal and Treaty rights.

In several key decisions, Canadian courts have said that the federal government must always uphold the honour of the Crown in its dealings with Aboriginal peoples. In *R. v. Sparrow* (1990), the Supreme Court ruled that "the Government has the responsibility to act in a fiduciary capacity with respect to aboriginal peoples. The relationship between the Government and aboriginals is trust-like, rather than adversarial ... the honour of the Crown is at stake in dealings with aboriginal peoples." In *Haida Nation v. British Columbia (Minister of Forests)* (2004), the Supreme Court ruled that "in all its dealings with Aboriginal peoples, from the assertion of sovereignty to the resolution of claims and the implementation of treaties, the Crown must act honourably," and that "the honour of the Crown ... is not a mere incantation, but rather a core precept that finds its application in concrete practices." In other words, the honour of the Crown is not merely an abstract principle but one that must be applied with diligence.[19]

In *Manitoba Métis Federation v. Canada (Attorney General)* (2013), the Métis Nation argued that when the Métis peoples negotiated an agreement with the federal government that would enable Manitoba to enter Confederation, "they trusted Canada to act in their best interests ... [and] to treat them fairly."[20] The Supreme Court said that in 1870, the

> broad purpose of S. 31 of the *Manitoba Act* was to reconcile the Métis community with the sovereignty of the Crown and to permit the creation of the province of Manitoba. This reconciliation was to be accomplished by a more concrete measure—the prompt and equitable transfer of the allotted public lands to the Métis children. (Para. 98)

Ruling in favour of the Manitoba Métis Nation, the court observed that its "submissions went beyond the argument that the honour of the Crown gave rise to a fiduciary duty, raising the broader issue of whether the government's conduct generally comported with the honour of the Crown" (para. 87). The court found that although Section 31 promised that land grants to Métis people would be implemented "in the most effectual and equitable manner," this did not happen. "Instead, the implementation was ineffectual and inequitable. This was not a matter of occasional negligence, but of repeated mistakes and inaction that persisted for more than a decade. A government sincerely intent on fulfilling the duty that its honour demanded could and should have done better" (para. 128).

For Treaty peoples or First Nations, the unilateral imposition of the *Indian Act*, including the residential school system, represents a fundamental breach of the

Crown's Treaty obligations and fiduciary duty to deal with them honourably in both principle and practice.

The Crown's position as a fiduciary with regard to Aboriginal peoples is clearly a complicated and potentially conflicting area of legal obligation. As a fiduciary, the Crown, through the Government of Canada, has a legal obligation to act in the best interests of Aboriginal peoples. This is the same case for the Bureau of Indian Affairs in the United States, which is commonly referred to as a "Trustee." As a trustee, the Bureau of Indian Affairs has a similar obligation to act in the best interests of Native Americans, and to ensure that other government departments do not act in a manner that contravenes tribal rights and interests or the government's lawful obligations.

In the United States, the "Solicitor's Opinions" issued from time to time by the Department of the Interior, which has authority over the Bureau of Indian Affairs, are used to give direction to government generally as well as to explain and justify government action. In Canada, it must be recognized that the federal Department of Justice has two important, and potentially conflicting, roles when it comes to Aboriginal peoples:

1. The Department of Justice Canada provides legal opinions to the Department of Aboriginal Affairs and Northern Development Canada (AANDC) in order to guide the department in its policy development, legislative initiatives, and actions. Those opinions, and the actions based on them, invariably affect Aboriginal governments and the lives of Aboriginal people significantly. Often those opinions are about the scope and extent of Aboriginal and Treaty rights, and often they form the basis upon which federal Aboriginal policy is developed and enacted.

2. Justice Canada also acts as the legal advocate for the AANDC and the government in legal disputes between the government and Aboriginal people. In this capacity, it takes instruction from senior officials within the Department of Aboriginal Affairs when the department is implicated in legal actions concerning its responsibilities. It gives advice about the conduct of litigation, the legal position to be advanced, the implementation of legal strategy, and the decision about whether to appeal a particular court ruling.

The necessity both to uphold the honour of the Crown and to dispute a legal challenge to an official's or department's action or decision can sometimes give rise to conflicting legal obligations.

In the Commission's view, these legal opinions should be available, as of right and upon request, to Aboriginal peoples, for whom the Crown is a fiduciary. Canadian governments and their law departments have a responsibility to discontinue acting as though they are in an adversarial relationship with Aboriginal peoples and to start acting as true fiduciaries. Canada's Department of Justice must be more transparent and accountable to Aboriginal peoples; this requirement includes sharing its legal opinions on Aboriginal rights. As noted above, there is precedent for making this change. Not only has the US Office of the Solicitor made public its legal opinions on a range of issues affecting Native Americans, but these opinions are now also widely available online.[21]

Call to action:

51) We call upon the Government of Canada, as an obligation of its fiduciary responsibility, to develop a policy of transparency by publishing legal opinions it develops and upon which it acts or intends to act, in regard to the scope and extent of Aboriginal and Treaty rights.

One aspect of the Doctrine of Discovery that continues to assert itself to this day is the fact that court cases involving Aboriginal territorial claims have placed a heavy requisite standard on Aboriginal claimants to prove that they were in occupation of land at first contact and that the rights claimed over the territory have continued from then to the present. The Commission believes that there is good reason to question this requirement, particularly in view of the fact that much of the record upon which courts rely is documentary proof or oral testimony from acknowledged Elder experts. History shows that for many years after Confederation, Aboriginal claimants were precluded from accessing legal advice or the courts to assert their claims, and that many of their best Elder experts have passed on without having had an opportunity to record their evidence.

The Commission believes that it is manifestly unfair for Aboriginal claimants to be held to the onus of proof throughout legal proceedings. However, it is reasonable to require that an Aboriginal claimant establish occupation of specified territory at the requisite period of time. This could be at the time of contact or at the time of Crown assertion of sovereignty. It is our view that once occupation has been proven, the onus should shift to the other party to show that the claim no longer exists, either through extinguishment, surrender, or some other valid legal means.[22] Therefore, we conclude that Aboriginal claims of title and rights should be accepted on assertion, with the burden of proof placed on those who object to such claims.

Call to action:

52) We call upon the Government of Canada, provincial and territorial governments, and the courts to adopt the following legal principles:

i. Aboriginal title claims are accepted once the Aboriginal claimant has established occupation over a particular territory at a particular point in time.

ii. Once Aboriginal title has been established, the burden of proving any limitation on any rights arising from the existence of that title shifts to the party asserting such a limitation.

The report of the Royal Commission on Aboriginal Peoples emphasized that the restoration of civic trust is essential to reconciliation. It concluded that "the purpose of engaging in a transaction of acknowledgement and forgiveness is not to bind Aboriginal and non-Aboriginal people in a repeating drama of blame and guilt, but jointly to acknowledge the past so that both sides are freed to embrace a shared future with a measure of trust." The report added that "the restoration of trust is essential to the great enterprise of forging peaceful relations."[23] The Truth and Reconciliation Commission of Canada agrees with these findings.

For reconciliation to take root, Canada, as the party to the relationship that has breached this trust, has the primary obligation to do the work needed to regain the trust of Aboriginal peoples. It is our view that at the time of Confederation, and in subsequent Treaty negotiations, Aboriginal peoples placed a great deal of faith in the words of those speaking for the Crown, and therefore expected that the new relationship would be a positive one for both of them. This faith was betrayed, however, by the imposition of the *Indian Act*, the development of the residential school system, and a series of other repressive measures.

Survivors have indicated that despite the Settlement Agreement and Canada's apology, trust has not yet been restored. Eugene Arcand of the Truth and Reconciliation Commission's Indian Residential Schools Survivor Committee said,

> I was there at the apology. I thought I was on my way to reconciliation when I heard the prime minister's words, in a way, when his voice trembled.... It would be remiss of me to the Survivors of Saskatchewan and Survivors across this country to not talk about what's happened since the apology. It's been difficult to talk on one side of my mouth about reconciliation and truth, and on the other side of my heart I have very intense feelings about the actions of the federal government, Prime Minister Harper who gave that apology, and the Ministry of Indian Affairs in the administration of this agreement and other acts of government that have been an assault on our people....

> [W]e as First Nations, Métis, and Inuit people, especially residential school Survivors, want to reconcile. We really, really want to. But it's difficult when we see, and feel, and read what's coming out of the House, provincially, federally, in regards to our well-being. First, with the cuts to the Aboriginal Healing

Foundation and other cuts that have happened in regards to education, in regards to our livelihood.[24]

In Winnipeg at the TRC Manitoba National Event, Survivor Allan Sutherland said, "I do teachings in schools. I ask the children when somebody gives you an apology, what are you looking for? They'll tell me—sincerity, do they mean it? And of course, behaviour. They don't repeat what they did, what they're doing. I had high hopes with the apology in 2008. I have since been dismayed about how slow we are moving."[25] At the TRC Victoria Regional Event in British Columbia, Survivor Lisa Scott said, "the apology was nice.... I'm glad somebody apologized, but how is it going to be accepted if it's just a statement and there is no action? ... The apology is just an apology.... Now show us. Make amends.[26]

Speaking to the Commission in Batoche, Saskatchewan, intergenerational Survivor Ron McHugh said,

> Reconciliation? I think there has to be a lot of integrity put behind that word. We're often given lip-service by the government in a lot ways, and even ... the national apology ... was a token event.... Action—that's what reconciliation means to me; it's action.... Action by both parties ... for us [Aboriginal peoples] to just put away [our] resentment and for the government to put away their devious, imperialistic mindset ... [We need to] come together and find a really solid solution.[27]

A government apology sends a powerful symbolic message to citizens that the state's actions were wrong.[28] As important as Canada's apology was, it did not simply mark a closure of the past. It also created an opening for Canadians to begin a national dialogue about restoring Aboriginal peoples to a just and rightful place within Canada. In their evaluation of where things stood in the years immediately following the apology, Aboriginal leaders identified a post-apology gap between the aspirational language of Canada's apology and Aboriginal peoples' continuing realities. Closing this gap is vital to reconciliation.

Speaking to the Senate on June 11, 2009, the first anniversary of Canada's apology, Assembly of First Nations National Chief Phil Fontaine, who is also a Survivor, said,

> In a post-apology era, the honour of the Crown must be a defining feature in the new relationship where legal obligations are vigilantly observed, where First Nations are diligently consulted and accommodated on all matters affecting our lives, and our right to free, prior and informed consent is respected.... Let it be clear that First Nations care deeply about our human rights—the human rights of the women in our communities, our children, our families and our communities.
>
> The principles of reconciliation, such as mutual respect, coexistence, fairness, meaningful dialogue, and mutual recognition, are not empty words. These prin-

ciples are about action; that is, they give shape and expression to the material, political and legal elements of reconciliation. It has been an eventful year in Canadian and global politics, society and the economy since last June. First Nations have been affected by the decisions of the Government of Canada during this time.... Given the level of poverty among First Nations, our economies and communities are at an alarmingly high risk of sinking further into the bleakness and despair of poverty. We, as a society, must not let this happen....

If this partnership between all founding peoples of the federation is to be meaningful, mutual responsibility and accountability must also define the relationship.... Reconciliation then, implies a solemn duty to act, a responsibility to engage, and an obligation to fulfill the promises inherent in an advanced democratic and ethical citizenship. That is, the Government of Canada—in fact, all, all members of Parliament in both houses—has a responsibility ... to bridge the past to a future in which the gap in the quality of life and well-being between Aboriginal and non-Aboriginal people vanishes, where First Nations poverty is eradicated, where our children have the same opportunities and life chances as other children, and the promises of our treaties are fulfilled.

Reconciliation must mean real change for all of our people in all the places we choose to live, change that addresses the wrongs in a way that brings all of us closer together. Human rights, hope, opportunity and human flourishing are not the privilege of one group or one segment of Canadian society; they belong to all of us. Achieving an apology is not an end point.[29]

National reconciliation involves respecting differences and finding common ground to build a better future together. Whether Survivors' hopes on the day of Canada's apology will ultimately be realized rests on our ability to find that common ground.

Therefore, we believe that all levels of government must make a new commitment to reconciliation and accountability. The federal government, First Nations, Inuit, and Métis peoples, and all Canadians will benefit from the establishment of an oversight body that will have a number of objectives, including assisting with discussions on reconciliation and making regular reports that evaluate progress on commitments to reconciliation. Progress on reconciliation at all levels of both government and civil society organizations needs vigilant attention and measurement to determine improvements. In terms of public education, it will be important to ensure that all Canadians have the educational resources and practical tools required to advance reconciliation.

Calls to action:

53) We call upon the Parliament of Canada, in consultation and collaboration with Aboriginal peoples, to enact legislation to establish a National Council for Reconciliation. The legislation would establish the council as an independent, national, oversight body with membership jointly appointed by the Government of Canada and national Aboriginal organizations, and consisting of Aboriginal and non-Aboriginal members. Its mandate would include, but not be limited to, the following:

   i. Monitor, evaluate, and report annually to Parliament and the people of Canada on the Government of Canada's post-apology progress on recon-ciliation to ensure that government accountability for reconciling the rela-tionship between Aboriginal peoples and the Crown is maintained in the coming years.

   ii. Monitor, evaluate, and report to Parliament and the people of Canada on reconciliation progress across all levels and sectors of Canadian society, including the implementation of the Truth and Reconciliation Commission of Canada's Calls to Action.

   iii. Develop and implement a multi-year National Action Plan for Reconciliation, which includes research and policy development, public education programs, and resources.

   iv. Promote public dialogue, public-private partnerships, and public initiatives for reconciliation.

54) We call upon the Government of Canada to provide multi-year funding for the National Council for Reconciliation to ensure that it has the financial, human, and technical resources required to conduct its work, including the endowment of a National Reconciliation Trust to advance the cause of reconciliation.

55) We call upon all levels of government to provide annual reports or any current data requested by the National Council for Reconciliation so that it can report on the progress towards reconciliation. The reports or data would include, but not be limited to:

i. The number of Aboriginal children—including Métis and Inuit children—in care compared with non-Aboriginal children, the reasons for apprehension, and the total spending on preventive and care services by child-welfare agencies.

ii. Comparative funding for the education of First Nations children on and off reserves.

iii. The educational and income attainments of Aboriginal peoples in Canada compared with non-Aboriginal people.

iv. Progress on closing the gaps between Aboriginal and non-Aboriginal communities in a number of health indicators, such as infant mortality, maternal health, suicide, mental health, addictions, life expectancy, birth rates, infant and child health issues, chronic diseases, illness and injury incidence, and the availability of appropriate health services.

v. Progress on eliminating the overrepresentation of Aboriginal children in youth custody over the next decade.

vi. Progress on reducing the rate of criminal victimization of Aboriginal people, including data related to homicide and family violence victimization and other crimes.

vii. Progress on reducing the overrepresentation of Aboriginal people in the justice and correctional systems.

56) We call upon the prime minister of Canada to formally respond to the report of the National Council for Reconciliation by issuing an annual "State of Aboriginal Peoples" report, which would outline the government's plans for advancing the cause of reconciliation.

These new frameworks and commitments will not succeed without more understanding and sensitivity among those who will administer them.

Call to action:

57) We call upon federal, provincial, territorial, and municipal governments to provide education to public servants on the history of Aboriginal peoples, including the history and legacy of residential schools, the *United Nations Declaration on the Rights of Indigenous Peoples*, Treaties and Aboriginal rights, Indigenous law, and Aboriginal–Crown relations. This will require skills-based training in intercultural competency, conflict resolution, human rights, and anti-racism.

The churches

Spiritual violence and residential schools

There is an old and well-accepted adage that states, "It takes a village to raise a child." The removal of Aboriginal children from their villages was seen as a necessary step in the achievement of assimilation. However, not only did the Government of Canada take the children from their homes and villages, but it also then proceeded to destroy the cultural and functional integrity of the villages from which the children came and to which they would return.

Christian teachings were a fundamental aspect of residential schools. Aboriginal children were taught to reject the spiritual ways of their parents and ancestors in favour of the religions that predominated among settler societies. As their traditional ways of worshipping the Creator were disparaged and rejected, so too were the children devalued. They were not respected as human beings who were loved by the Creator just as they were—as First Nations, Inuit, or Métis peoples. Rather, their Christian teachers saw them as inferior humans in need of being 'raised up' through Christianity, and therefore tried to mould them into models of Christianity according to the racist ideals that prevailed at the time. The impact of such treatment was amplified by federal laws and policies that banned traditional Indigenous spiritual practices in the children's home communities for much of the residential school era.

Spiritual violence occurs when

- a person is not permitted to follow her or his preferred spiritual or religious tradition;
- a different spiritual or religious path or practice is forced on a person;
- a person's spiritual or religious tradition, beliefs, or practices are demeaned or belittled; or
- a person is made to feel shame for practising his or her traditional or family beliefs.

There is plenty of evidence to support our conclusion that spiritual violence was common in residential schools.

The effects of this spiritual violence have been profound and did not end with the schools. At the Alberta National Event, Survivor Theodore (Ted) Fontaine could have spoken for many Survivors when he said, "I went through sexual abuse. I went through physical abuse, mental, spiritual. And I'll tell you ... the one thing that we suffered [from] the most is the mental and spiritual abuse that we carried for the rest of our lives."[30]

At the Saskatchewan National Event, Survivor and Elder Noel Starblanket, National Chief of the National Indian Brotherhood (later the Assembly of First Nations), talked about the intergenerational spiritual impacts of the residential schools: "My great-grandfather ... was the first one to be abused by these churches and by these governments, and they forced his children into an Indian residential school and this began that legacy. They called him a pagan, a heathen ... and that was in the late 1800s. So I've been living with that in my family since then."[31]

Across the country, Survivors described how school staff demonized, punished, and terrorized them into accepting Christian beliefs.

Geraldine Bob told us,

> The first thing we did was pray ... and we prayed again after breakfast ... [We] went to school and we prayed before school; we had catechism. And before we went for lunch, we prayed again; after lunch we prayed again. After school, we went to more catechism lessons. And we prayed again before dinner, after dinner, and then in the evening. The reason I remember all that praying was because I didn't accept or acknowledge their God or their religion ... I didn't want to partake of [communion, but] we were forced to, and physically beaten if we didn't ... It was a kind of spiritual brutality that I experienced there.[32]

Survivor and former premier of the Northwest Territories Stephen Kakfwi said,

> The nun used to say, "You know, Steve, you don't listen. You're just like a devil." And I often wondered about it. You know, you go through depression and all these things, and you think, maybe she was right, you know, maybe as a nine year old, maybe I was a devil. Why else would I be punished by a nun? Why would she hit me? Why would she beat me? I must be so bad that God's people would do that [to me].[33]

Robert Keesick said,

> After arriving at the residential school, two nuns met me. I wasn't welcomed. One said, ... "Do you know your parents?" I said, "I know my mom." She asked again, "Do you know your dad?" [I said,] "Not really." She said, "So you are a bastard. We don't accept the devil's work in this school." ... From then on, it was pure hell. I was called bastard, savage, devil. I was not allowed to play with the other kids.[34]

Elaine Durocher said,

> We were always praying. We were always on our knees. We were told we were little stupid savages and that they had to educate us. And because we were Métis kids, we should know more than the Indian kids because we have white blood in us. So because we were so stupid, they were going to beat us, beat it into us. We were always praying because we were devilish children. Because we were born Métis, we were stupid, they had to teach us.[35]

Not only was spiritual violence practised in the schools and imposed by the teachers, but the children themselves also learned and accepted such violence as part of their lives, and perpetuated its practice once they returned to their communities and became parents and adults. Intergenerational Survivor Ava Bear told us that her grandfather and father had both attended residential school.

> My dad couldn't get over being in residence [residential school], and he used to call our own people dirty heathens because that's what he had been taught at school … My dad never believed in anything cultural. We never ever had wild meat. We never spoke our language. And when the powwow first came to our community, me and my sister both got involved on the Powwow Committee, and then one day my mother said, "Dad said you girls aren't supposed to be involved with the Powwow Committee because it's too pagan." So I quit, but my sister's still involved. So we lost our culture. We lost our language.[36]

Survivor Iris Nicholas explained that, as adults, she and other Survivors still carried a deep fear of the church that had been instilled in them as children.

> At the residential school we were told we were pagans, and would grow up to be good-for-nothing Indians. Did they realize the impact their words had on us? It didn't help the children, knowing that we were going to hell if we didn't do what the nuns demanded. This fear is still inside of me. I'm sure that other Survivors still feel the fear, especially now that we are revealing the true nature of the government and the Catholic church [which were] using force and fear as a tactic to control innocent Indian children.[37]

That Christians in Canada, in the name of their religion, inflicted serious harms on Aboriginal children, their families, and their communities was in fundamental contradiction to what they purported their core beliefs to be. For the churches to avoid repeating their failures of the past, understanding how and why they perverted Christian doctrine to justify their actions is critical knowledge to be gained from the residential school experience.

Church apologies

Survivors, who for so many years were not believed by church officials when they revealed the abuses they had suffered in the schools, needed to hear the churches tell the truth. They needed to see that the churches now held themselves accountable both in words and by their actions. Between 1986 and 1998, all four Settlement Agreement churches offered apologies or statements of regret, in one form or another, for their attempts to destroy Indigenous cultures, languages, spirituality, and ways of life, and, more specifically, for their involvement in residential schools.

The United, Anglican, and Presbyterian Churches followed similar pathways: individuals or committees at the national level of each church became aware that there might be a need to apologize, a decision-making process was established at the highest levels of the church, and the apology was subsequently issued through the moderator or primate, who spoke for the whole church.

Unlike the three Protestant denominations, the Roman Catholic Church in Canada does not have a single spokesperson with authority to represent all of its many dioceses and distinct religious orders. The issuing of apologies or statements of regret was left up to each of them individually. The result has been a patchwork of apologies or statements of regret that few Survivors or church members may even know exist.

Roman Catholics in Canada and across the globe look to the Pope as their spiritual and moral leader. Therefore, it has been disappointing to Survivors and others that the Pope has not yet made a clear and emphatic public apology in Canada for the abuses perpetrated in Catholic-run residential schools throughout the country.

On April 29, 2009, National Chief of the Assembly of First Nations Phil Fontaine, four other Aboriginal leaders, and five leaders from the Roman Catholic community in Canada travelled to Rome for a private audience with Pope Benedict XVI. No recording of the private meeting was permitted, but the Vatican issued a communiqué describing what the Pope had said.

> Given the sufferings that some indigenous children experienced in the Canadian Residential School system, the Holy Father expressed his sorrow at the anguish caused by the deplorable conduct of some members of the Church and he offered his sympathy and prayerful solidarity. His Holiness emphasized that acts of abuse cannot be tolerated in society. He prayed that all those affected would experience healing, and he encouraged First Nations people to continue to move forward with renewed hope.[38]

The media reported that National Chief Fontaine and other Aboriginal leaders who had met with the Pope said that the statement was significant for all Survivors. Fontaine told CBC News that although it was not an official apology, he hoped that the Pope's statement of regret would bring closure to the issue for residential school Survivors. "The fact that the word 'apology' was not used does not diminish this moment in any way," he said. "This experience gives me great comfort."[39]

The Pope's statement of regret was significant to those who were present, and was reported widely in the media, but it is unclear what, if any, impact it had on Survivors, their families, and their communities, who were not able to hear the Pope's words themselves. Many Survivors raised the lack of a clear Catholic apology from the Vatican as evidence that the Catholic Church still has not come to terms with its own wrongdoing in residential schools, and has permitted many Catholic nuns and priests to maintain that the allegations against their colleagues are false. A statement of regret that children were harmed in the schools is a far cry from a full and proper apology that takes responsibility for the harms that occurred.

The Commission notes that in 2010 Pope Benedict XVI responded to the issue of the abuse of children in Ireland differently and more clearly when he issued a pastoral letter, a public statement that was distributed through the churches to all Catholics in Ireland. He acknowledged that the church had failed to address the issue of child abuse in Catholic institutions.

> Only by examining carefully the many elements that gave rise to the present crisis can a clear-sighted diagnosis of its causes be undertaken and effective remedies be found. Certainly, among the contributing factors we can include: inadequate procedures for determining the suitability of candidates for the priesthood and the religious life; insufficient human, moral, intellectual and spiritual formation in seminaries and novitiates; a tendency in society to favour the clergy and other authority figures; and a misplaced concern for the reputation of the Church and the avoidance of scandal, resulting in failure to apply existing canonical penalties and to safeguard the dignity of every person. Urgent action is required to address these factors, which have had such tragic consequences in the lives of victims and their families.[40]

He directly addressed those who were abused as children by church clergy.

> You have suffered grievously and I am truly sorry. I know that nothing can undo the wrong you have endured. Your trust has been betrayed and your dignity has been violated. Many of you found that, when you were courageous enough to speak of what happened to you, no one would listen. Those of you who were abused in residential institutions must have felt that there was no escape from your sufferings. It is understandable that you find it hard to forgive or be reconciled with the Church. In her name, I openly express the shame and remorse that we all feel. At the same time, I ask you not to lose hope.... Speaking to you as a pastor concerned for the good of all God's children, I humbly ask you to consider what I have said ... [and that] you will be able to find reconciliation, deep inner healing and peace.[41]

In Canada, for more than a century, thousands of First Nations, Inuit, and Métis children were subjected to spiritual, emotional, physical, and sexual abuse in Catholic-run residential schools. Other than a small private audience with Pope Benedict XVI in 2009, the Vatican has remained silent on the Roman Catholic Church's involvement in the Canadian residential school system. During the Commission's hearings, many Survivors told us that they knew that the Pope had apologized to Survivors of Catholic-run schools in Ireland. They wondered why no similar apology had been extended to them. They said, "I did not hear the Pope say to me, 'I am sorry.' Those words are very important to me ... but he didn't say that to the First Nations people."[42]

Call to action:

58) We call upon the Pope to issue an apology to Survivors, their families, and communities for the Roman Catholic Church's role in the spiritual, cultural, emotional, physical, and sexual abuse of First Nations, Inuit, and Métis children in Catholic-run residential schools. We call for that apology to be similar to the 2010 apology issued to Irish victims of abuse and to occur within one year of the issuing of this final report and to be delivered by the Pope in Canada.

Survivors' responses to church apologies

Survivors made many statements to the Commission about Canada's apology, but the same cannot be said of their response to church apologies. It is striking that although Survivors told us a great deal about how churches have affected their lives, and about how, as adults, they may or may not practise Christianity, they seldom mentioned the churches' apologies or healing and reconciliation activities. This was the case even though they heard church representatives offer apologies at the TRC's National Events. Their engagement with the churches was often more informal and personal. Survivors who visited the churches' archival displays in the TRC's Learning Places picked up copies of the apologies and talked directly with church representatives. They also had conversations with church representatives in the Churches Listening Areas and in public Sharing Circles.[43]

When the late Alvin Dixon, chair of the United Church of Canada's Indian Residential School Survivors Committee, spoke to the Commission at the Northern National Event in Inuvik in 2011, he expressed what many other Survivors may have thought about all of the churches' apologies.

> The apologies don't come readily. They don't come easily. And when we heard the apology in 1986, those of us First Nations members of the United Church didn't accept the apology, but we agreed to receive it and watch, and wait, and work with the United Church to put some flesh, to put some substance, to that apology. And we all believed that apologies should be words of action, words of sincerity that should mean something.... Our task is to make sure that the United Church lives up to that apology in meaningful ways....

> You know, our work is just beginning and we're going to hold the church's feet to the fire, other churches, and Canada to make sure that this whole exercise of healing goes on for as long as it takes for us to recover from the impacts of our experiences in those residential schools.

The other issue that comes up that we are addressing is having our Native spiritual practice condemned initially not just by the United Church but all churches ... [W]ell, we now have our church supporting Native spiritual gatherings, and we're going to host a national Native spiritual gathering in Prince Rupert this summer.... So we are very much holding the church's feet to the fire and making sure that there are real commitments to putting life to the apologies.[44]

What Alvin Dixon told us is consistent with what the Commission heard from Survivors about Canada's apology. Official apologies made on behalf of institutions or governments may be graciously received but are also understandably viewed with some skepticism. When trust has been so badly broken, it can be restored only over time as Survivors observe how the churches interact with them in daily life. He explained, in practical terms, how Survivors would continue to hold the churches accountable. Apologies mark only a beginning point on pathways of reconciliation; the proof of their authenticity lies in putting words into action. He emphasized how important it was to Survivors not only that the churches admit that condemning Indigenous spirituality was wrong but also that they go one step further and actively support traditional spiritual gatherings. This action, however, calls for ongoing commitment to educating church congregations into the future about the need for such action.

Call to action:

59) We call upon church parties to the Settlement Agreement to develop ongoing education strategies to ensure that their respective congregations learn about their church's role in colonization, the history and legacy of residential schools, and why apologies to former residential school students, their families, and communities were necessary.

Honouring Indigenous spirituality

Many Survivors told the Commission that reconnecting with traditional Indigenous spiritual teachings and practices has been essential to their healing, with some going so far as to say, "It saved my life." One Survivor said, "The Sun Dances and all the other teachings, the healing lodges, sweat lodges ... I know that's what helped me keep my sanity; to keep me from breaking down and being a total basket case. That's what has helped me—the teachings of our Aboriginal culture and language."[45]

Losing the connections to their languages and cultures in the residential schools had devastating impacts on Survivors, their families, and their communities. Land, language, culture, and identity are inseparable from spirituality; all are necessary elements of a whole way of being, of living on the land as Indigenous peoples. As Survivor and Anishinaabe Elder Fred Kelly has explained,

> To take the territorial lands away from a people whose very spirit is so intrinsically connected to Mother Earth was to actually dispossess them of their very soul and being; it was to destroy whole Indigenous nations. Weakened by disease and separated from their traditional foods and medicines, First Nations peoples had no defence against further government encroachments on their lives. Yet they continued to abide by the terms of the treaties trusting in the honour of the Crown to no avail. They were mortally wounded in mind, body, heart, and spirit [and] that turned them into the walking dead. Recovery would take time, and fortunately they took their sacred traditions underground to be practiced in secret until the day of revival that would surely come.... I am happy that my ancestors saw fit to bring their sacred beliefs underground when they were banned and persecuted. Because of them and the Creator, my people are alive and in them I have found my answers.[46]

Jennie Blackbird, who attended the Mohawk Institute in Brantford, Ontario, explained it this way:

> Our Elders taught us that language is the soul of the nation, and the sound of our language is its cement. Anishinaabemowin gives [us] the ability to see into our future.... Anishinaabemowin gives us the ability to listen ... to what is going on around us and the ability to listen to what is happening inside of us. Through seeing and listening, we can harvest what we need to sustain ourselves, and to secure the properties that will heal us. Ever since I can remember as a child speaking my language, it helped me to restore my inner harmony by maintaining my mental, emotional, physical, and spiritual well-being.[47]

Spiritual fear, confusion, and conflict are the direct consequences of the violence with which traditional beliefs were stripped away from Indigenous peoples. This turmoil gives particular urgency to understanding the role of Canada's churches in effecting reconciliation with Indigenous peoples. A number of Survivors spoke to us about the many contradictions they now see between their adult knowledge of Christian ethics and biblical teachings and how they were treated in the schools. These contradictions indicate the spiritual fear and confusion that so many Survivors have experienced.

Children who returned home from the residential schools were unable to relate to families who still spoke their traditional languages and practised traditional spirituality. Survivors who wanted to learn the spiritual teachings of their ancestors were criticized and sometimes ostracized by their own family members who were Christian, and by the church. Survivors and their relatives reported that these tensions led to family breakdown—such is the depth of this spiritual conflict.

Survivor Martina Fisher said that as an adult, she had approached Indigenous spiritual practices with trepidation. She was afraid that the church and her family would disapprove of what she was doing.

> When I went to my first sweat lodge, I was just shaking. I was so scared. And [my youngest sister] asked me ... why I was afraid. And I said, "Well, I'll hurt the church and I'll hurt Mom and Dad." And she said, "No. You'll be okay." ... And here I was already in my thirties, and I was still afraid. And then I went into the sweat lodge with her. And I'm so happy I went in ... 'cause when it was done ... it was like everything was lifted. I felt so much lighter, and I felt like I found my home ... I tried to continue to go to church but once they knew that I was going to the Sun Dance, that I was going to the sweat lodge ... I was being told here in my own community ... that I was evil.... When we had our sweat lodge ... and then somebody died, they blamed us. They thought that we were bringing evil into the community. That's how Christianized our little community is. It's hard for them to accept who they are. I keep telling them, "You have to be proud of who you are. You're Anishinaabe. You can't be somebody else."[48]

The cumulative impact of the residential schools was to deny First Nations, Inuit, and Métis peoples their spiritual birthright and heritage. In our view, supporting the right of Indigenous peoples to self-determination in spiritual matters must be a high priority in the reconciliation process if it is to be undertaken in a manner consistent with the *United Nations Declaration on the Rights of Indigenous Peoples*. Indigenous peoples, who were denied the right to practise and teach their own spiritual and religious beliefs and traditions, must now be able to do so freely and on their own terms.[49] For many, this is not easily achieved.

Many Survivors and their families continue to live in spiritual fear of their own traditions. Such fear is a direct result of the religious beliefs imposed on them by those who ran the residential schools. This long-internalized fear has spanned several generations and is difficult to shed. It is exacerbated by the fact that Christian doctrine today still fails to accord full and proper respect to Indigenous spiritual belief systems.

If it were the Survivors alone who faced this dilemma, one could argue that they should be able to resolve this for themselves in whatever way they can, including with the assistance of trusted church allies. However, the dilemma of spiritual conflict is more than a personal one to Survivors. It is one that extends to their children and grandchildren, who, in these modern times, realize that there is much more to their personal histories than what they have inherited from the residential schools and Canadian society. They realize that each Indigenous nation also has its own history and that such histories are part of who they are. Young First Nations, Inuit, and Métis people today are searching for their identities, which include their own languages and cultures.

Aboriginal parents want their children raised in a community environment that provides all of this. However, there is often conflict within communities when those who have been influenced by the doctrines of the churches feel that to teach Indigenous cultural beliefs to their children is to propagate evil. There are those who continue to actively speak out against Indigenous spiritual beliefs and to block or prohibit their practice.[50]

To have a right that you are afraid to exercise is to have no right at all. The *Declaration* asserts that governments (and other parties) now have an obligation to assist Indigenous communities to restore their own spiritual belief systems and faith practices, where these have been damaged or subjected to spiritual violence through past laws, policies, and practices. No one should be told who is, or how to worship, their Creator. This is an individual choice, and for Indigenous peoples it is also a collective right. However, First Nations, Inuit, and Métis people need to be assured that they do indeed have the freedom to choose and that their choice will be respected.

All religious denominations in Canada must respect this right, but the United, Anglican, Presbyterian, and Catholic Churches, as parties to the Settlement Agreement, bear a particular responsibility to formally recognize Indigenous spirituality as a valid form of worship that is equal to their own. It cannot be left up to individuals in the churches to speak out when such freedom to worship is denied. Rather, the churches, as religious institutions, must affirm Indigenous spirituality in its own right. Without such formal recognition, a full and robust reconciliation will be impossible. Healing and reconciliation have a spiritual dimension that must continue to be addressed by the churches in partnership with Indigenous spiritual leaders, Survivors, their families, and their communities.

Many Indigenous people who no longer subscribe to Christian teachings have found the reclaiming of their Indigenous spirituality important to their healing and sense of identity. Some have no desire to integrate Indigenous spirituality into Christian religious institutions. Rather, they believe that Indigenous spirituality and Western religion should coexist on separate but parallel paths.

Elder Jim Dumont told the Commission about the importance of non-interference and mutual respect.

> [The] abuse and the damage that has been done in residential schools, one of the primary sources of that is the church. And the church has to take ownership for that. But what bothers me about it is that the church continues to have a hold on our people.... Just get out of the way for awhile so that we can do what we need to do because as long as you are standing there thinking that you are supporting us, you are actually preventing us from getting to our own truth about this and our own healing about this, but I think the other thing that's being avoided by the church is their need to reconcile with the Spirit.... I think that the church has to reconcile with the Creator.... I'm not a Christian but I have a high regard for this

Spirit ... who is called Jesus.... What I think is that when the church can reconcile with their God and their Saviour for what they have done, then maybe we can talk to them about reconciling amongst ourselves.[51]

In contrast, Aboriginal Christians who also practise Indigenous spirituality seek Indigenous and Christian spiritual and religious coexistence within the churches themselves. United Church reverend Alf Dumont, the first speaker of the All Native Circle Conference, said,

Respect is one of the greatest teachings that come from the original people of this land. Our ancestors followed that teaching when they met with their Christian brothers and sisters so many years ago. They saw a truth and a sacredness they could not deny in Christian teachings. Many were willing to embrace these teachings and leave their traditional teachings. Some were willing to embrace the teachings but still wanted to hold to their own. Some did not leave their own traditions, and when persecuted, went into hiding either deep in the mountains or deep inside themselves. Many were suspicious of the way the [Christian] teachings were presented and how they were lived. They were suspicious of the fact that they were asked to deny their own sacred teachings and ways and adopt *only* the new teachings they were given. Why could they not take what they needed from these new understandings and still live from their own? That was the understanding and teaching of holding respect for others' beliefs. It was the way of the first people.[52]

Presbyterian reverend Margaret Mullin (Thundering Eagle Woman) put it this way:

Can the Rev. Margaret Mullin/Thundering Eagle [W]oman from the Bear Clan be a strong Anishinaabe woman and a Christian simultaneously? Yes I can, because I do not have my feet in two different worlds, two different religions, or two different understandings of God. The two halves of me are one in the same Spirit. I can learn from my grandparents, European and Indigenous Canadian, who have all walked on the same path ahead of me. I can learn from Jesus and I can learn from my Elders.[53]

Each of the Settlement Agreement churches has wrestled with the theological challenges and necessary institutional reforms that arise with regard to Indigenous spiritual beliefs and practices. At the same time, Aboriginal church members have taken a leadership role in advocating for Indigenous perspectives and ensuring that they are fully represented in the institutional structures, programs, and services of their respective churches.

The General Assembly of the Presbyterian Church of Canada in 2013 endorsed a report on the development of a theological framework for Aboriginal spirituality within the church. The report noted "the need for Aboriginal Christians to be true to both their *Indigenous identity* and to their [Christian] faith," and concluded, among other things, that "this conversation has the potential not simply to help us address our relationship as Presbyterians with Aboriginal people; it has the potential to contribute to the renewal of our church."[54]

The Anglican Church has developed a vision for a self-governing Indigenous church to coexist within the broader institutional structure of the church. In 2001, a strategic plan called "A New Agape" was formally adopted by the church's General Synod meeting. The plan set out the church's vision for a

> new relationship ... based on a partnership which focuses on the cultural, spiritual, social and economic independence of Indigenous communities. To give expression to this new relationship the Anglican Church of Canada will work primarily with ... Indigenous peoples for a truly Anglican Indigenous Church in Canada. It is an important step in the overall quest for self-governance.[55]

In 2007, the church appointed the Reverend Mark MacDonald as its first Indigenous National Bishop.

The United Church has likewise examined its theological foundations. In a 2007 report, "Living Faithfully in the Midst of Empire: Report to the 39th General Council 2006," the United Church responded to an earlier call from the World Council of Churches "to reflect on the question of power and empire from a biblical and theological perspective and take a firm faith stance against hegemonic powers because all power is accountable to God."[56] The report recommended that further work be done, and a follow-up report, "Reviewing Partnership in the Context of Empire," was issued in 2009. The report's theological reflection noted,

> Our development of the partnership model was an attempt to move beyond the paternalism and colonialism of 19th century missions. The current work to develop right relations with Aboriginal peoples is an attempt to move beyond a history of colonization and racism. This ongoing struggle to move beyond empire involves the recognition that our theology and biblical interpretation have often supported sexism, racism, colonialism, and the exploitation of creation.... Theologies of empire have understood God and men as separate from and superior to women, Indigenous peoples, and nature.[57]

In 2012, the Executive of the General Council reported on the follow-up to the 2006 and 2009 reports on how to re-envision the church's theological purpose and restructure its institutions by shifting from a theology of empire to a theology of partnership.[58]

The Commission asked all the Settlement Agreement churches to tell us their views on Indigenous spirituality and what steps were being taken within their respective institutions to respect Indigenous spiritual practices. In 2015, two of the Settlement Agreement churches responded to this call.

On January 29, 2015, the Presbyterian Church in Canada issued a "Statement on Aboriginal Spiritual Practices." Among other things, the church said,

> As part of the Churches' commitment to a journey of truth and reconciliation, the Presbyterian Church in Canada has learned that many facets of Aboriginal traditional spiritualities bring life and oneness with creation. Accepting this has sometimes been a challenge for the Presbyterian Church in Canada. We are now aware that there is a wide variety of Aboriginal spiritual practices and we acknowledge that it is for our church to continue in humility to learn the deep significance of these practices and to respect them and the Aboriginal elders who are the keepers of their traditional sacred truths....
>
> We acknowledge and respect both Aboriginal members of the Presbyterian Church in Canada who wish to bring traditional practices into their congregations and those Aboriginal members who are not comfortable or willing to do so. The church must be a community where all are valued and respected. It is not for the Presbyterian Church in Canada to validate or invalidate Aboriginal spiritualities and practices. Our church, however, is deeply respectful of these traditions.[59]

On February 18, 2015, the United Church of Canada issued a statement, "Affirming Other Spiritual Paths." The document sets out various statements and apologies made by the church with regard to Indigenous spirituality, including an expression of reconciliation at the TRC's Alberta National Event on March 27, 2014. Among other things, the church said,

> In humility, the Church acknowledges its complicity in the degradation of Aboriginal wisdom and spirituality, and offers the following statements from its recent history. In doing so, the Church recognizes with pain that this is a complex and sensitive issue for some within Aboriginal communities of faith, who as a result of our Christianizing work, and the legacy of colonialism, are on a journey to restore harmony and spiritual balance....
>
> We have learned that 'good intentions' are never enough, especially when wrapped in the misguided zeal of cultural and spiritual superiority. Thus, we have learned that we were wrong to reject, discredit, and yes, even outlaw traditional indigenous spiritual practice and ceremony; in amazing circles of grace, as we have begun to listen to the wisdom of the elders, we have found our own faith enriched and deepened. And we are grateful. We know we have a long journey ahead of us. We are committed to make that journey in humility and partnership, engaging in the healing work of making "whole" our own spirituality, and acknowledging that holding both your spirituality and ours is possible through listening and learning with open hearts.[60]

Unlike the Protestant churches, in which theological reflection and institutional reform have been undertaken at the national level, the Roman Catholic Church in Canada's approach to Indigenous spirituality has emphasized decision making at the local diocesan level. However, in a submission to the Royal Commission on Aboriginal

Peoples in 1993, the Canadian Conference of Catholic Bishops expressed its views on Indigenous spirituality.

> The Native spiritual voice is now finding greater resonance in the broader Christian and social worlds. Native Christianity today is marked by the development of a theology that comes from Native prayer, culture, and experience.... As bishops, we have encouraged Native Catholic leaders to take increasing responsibility for the faith life of their communities....
>
> We also recognize that for some Native Peoples, Christianity and Native spirituality are mutually exclusive. We are committed to responding to this belief in a spirit of dialogue and respect, and to encouraging Native Peoples to join in conversation between Christianity and Native spirituality.... We will continue to explore the possibility of establishing channels of communication between our own spiritual heritage and Aboriginal spiritualities.[61]

In terms of institutional reform, the Canadian Catholic Aboriginal Council, established in 1998, advises the Canadian Conference of Catholic Bishops on issues regarding Aboriginal peoples within the Catholic Church. The council's mandate is to study and analyze "issues related to Catholic Aboriginal spirituality and education," encourage "Aboriginal leadership in the Christian community," support and promote "reconciliation in the context of the Catholic reality," and serve "as an important link between Aboriginal Catholics and non-Aboriginal Catholics."[62]

The Commission notes that all the Settlement Agreement churches have recognized the need to provide Aboriginal church members with theological education and training for leadership positions within the churches and for work in Aboriginal ministry programs. Beginning in 2007, the Churches' Council on Theological Education in Canada held a series of conferences that sought to encourage and deepen the exploration of questions with respect to Indigenous and Christian beliefs and the incorporation of Indigenous cultural and spiritual practices into Christian practices. Through these events, the council also sought to challenge post-secondary institutions to consider how best to prepare theological students for ministry in Canada, in consideration not only of Indigenous people, their culture, and their spirituality but also of the need for churches to engage in healing and reconciliation between Aboriginal and non-Aboriginal peoples.

The Toronto School of Theology made a public commitment to giving the same academic respect to Indigenous knowledge, including traditional Indigenous spiritual teachings, as is given to "traditions of Greek philosophy and modern science."[63] This pledge was made at the Meeting Place, an event co-sponsored by Council Fire Native Cultural Centre and the Toronto Conference of the United Church of Canada in June 2012.

Yet more remains to be done in education and training with regard to reconciling Indigenous spirituality and Christianity in ways that support Indigenous self-determination. Writing in 2009, the former Archdeacon for the Anglican Church and founding member of the Indian Ecumenical Conference, the Reverend John A. (Ian) MacKenzie, said,

> Most urgently, churches need to consider opening a serious dialogue with Aboriginal theologians, doctors, and healers who represent ... the North American intellectual tradition.... [Aboriginal peoples] call for recognition of the truth of past injustices and respect for their civilizations. Most of all, this is a call for respect for their traditional religious thoughts and practices. The only legitimate North American intellectual tradition comes from the diverse tribal societies in our midst! ...
>
> Sustainable reconciliation will only take place when every Canadian seminary includes a course on Aboriginal religious traditions; when every congregation ... reflect[s] on North American intellectual tradition by initiating and inviting Aboriginal religious leaders to lead such discussions ... when Aboriginal peoples achieve real self-government within their churches; and when Christian theology not only respects Aboriginal thought, but learns from it.[64]

Call to action:

60) We call upon leaders of the church parties to the Settlement Agreement and all other faiths, in collaboration with Indigenous spiritual leaders, Survivors, schools of theology, seminaries, and other religious training centres, to develop and teach curriculum for all student clergy, and all clergy and staff who work in Aboriginal communities, on the need to respect Indigenous spirituality in its own right, the history and legacy of residential schools and the roles of the church parties in that system, the history and legacy of religious conflict in Aboriginal families and communities, and the responsibility that churches have to mitigate such conflicts and prevent spiritual violence.

Church healing and reconciliation projects

Beginning in the 1990s, the four Settlement Agreement churches began allocating specific funds for community-based healing and reconciliation projects. This work continued under the terms of the Settlement Agreement. Each of the defendant churches agreed to provide and manage funds specifically dedicated to healing and reconciliation. All the churches established committees, including Aboriginal representatives, to review and approve projects. Those listed below are representative of hundreds of projects across the country. In broad terms, the reconciliation projects funded by the Settlement Agreement churches have had three primary purposes:

1. **Healing.** The Toronto Urban Native Ministry, funded by Anglican, United, and Roman Catholic churches, "reaches out to Aboriginal people on the street, in hospitals, in jails, shelters and hostels."65 The ministry works with all Aboriginal people who are socially marginalized and impoverished, including Survivors and intergenerational family members who have been impacted by residential schools. Anamiewigumming Kenora Fellowship Centre, with funds from the Presbyterian Church in Canada, developed "A Step Up ... Tools for the Soul," in partnership with local Aboriginal organizations. Under the program, a series of ten teaching events led by Aboriginal Elders, teachers, and professionals were held to support Survivors and family members on their healing journey, featuring education about culture and tradition, with the goal of fostering reconciliation.[66]

2. **Language and culture revitalization.** The Language Immersion Canoe Course in Tofino, British Columbia, funded by the United Church, focused on reconnecting Aboriginal youth to their homelands and cultures. For one month, young Aboriginal people from Vancouver Island, including the community of Ahousaht, where the United Church operated a school, were taken to a remote and ancient Hesquiaht village site to learn the Hesquiah language through the art of canoe making.[67]

    The Four Season Cultural Camps of the Serpent River First Nation in Ontario, funded by the Anglican Church, used traditional practices of harvesting, food storage, storytelling, and related ceremonies to promote language and culture.[68] The Anglicans also supported a wilderness retreat for young people at the Nibinamik First Nation at Summer Beaver, Ontario. It taught traditional life ways, while instilling a sense of self-confidence in the youth as they successfully completed the activities at the camp.[69]

3. **Education and relationship building.** The Anglican and Roman Catholic Churches still have relatively large numbers of Aboriginal members, so many of their initiatives focused on bringing their own Aboriginal and non-Aboriginal members together. The Anglican Church has worked to help build understanding and counter stereotypes among its members through anti-racism training. The Roman Catholic entities were among the core funders of the Returning to Spirit: Residential School Healing and Reconciliation Program. The program brings Aboriginal and non-Aboriginal participants together to

gain new insights into the residential school experience and to develop new communication and relationship-building skills.[70]

The Settlement Agreement churches bear a special responsibility to continue to support the long-term healing needs of Survivors, their families, and their communities, where people are still struggling with a range of health, social, and economic impacts. The closure of the national Aboriginal Healing Foundation in 2014 when government funding ended has left a significant gap in funding for community-based healing projects, at the very time when healing for many individuals and communities is still just beginning.[71]

The churches must also continue to educate their own congregations and facilitate dialogue between Aboriginal and non-Aboriginal peoples. Much has been accomplished through the healing and reconciliation projects of the Settlement Agreement churches, but more remains to be done.

Call to action:

61) We call upon church parties to the Settlement Agreement, in collaboration with Survivors and representatives of Aboriginal organizations, to establish permanent funding to Aboriginal people for:

    i. Community-controlled healing and reconciliation projects.

    ii. Community-controlled culture- and language-revitalization projects.

    iii. Community-controlled education and relationship-building projects.

    iv. Regional dialogues for Indigenous spiritual leaders and youth to discuss Indigenous spirituality, self-determination, and reconciliation.

Expanding the circle

The Commission believes that the circle of reconciliation must grow beyond the Settlement Agreement churches to include all faith communities. Together all peoples of faith have a critical role to play in the reconciliation process. Many faith communities offered expressions of reconciliation at TRC National Events. The following representative examples convey a sense of the range and scope of these public statements.

At the Saskatchewan National Event, the Reverend Bruce Adema, of the Christian Reformed Church of North American, presented a book on a series of paintings, Kisemanito Pakitinasuwin—The Creator's Sacrifice, by Cree artist Ovide Bigetty. In presenting the book, Adema, as the director of Canadian Ministries, offered the first apology for residential schools and colonial policies from a church that had not run any residential schools.

> Our church does not have a direct history of running Residential Schools in Canada. However, as members of the body of Christ in Canada we confess that the sins of assimilation and paternalism in Indian Residential Schools, and in wider government policy, are ours as the Christian Reformed Church. We are deeply sorry and pledge to walk the journey of reconciliation and healing with you.

> This art also testifies to the presence of the Creator's truth and beauty in Indigenous culture. It reminds us that the journey of faith, healing and reconciliation is one of sharing and mutual respect. The church and the nation of Canada are poorer because we refused to acknowledge the Creator's truth and way as revealed to Indigenous people.[72]

Members of the Mennonite Central Committee Saskatchewan served on the regional working group and subcommittees that helped to plan the Saskatchewan National Event. They also worked as volunteers at the event. On their behalf, the Reverend Claire Ewert Fisher, the committee's executive director, spoke about the complicity of Mennonites as members of the dominant Euro-Canadian society in supporting government policies of assimilation, including the residential school system.

> Many people from the Mennonite community have come to this gathering to volunteer, to listen, to learn. We are on a path leading us to greater understanding. As members of the dominant culture, we regret our part in an assimilation practice that took away language use and cultural practice. We repent of our participation in the destructive acts of the dominant society. We thank you for your welcome to walk this path together as we move to a better and healthier tomorrow. We commit ourselves to walk with you, with your help.[73]

At the British Columbia National Event, representatives from the Jewish, Bahá'í, and Sikh faith communities offered expressions of reconciliation that made connections between their spiritual beliefs and the need for justice, healing, and reconciliation.

Rabbi Jonathan Infeld of Vancouver's Congregation Beth Israel spoke about the importance of cultivating empathy from one's own experience of suffering to become an effective witness to the stories of how others have suffered historically. For members of the Jewish community, their experience of the Holocaust is a source of empathy in approaching the topic of the residential schools. As an expression of the Jewish community's desire for reconciliation in Canada, he invited all gathered to stand for a sacred moment as he blew a shofar—a trumpet made from a ram's horn—which he then presented to the TRC. Rabbi Infeld explained that the shofar had been sounded over the preceding two weeks during the Jewish High Holy Days, including Rosh Hashanah and Yom Kippur—the Day of Atonement—which calls the faithful to repent of sins that have been committed. Quoting from the teaching of twelfth-century Jewish rabbi Maimonides, Infeld noted, "like an alarm clock, the shofar is meant to wake us up to the need to sacrifice, to give up or forsake former ways of thinking and acting, to atone for how we have wronged others."[74]

Deloria Bighorn, chair of the National Spiritual Assembly of the Bahá'í of Canada, who is also a Survivor, spoke about some of the teachings of the Bahá'í faith concerning the process of reconciliation and its spiritual importance. The assembly's expression of reconciliation said, among other things,

> We believe that the pursuit of truth and reconciliation is intimately connected with the principle of justice. Justice is essential to truth and reconciliation alike. Justice is, first, made possible by developing the capacity to seek truth through our own eyes ... [W]e must seek to recognize injustice and then see that justice is restored within our society and institutions ...

> When we speak of reconciliation we are referring to the movement towards peace and unity, and the individual and collective transformation that is required in order to achieve that goal. Reconciliation involves a process that contributes to the achievement of progressively greater degrees of unity and trust. Fundamentally, reconciliation is a spiritual process. It is the process of realizing the essential oneness of humanity in all dimensions of human life ...

> Canada shares the challenge of reconciliation with the rest of the human family. In our international relations, just as in our domestic ones, we need to recognize that we are all parts of an organic whole. How do we forge bonds of unity that respect and draw strength from our diversity? How can we overcome the forces of paternalism and prejudice with the powers of love and justice? What changes do we need to make to the structures of governance and the use of material resources in order to redress past injustices and social inequities? These are questions that we ask ourselves as citizens of a country that seeks reconciliation.[75]

Eight leaders of the Sikh community, including Prem Singh Vinning, as president of the World Sikh Organization of Canada, and leaders from Sikh *gurdwaras* in the Lower Mainland of British Columbia, presented a statement and four videos to the TRC as an expression of reconciliation. The videos explore why the residential schools matter to Sikhs as Canadians, as peoples of faith, and as Sikhs—and serve to educate other members of the Sikh community by comparing the residential school story with the historical Sikh experiences of discrimination and cultural oppression. The Sikh leaders expressed their commitment to reconciliation in Canada.

> Our faith requires us to come to the aid of our neighbours in their time of need. As a community, we Sikhs also know what it is like to have loved ones taken away, never to be seen again. Throughout our history we have also lost generations, and understand the struggle to freely practice our faith and preserve our language.

It takes incredible determination and fortitude to shine a light on a deep wound that has been hidden for so long. We would like to acknowledge all the survivors that stood up and began this process. It is not easy to be first. Your courage, tenacity and strength have helped pave the way for other residential school survivors to come forward as well.

But that is not all that you have accomplished. Your enduring valour has set an example and created a space in Canada where Canadians from diverse backgrounds can talk about their own experiences of genocide, tyranny and persecution. Many immigrants to this country understand these all too well.

As Sikhs, we have not yet had the opportunity to engage in truth telling and reconciliation as a community with respect to the thousands lost in India in 1984 and later. In this we will be looking to our Métis, First Nations, and Inuit brothers and sisters for inspiration as we work together to lay a foundation for a new way forward.[76]

At the Alberta National Event, representatives of the Canadian Council of Churches read a statement signed by the heads of the twenty-five denominations making up the council, an organization that represents 85% of Canadian Christians.

As Christians, we have been part of communities and governments that brought tremendous pressure to bear on you, and through actions of privilege, prejudice and discrimination sought to assimilate the Indigenous Peoples in this country. One of the most destructive of these actions was the creation of Indian Residential Schools, a system of assimilation in which a number of member churches of the Canadian Council of Churches played a prominent role....

Christian denominations who were not involved directly in the creation and running of the Indian Residential Schools are also represented here today [in this statement]. As willing or unwilling accomplices to the terrible effects that so called Christian attitudes and policies had on your life and the lives of your peoples, we, too, live with the legacy of Indian Residential Schools ...

We commit to respect the right and freedom of Indigenous communities to practise traditional spirituality and teachings. We commit to value the gifts of Indigenous traditional teachings in Christian worship and pastoral practices, where appropriate, in consultation with your Elders.[77]

A group of young Christians, including Mennonites, called the Honour Walkers told the Commission about their 550-kilometre walk from Stony Knoll, Saskatchewan, to the Alberta National Event in Edmonton to honour the stories of Survivors. One walker explained,

Although there were only four walkers walking for twenty days, there were also groups of students and congregations back home that fasted and prayed to recognize residential and day school Survivors. As a group of walkers, we represent communities that are wanting and needing to learn the history of residential schools. As our group walked across Treaty 6 [lands], we further learned the difficult history of the residential schools through community gatherings and passersby who stopped to share their stories. We celebrated the strengths and gifts of Indigenous peoples through ceremony and hospitality. We were also blessed by the many congregations who opened their doors for conversations on settler-Indigenous issues, including discussions on residential schools, Treaties, and land justice.[78]

Expressions of reconciliation offered at TRC National Events are an indicator that the circle is growing as other faith groups recognize that they must be involved in reconciliation concerning matters both of spirituality and of social justice.

CHAPTER 4

———

Education for reconciliation

Much of the current state of troubled relations between Aboriginal and non-Aboriginal Canadians is attributable to educational institutions and what they have taught, or failed to teach, over many generations. Despite this history—or, perhaps more correctly, because of its potential—the Truth and Reconciliation Commission (TRC) believes that education is also the key to reconciliation. Educating Canadians for reconciliation involves not only schools and post-secondary institutions but also dialogue forums and public history institutions such as museums and archives. Education must remedy the gaps in historical knowledge that perpetuate ignorance and racism.

But education for reconciliation must do even more. Survivors told us that Canadians must learn about the history and legacy of residential schools in ways that change both minds *and* hearts. At the Manitoba National Event in Winnipeg, Allan Sutherland said,

> There are still a lot of emotions [that are] unresolved. People need to tell their stories.... We need the ability to move forward together, but you have to understand how it all began [starting with] Christopher Columbus, from Christianization, then colonization, and then assimilation.... If we put our minds and hearts to it, we can [change] the status quo.[1]

At the Commission's Community Hearing in Thunder Bay, Ontario, in 2010, Esther Lachinette-Diabo said,

> I'm doing this interview in hope that we could use this as an educational tool to educate our youth about what happened.... Maybe one day the Ministry of Education can work with the TRC and develop some kind of curriculum for Native Studies, Indigenous learning. So that not only Aboriginal people can understand, you know, what we had to go through—the experiences of all the Anishinaabe people that attended—but for the Canadian people as well to understand that the residential schools did happen. And through this sharing, they can understand and hear stories from Survivors like me.[2]

In Lethbridge, Alberta, in 2013, Charlotte Marten said,

> I would like to see action taken as a result of the findings of this Commission. I would like to see the history of the residential school system be part of the school curriculum across Canada. I want my grandchildren and the future generations of our society to know the whole truth behind Canada's residential school policy and how it destroyed generations of our people. It is my hope that by sharing the truth ... it will help the public gain a better understanding of the struggles we face as First Nations.[3]

Non-Aboriginal Canadians hear about the problems faced by Aboriginal communities, but they have almost no idea how these problems developed. There is little understanding of how the federal government contributed to this reality through the residential schools and the policies and laws in place during their existence. Our education system, through omission or commission, has failed to teach this history. It bears a large share of the responsibility for the current state of affairs.

It became clear over the course of the Commission's work that most adult Canadians have been taught little or nothing about the residential schools. More typically, they were taught that the history of Canada began when the first European explorers set foot in the New World. Nation building has been the main theme of Canada's history curricula for a long time, and Aboriginal peoples, with a few notable exceptions, have been portrayed as bystanders, if not obstacles, to this enterprise.

Prior to 1970, school textbooks across the country depicted Aboriginal peoples as being either savage warriors or onlookers who were irrelevant to the more important history of Canada: the story of European settlement. Beginning in the 1980s, the history of Aboriginal peoples was sometimes cast in a more positive light, but the poverty and social dysfunction in Aboriginal communities were emphasized without any historical context to help students understand how or why these conditions came about. This omission has left most Canadians with the view that Aboriginal people were and are to blame for the situations in which they find themselves, as though there were no external causes. Aboriginal peoples have therefore been characterized as a social and economic problem that must be solved.

By the 1990s, textbooks emphasized the role of Aboriginal peoples as protestors advocating for rights. Most Canadians failed to understand or appreciate the significance of these rights, given the overriding perspective of Aboriginal assimilation in Canada's education system.

Although textbooks have become more inclusive of Aboriginal perspectives over the past three decades, the role of Aboriginal peoples in Canadian history during much of the twentieth century remains invisible. Students learn something about Aboriginal peoples prior to contact and during the exploration, fur trade, and settlement periods. They learn about Métis resistance in the 1880s, and the signing of Treaties. Then Aboriginal peoples virtually disappear until the 1960s and 1970s, when they resurface as political and social justice activists. The defining period in between remains largely unmentioned.[4] Thus much of the story of Aboriginal peoples, as seen through their own eyes, is still missing from Canadian history.

In the Commission's view, all students—Aboriginal and non-Aboriginal—need to learn that the history of this country did not begin with the arrival of Jacques Cartier on the banks of the St. Lawrence River. They need to learn about the Indigenous nations the Europeans met, about their rich linguistic and cultural heritage, about what they felt and thought as they dealt with early explorers like Samuel de Champlain and Pierre Gaultier de Varennes et de La Vérendrye, or with the representatives of the Hudson's Bay Company. Canadians need to learn why Indigenous nations negotiated the Treaties and to understand that they negotiated with integrity and in good faith. They need to learn about why Aboriginal leaders and Elders still fight so hard to defend these Treaties, what these agreements represent to them, and why they have been ignored by European settlers or governments. They need to learn about what it means to have inherent rights, what those are for Aboriginal peoples, and what the settler government's political and legal obligations are in those areas where Treaties were never negotiated. They need to learn why so many of these issues are ongoing. They need to learn about the Doctrine of Discovery—the politically and socially accepted basis for presumptive European claims to the land and riches of this country—and to understand that this same doctrine is now being repudiated around the world, most recently by the United Nations and the World Council of Churches.

Survivors have also said that knowing about these things is not enough. Our public education system also needs to influence behaviour by undertaking to teach our children—Aboriginal and non-Aboriginal—how to speak respectfully to, and about, each other in the future. Reconciliation is all about respect.

The Commission's 2012 Interim Report made three recommendations directed at provincial and territorial governments:

> Recommendation 4: The Commission recommends that each provincial and territorial government undertake a review of the curriculum materials currently in use in public schools to assess what, if anything, they teach about residential schools.

> Recommendation 5: The Commission recommends that provincial and territorial departments of education work in concert with the Commission to develop age-appropriate educational materials about residential schools for use in public schools.

> Recommendation 6: The Commission recommends that each provincial and territorial government work with the Commission to develop public education campaigns to inform the general public about the history and impact of residential schools in their respective jurisdictions.

At various times, the Commission met with provincial and territorial education ministers from across Canada. In July 2014, the Council of Ministers of Education, Canada gave us an update on the status of curriculum-development commitments across the country.[5] The Commission was encouraged to see that progress has been made. We note, however, that not all provinces and territories have yet made curriculum about residential schools mandatory, and not all courses cover the subject in depth.

The Northwest Territories and Nunavut have taken a leadership role in developing and implementing mandatory curriculum about residential schools for all high school students, in engaging Survivors directly in the development of new materials, and in ensuring that teachers receive appropriate training and support, including direct dialogues with Survivors. Working in partnership with the Legacy of Hope Foundation, the Governments of the Northwest Territories and Nunavut unveiled the new curriculum, *The Residential School System in Canada: Understanding the Past— Seeking Reconciliation—Building Hope for Tomorrow*, in October 2012.[6] At the time of this writing, Yukon had begun the process of adapting the Northwest Territories and Nunavut materials for mandatory use in its territory. Among the provinces, Alberta has publicly declared that it is launching its own initiative to develop mandatory curriculum on the Treaties and residential schools for all students.

These education initiatives are significant, but it will be essential to ensure that momentum is not lost in the years following the end of the Commission's mandate. To be successful over the long term, this and similar initiatives will require substantive and sustained support from provincial and territorial governments, educators, and local school districts. An ongoing commitment from ministers of education throughout the country is critical. The Commission notes that on July 9, 2014, the Council of Ministers of Education, Canada announced that education ministers

> agreed to additional pan-Canadian work in Aboriginal education to take place over the next two years, which will focus on four key directional ideas: support for Aboriginal students interested in pursuing teaching as a career; development of learning resources on Canadian history and the legacy of Indian Residential Schools that could be used by teacher training programs; sharing of promising practices in Aboriginal education; and ongoing promotion of learning about Indian Residential Schools in K–12 education systems.[7]

In regions where curriculum and teacher training on residential schools have been introduced, it will be necessary to build on these early successes and evaluate progress on an ongoing basis. Where education about residential schools is minimal, provincial and territorial governments can benefit from the lessons learned in jurisdictions that have made this material a mandatory requirement.

The Commission notes that throughout the residential school era, Catholic and Protestant religious schools taught students only about their own religions. Students were ill prepared to understand or respect other religious or spiritual perspectives, including those of Aboriginal peoples. In our view, no religious school receiving public funding should be allowed to teach one religion to the complete exclusion of all other religions. This is consistent with the Supreme Court of Canada decision in *S. L. v. Commission scolaire des Chênes* in 2012. At issue was whether Québec's mandatory Ethics and Religious Cultures Program, which was introduced in 2008 to replace Catholic and Protestant programs of religious and moral instruction with a comparative religions course taught from a neutral and objective perspective, violated the charter right of Catholic parents and children to be taught only Catholic religious beliefs.[8] However, the court ruled,

> Exposing children to a comprehensive presentation of various religions without forcing the children to join them does not constitute an indoctrination of students that would infringe the freedom of religion.... Furthermore, the early exposure of children to realities that differ from those in their immediate family environment is a fact of life in society. The suggestion that exposing children to a variety of religious facts in itself infringes on religious freedom or that of their parents amounts to a rejection of the multicultural reality of Canadian society and ignores the Quebec government's obligations with regard to public education.[9]

The Commission believes that religious diversity courses must be mandatory in all provinces and territories. Any religious school receiving public funding must be required to teach at least one course on comparative religious studies, which must include a segment on Aboriginal spiritual beliefs and practices.

Calls to action:

62) We call upon the federal, provincial, and territorial governments, in consultation and collaboration with Survivors, Aboriginal peoples, and educators, to:

  i. Make age-appropriate curriculum on residential schools, Treaties, and Aboriginal peoples' historical and contemporary contributions to Canada a mandatory education requirement for Kindergarten to Grade Twelve students.

  ii. Provide the necessary funding to post-secondary institutions to educate teachers on how to integrate Indigenous knowledge and teaching methods into classrooms.

  iii. Provide the necessary funding to Aboriginal schools to utilize Indigenous knowledge and teaching methods in classrooms.

  iv. Establish senior-level positions in government at the assistant deputy minister level or higher dedicated to Aboriginal content in education.

63) We call upon the Council of Ministers of Education, Canada to maintain an annual commitment to Aboriginal education issues, including:

 i. Developing and implementing Kindergarten to Grade Twelve curriculum and learning resources on Aboriginal peoples in Canadian history, and the history and legacy of residential schools.

 ii. Sharing information and best practices on teaching curriculum related to residential schools and Aboriginal history.

 iii. Building student capacity for intercultural understanding, empathy, and mutual respect.

 iv. Identifying teacher-training needs relating to the above.

64) We call upon all levels of government that provide public funds to denominational schools to require such schools to provide an education on comparative religious studies, which must include a segment on Aboriginal spiritual beliefs and practices developed in collaboration with Aboriginal Elders.

Transforming the education system: Creating respectful learning environments

The Commission believes that to be an effective force for reconciliation, curriculum about residential schools must be part of a broader history education that integrates First Nations, Inuit, and Métis voices, perspectives, and experiences, and that builds common ground between Aboriginal and non-Aboriginal peoples. The education system itself must be transformed into one that rejects the racism embedded in colonial systems of education and treats Aboriginal and Euro-Canadian knowledge systems with equal respect.[10]

This is consistent with the *United Nations Declaration on the Rights of Indigenous Peoples*, which articulates the state's responsibility with regard to public education and the promotion of respectful relationships between citizens.

> Indigenous peoples have the right to the dignity and diversity of their cultures, traditions, histories and aspirations which shall be appropriately reflected in education and public information [Article 15:1].

> States shall take effective measures, in consultation and cooperation with the indigenous peoples concerned, to combat prejudice and eliminate discrimination

and to promote tolerance, understanding and good relations among indigenous peoples and all other segments of society [Article 15:2].

Fully implementing this national education framework will take many years, but it will ensure that Aboriginal children and youth see themselves and their cultures, languages, and histories respectfully reflected in the classroom. Non-Aboriginal learners will benefit as well. Taught in this way, all students, both Aboriginal and non-Aboriginal, will gain historical knowledge while also developing respect and empathy for each other. Both elements will be vital to supporting reconciliation in the coming years.

Developing respect for, and an understanding of, the situation of others is an important but often ignored part of the reconciliation process. Survivors' testimonies compelled those who listened to think deeply about what justice really means in the face of mass human rights violations. Teaching and learning about the residential schools are difficult for educators and students alike. They can bring up feelings of anger, grief, shame, guilt, and denial. But they can also shift understanding and alter worldviews.[11]

Education for reconciliation requires not only age-appropriate curriculum but also ensuring that teachers have the necessary skills, supports, and resources to teach Canadian students about the residential school system in a manner that fosters constructive dialogue and mutual respect. Educating the heart as well as the mind helps young people to become critical thinkers who are also engaged, compassionate citizens.[12]

In 2008, Ottawa teacher Sylvia Smith, troubled by the lack of knowledge about residential schools in the Ontario education system, created Project of Heart. This hands-on collaborative approach to learning about residential schools combines history, art, and social action. The project grew, and eventually hundreds of schools and community groups across the country participated.

Through Project of Heart, students and teachers have come together with Survivors and Elders to learn about the history and legacy of residential schools and to find out more about Aboriginal languages, values, cultural traditions, and teachings. Together they have created a national network of commemorative works that remember and honour those children who did not return home from the residential schools, and all Survivors. By bearing witness, the project enables participants to transform empathy into action and solidarity on social justice issues affecting the lives of First Nations, Inuit, and Métis peoples across the country.[13]

In 2011, Ms. Smith won the Governor General's Award for Excellence in Teaching for her work on Project of Heart. In a subsequent interview, she spoke of the importance of young people learning the truth of their own history and using this learning as the basis for action.

> Change doesn't happen by just wanting things to change. Caring isn't enough.
> Caring is good, but it's not enough. We actually have to do something with our

caring, and young people understand that. Students want to inherit a world that's better than the one they've got right now. Once they actually get their feet dirty, once they actually start doing these kinds of things, it's catching. It travels from student to student, it travels to the schools, and it travels outside the school. I think Project of Heart actually has proven that. We've got schools that have adopted this in most of the provinces, or church groups, or whatever. So you know you've got a good thing when people can make it their own, and when it can be contextualized to meet the needs of that particular group.... This kind of learning is something we can't get from books. A lot of our teaching experiences don't touch on the heart and the spirit. And yet, as teachers, I think that we all know that the affective component is the most important component. It's what stays with you ... [W]e can teach empathy, we can teach compassion, we can teach social justice through history.[14]

The Commission has been privileged to see many of the works created by the Project of Heart. At the TRC's Final Event in June 2015 in Ottawa, the Commission inducted Ms. Smith as an Honorary Witness in recognition of her leadership in education for reconciliation.

Aboriginal and non-Aboriginal youth are also finding their own ways to learn about the residential school history and legacy. Through dialogue, they are building new relationships that strengthen mutual respect and initiate action.

At the Alberta National Event, a youth delegation from Feathers of Hope, a project sponsored by Ontario's Provincial Advocate for Children and Youth, offered an expression of reconciliation. Samantha Crowe said,

Feathers of Hope began as a First Nations youth forum, but it quickly [became] a movement of hope, healing, and positive change within northern Ontario's First Nations communities. You spoke passionately about wanting to learn about the past, and said that First Nations and non-First Nations people alike need to understand our history, and the impacts it still has on everything around us.... First Nations and non-First Nations people need to understand how colonization, racism, [and] residential schools still continue to negatively impact the quality of life in our communities.

Everyone, especially the young people ... need to learn of Canada's history, of our past, to truly try and understand our present. This needs to be taught in school, but it also needs to be heard first-hand from our family, our friends, and our other community members. This will begin the journey of healing together as a family or as a community because we can no longer live [with] a silence that hides our pain. So while youth want to know of their past, they are ready to move forward. They understand they need positive change, but they don't want to do this alone. We all need to come together so we can share, so we can grow, and then we can uplift one another, because that's what reconciliation is about.[15]

Learning *about* the residential schools' history is crucial to reconciliation, but it can be effective only if Canadians also learn *from* this history in terms of repairing broken trust, strengthening a sense of civic responsibility, and spurring remedial and constructive action.[16] In the digital world, where students have ready access to a barrage of information concerning Treaties, Aboriginal rights, or historical wrongs such as the residential schools, they must know how to assess the credibility of these sources for themselves. As active citizens, they must be able to engage in debates on these issues, armed with real knowledge and deepened understanding about the past.

Understanding the ethical dimension of history is especially important. Students must be able to make ethical judgments about the actions of their ancestors while recognizing that the moral sensibilities of the past may have been quite different from their own. They must be able to make informed decisions about what responsibility today's society has to address historical injustices.[17] This ethical awareness will ensure that tomorrow's citizens both know and care about the injustices of the past as they relate to their own futures.

Gathering new knowledge: Research on reconciliation

For reconciliation to thrive in the coming years, it will also be necessary for federal, provincial, and territorial governments, universities, and funding agencies to invest in and support new research on reconciliation. Over the course of the Commission's work, a wide range of research projects across the country have examined the meaning, concepts, and practices of reconciliation. Yet there remains much to learn about the circumstances and conditions in which reconciliation either fails or flourishes. Equally important, there are rich insights into healing and reconciliation that emerge from the research process itself. Two research projects sponsored by the Commission illustrate this point.

Through a TRC-sponsored project at the Centre for Youth and Society at the University of Victoria, seven Aboriginal youth researchers embarked on a digital storytelling project, "Residential Schools Resistance Narratives: Significance and Strategies for Indigenous Youth." The project enabled youth researchers to learn about the critical role that resistance and resilience played in the residential schools and beyond, but it also allowed them to reflect on their own identities and roles within their families and communities. One youth researcher said that "what started as a research job turned into a personal hunt for knowledge of my own family's history with residential schools." Others noted the importance of respecting and incorporating ceremony and protocols into their digital storytelling project. Asma Antoine, the project coordinator, reported that the group learned the importance of

> knowing that when speaking to a Survivor ... you have to hear their past before you can hear their understanding of resistance. This project allowed the group [to have] a learning process that weaves [together] traditional [Indigenous] and Western knowledge to build our stories of resistance.... This research project has ignited a fire that shows in each digital story. The passion of resistance that validates the survival and resiliency of First Nations people and communities provides hope for healing and reconciliation over the next seven generations.[18]

In 2012, a digital storytelling project was undertaken by Aboriginal women at the Prairie Women's Health Centre of Excellence, "Nitâpwewininân: Ongoing Effects of Residential Schools on Aboriginal Women—Towards Inter-generational Reconciliation." Consistent with the use of ceremony and protocols throughout the project, the first workshop began with a pipe ceremony, followed by a Sharing Circle in which participants talked about their lives and group members discussed their individual and collective need for support. They later moved on to making videos of their individual stories, which were screened in March 2012 at the University of Winnipeg.[19] One of the participants, Lorena Fontaine, said,

> Reconciliation is about stories and our ability to tell stories. I think the intellectual part of ourselves wants to start looking for words to define reconciliation. And then there is the heart knowledge that comes from our life experiences. It's challenging to connect the two and relate it to reconciliation.... Without even thinking of the term reconciliation, I'm reminded about the power of story.... [People who watched the videos] said that when they saw the faces of Aboriginal women and heard their voices in the videos they understood assimilation in a different way. They felt the impact of assimilation.... It's far more powerful to have Aboriginal peoples talk about the impact of assimilation and hope for reconciliation than having words written down in a report.[20]

Research is vital to reconciliation. It provides insights and practical examples of why and how educating Canadians about the diverse concepts, principles, and practices of reconciliation contributes to healing and transformative social change.

The benefits of research extend beyond addressing the legacy of residential schools. Research on the reconciliation process can inform how Canadian society can mitigate intercultural conflicts, strengthen civic trust, and build social capacity and practical skills for long-term reconciliation. First Nations, Inuit, and Métis peoples have an especially strong contribution to make to this work.

Research partnerships between universities and communities or organizations are fruitful collaborations and can provide the necessary structure to document, analyze, and report research findings on reconciliation for a broader audience.

Call to action:

65) We call upon the federal government, through the Social Sciences and Humanities Research Council, and in collaboration with Aboriginal peoples, post-secondary institutions and educators, and the National Centre for Truth and Reconciliation and its partner institutions, to establish a national research program with multi-year funding to advance understanding of reconciliation.

TRC public education forums: Education days and youth dialogues

Education for reconciliation must happen not only in formal education settings, such as elementary and secondary schools and post-secondary institutions, but also in more informal places. One of the ways that the Commission fulfilled its public education mandate was through forums such as National Event Education Days and Youth Dialogues. The Commission believes that establishing a strong foundation for reconciliation depends on the achievement of individual self-respect and mutual respect between Aboriginal and non-Aboriginal Canadians. Although this is true for adults, it is particularly urgent for young people; they are the lifeblood of reconciliation into the future.

Mary Ellen Turpel-Lafond is a member of the Muskeg Lake Cree Nation, a former judge of the Saskatchewan Provincial Court, and now the British Columbia representative for children and youth. Her children's great-great-grandparents attended the St. Michael's Residential School in Duck Lake, Saskatchewan.[21] In a written submission following her attendance at the TRC's Victoria Regional Event in April, 2012, she noted that the *UN Convention on the Rights of the Child* and the *UN Declaration on the Rights of Indigenous Peoples* are essential tools for "[a]pplying a human rights lens to Aboriginal children's lives [that] encourages us to expand our understanding about past injustices, to recognize the full extent of abuses of their human rights, and to seek ways to remedy those abuses."[22] With regard to the importance of engaging children and youth in reconciliation, she said, "There are many dimensions to reconciliation, which can occur within families, communities, Canadian society and the international community.... There is developing awareness about children's potential role in societal reconciliation processes and the need to pay particular attention to children's special considerations."[23]

The Commission concurs with these findings. There is also a growing international consensus that children and youth must be involved in the reconciliation process itself.[24] Findings from earlier truth and reconciliation commissions indicate that children have often been marginalized in the very processes that are designed to remedy the impacts of violence on young lives. As both victims and witnesses of violence, children and youth bring unique perspectives to what is needed to address intergenerational harms and to promote reconciliation in their families, their communities, and broader society.[25]

At the Saskatchewan National Event, Grade Eight student Brooklyn Rae, who attended the Education Day, said, "I think it's really important for youth to voice their opinions, to not only prove to themselves that they can, that their voice is important, but to prove to adults that they have a voice and that they have a strong opinion that is important in the world."[26] Elder Barney Williams, a member of the TRC's Survivor Committee and one of the panelists at the Education Day Youth Dialogue, said,

> I think more and more people are realizing that the engagement of youth is crucial. For me, as a Survivor, I'm really impressed with how much they knew. I was very impressed with the type of questions the audience asked. It tells me, as somebody who's carried this pain for over sixty-eight years, that there's hope. Finally there's hope on the horizon and it's coming from the right place. It's coming from the youth.[27]

The Commission agrees. We believe that children and youth must have a strong voice in developing reconciliation policy, programs, and practices into the future. It is therefore vital to develop appropriate public education strategies to support the ongoing involvement of children and youth in age-appropriate reconciliation initiatives and projects at community, regional, and national levels.

Through direct participation in the TRC's National Events, thousands of young people and their teachers across the country had the opportunity to learn about the residential schools and think about their own role and responsibility in reconciliation. The TRC's Education Days were designed specifically for elementary and high school students and their teachers. Young people had the opportunity to listen to, and interact with, Elders and Survivors. They attended interactive workshops where they learned about the residential school history, resilience, and healing through the arts—painting, carving, storytelling, music, and film. They visited the Learning Places to walk through the Legacy of Hope Foundation display, "One Hundred Years of Loss," and to see posters and archival photographs of the residential schools from their own region.

Education Days were well attended. For example, at the British Columbia National Event in Vancouver, approximately 5,000 elementary and high school students from across the province spent the day at the National Event. In advance of Education Day, teachers in each region were given orientation materials to help prepare their students and themselves. In total, close to 15,000 young people across the country have participated in such Education Days, most with a commitment to take what they learned and witnessed back to their home schools to share with thousands more of their fellow students.

Over the course of the TRC's mandate, the Commission worked in partnership with the International Center for Transitional Justice's (ICTJ) Children and Youth Program to host a series of small retreats and workshops. Youth Dialogues were also integrated into Education Day activities at National Events. Their purpose was to engage youth in dialogue and to support their efforts to make their own submissions to the TRC. For example, in October 2010, the Commission co-sponsored a retreat for Aboriginal and non-Aboriginal youth near Vancouver, British Columbia. Young people came together to learn about the residential schools, talk with Elders, and share team-building activities. One young participant said that during the retreat, "we learn[ed] more about each other and the past. It's really important because it actually teaches us, the stories that we heard it touched us, and it inspired us to become better people."[28]

In June 2011, Molly Tilden and Marlisa Brown, two young women who attended this retreat, produced their own video documentary, *Our Truth: The Youth Perspective on Residential Schools*. The production featured interviews with their classmates in Yellowknife about what they knew about the residential schools. They presented the video at the Northern National Event in Inuvik, Northwest Territories.[29] Virginie Ladisch, director of ICTJ's Children and Youth Program, summarized what the two young women found and the subsequent impact of the project.

> The answers are shocking: some students had no knowledge, or simply complete indifference; those are largely the non-Aboriginal youth interviewed. Other students talk about the enduring impact they see in terms of high rates of alcoholism, suicide, and teenage pregnancies.
>
> So there's a huge disconnect in terms of how the young people view the relevance of this legacy and what knowledge they have of it. When that video was shared with people involved in designing the secondary school curriculum for the Northwest Territories and Nunavut, they could not believe that their youth had such reactions.
>
> So the curriculum on residential schools, which was previously barely addressed in the classroom, was revised to be a mandatory 25 hours of instruction, of which Ms. Brown and Ms. Tilden's video is a critical component.[30]

In October 2011, the TRC–ICTJ initiative prepared and supported a group of Mi'kmaq youth reporters at the Atlantic National Event in Halifax, Nova Scotia. They interviewed Survivors and documented the TRC event. At a follow-up retreat in the community, the young reporters discussed their experiences and produced a documentary called *Our Legacy, Our Hope*.[31] In 2012, the documentary was presented at the Youth Dialogue during the TRC's National Event in Saskatchewan.[32] Some of the youth also presented this documentary to international policymakers at the United Nations Permanent Forum on Indigenous Issues in 2012.[33]

The Commission's interactions with youth indicated that young people care deeply about the past. They understand that knowing the whole story about Canada's history is relevant for today and crucial for their future. In a Youth Dialogue forum at the TRC British Columbia National Event, Rory Shade told the Commission,

> I strongly believe that all youth should learn of what happened with the residential schools ... because it is a part of our history as a nation. We cannot progress as a society until we learn from the mistakes made in the past.... Knowledge is power and knowledge should be shared. The history and impacts of the residential school system must be taught because to deny a part of our history simply because it is unpleasant or controversial means to deny ourselves the chance to grow as a society.... Reconciliation is the process of accepting what happened and growing from it.... We must listen to the testimonies of those who survived such events.... We must learn to live together, and to do that, we must first reconcile with our past.[34]

In an expression of reconciliation made to the TRC at the Alberta National Event on March 27, 2014, by a group of Aboriginal and non-Aboriginal youth from the Centre for Global Citizenship Education and Research in Edmonton, one of the non-Aboriginal youth, Hanshi Liu, told us about their project. First, the group—made up of youth from First Nations reserves, the rural communities of High Prairie and Fort MacLeod, and the city of Edmonton—spent a month studying and talking about residential schools and their shared history. They then held a virtual town hall where over 300 students talked about their vision for reconciliation.

Emerald Blesse from Little River Cree Nation told us that "youth believe that reconciliation is the way to re-establish lost trust and open doors to positive and productive communications. When we affirm every culture's pride in their heritage, healing can take place." Hayley Grier-Stewart, representing the Kainai, Siksika, Tsuu T'ina, and Stony First Nations, said,

> The youth believe that within our communities, we need to teach and create awareness, cultural appreciation, as well as healing and restoration. If we introduce youth to the culture at a young age in our schools, through curriculum and the practice of restorative justice, it will teach the younger generation to be proactive instead of reactive.

Métis youth Shelby Lachlan said,

> The youth of Alberta believe that in order to move forward, towards healing and reconciliation, it is important for action to be taken on a national and provincial level. First we must re-establish trust between these two [Aboriginal and non-Aboriginal] collectives, and through the honouring, acknowledgement, and respect of all Treaties and settlements, we believe this can be achieved.

Hanshi Liu then spoke again.

We, the youth of Alberta, came together as a diverse and dynamic group. With representatives from Treaty 6, 7, and 8, a Métis settlement, and non-Aboriginal communities, together we created our vision for the future. This will serve as hope for our province and nations as we seek to facilitate healing and reconciliation for the Survivors of the Indian residential school system. This will take the commitment of multiple generations and many stakeholders, but when reconciliation is achieved, it will make for a better Canada. Today, we [the youth] are 11% of the population ... [but] we are 100% of the future and we will be a powerful ally. We only have one request. We want to be an active part of the conversation. We want to be an active part of the solution. We want to be part of making that better, stronger Canada that everyone is proud to call home.[35]

This project is one example of the significant work being undertaken by non-profit organizations that work with youth on issues related to intercultural understanding, reconciliation, and peace building. There are many others across the country.

The Canadian Roots Exchange began a Youth Reconciliation Initiative in 2012. This nationwide initiative provides Aboriginal and non-Aboriginal youth with volunteer opportunities to work together on reconciliation and education activities in their region. The initiative provides youth with leadership development, experience delivering community workshops, opportunities to plan and organize reciprocal exchanges, and participation in a national leadership exchange or youth conference.[36]

In 2014, Reconciliation Canada introduced a new youth program, "Through Our Eyes: Changing the Canadian Lens." The program provides opportunities for youth from diverse communities in British Columbia to build leadership and develop filmmaking and video production skills while learning about residential schools and the truth and reconciliation process. Participants also received training to deliver reconciliation dialogue workshops.[37]

Youth forums and dialogues are a vital component of education for reconciliation. Non-profit organizations can play a key role in providing ongoing opportunities for Aboriginal and non-Aboriginal youth to participate in intercultural dialogue and work actively together to foster reconciliation.

Call to action:

66) We call upon the federal government to establish multi-year funding for community-based youth organizations to deliver programs on reconciliation, and establish a national network to share information and best practices.

The role of Canada's museums and archives in education for reconciliation

Museums and archives, as sites of public memory and national history, have a key role to play in national reconciliation. As publicly funded institutions, museums and archives in settler colonial states such as Canada, New Zealand, Australia, and the United States have interpreted the past in ways that have excluded or marginalized Aboriginal peoples' cultural perspectives and historical experience. Museums have traditionally been thought of as places where a nation's history is presented in neutral, objective terms. Yet, as history that had formerly been silenced was revealed, it became evident that Canada's museums had told only part of the story.[38]

In a similar vein, archives have been part of the "architecture of imperialism"—institutions that held the historical documents of the state.[39] As Canada confronts its settler colonial past, museums and archives have been gradually transforming from institutions of colony and empire into more inclusive institutions that better reflect the full richness of Canadian history.

Political and legal developments on international and national fronts have contributed to this change. Around the globe, the adoption of the *United Nations Declaration on the Rights of Indigenous Peoples* has resulted in the growing recognition that Indigenous peoples have the right to be self-determining peoples and that the state has a duty to protect Indigenous traditional knowledge and cultural rights. The *Declaration* also establishes that actions by the state that affect Indigenous peoples require their free, prior, and informed consent. States have an obligation to take effective measures to protect the rights of Indigenous peoples or to make reparations where traditional knowledge or cultural rights have been violated. These provisions have significant implications for national museums and archives and for the public servants who work in them.[40]

The Commission emphasizes that several articles under the *Declaration* have particular relevance for national museums and archives in Canada. These include:

- Indigenous peoples have the right to practise and revitalize their cultural traditions and customs. This includes the right to maintain, protect and develop the past, present and future manifestations of their cultures, such as archaeological and historical sites, artefacts, designs, ceremonies, technologies and visual and performing arts and literature [Article 11:1].

- States shall provide redress through effective mechanisms which may include restitution, developed in conjunction with indigenous peoples, with respect to their cultural, intellectual, religious and spiritual property taken without their free, prior and informed consent or in violation of their laws, traditions and customs [Article 11:2].

- Indigenous peoples have the right to manifest, practise, develop and teach their spiritual and religious traditions, customs and ceremonies; the right to maintain, protect and have access in privacy to their religious and cultural sites; the right to use and control of their ceremonial objects; and the right to the repatriation of their human remains [Article 12:1].

- States shall seek to enable the access and/or repatriation of ceremonial objects and human remains in their possession through fair, transparent and effective mechanisms developed in conjunction with indigenous peoples concerned [Article 12:2].

The *Declaration*, in conjunction with Section 35 of Canada's *Constitution Act, 1982*, which recognizes and affirms existing Aboriginal and Treaty rights, and various court rulings related to Aboriginal rights have fundamentally altered the landscape in Canada's public history institutions. In light of court decisions that have declared that the principle of the honour of the Crown must be upheld by the state in all its dealings with Aboriginal peoples and that Aboriginal peoples' oral history must be "placed on an equal footing" with written historical documents, national museums and archives have been compelled to respond accordingly.[41] The governance structures, policies, ethical codes, and daily operations of national museums and archives have had to adapt to accommodate the constitutional and legal realities of Canada's changing relationship with Aboriginal peoples.[42]

Canada's national museums

The 1996 *Report of the Royal Commission on Aboriginal Peoples* made a specific recommendation to Canada's museums.

> Museums and cultural institutions [should] adopt ethical guidelines governing all aspects of collection, disposition, display and interpretation of artifacts related to Aboriginal culture and heritage, including the following:
>
> a) Involving Aboriginal people in drafting, endorsing and implementing the guidelines;
>
> b) Creating inventories of relevant holdings and making such inventories freely accessible to Aboriginal people;
>
> c) Cataloguing and designating appropriate use and display of relevant holdings;
>
> d) Repatriating, on request, objects that are sacred or integral to the history and continuity of particular nations and communities;
>
> e) Returning human remains to the family, community or nation of origin, on

request, or consulting with Aboriginal advisers on appropriate disposition,
where remains cannot be associated with a particular nation;

f) Ensuring that Aboriginal people and communities have effective access to
cultural education and training opportunities available through museums
and cultural institutions [Recommendation 3.6.4].[43]

In the years following the Royal Commission's report, museums across the country
have implemented many of its recommendations.[44] Many have worked with communities to repatriate human remains or cultural artifacts. For some institutions, consultation and collaborative partnerships with Aboriginal communities have become
standard practice, and Aboriginal internships and other training opportunities have
been established. Yet more is still needed, even as museums are faced with significant
challenges in obtaining adequate and stable multi-year funding to properly support
these critical initiatives.[45]

Over the past three decades, Canadian museums that used to tell the story of
the nation's past with little regard for the histories of First Nations, Inuit, and Métis
peoples have been slowly transforming. Although dialogue between museums and
Aboriginal peoples has improved substantially since the 1980s, the broader debate
continues over whose history is told and how it is interpreted. Here, we focus on
two national museums: the Canadian Museum of History, formerly the Canadian
Museum of Civilization;[46] and the Canadian Museum for Human Rights. As national
public history institutions, they bear a particular responsibility to retell the story of
Canada's past so that it reflects not only diverse cultures, histories, and experiences of
First Nations, Inuit, and Métis peoples but also the collective violence and historical
injustices that they have suffered at the hands of the state. It is instructive to examine
how these two public history institutions plan to interpret the history of Aboriginal
peoples and address historical injustices in the coming years.

Canadian Museum of History

Appearing before the House of Commons Standing Committee on Canadian
Heritage in June 2013, Mark O'Neill, president and chief executive officer of the
Canadian Museum of Civilization Corporation, acknowledged that many important
aspects and milestones of Canadian history—including the residential schools—have
been missing from the museum.

[P]erhaps the most egregious flaw in the Canada Hall is its starting point. If
you've been there, you will know that its telling of our national story begins not
with the arrival of First Peoples but with the arrival of Europeans in the elev-

enth century. Colonization as a term or concept is not mentioned in Canada Hall. This is something we intend to correct. Canadians made it very clear to us during the public engagement process that the voices and the experiences of First Peoples must have a place in any narrative of Canadian history.... Canadians want us to be comprehensive, frank and fair in our presentation of their history. They want us to examine both the good and the bad from our past. We were urged to foster a sense of national pride without ignoring our failings, mistakes and controversies.[47]

In July 2013, the Canadian Museum of Civilization and its partner, the Canadian War Museum, released a joint research strategy intended to guide the research activities at both institutions until 2023. "Memory and commemoration" are a key research theme; objectives include the presentation of competing and contentious historical narratives of Confederation and the two world wars, and the use of "selected commemorations to explore concepts of myth, memory, and nation." The museums intended to "present honestly, but respectfully, for public understanding issues of contention or debate ... [through] deliberate exploration of traumatic pasts (e.g. Africville or residential schools)."[48]

Drawing on research showing that Canadians valued their "personal and family connections to history," the Canadian Museum of History said that it intended to "explore the realities of contemporary life for Canada's First Peoples [including] cultural engagements with modernity, environmental change, and globalization, evolving concepts of tradition, political mobilization, and new avenues of social expression ... [and] the impact of rapid change in Canada's North, especially for Inuit."[49] Another key research theme is "First Peoples," with a particular focus on Aboriginal histories.

> The histories and cultures of Aboriginal peoples are central to all Canadians' understanding of their shared past. Respectful exploration of the interwoven, often difficult histories of Aboriginal and non-Aboriginal Peoples is a responsible, timely contribution to contemporary Canada, and to global understanding of Aboriginal Peoples.... There are four principal objectives in exploring and sharing Aboriginal narratives.... 1) Represent Aboriginal histories and cultures within broader Canadian narratives ... 2) Explore inter-cultural engagement and its continuing impacts ... 3) Broaden understanding of Aboriginal history before European contact ... [and] 4) Deepen efforts to support First Peoples' stewardship.[50]

We are encouraged to note that much of what the museum's research strategy emphasizes is consistent with our own findings: Canadians, including youth and teachers, think they should learn about the history and legacy of residential schools, and about Aboriginal history more broadly. We take particular note of the prominence given to presenting both the positive and negative aspects of Canada's history, demonstrating the relevance of the past to the present, including marginalized voices and perspectives, encouraging collaboration, and making connections between personal and public history.

The Canadian Museum for Human Rights

As a national public history institution, the new Canadian Museum for Human Rights (CMHR) in Winnipeg is mandated to "explore the subject of human rights, with special but not exclusive reference to Canada, in order to enhance the public's understanding of human rights, to promote respect for others, and to encourage reflection and dialogue."[51] Speaking at the TRC's Forum at the National Research Centre in Vancouver on March 3, 2011, CMHR president and chief executive officer Stuart Murray talked about the museum's vision for, and role in, national reconciliation. He emphasized the prominent role of the CMHR's First Nations, Inuit, and Métis advisors, as well as the Elders Advisory Council, Aboriginal Youth Council, and the broader Aboriginal community, in the planning and programs developed by the museum.[52]

Given the deep controversies that exist regarding the history of the residential school system, it is perhaps not surprising that the CMHR was criticized by the Southern Chiefs Organization in Manitoba in June 2013 after media reports that the museum would not "label human rights violations against First Nations as genocide." From the perspective of the Southern Chiefs Organization, the museum was "sanitizing the true history of Canada's shameful treatment of First Nations."[53] Stuart Murray issued a statement on July 26, 2013, clarifying the museum's position.

> In the Museum, we will examine the gross and systemic human rights violation of Indigenous peoples. This will include information about the efforts of the Aboriginal community, and others, to gain recognition of these violations as genocide—and we will use that word. We will look at the ways this recognition can occur when people combat denial and work to break the silence surrounding such horrific abuses…. We have chosen, at present, not to use the word "genocide" in the title for one of the exhibits about this experience, but will be using the term in the exhibit itself when describing community efforts for this recognition. Historical fact and emerging information will be presented to help visitors reach their own conclusions. While a museum does not have the power to make declarations of genocide, we can certainly encourage—through ongoing partnership with the Indigenous community itself—an honest examination of Canada's human rights history, in hopes that respect and reconciliation will prevail.[54]

The museum signalled its intention to create opportunities for Canadians to engage in a much broader and long-overdue public dialogue about the issue of genocide as it relates to the residential school system. The CMHR envisioned creating a public education venue for teaching all Canadians to think more critically about the history of human rights violations against Aboriginal peoples.

Speaking about the forthcoming 2017 commemoration of Canada's Confederation, Murray observed that Canada's human rights record is not unblemished, and that

> for many Aboriginal communities, this is not necessarily an event that warrants celebration. But by looking honestly and openly at our past, by engaging a diversity of voices and perspectives, and by celebrating what has been accomplished to overcome these mistakes, we will serve to make our nation more united, more proud, and more just. We can use this anniversary to continue on a journey of reconciliation.[55]

The Commission believes that, as Canada's 150th anniversary approaches in 2017, national reconciliation is the most suitable framework to guide commemoration of this significant historical benchmark in Canada's history. This intended celebration can be an opportunity for Canadians to take stock of the past, celebrating the country's accomplishments without shirking responsibility for its failures. Fostering more inclusive public discourse about the past through a reconciliation lens would open up new and exciting possibilities for a future in which Aboriginal peoples take their rightful place in Canada's history as founding nations who have strong and unique contributions to make to this country.

In the Commission's view, there is an urgent need in Canada to develop historically literate citizens who understand why and how the past is relevant to their own lives and the future of the country. Museums have an ethical responsibility to foster national reconciliation, and not simply tell one party's version of the past. This can be accomplished by representing the history of the residential schools and of Aboriginal peoples in ways that invite multiple, sometimes conflicting, perspectives, yet ultimately facilitate empathy, mutual respect, and a desire for reconciliation that is rooted in justice.

The Canadian Museum of History and the Canadian Museum for Human Rights, working collaboratively with Aboriginal peoples, regional and local museums, and the Canadian Museums Association, should take a leadership role in making reconciliation a central theme in the commemoration of the 150th anniversary of Canada's Confederation in 2017.

It must be noted that although we have focused on national museums here, regional and local museums also have a critical role to play in creating opportunities for Canadians to examine the historical injustices suffered by First Nations, Inuit, and Métis peoples, engage in public dialogue about what has been done and what remains to be done to remedy these harms, and reflect on the spirit and intent of reconciliation. Through their exhibits, education outreach, and research programs, all museums are well positioned to contribute to education for reconciliation.

Calls to action:

67) We call upon the federal government to provide funding to the Canadian Museums Association to undertake, in collaboration with Aboriginal peoples, a national review of museum policies and best practices to determine the level of compliance with the *United Nations Declaration on the Rights of Indigenous Peoples* and to make recommendations.

68) We call upon the federal government, in collaboration with Aboriginal peoples, and the Canadian Museums Association to mark the 150th anniversary of Canadian Confederation in 2017 by establishing a dedicated national funding program for commemoration projects on the theme of reconciliation.

Canada's national archives: Sharing Aboriginal history versus keeping state records

As Canada's national archives, Library and Archives Canada (LAC) has a dual function with regard to its holdings on Aboriginal peoples. It is both a public history institution tasked with making documents relevant to Aboriginal history accessible to the public, and it is the custodian of federal government departmental historical records.

In 2005, LAC issued a "Collection Development Framework," which set out the principles and practices that would guide the institution's acquisition and preservation of its holdings. The framework made specific commitments regarding materials related to Aboriginal peoples.

> LAC recognizes the contributions of Aboriginal peoples to the documentary heritage of Canada, and realizes that, in building its collection of materials, it must take into account the diversity of Aboriginal cultures, the relationship the Government of Canada has with Aboriginal peoples, and the unique needs and realities of Aboriginal communities. The development of a national strategy will be done in consultation and collaboration with Aboriginal communities and organizations, and will respect the ways in which indigenous knowledge and heritage is preserved or ought to be preserved and protected within or outside of Aboriginal communities.[56]

Library and Archives Canada has developed various guides and resources related to researching Aboriginal heritage.[57] But a fundamental tension exists between LAC's public education mandate to work collaboratively with Aboriginal peoples in order to document their cultural and social history and LAC's legal obligation to serve the state. This tension is most evident where archived documents are relevant to various historical injustices involving Aboriginal peoples. Historical records housed at LAC have been used extensively as evidence by both Aboriginal claimants and Crown defendants in litigation involving residential schools, Treaties, Aboriginal title and rights cases, and land claims.

In the case of documents related to residential schools, the problems associated with LAC's dual function became apparent during the litigation period prior to the Settlement Agreement. During this time, with regard to its public education mandate, LAC produced "Native Residential Schools in Canada: A Selective Bibliography" in 2002, and assisted Aboriginal people, academics, and other researchers who wished to access these holdings.[58] But because the residential schools litigation put the federal government in the position of being the major defendant in the court cases, the overriding priority for LAC, as the custodian of federal government departmental records, was to meet its legal obligations to the Crown.

Librarian and Archivist Emeritus Dr. Ian Wilson, Canada's former national archivist, described this tension. He explained that, as the residential school litigation intensified,

> Lawyers besieged the archives. Archivists, caught between the vagaries of old informal recordkeeping practices in church schools across the country, legal demands for instant and full access and obligations to employer and profession, struggled to uphold their ideal of the honest stewardship of the records.... This process has tested the capacity of the archives and our professional ability to respond.[59]

These challenges did not end with the implementation of the 2007 Settlement Agreement. The TRC's own difficulties in gaining access to government records held at LAC demonstrated why state-controlled archives are not necessarily best suited to meet the needs of Survivors, their families, and their communities.

By 2009, in terms of public education, LAC had partnered with the Legacy of Hope Foundation and the Aboriginal Healing Foundation on two exhibitions: *Where Are the Children? Healing the Legacy of the Residential Schools*; and *"We were so far away": The Inuit Experience of Residential Schools*.[60] Library and Archives Canada also produced an updated online version of "The Legacy of the Residential School System in Canada: A Selective Bibliography."[61] In 2010, LAC made an online finding aid available, "Conducting Research on Residential Schools: A Guide to the Records of the Indian and Inuit Affairs Program and Related Resources at Library and Archives Canada."[62]

In the spirit of reconciliation, LAC archivists (along with church archivists) brought binders of residential school photographs to the Learning Places at the TRC's National Events, where Survivors and others could see them and get copies of their class pictures and other school activities. For many Survivors, especially those who had no visual record of their own childhood or no pictures of siblings who have since passed away, this proved to be one of the most treasured aspects of the National Events experience. However, during this same time period, LAC's holdings and its role in complying with the federal government's legal obligations for document production, under the terms of the Settlement Agreement, became the focus of court proceedings between the TRC and the federal government.

The TRC seeks full access to LAC records

Schedule N of the Indian Residential Schools Settlement Agreement describes the mandate of the TRC as well as the obligations of the parties to the Agreement to assist the Commission in its work. There is a provision that deals with the obligation of the parties to provide relevant records to the Commission.

> In order to ensure the efficacy of the truth and reconciliation process, Canada and the churches will provide all relevant documents in their possession or control to and for the use of the Truth and Reconciliation Commission, subject to the privacy interests of an individual as provided by applicable privacy legislation, and subject to and in compliance with applicable privacy and access to information legislation, and except for those documents for which solicitor-client privilege applies and is asserted.

> In cases where privacy interests of an individual exist, and subject to and in compliance with applicable privacy legislation and access to information legislation, researchers for the Commission shall have access to the documents, provided privacy is protected. In cases where solicitor-client privilege is asserted, the asserting party will provide a list of all documents for which the privilege is claimed.

> Canada and the churches are not required to give up possession of their original documents to the Commission. They are required to compile all relevant documents in an organized manner for review by the Commission and to provide access to their archives for the Commission to carry out its mandate. Provision of documents does not require provision of original documents. Originals or true copies may be provided or originals may be provided temporarily for copying purposes if the original documents are not to be housed with the Commission.

> Insofar as agreed to by the individuals affected and as permitted by process requirements, information from the Independent Assessment Process (IAP), existing litigation and Dispute Resolution processes may be transferred to the Commission for research and archiving purposes.[63]

Gaining access to archival government records about the administration of the residential school system has been an important part of the mandate of the Truth and Reconciliation Commission of Canada. Such access has been essential for our own understanding of the history of government policy and practice in relation to

Aboriginal peoples in general and the residential schools in particular. But it has also been necessary to fulfilling our mandate obligation to ensure ongoing public access to the records through the National Centre for Truth and Reconciliation. The Commission's attempts to obtain records were frustrated by a series of bureaucratic and legal roadblocks.

In April 2012, the Commission was compelled to file a "Request for Direction" in the Ontario Superior Court of Justice regarding access to relevant federal records housed in the national archives. At issue was the question of what Canada's obligations were under the Settlement Agreement with respect to providing to the TRC archived government documents housed at Library and Archives Canada. The Commission, Aboriginal Affairs and Northern Development Canada, the Department of Justice, and Library and Archives Canada had very different views as to how the TRC should acquire these records.

In LAC's view, its role was that of the neutral keeper of government records, whose task was to facilitate and empower federal government departments to canvass their own archival holdings.

Faced with the onerous task of conducting its own research through LAC's vast holdings, Canada's position was that its obligation was limited to locating and producing relevant documents from the active and semi-active files in various departments. The government's view became that departments needed to provide the TRC only with departmental researcher status in order for the Commission to access their archived documents at LAC and conduct its own research.

The TRC's position was that Canada was obligated to produce all relevant documents, including those at LAC, and had an additional obligation to provide the Commission with access to LAC in order to conduct its own research. Although the TRC, in the spirit of co-operation, had agreed to obtain departmental researcher status, it maintained that this was unnecessary because the Settlement Agreement already gave the Commission unconditional access to the archives. The end result was that Canada had effectively shifted its responsibility to produce LAC documents onto the TRC.

In rendering his decision in favour of the Commission, Justice Stephen Goudge said,

> In my view, the first paragraph of section 11 sets out Canada's basic obligation concerning documents in its possession or control. The plain meaning of the language is straightforward. It is to provide all relevant documents to the TRC. The obligation is in unqualified language unlimited by where the documents are located within the government of Canada. Nor is the obligation limited to the documents assembled by Canada for production in the underlying litigation [para. 69].

I therefore conclude that given their meaning, the language in section 11 of Schedule N does not exclude documents archived at LAC from Canada's obligation to the TRC. The context in which the Settlement Agreement was created provides further important support for that conclusion in several ways [para. 71].

First, telling the history of Indian Residential Schools was clearly seen as a central aspect of the mandate of the TRC when the Settlement Agreement was made. Since Canada played a vital role in the IRS [Indian Residential School] system, Canada's documents wherever they were held, would have been understood as a very important historical resource for this purpose [para. 72].

Second, the Settlement Agreement charged the TRC with compiling an historical record of the IRS system to be accessible to the public in the future. Here too, Canada's documents, wherever housed, would have been seen to be vital to this task [para. 73].

Third, the story of the history and the historical record to be compiled cover[s] over 100 years and dates back to the nineteenth century. In light of this time span, it would have been understood at the time of the Settlement Agreement that much of the relevant documentary record in Canada's possession would be archived in LAC and would no longer be in the active or semi-active files of the departments of the Government of Canada [para. 74].

Fourth, it would have been obvious that the experienced staff at LAC would have vastly more ability to identify and organize the relevant documents at LAC than would the newly hired staff of the newly formed TRC. It would have made little sense to give that task to the latter rather than the former, particularly given its importance to the TRC's mandate [para. 75].[64]

In 2014, the auditor general of Canada's report "Documentary Heritage of the Government of Canada: Library and Archives Canada" concluded that systemic problems within LAC presented significant obstacles to accessing archival records.

Overall, we found that Library and Archives Canada was not acquiring all the archival records it should from federal institutions.... Of those records it had acquired, Library and Archives Canada had a backlog of some 98,000 boxes of government archival records as of April 2014, and does not know when it will be able to complete the processing of these records and facilitate public access to them. This is important because Canadians do not have knowledge of the government's archival records that have not yet been transferred from the institutions to Library and Archives Canada, nor of records still in Library and Archives Canada's backlog.[65]

More specifically, with regard to the TRC, the auditor general found that the Commission's research had been impeded by deficiencies in the quality of research finding aids that researchers use to identify relevant records.

> In the fall of 2013, the researchers conducted a pilot project to identify as many student health care records as possible. The pilot project demonstrated that 77 percent of the health care records had either non-existent or incomplete finding aids.... As an example, one of the researchers found an undescribed box to contain three years of reports that confirmed students' attendance in residential schools. In the spring of 2014, Library and Archives Canada drafted a work plan to identify and correct the deficiencies of the finding aids.[66]

Although the difficulties that the TRC encountered in obtaining LAC documents were specific to the Commission's mandate, they highlight broader questions concerning the role of state archives and archivists in providing access to documents that reveal the facts of why and how a targeted group of people has suffered harms on a massive scale. As part of a growing trend towards demanding better government accountability and transparency, and the evolution of new privacy and freedom of information legislation, archives have become more directly connected to struggles for human rights and justice.[67]

Archives and access to justice

Library and Archives Canada's federal government departmental records pertaining to Aboriginal peoples are vital to understanding how human rights violations occurred and their subsequent impacts. In 2005, the United Nations adopted the *Joinet-Orentlicher Principles*, which set out remedial measures that states must undertake to satisfy their duty to guard against impunity from past human rights violations and prevent their reoccurrence. This includes victims' right to know the truth about what happened to them and their missing family members. Society at large also has the right to know the truth about what happened in the past and what circumstances led to mass human rights violations. The state has a duty to safeguard this knowledge and to ensure that proper documentation is preserved in archives and history books.

The *Joinet-Orentlicher Principles* state, "The full and effective exercise of the right to truth is ensured through preservation of archives." Equally important, ready access to the archives must be facilitated for victims and their relatives, and for the purposes of research (Principles 5, 14, 15, 16).[68]

The Commission notes that in his August 2013 report to the United Nations Human Rights Council, Pablo de Greiff, Special Rapporteur on the Promotion of Truth, Justice, Reparation and Guarantees of Non-Recurrence, made specific reference to the importance of archives. He found that both a truth commission's own records and those housed in national, regional, and local archives extend the life and legacy of the truth commission's work. Archives can serve as permanent sites where post-commission accountability and the right to truth can be realized.[69] He further explained that archives "are a means of guaranteeing that the voices of victims will not be lost, and they contribute to a culture of memorialisation and remembrance. They also provide a safeguard against revisionism and denial—essential given the long duration and non-linearity of social reconciliation and integration processes."[70] He concluded that "truth commissions and national archives contribute in a substantial manner to realizing the right to truth and may further criminal prosecutions, reparations, and institutional and personnel reforms," and he recommended that international archival standards be established.[71]

Although de Greiff does not reference Indigenous peoples specifically, we note that in many countries, including Canada, access to protected historical records has been instrumental in advancing the rights of Indigenous peoples and documenting the state's wrongful actions. In the wake of the South African and other truth commissions, some archivists have come to see themselves not simply as neutral custodians of national history but also as professionals who are responsible for ensuring that records documenting past injustices are preserved and used to strengthen government accountability and support justice.[72]

Calls to action:

69) We call upon Library and Archives Canada to:

 i. Fully adopt and implement the *United Nations Declaration on the Rights of Indigenous Peoples* and the *United Nations Joinet-Orentlicher Principles,* as related to Aboriginal peoples' inalienable right to know the truth about what happened and why, with regard to human rights violations committed against them in the residential schools.

 ii. Ensure that its record holdings related to residential schools are accessible to the public.

 iii. Commit more resources to its public education materials and programming on residential schools.

70) We call upon the federal government to provide funding to the Canadian Association of Archivists to undertake, in collaboration with Aboriginal peoples, a national review of archival policies and best practices to:

i. Determine the level of compliance with the *United Nations Declaration on the Rights of Indigenous Peoples* and the *United Nations Joinet-Orentlicher Principles*, as related to Aboriginal peoples' inalienable right to know the truth about what happened and why, with regard to human rights violations committed against them in the residential schools.

ii. Produce a report with recommendations for full implementation of these international mechanisms as a reconciliation framework for Canadian archives.

Missing children, unmarked graves, and residential school cemeteries

Over the course of the Commission's work, many Aboriginal people spoke to us about the children who never came home from residential school. The question of what happened to their loved ones and where they were laid to rest has haunted families and communities. Throughout the history of Canada's residential school system, there was no effort to record across the entire system the number of students who died while attending the schools each year.

The National Residential School Student Death Register, established by the Truth and Reconciliation Commission of Canada, represents the first national effort to record the names of the students who died at school. The register is far from complete: there are, for example, many relevant documents that have yet to be received, collected, and reviewed.

Some of these records have been located in provincial records. In June 2012, at their annual general meeting, the Chief Coroners and Medical Examiners of Canada approved a unanimous resolution to support the TRC's Missing Children Project by making available to the Commission their records on the deaths of Aboriginal children in the care of residential school authorities. The Office of the Chief Coroner of Ontario had already done some groundbreaking work in terms of screening and reviewing its records, and identifying 120 possible cases of death of an Aboriginal residential school student. The TRC subsequently contacted chief coroners across the country to request their assistance in locating records related to deaths at residential schools. As of 2014, chief coroners' offices in Saskatchewan, the Northwest Territories, Manitoba, and Nova Scotia had also responded to the Commission's request for records.

Other regional agencies also hold critical information in their records. The TRC contacted offices of provincial vital statistics across the country. At the Alberta National Event, Assistant Deputy Minister Peter Cunningham, from the Ministry of Aboriginal

Relations and Reconciliation in British Columbia, offered a flash drive in a small, carved, Bentwood Box as an expression of reconciliation.

> I think it's incredibly important that all of the information comes out about what was a very deeply dark and disturbing event in Canadian history ... residential schools.... I'm here today to add to that body of knowledge on behalf of the government of British Columbia and the Vital Statistics Agency of BC.... The information on this flash drive is information about Aboriginal children between the ages of four and nineteen years of age who died in British Columbia between the years 1870 and 1984.[73]

As of 2014, in addition to the office in British Columbia, vital statistics offices in Alberta, Nova Scotia, Ontario, Saskatchewan, Yukon, and Nunavut had responded to the Commission's request for records. To complete the work begun by the Commission on the National Residential School Student Death Register, it will be critical for the National Centre for Truth and Reconciliation to obtain all records related to the deaths of residential school students.

Call to action:

71) We call upon all chief coroners and provincial vital statistics agencies that have not provided to the Truth and Reconciliation Commission of Canada their records on the deaths of Aboriginal children in the care of residential school authorities to make these documents available to the National Centre for Truth and Reconciliation.

The completion and maintenance of the National Residential School Student Death Register will require ongoing financial support.

Call to action:

72) We call upon the federal government to allocate sufficient resources to the National Centre for Truth and Reconciliation to allow it to develop and maintain the National Residential School Student Death Register established by the Truth and Reconciliation Commission of Canada.

There is also a need for information sharing with the families of those who died at the schools. As the historical record indicates, families were not adequately informed of the health condition of their children. There is a need for the federal government to ensure that appropriate measures are undertaken to inform families of the fate of their children and to ensure that the children are commemorated in a way that is acceptable to their families.

Calls to action:

73) We call upon the federal government to work with churches, Aboriginal communities, and former residential school students to establish and maintain an online registry of residential school cemeteries, including, where possible, plot maps showing the location of deceased residential school children.

74) We call upon the federal government to work with the churches and Aboriginal community leaders to inform the families of children who died at residential schools of the child's burial location, and to respond to families' wishes for appropriate commemoration ceremonies and markers, and reburial in home communities where requested.

As Commissioners, we have been honoured to bear witness to commemoration ceremonies held by communities to remember and honour children who died in residential schools. Such ceremonies have played an important role in the reconciliation process. At the Alberta National Event, the board members of the Remembering the Children Society offered an expression of reconciliation. They spoke about the process they undertook to identify children who had died while attending the Red Deer Industrial School. Richard Lightning said,

> My father, Albert Lightning, and his younger brother, David, from Samson First Nation, went to the Red Deer Industrial School, which was operated by the Methodist Church from 1893 to 1919. Albert Lightning survived this school experience, but David died of Spanish flu in 1918. In 1986, Albert visited the Red Deer and District Museum and Archives, saying to the staff person, Lyle Keewatin-Richards, "Oh, there you are. You're the one who is going to find my little brother." Lyle learned that along with three other students who had died at the same time, David was buried in the Red Deer City Cemetery. Lyle also became aware of the existence of the school cemetery beside Sylvan Creek.

The Reverend Cecile Fausak[74] explained,

> Around 2004 ... people at Sunnybrook United Church began to ask themselves, "Is there anything we can do to build better relations with First Nations peoples in this area?" And Lyle, remembering back, suggested then, "There is this little project. The children who were buried at the long-neglected [residential] school cemetery and in this city need to be remembered." So the church formed a committee ... and over the next few years, we researched the site and the school

records, personally visited the seven Cree and Stony communities and the Métis nation from which all the students had come. In September 2009, over thirty people from those concerned First Nations and Métis communities travelled to Red Deer, had stew and bannock at Sunnybrook United Church, and visited the school cemetery for the first time, where we were welcomed by the [current] landowner.

Muriel Stanley Venne, from the Sunnybrook United Church, continued,

A working group was formed to organize the first [commemoration] feast, which was held at Fort Normandeau, on June 30, 2010. As the more than 325 names of students were read, a hush fell over the crowd…. Since then the collaboration [has] continued, with First Nations Treaty 6 and 7, Métis Nation of Alberta, United Church members, the Red Deer Museum and Art Gallery, the City and County [of Red Deer], the [Indian] Friendship Centre, and school boards. This led to the formation of the Remembering the Children Society in 2011…. Our society's objectives include: continued support for recovering Indian residential school cemeteries and histories in Alberta; educating the public about the same; honouring the Survivors, and those who died in the schools; as well as identifying the unmarked graves. Each year for the next three years, a commemorative feast was held. At the third gathering, many descendants shared stories of the impact on them, their parents, and grandparents, because they attended the Red Deer Industrial School.

Charles Wood then said,

The society has worked with the museum in developing a new standing exhibit and with the Waskasoo Park administration in the preparation of new interpretive signage at Fort Normandeau regarding the school history. We are grateful for the truth spoken of a painful shared history, the friendships we have formed, and the healing that has happened as a result of working together for over five years. We will continue to remember the children of the past and present. In the Bentwood Box, as symbols of our work together, we place a program of the first ceremony, a DVD from the museum display, flower and ribbon pins from the third feast, and a copy of guidelines we have published of our experience for those who wish to undertake a similar recovery of a residential school cemetery.[75]

For the most part, the residential school cemeteries and burial sites that the Commission documented are abandoned, disused, and vulnerable to disturbance. Although there have been community commemoration measures undertaken in some locations, there is an overall need for a national strategy for the documentation, maintenance, commemoration, and protection of residential school cemeteries. This work is complex and sensitive. Although former schools might be associated with specific Aboriginal communities, the cemeteries may contain the bodies of children from many communities. They may also contain the bodies of teachers (or their children) who died while working at the institutions. No one set of recommendations will serve all circumstances.

Call to action:

75) We call upon the federal government to work with provincial, territorial, and municipal governments, churches, Aboriginal communities, former residential school students, and current landowners to develop and implement strategies and procedures for the ongoing identification, documentation, maintenance, commemoration, and protection of residential school cemeteries or other sites at which residential school children were buried. This is to include the provision of appropriate memorial ceremonies and commemorative markers to honour the deceased children.

As infrastructure and resource development accelerates throughout Canada, the risk of damage to undocumented residential school cemeteries increases. Depending on the jurisdiction, environmental impact assessments, which include the assessment of heritage sites, are usually required prior to development. This generally involves a review of existing documentation, an evaluation of the potential for heritage sites within the development zone, and a physical search. Such work is often done in phases, with a preliminary review of centralized archives and databases informing subsequent investigation. Local knowledge about residential cemeteries might not be readily accessible to non-local planners, resource managers, and impact assessors. Therefore, it is important that locally collected information is shared with agencies responsible for land-use planning, environmental impact assessment, and protection and regulation of cemeteries.

Such information sharing is hindered by limited documentation, unclear jurisdictional responsibility, and uncoordinated consolidation of information. These problems could be addressed through the establishment of a registry of residential school cemeteries that could be available online. At a minimum, such a registry should include the identification, duration, and affiliation of each cemetery, its legal description, its current land ownership and condition, and its location coordinates.

The complex and sensitive work of documenting, maintaining, commemorating, and protecting residential school cemeteries must be undertaken according to a set of guiding principles that are based on community priorities and knowledge. Any physical investigation of the cemeteries must involve close consultation with interested communities, identification of community-driven objectives, suitable methodologies, and attention to spiritual and emotional sensitivities.

The generally sparse written documentation must be combined with locally held knowledge. Often, this information will be unwritten, and held by Survivors, the families of Survivors, staff, or local residents. This locally held information can be used to verify, correct, and amplify archival information. This work might involve local initiatives to physically document a cemetery's extent and location, and also to identify individual graves within or around the cemetery area. When undertaking physical inspection and documentation of the cemeteries, the most cost-effective strategy involves collection and consolidation of both documentary and locally held knowledge prior to initiating fieldwork. This will improve efficiency of the physical search, and aid selection of the most effective field methodologies. It will also enable researchers to determine community wishes regarding the most appropriate approaches to site investigation. These approaches include adherence to preferred protocols regarding prayers and ceremonial observance prior to a site visit.

Call to action:

76) We call upon the parties engaged in the work of documenting, maintaining, commemorating, and protecting residential school cemeteries to adopt strategies in accordance with the following principles:

   i. The Aboriginal community most affected shall lead the development of such strategies.

   ii. Information shall be sought from residential school Survivors and other Knowledge Keepers in the development of such strategies.

   iii. Aboriginal protocols shall be respected before any potentially invasive technical inspection and investigation of a cemetery site.

The Commission believes that assisting families to learn the fate of children who died in residential schools, locating unmarked graves, and maintaining, protecting, and commemorating residential school cemeteries are vital to healing and reconciliation. Archives and government departments and agencies have a crucial role to play in this process. Equally important, archival records can help Survivors, their families, and their communities to reconstruct their family and community histories. Yet accessing such holdings is not without problems.

The limitations of archives

We have outlined how Library and Archives Canada has dealt with its residential school records. Other records that are relevant to the history and legacy of the residential school system are scattered across the country in provincial, territorial, municipal, and local archives, as well as in government departments and agencies that were not parties to the Settlement Agreement. All this has made it extremely difficult for Survivors, their families, and their communities to access records that hold critical pieces of information about their own lives and the history of their communities.

The Settlement Agreement church archives, to varying degrees, have endeavoured to make their residential school records more accessible to Survivors, their families and communities, researchers, and the general public.[76] For example, the United Church of Canada, "as a form of repatriation to First Nations communities,"[77] has put all of its residential school photographs and school histories online to make them more accessible to Survivors and others.

The National Centre for Truth and Reconciliation: An emerging model

Archives may be viewed with distrust by First Nations, Inuit, and Métis peoples. Many feel that much of their lives is contained in documents (most of which they have never seen) kept by the state in order to study and categorize them in a depersonalized manner.[78] In various ways, existing archives have been ill suited to serving the needs of Survivors, their families, and their communities. What Aboriginal peoples require is a centre of their own—a cultural space that will serve as both an archive and a museum to hold the collective memory of Survivors and others whose lives were touched by the history and legacy of the residential school system.

With this understanding, the TRC mandate called for the establishment of a new National Research Centre (NRC) to hold all the historical and newly created documents and oral statements related to residential schools, and to make them accessible for the future. This NRC, as created by the Truth and Reconciliation Commission of Canada, and now renamed the National Centre for Truth and Reconciliation (NCTR), is an evolving, Survivor-centred model of education for reconciliation. Implementing a new approach to public education, research, and recordkeeping, the centre will serve as a public memory "site of conscience," bearing permanent witness to Survivors' testimonies and the history and legacy of the residential school system.[79] Along with other museums and archives across the country, the centre will shape how the residential school era is understood and remembered.

The concept of the National Centre for Truth and Reconciliation has deep roots. For many years, Survivors and their supporters called for a centre that would be a lasting legacy to Survivors' own history and to Canada's national memory. In March 2011, the TRC hosted an international forum in Vancouver, "Sharing Truth: Creating a National Research Centre on Residential Schools," to study how records and other materials from truth and reconciliation commissions around the world have been archived.[80]

Several speakers talked about their vision for the NCTR. Georges Erasmus, former co-chair of the Royal Commission on Aboriginal Peoples, and then president of the Aboriginal Healing Foundation, said,

> Those who become the keepers of the archives become stewards of human stories and relationships, of what has been an endowment to what will be. Because no legacy is enriched by counterfeit, a nation is ill served by a history which is not genuine. This is a high calling indeed and it must be said that too often the promise and the potential of this stewardship has gone unrealized.... If the stories of our people are not accessible to the general public, it will be as if their experiences never occurred. And if their voices are rendered as museum pieces, it will be as if their experience is frozen in time. What we need are open, dynamic, interactive spaces and participatory forms of narrative, knowledge, and research. This would be a fitting way to step into the twenty-first century and into a new kind of relationship.... The National Research Centre ought to be a treasure valued by all sorts of people.[81]

Charlene Belleau, a Survivor and manager of the Assembly of First Nations Residential Schools Unit, talked about how important it was for the centre to provide access to communities and individual Survivors.

> When I thought about the National Research Centre, coming from a community-based process and Tribal Council work, I really feel that the National Research Centre has to be regionally based or tribally based where possible so that it is accessible to the former students or to the public within our areas.... If we put all our eggs in one basket and put a thirty million dollar project in Alberta or Saskatchewan, who has access to it? For sure, the Survivors that are on welfare, the Survivors who have no money will never get to see a place like that. I think we need to be real and make sure that we have that access so that we can continue to heal and work together.[82]

James Scott, General Council officer for the United Church of Canada, was involved in the Settlement Agreement negotiations. He recalled,

> We [the parties] wanted to honour and acknowledge the experience of Survivors, their families, and communities, and we wanted to create a vehicle through which that history would forever be protected and available in order that it be understood, that it not be forgotten, and that it never happen again. The National Research Centre was, and is, to be that vehicle ...
>
> The Research Centre can be so much more than an archive or museum. It can ... be a catalyst for education and transformation.... While the residential school system no longer exists as a system, other tools used by the settler population to dominate, dispossess, and assimilate Aboriginal peoples in this country still operate. So the National Research Centre, in my view, must be a striking and

visible reminder to all Canadians that the battle for justice, equality, respect and self-determination for Aboriginal people is not over. It must be fought on a daily basis for the sake of the future of our country, for our children, and for our children's children.[83]

The Commission subsequently issued an open invitation for organizations to submit proposals for the NCTR based on specific criteria. In June 2013, the TRC announced that the University of Manitoba would house the new centre.

The National Centre for Truth and Reconciliation will play a key educational role in ensuring that historic harms and Treaty, constitutional, and human rights violations against Aboriginal peoples are not repeated. As a highly visible site of conscience, it will serve as an intervention in the country's public memory and national history. The centre is independent from government. It is guided by a Governing Circle, the majority of whose members must be Aboriginal and which includes Survivor representatives. Among its various responsibilities, this governing body will make decisions, provide advice on ceremonies and protocols, and establish a Survivors' Circle.[84]

The centre will house TRC records, including Survivors' oral history statements, artworks, expressions of reconciliation, and other materials gathered by the Commission, as well as government and church documents. It is intended to be a welcoming and safe place for Survivors, their families, and their communities to have access to their own history. The centre has committed to creating a culturally rooted and healing environment where all Canadians can honour, learn from, and commemorate the history and legacy of the residential schools.

Once the centre is fully operational, it will be well positioned to take a leadership role in forging new directions for research on residential schools and on Indigenous rights, and in establishing new standards and benchmarks for archival and museum policy, management, and operations based on Indigenous and Western principles and best practices.

The University of Manitoba and its partners[85] have emphasized that the centre recognizes the

> paramount importance of accessibility [for] the Aboriginal survivor, family member [or] researcher, [and is] committed to recognition of Aboriginal peoples as co-creators of the IRS records, through co-curation and participatory archiving; and committed to continuing the work of the TRC of statement-gathering, public education, engagement and outreach.[86]

The NCTR will incorporate an

> archival system and approach which is devoted to "reconciling records"; [it] will ... support Indigenous frameworks of knowledge, memory and evidence, and reposition ... Indigenous communities as co-creators of archival records that relate to them, including government archives. Such approaches acknowledge rights

in records that extend beyond access to working in partnership with archival institutions to manage appraisal, description and accessibility of records relating to Indigenous communities.[87]

The centre is committed to "establish[ing] trust with Aboriginal communities by working with these communities to realize their own goals through participatory archiving.... The process of participatory archiving, interacting with as complete a record as possible, will be a powerful force for reconciliation and healing."[88] As well, the Centre for Truth and Reconciliation is committed to

> personally supporting survivors, their families, and all researchers in navigating, using, and understanding the records, in a culturally sensitive environment. The support that the NRC will provide includes emotionally-sensitive support, acknowledging that accessing the NRC documents may be traumatic, difficult or otherwise emotional experiences for many users. An Elder will be present or on call (from a nearby building) most of the time the NRC is open to the public. LAC and other government departments have no mandate or capacity to offer these various supports, which are critical to relationship-building and overcoming the perception of archives as yet another mechanism of colonization, cultural appropriation by Western society and hyper-surveillance and objectification of Aboriginal peoples.[89]

On October 27, 2011, at the Atlantic National Event, David T. Barnard, president and vice chancellor of the University of Manitoba, offered an apology on behalf of the university to Survivors, to their families and communities, and to Aboriginal students, faculty, and staff. He acknowledged the university's complicity in the residential school system and the role of all educational institutions in "perpetuating the misguided and failed system of assimilation that was at the heart of the Indian residential school system." He further noted that this complicity did not end with the residential school system but continued through the "Sixties Scoop" adoption policy, which forcibly removed thousands of Aboriginal children from their families. He admitted that "the University of Manitoba educated and mentored individuals who became clergy, teachers, social workers, civil servants and politicians. They carried out assimilation policies aimed at the Aboriginal peoples of Manitoba."[90]

By acknowledging the pain that the university had inflicted, President Barnard hoped that "we can begin the process of restoring trust." He committed the university to ensuring that "the values of First Nations, Métis, and Inuit cultures and communities are included in scholarship and research across the university." To do so, he said that "we must acknowledge our mistakes, learn from them, apologize and move forward in a spirit of reconciliation."[91]

The National Research Centre for Truth and Reconciliation is not only a tangible and long-term demonstration of how the university is putting the words of its apology into action; it is also an example of the substantive and concrete contributions that universities can make to education for reconciliation.

On June 21, 2013, First Nations, Inuit, and Métis Survivors, Elders, the TRC, and the University of Manitoba and its partner institutions, along with other dignitaries, gathered in Treaty 1 territory of the Anishinaabe peoples and homeland of the Métis Nation for a signing ceremony at the University of Manitoba.[92] This signing of a "Trust Deed" with the university marked the transfer of a sacred trust—a solemn promise that the Truth and Reconciliation Commission made to Survivors and all those affected by the residential schools as it travelled across the country bearing witness to their testimonies.

The NCTR is committed to making all its holdings readily accessible to Survivors, their families, and their communities, as well as to the public, educators, and researchers.[93] To support reconciliation at the local level, the Commission believes, it will be especially important to ensure that communities are able to access the centre's holdings and resources in order to produce histories of their own residential school experiences and their involvement in the truth, healing, and reconciliation process.

The centre will be a living legacy, a teaching and learning place for public education that will promote understanding and reconciliation through ongoing statement gathering, new research, commemoration ceremonies, dialogues on reconciliation, and celebrations of Indigenous cultures, oral histories, and legal traditions.[94]

Calls to action:

77) We call upon provincial, territorial, municipal, and community archives to work collaboratively with the National Centre for Truth and Reconciliation to identify and collect copies of all records relevant to the history and legacy of the residential school system, and to provide these to the National Centre for Truth and Reconciliation.

78) We call upon the Government of Canada to commit to making a funding contribution of $10 million over seven years to the National Centre for Truth and Reconciliation, plus an additional amount to assist communities to research and produce histories of their own Indian residential school experience and their involvement in truth, healing, and reconciliation.

CHAPTER 5

Public memory: Dialogue, the arts, and commemoration

For Survivors who came forward at the Truth and Reconciliation Commission (TRC) National Events and Community Hearings, remembering their childhood often meant reliving horrific memories of abuse, hunger, and neglect. It meant dredging up painful feelings of loneliness, abandonment, and shame. Many still struggle to heal deep wounds of the past. Words fail to do justice to their courage in standing up and speaking out.

There were other memories too—of resilience, of lifetime friendships forged with classmates and teachers, of taking pride in art, music, or sports accomplishments, and of becoming leaders in their communities and in the life of the nation. Survivors shared their memories with Canada and the world so that the truth could no longer be denied. Survivors also remembered so that other Canadians could learn from these hard lessons of the past. They want Canadians to know, to remember, to care, and to change.

One of the most significant harms to come out of the residential schools was the attack on Indigenous memory. The federal government's policy of assimilation sought to break the chain of memory that connected the hearts, minds, and spirits of Aboriginal children to their families, communities, and nations. Many, but not all, Survivors have found ways to restore these connections. They believe that reconciliation with other Canadians calls for changing the country's collective, national history so that it is based on the truth about what happened to them as children, and to their families, communities, and nations.

Public memory is important. It is especially important to recognize that the transmission of this collective memory from generation to generation of First Nations, Inuit, and Métis individuals, families, and communities was impaired by the actions of those who ran residential schools.

In order for any society to function properly and to its full capacity, it must raise and educate its children so that they can answer what philosophers and Elders call 'the great questions of life.' Those questions are:

Where do I come from?

Where am I going?

Why am I here?

Who am I?

Children need to know their personal story, including the part that precedes their birth. We need to know the stories of our parents and grandparents, our direct and indirect ancestors, and our real and mythological villains and heroes. As part of this story, we also need to know about the community of people to which we are attached—our collective story—all the way back to our place in the creation of this world. We all have a creation story, and we all need to understand it. We also need to learn that although not all creation stories are the same, they all have truth. This is an important teaching about respect.

Knowing where we are going is a natural outcome of knowing where we have come from. It is not just about where we are going to be next week, or next year, or in twenty-five years. It is also about what happens to us when we die. It is about the spirit world, and life after death, and a reaffirmation of the role of the Creator in matters of life and death. It is about belief, and faith, and hope.

Knowing why we are here is also related to the other two questions. Knowing one's creation story is always imbued with teachings about why the Creator made this world to begin with and what our place as human beings was intended to be within it. But the answer to this question is also about knowing what role we play in the overall collective. It is about knowing whether our purpose is fulfilled through being an artist, or a leader, or a warrior, or a caregiver, or a healer, or a helper. Clan teachings and naming ceremonies in Indigenous cultures provide answers to this question, but the answer is also influenced by knowing what our family and community need, and then filling this need and feeling the satisfaction that results.

The fourth question—"Who am I?"—is the most important, because it is the constant question. It is influenced by everything and everyone. We fight to maintain the answer we like, and we fight to change and improve the answer we dislike. We strive to attain the perfect answer by the time we die, not realizing that in fact there is no right or wrong answer. It is a question about understanding our life. It is about identity. It is about what we have become, but it is also about what we want to become. This is why it is constant. In many ways, it is the answer that derives from knowing the answers to the other three questions. If one of them is unanswered or the answer is in doubt, this question remains unfulfilled. Our life is not in balance.

For children in the residential schools, these questions went unanswered, and their sense of belonging to a collective community went unfulfilled. The answers that they were forced to accept ran counter to much of the knowledge they carried. The schools were about changing their identities, and the potential for internal conflict was enormous. Their loss of a sense of collective memory was a loss that directly resulted from the breaking of family ties, the attack on their languages and cultures, and the denial of access to any information about their own unique and special histories. These losses were carried forward to the next generation.

As youngsters, Survivors were vulnerable rememberers.[1] That is, their connection to their own family and community memory was more easily severed or damaged than it would have been if they had been adults. This ruptured memory also had a significant impact on their children and grandchildren, who lost their culture and language, which were normally transmitted through family and community memory, and often knew nothing about the residential school system or what their older relatives had gone through. Generations of young people have grown up not knowing the history of their own families and communities, and feeling excluded from Canada's history as well. At the TRC Alberta National Event in Edmonton, at a panel on "Recollection and Collective Memory in a Divided Society," Métis scholar Jennifer Adese said,

> It's an honour to be here with you ... in ... Métis [and] Treaty 6 territory ... so close to the homes of the lands where my father ... and grandmother were born ... and so close to the home of all our relations that have come before us ... I was lucky to grow up connected to an active urban Native community, but it's taken me at least the last ten years to reconnect to my family here, close and extended, and to ... reweave myself back into the web of kinship ties that I was separated from at a young age....
>
> I can't tell you how to bridge the gap and the memories of Métis and settler people ... [but] when I was thinking about what I would share with you today, I kept thinking of the phrase "the train left without me." ... The role that Canadian prime minister Sir John A. Macdonald's vision for building a railway through First Nation and Métis territory [played in] the displacing of our relations ... It also speaks to the use of the railway to transport Métis into the farming colonies in the twentieth century, displacing them from the homes they kept trying to make for themselves in the wake of their displacements in 1869–70 and in 1885 ...
>
> For Métis, we're moving into an era of reconciliation when the intergenerational impacts of broader systems of colonization on Métis peoples have scarcely been addressed. When talk of reconciliation and remembering come up, people often forget the very important reality that residential schools were just one of hundreds of different paths taken by church and state in efforts to change and assimilate Indigenous peoples....
>
> The assimilation of Indigenous peoples didn't begin or end with schooling. It's ongoing now. It also didn't exist in isolation, and it didn't target only culture. Its purpose was to take everything: language, family ties, stories, memories, political

structures, governing structures, and economic relationships. These are things we need to remember.[2]

Aboriginal women—those who are Elders and Knowledge Keepers in their communities as well as those who are disconnected from their roots—are vital to national reconciliation.

Aboriginal women told the Commission about damaged relationships with female relatives, high levels of domestic and societal violence, and the gendered racism they have experienced throughout their lives. They also told us that learning about their own history—women's traditional roles in the political, cultural, social, and economic life of their communities—was an empowering catalyst for healing. They emphasized the importance of storytelling to restoring their dignity and repairing family relationships. Aboriginal women, storytellers, scholars, and activists are themselves at the forefront of this work, reshaping public memory and national history through storytelling and ceremonies that remember and honour the life stories, experiences, and struggles of their grandmothers, mothers, sisters, daughters, and aunties. Although much has been lost from family and community memory, much still remains. In many communities, women continue to hold positions of status and power that have been passed down through the generations.[3]

The power of women's stories and the process of sharing these stories strengthen healing, resilience, and reconciliation at the family, community, and national levels. Saulteaux Elder Danny Musqua explains,

> We never had any doubt that women were the centre and core of our community and nation. No nation ever existed without the fortitude of our grandmothers, and all of those teachings have to somehow be recovered. And it will be up to these young people ... they've got to *dig up the medicines*, to heal the people. And the medicines in this case are the teachings.[4]

The concept of women's stories as medicine resonates with us as Commissioners. At TRC National and Regional Events and at Community Hearings, as well as in public and private statements and written submissions, the Commission heard from thousands of Aboriginal women from all walks of life across the country.

At the British Columbia National Event in Vancouver, a dialogue panel, "Honouring Women's Wisdom: Pathways of Truth, Resilience and Reconciliation," took place on September 21, 2013. One of the panelists, Sharon Jinkerson-Brass, community health liaison for the Pacific Association of First Nations Women, observed that many urban Aboriginal women have lost touch with the teachings and ceremonies of their grandmothers. She emphasized the importance of reviving matriarchal cultural traditions in contemporary contexts. She said that women are the "seed-carriers" of cultural knowledge and explained that although "many of our ceremonies are still sleeping ... many strands are missing, we walk on the breath of our ancestors and we are here to bring beauty into the world." She spoke of bringing an urban group of Aboriginal women together to weave cedar capes for a grandmother ceremony held on the Musqueam reserve. After the ceremony, the capes became a community bundle for women to use in rites-of-passage ceremonies.

The importance of women's ceremonies to healing was evident in the discussion that followed the panel presentations. One speaker said that all women have a responsibility to ensure that their children have a grandmother influence in their lives, and she explained that "cedar weaving has become our medicine."[5]

For many years, Aboriginal women have taken a strong political leadership role in advocating for real change in their communities and the nation. Aboriginal women are inspiring models of resilience who work to address legacy issues even as they revitalize matriarchal systems, cultural traditions, ceremonies, and laws that ensured gender equity prior to colonization. They are Elders, Clan Mothers, Knowledge Keepers, and teachers who draw on the collective wisdom of their grandmothers from seven generations past. They are carriers of memory whose ability to transmit family and community history to their children and grandchildren was severely impacted by the residential schools.

Despite making inroads over the past three decades, Aboriginal women continue to be marginalized and misrepresented in Canada's public memory and national history. Over time, popular history and the media have reinforced misperceptions of Aboriginal women, often portraying them either as 'noble Indian princesses' or in derogatory and racist terms.[6] It is clear that the negative stereotypes and social attitudes that fuel racist and gendered violence persist.

Although a direct causal link cannot be drawn between the harmful stereotypes of Aboriginal women that are deeply embedded in the Canadian psyche and the ongoing violence against Aboriginal women and girls, the Commission believes that it is a significant factor. We concur with law professor and legal historian Constance Backhouse, who argues that Canada's lack of action on missing and murdered Aboriginal women and girls and other forms of systemic violence can be attributed in part to "the legacy of misogyny and racism that runs through the heart of Canadian history."[7] The Commission believes that correcting the historical record concerning Aboriginal women is essential to reconciliation.

As Commissioners, we are governed in our approach to reconciliation with this thought: the way that we all have been educated in this country—Aboriginal children in residential schools and Aboriginal and non-Aboriginal children in public and other schools—has brought us to where we are today: to a point where the psychological and emotional well-being of Aboriginal children has been harmed, and the relationship between Aboriginal and non-Aboriginal peoples has been seriously damaged. We believe that true reconciliation can take place only through a reshaping of a shared, national, collective memory of who we are and what has come before. The youth of this country are taking up this challenge.

Reshaping national history is a public process, one that happens through discussion, sharing, and commemoration. As Canadians gather in public spaces to share their memories, beliefs, and ideas about the past with others, our collective understanding of the present and future is formed.[8] As citizens, our ideas, worldviews, cultural identities, and values are shaped not only in classrooms and museums or by popular culture but also in everyday social relationships and patterns of living that become our way of life.[9]

Public memory is dynamic—it changes over time as new understandings, dialogues, artistic expressions, and commemorations emerge. Public memory, much like national history, is often contentious. Although public memory can simply reinforce the colonial story of how Canada began with European settlement and became a nation, the process of remembering the past together also invites people to question this limited version of history.

Unlike some truth and reconciliation commissions that have focused on individual victims of human rights violations committed over a short period of time, this Commission has examined both the individual and collective harms perpetrated against Aboriginal families, communities, and nations for well over a century, as well as the preconditions that enabled such violence and oppression to occur.

Of course, previously inaccessible archival documents are critically important to correcting the historical record, but we have given equal weight and greater voice to Indigenous oral-based history, legal traditions, and memory practices in our work and in this final report since these sources represent previously unheard and unrecorded versions of history, knowledge, and wisdom.[10] This has significantly informed our thinking about why repairing and revitalizing individual, family, and community memory are so crucial to the truth and reconciliation process.

Dialogue: Ceremony, testimony, and witnessing

Just as Survivors were involved in the long struggle to achieve a legally binding Settlement Agreement for the harms they have experienced, and an official apology, they have also continued to advise the Commission as it has implemented its mandate. Guided by Elders, Knowledge Keepers, and the members of the TRC Survivor Committee, the Commission has made Aboriginal oral history, legal traditions, and memory practices—ceremony, protocols, and the rituals of storytelling and testimonial witnessing—central to the TRC's National Events, Community Hearings, forums, and dialogues.

The Commission's proceedings themselves constitute an oral history record, duly witnessed by all those in attendance. Working with local communities in each region, sacred ceremonies and protocols were performed and followed at all TRC events. Elders and traditional healers ensured that a safe environment was created for truth sharing, apology, healing, and acts of reconciliation.

The power of ceremony

Sacred ceremony has always been at the heart of Indigenous cultures, law, and political life. When ceremonies were outlawed by the federal government, they were hidden away until the law was repealed. Historically and, to a certain degree, even at present, Indigenous ceremonies that create community bonds, sanctify laws, and ratify Treaty making have been misunderstood, disrespected, and disregarded by Canada. These ceremonies must now be recognized and honoured as an integral, vital, ongoing dimension of the truth and reconciliation process.

Ceremonies also reach across cultures to bridge the divide between Aboriginal and non-Aboriginal peoples. They are vital to reconciliation because of their sacred nature and because they connect people, preparing them to listen respectfully to each other in a difficult dialogue. Ceremonies are an affirmation of human dignity; they feed our spirits and comfort us even as they call on us to reimagine or envision finding common ground. Ceremonies validate and legitimize Treaties, family and kinship lines, and connections to the land. Ceremonies are also acts of memory sharing, mourning, healing, and renewal; they express the collective memory of families, communities, and nations.

Ceremonies enable us to set aside, however briefly, our cynicism, doubts, and disbelief, even as they console us, educate us, and inspire hope.[11] They have an intangible quality that moves us from our heads to our hearts. They teach us about ourselves, our histories, and our lives. Ceremony and ritual have played an important role in various conflict and peace-building settings across the globe, including North America, where Indigenous nations have their own long histories of diplomacy and peacemaking.

Ceremonial rituals have three functions in the peacemaking process. First, they create a safe space for people to interact and learn as they take part in the ceremony. Second, they enable people to communicate non-verbally and process their emotions. Third, ceremonies create an environment where change is made possible; worldviews, identities, and relationships with others are transformed.[12]

Those in attendance at TRC events learned to acknowledge and respect Indigenous ceremonies and protocols by participating in them. The Commission intentionally made ceremonies the spiritual and ethical framework of our public education work, creating a safe space for sharing life stories and bearing testimonial witness to the past for the future.

The Commission's National Events were designed to inspire reconciliation and shape individual and collective memory by demonstrating the core values that lie at the heart of reconciliation: wisdom, love, respect, courage, humility, honesty, and truth. These values are known by many Aboriginal peoples as the Seven Grandfather and Grandmother Teachings or Seven Sacred Teachings. They are also in the ancient teachings of most world religions.[13] Each National Event focused on one of these teachings.

Working closely with local Aboriginal communities and various regional organizations, representatives of the parties to the Settlement Agreement, and other government and community networks, the Commission took great care to ensure that the proper ceremonies and protocols were understood and followed throughout every National Event. Elders offered prayers and teachings at the opening and closing of each event. Smudges, sacred pipe and water ceremonies, cedar brushings, songs, and drumming occurred on a regular basis throughout.

At each event, a sacred fire was lit and cared for by Elders and Fire Keepers. Water ceremonies were performed by women who were recognized as the Protectors of the Waters. The sacred fire was also used for ongoing prayers and tobacco offerings, as well as to receive the tissues from the many tears shed during each event. The ashes from each of the sacred fires were then carried forward to the next National Event, to be added in turn to its sacred fire, thus gathering in sacred ceremony the tears of an entire country.

At the Manitoba National Event, a young Métis woman, Ms. Lussier, who had grown up with little knowledge of Métis culture, said,

> I can't express the emotion and the power that I've felt in the past week here. I was given an opportunity yesterday to make an offering to the sacred fire. What I felt was unexplainable. The wind blew the fire in my direction, and I closed my eyes and I breathed deep, and I felt for the first time I could really feel my father's heritage.[14]

That same day, Ms. Kenny, a first-generation Irish Canadian, said,

> I have learned the traditions ... Thank you for teaching me the water ceremony. In these past few days, what I've learned of Aboriginal culture, I just feel it has enriched my life so much. For them to be made to feel ashamed of that culture, it just makes me feel angry and it makes me feel sadness. And I just would like to say thank you to all of them for sharing their stories, and I wish for all of them, all the healing in the world.[15]

The Commission's mandate also instructed that there be a "ceremonial transfer of knowledge" at the National Events. Coast Salish artist Luke Marston was commissioned by the TRC to design and carve a Bentwood Box as a symbol of this transfer. The box was steamed and bent in the traditional way from a single piece of western redcedar. Its intricately carved and beautifully painted wood panels represent First Nations, Inuit, and Métis cultures.

The Bentwood Box is a lasting tribute to all residential school Survivors and their families, both those who are living and those who have passed on, including the artist's grandmother, who attended the Kuper Island Residential School. This ceremonial box travelled with the Commission to every one of its seven National Events, where offerings—public expressions of reconciliation—were made by governments, churches and other faith communities, educational institutions, the business sector, municipalities, youth groups, and various other groups and organizations.

The Truth and Reconciliation Bentwood Box, along with the many other sacred items that the TRC received, will be housed permanently in the National Centre for Truth and Reconciliation at the University of Manitoba in Winnipeg.[16]

Life stories, testimonies, and witnessing as teachings

Reconciliation is not possible without knowing the truth. To determine the truth and to be able to tell the full story of the residential schools in this country, it was fundamentally important to the Commission's work to be able to hear the stories of Survivors and their families. It was also important to hear the stories of those who worked in the schools—the teachers, the administrators, the cooks, the janitors—as well as their family members. Canada's national history must reflect this complex truth so that 50 or 100 years from now, our children's children and their children will know what happened. They will inherit the responsibility to ensure that it never happens again.

Regardless of the different individual experiences that children had as students in the schools, they shared the common experience of being exploited. They were victims of a system intent on destroying intergenerational links of memory to their families, communities, and nations. The process of assimilation also profoundly disrespected parents, grandparents, and Elders in their rightful roles as the carriers of memory, through which culture, language, and identity are transmitted from one generation to the next.[17]

In providing their testimonies to the TRC, Survivors reclaimed their rightful place as members of intergenerational communities of memory. They remembered so that their families could understand what happened. They remembered so that their cultures, histories, laws, and nations can once again thrive for the benefit of future generations. They remembered so that Canada will know the truth and never forget.

The residential school story is complicated. Stories of abuse stand in sharp contradiction to the happier memories of some Survivors. The statements of former residential school staff also varied. Some were remorseful, whereas others were defensive. Some were proud of their students and their own efforts to support them, whereas others were critical of their own school and government authorities for their lack of attention, care, and resources.

The stories of government and church officials involved acknowledgement, apology, and promises not to repeat history. Some non-Aboriginal Canadians expressed outrage at what had happened in the schools and shared their feelings of guilt and shame that they had not known this. Others denied or minimized the destructive impacts of residential schools. These conflicting stories, based on different experiences, locations, time periods, and perspectives, all feed into a national historical narrative.

Developing this narrative through public dialogue can strengthen civic capacity for accountability and thereby do justice to victims not just in the legal sense but also in terms of restoring human dignity, nurturing mutual respect, and supporting healing. As citizens use ceremony and testimony to remember, witness, and commemorate, they learn how to put the principles of accountability, justice, and reconciliation into everyday practice. They become active agents in the truth and reconciliation process.

Participants at Commission events learned from the Survivors themselves by interacting directly with them. Survivors, whose memories are still alive, demonstrated in the most powerful and compelling terms that by sitting together in Sharing Circles, people gain a much deeper knowledge and understanding of what happened in the residential schools than can ever be acquired at a distance by studying books, reading newspapers, or watching television reports.

For Indigenous peoples, stories and teachings are rooted in relationships. Through stories, knowledge and understanding about what happened and why are acquired, validated, and shared with others. Writing about her work with Survivors from her own community, social work scholar Qwul'sih'yah'maht (Dr. Robina Anne Thomas) said,

> I never dreamed of learning to listen in such a powerful way. Storytelling, despite all the struggles, enabled me to respect and honour the Ancestors and the storytellers while at the same time sharing tragic, traumatic, inhumanely unbelievable truths that our people had lived. It was this level of integrity that was essential to storytelling.... When we make personal what we teach ... we touch people in a different and more profound way.[18]

At a Community Hearing in St. Paul, Alberta, in January 2011, Charles Cardinal explained that although he did not want to remember his residential school experiences, he came forward because "we've got to let other people hear our voices." When he was asked how, given the history of the residential schools, Canada could be a better place, he replied that we must "listen to the people."[19] When asked the same question in Beausejour, Manitoba, Laurie McDonald said that Canada must begin by "doing exactly what is happening now ... Governments ... [have got to know] that they can never, ever, ever do this again."[20] In Ottawa, Survivor Victoria Grant-Boucher said,

> I'm telling my story ... for the education of the Canadian general public ... [so that they] can understand what stolen identity is, you know, how it affects people, how it affects an individual, how it affects family, how it affects community....
> I think the non-Aboriginal person, Canadian, has to understand that a First Nations person has a culture.... And I think that we, as Aboriginal people, have so much to share if you just let us regain that knowledge.... And I also take to heart what Elders talk about ... We have to heal ourselves. We have to heal each other. And for Canada to heal, they have to allow us to heal before we can contribute. That's what reconciliation means to me.[21]

Survivors told the Commission that an important reason for breaking their silence was to educate their own children and grandchildren by publicly sharing their life stories with them. The effect of this testimony on intergenerational Survivors was significant. At the Manitoba National Event, Desarae Eashappie said,

> I have sat through this week having the honour of listening to the stories from Survivors. And I just feel—I just really want to acknowledge everybody in this room, you know, all of our Elders, all of our Survivors, all of our intergenerational Survivors.... We are all sitting here in solidarity right now ... and we are all on our own journey, and [yet we are] sitting here together ... with so much strength in this room, it really is phenomenal. And I just want to acknowledge that and thank everybody here. And to be given this experience, this opportunity, you know, to sit here ... and to listen to other people and listen to their stories and their experiences, you know, it has really humbled me as a person in such a way that is indescribable.... And I can take this home with me now and I can take it into my own home. Because my dad is a residential school Survivor, I have lived the traumas, but I have lived the history without the context.[22]

Survivors' life stories are teachings rooted in personal experience; the human relationships of their childhoods were scarred by those who harmed them in the schools. Their stories teach us about what it means to lose family, culture, community, self-esteem, and human dignity. They also teach us about courage, resilience, and resistance to violence and oppression.

An ethical response to Survivors' life stories requires the listener to respond in ways that recognize the teller's dignity and affirm that injustices were committed. Non-Indigenous witnesses must be willing to "risk interacting differently with Indigenous people—with vulnerability, humility, and a willingness to stay in the decolonizing struggle of our own discomfort ... [and] to embrace [residential school] stories as powerful teachings—disquieting moments [that] can change our beliefs, attitudes, and actions."[23]

Former residential school staff and their families

Relatively few former residential school staff or their family members came forward publicly at TRC events; some staff are deceased, others are now elderly or ill, and a small minority refused to admit, despite overwhelming evidence to the contrary, that the schools were destructive. Still others gave private statements to the Commission so that their memories would be preserved at the National Centre for Truth and Reconciliation.

The Commission observed that many former residential school staff expressed mixed feelings about their residential school experiences in the wake of revelations of widespread abuse. Whereas some remembered their time at the schools as a positive experience, others felt shame. They were haunted by knowing that they had failed to intervene on behalf of young students. They saw this as a stain on their lifework. The stories of the family members of staff are just beginning to surface. They too have been affected and must grapple with trying to reconcile their own family memories of relatives with what they now know about the schools.

In May 2011, in St. Albert, Alberta, the Commission met with a group of priests of the Missionary Oblates of Mary Immaculate and nuns of the Sisters of Providence and Grey Nuns. Many of the priests and nuns who attended the meeting had either taught at the residential schools or worked in Aboriginal communities for many years. Two key issues of concern were raised. First, the majority of those present felt that positive experiences at the schools were being ignored; second, they felt that many of their colleagues had been unjustly accused of abuse. One of the speakers said that in listening to what was being said about the residential schools,

> I felt that there is so much negativeness, like we did everything wrong, everything wrong, and I don't believe in that. I believe in the reconciliation, that's for sure. But you know, we talk about apologies, apologies. When do we talk a little bit about gratitude for what we did? Because we certainly did something right. We never hear about that ... We made mistakes, I'm sure, and many have been accused of sexual abuse that wasn't true. What do you think of that, I wonder? I feel very bad for some people because I heard them, they talked to me. I heard them, and they're destroyed.[24]

Another speaker said,

> When Sister expressed the pain she was holding of a particular community member that has been falsely accused, it wasn't that she was saying that those coming forth haven't experienced abuse, she was saying that it happened in

reverse as well, where some of us experienced accusations that were unfounded, and that's the one she said she was prepared to walk through fire because she knew they were innocent, and she holds their pain. It wasn't denying the fact that abuse happened to people that have the courage to stand up and express it in the wide public forums.[25]

Although the majority of Survivors who testified at TRC sessions described the individual and collective abuses that they experienced in the schools, the Commission also heard appreciation and gratitude from many Survivors for the education they received, and for individual teachers who were kind to them and very important to their success.

At the Northern National Event in Inuvik, Survivor Agnes Moses said,

Even though there was a lot of things that we didn't like about residential schools, there were some good people in there that helped us…. When I went to live in Ottawa, who do I run into but my two teachers, and I knew them until they passed away just in the last couple of years. I've had contact with them.[26]

In Chisasabi, Québec, Survivor Samuel Tapiatic told the Commission that he was abused and bullied at residential school. He also said, "Now I realize that some of the things that happened in that residential school were good for the education I got…. So anyway, I'm grateful for what I have learned in the residential school."[27]

A number of former residential school staff came to the Commission to speak not only about their perspectives on the time they spent at the schools but also about their struggles to come to terms with their own past. Florence Kaefer, a former teacher, spoke at the Manitoba National Event.

And from my English ancestors, I apologize today for what my people did to you. I taught in two residential schools. In 1954, I taught in Norway House United Church Residential School for three or four years, and then I taught in the Alberni United Church Indian Residential School in BC. I worked very hard to be the best teacher I could be, and I did not know about the violence and cruelty going on in the dormitories and in the playrooms. But I have found out through one of my former students, who was five years old when he came to Norway House, his name is Edward Gamblin, and Edward Gamblin and I have gone through a personal truth and reconciliation.[28]

In a media interview afterwards, Ms. Kaefer said that she had contacted Mr. Gamblin after

hearing his song a few years ago describing the cultural, physical and sexual abuse he had suffered at Norway House school. She said, "I just cried. I told my sister that I can never think of teaching in the residential school in the same way again." She called Gamblin after hearing the song. He told her he had to hide his abuse from the good teachers for fear he would lose them if they found out what was happening and left. He invited Kaefer to a healing circle in 2006 and they became close friends. Kaefer said Gamblin taught her not to be embarrassed about her past, being part of a school where abuse took place. "I was 19 and you don't question your church and your government when you're 19, but I certainly question my church and my government today." … Gamblin said Kaefer taught him how to forgive. "There are good people [teachers] who don't deserve to be labeled," he said.[29]

Some family members of former staff also came forward. At the Manitoba National Event, Jack Lee told the Commission,

My parents were staff members of the Indian residential school in Norway House. I was born on a reserve in Ontario and I moved with my family to Norway House when I was about one or two years old, and started school in the Indian residential school system, basically, at the very start as a day student … as a white boy…. My father agonized very much over his role…. But I just want everyone to know that my father tried his best, as many other staff members tried their best, but they were working with so limited resources, and many of them felt very bad about their role in it, but they chose to stay in the system because it was still better than nothing, it was still better than abandoning the system, and abandoning the students that were in it.[30]

At the Atlantic National Event, Mark DeWolf spoke to us about his father, the Reverend James Edward DeWolf, who was the principal at two residential schools: St. Paul's in Alberta and La Tuque in Québec.

I'm quite hesitant to speak here this morning … I'm not here to defend my father [but] to speak part of the truth about the kind of person my father was. I think he was an exemplary principal of an Indian residential school…. Part of the story will be about what I saw around me, what my parents tried to do, however effective that was, however well-intentioned that was, however beneficial or not beneficial it was, you will at least, when you leave here today, have a bit more of the story and you may judge for yourselves. I hope you will judge with kindness, understanding, and generosity of spirit….

[My father] did so many things, coached the teams, blew the whistle or shot off the starting pistol at the sports days. Twelve o'clock at midnight, on the coldest of winter days, he would be out on the rink that he had constructed behind the school, flooding it so that the children could skate. He devoted his life to the service of his church, his God, and those that he thought had been marginalized, oppressed…. It is a terrible shame there were not more like him. When we leave today, though, let's remember that when you have a system like the residential school, there are the individuals within the system, some of whom are good, decent, loving, caring people, and some of whom are blind, intolerant, predatory…. My father worked within the system trying to make it a better one.[31]

Church and government officials

In the introduction to this volume, we emphasized that the issue of timing is critical in the truth and reconciliation process. There is a time for speaking, a time for listening, and a time for reflection. Church and government officials sometimes spoke about how important it was for them just to listen to Survivors and to think about how to take action on reconciliation in their own institutions.

At the Saskatchewan National Event, the Reverend Dr. John Vissers, principal of the Presbyterian College in Montreal and director of the Montreal School of Theology, said,

> How do communities reconcile? Survivors, as we've learned, have had to keep the painful experiences of residential schools a secret for many years. Family members, in many cases, knew little or nothing about what had happened to their parents or their grandparents. The Truth and Reconciliation Commission of Canada is giving Survivors this opportunity to share what has happened to them, to share painful memories with family members, with friends, and with Canadian society....
>
> Reconciliation is a conscious act involving two or more parties.... And reconciliation, of course, must be rooted in truth, in truth that comes from deep listening and deep respect for the other. For the members of the churches than ran the schools on behalf of the government of Canada and therefore the people of Canada, we need to listen deeply and profoundly to the stories of Survivors....
>
> Reconciliation between Indigenous and non-Indigenous peoples in Canada, if it is to have any meaning, must be mutual. When there is mutuality, the journey then may begin. We understand, as churches, and we acknowledge that many Survivors are not yet prepared to participate in this journey in this way. But we must continue as churches to listen deeply and profoundly and to live into the reconciliation that we believe lies ahead of us.[32]

At the same event, Bishop Don Bolen, the Roman Catholic Bishop of Saskatoon, spoke about the importance of the church's active participation in the truth and reconciliation process. He said that this involved

> [b]earing witness to what happened at the residential schools and doing so in a way that tells the truth and which fosters genuine reconciliation. Those witnesses need to be heard. And we embrace the invitation to listen, to engage in a relationship-building process, to join in bearing witness, to working together toward a new future based on an honest dealing with the past.[33]

At the Atlantic National Event, Ian Gray, the regional director general of Aboriginal Affairs and Northern Development Canada for the Atlantic region, said that it was important for government officials to hear directly from Survivors.

[A]s an official within the department, you know, we all have our spheres of influence. We all work in a cubicle, [a] physical cubicle, but also a cubicle of terms and conditions, programs, legislation, rules, regulations, bosses, people that report to us.... So often we have our head down in dealing with those things. That's the day-to-day stuff that we grind through as public servants in a department. And it's just so special to have that opportunity and occasions like this to be able to rise above that [and] to really think about and talk about and hear from people about the real big issues about reconciliation.[34]

At the British Columbia National Event, a group of resolution managers from the BC Regional Office of Resolution and Individual Affairs, Aboriginal Affairs and Northern Development Canada, offered an expression of reconciliation to Survivors.

We work to resolve claims of abuse made under the Settlement Agreement. This work includes attending former students' Independent Assessment Process [IAP] hearings where we represent Canada....

Listening carefully to your experiences and remembering what we have heard is critical. We leave each hearing as changed people. We want you to know that your courage and strength in coming forward to share your testimony transform each and every one of us.... The people we encounter in this work show a strength of character, a deep love of family and community, and a commitment to culture and healing that touches our hearts and teaches us to be better people....

As resolution managers, our focus is always on reconciliation, while understanding that reconciliation means different things to different people. Reconciliation is something that grows, rather than something that is imposed. We acknowledge that while many [Survivors] come through the hearing process feeling lighter of heart and mind, and perhaps even feeling a measure of healing, this has not been everyone's experience. We know that, in our role as Canada's representatives, we cannot take away the hurt or give anyone back the childhood that was lost.

We sincerely hope to leave a legacy within the Canadian public service when the work of resolving IAP claims is complete. For this legacy, we will spread knowledge among people in Canada in the public service and beyond of the impact of Indian residential schools. We will bring an atmosphere of caring and respect with us in whatever work we do, as we have learned from Survivors and their families.[35]

TRC Honorary Witnesses

The mandate of the Truth and Reconciliation Commission describes reconciliation as an ongoing individual and collective process involving all the people of Canada. To help ensure that reconciliation will indeed be ongoing, even after the TRC's own official work is done, the Commissioners decided early on to implement a public education and advocacy strategy for engaging high-profile supporters, each willing to foster the continuing work of public education and dialogue. We called upon more than seventy of them across the country and internationally, and inducted them as Honorary Witnesses in a public ceremony at each of the National Events.

Together, the Honorary Witnesses represent accomplished and influential leaders from all walks of life, now serving as ambassadors in educating the broader public about why reconciliation is necessary. Most of them, including some who had worked with Aboriginal people in the past, frankly admitted to their own prior gaps in knowledge and understanding of the residential school system and its continuing legacy. They now encourage the broader Canadian public to do what they have done: to learn and to be transformed in understanding and in commitment to societal change.

CBC broadcaster Shelagh Rogers, OC, who became an Honorary Witness at the Northern National Event, has said about the role and responsibility of witnessing, "Witnessing is an active verb ... And if you're seriously committed to the retelling of what you've seen and heard, it's not always comfortable."[36]

> As a Witness, you keep the memory and you take the story further down the road and deliver it to more people. I have been very busy talking in churches, doing dialogues, meeting in community hall basements, [and] book clubs—just trying to get the real story of our country out to as many people as possible. It has really taken over my heart. It is bigger than just telling the story—I want to see policy change, curriculum change, to see concrete fixes in civil society that will enable us to have much better partnerships than we have right now.[37]

Speaking at the Saskatchewan National Event, TRC Honorary Witness and former member of Parliament the Honourable Tina Keeper, who is also a member of the Norway House Cree Nation, talked about the importance of honouring individual, family, and community relationships and memory, her own emotional involvement in the ratification of the Settlement Agreement, and the struggles surrounding Canada's apology. She underscored the strong contributions that Aboriginal peoples have to make to national healing and reconciliation.

> Yesterday was an incredible opportunity for me personally to let the tears flow, and they flowed all day long. And I didn't do that when I was in the House of Commons. I had the privilege of delivering the speech on behalf of the official opposition when the Agreement was tabled in the House, and during that speech I had to stop midway and breathe ... because I didn't think I could do it. I

kept thinking of my family, and my extended family, and my grandparents, and
so many of the people in the communities.... Our cultures, our languages, our
values, and spiritual beliefs that have taken care of us at this gathering ... they
will become tools for the healing of a nation.[38]

At the Québec National Event, TRC Honorary Witness and former prime minister
the Right Honourable Paul Martin reminded participants about the role that education played in the attempted destruction of Aboriginal families, communities, and
nations, and the role it must play in repairing this damage.

I've talked to a number of the people here, some of the members of Parliament
are here ... and the question we asked ourselves is, "How come we didn't know
what happened?" ... I still can't answer that.... [L]et us understand that what happened at the residential schools was the use of education for cultural genocide
... [Let's] call a spade a spade. What that really means is that we've got to offer
Aboriginal Canadians, without any shadow of a doubt, the best education system
that [it] is possible to have.[39]

Although some Honorary Witnesses already had significant knowledge of Aboriginal
issues, including residential schools, through the act of witnessing Survivors' testimonies, they learned about this history in a different way. At the Saskatchewan National
Event, former prime minister the Right Honourable Joe Clark said that the event gave
him a better understanding of the intergenerational impacts of the residential schools,
and a better sense of the challenges and opportunities for reconciliation with the rest
of Canada.

When I came to take my place this morning, I knew the storyline, if you will. I
knew what had happened. I had some idea of the consequences it [the residential school system] involved, but I had no real idea because I had not been able
to witness it before ... the multi-generational emotion that is involved in what has
happened to so many of the victims of the residential schools.... [Today] I heard,
"We are only as sick as our secrets." That is an incentive to all that have kept these
emotions and this history too secret, too long, to show the courage that so many
of you have shown, and let those facts be known....

There are cross-cultural difficulties here as we seek reconciliation, the reconciliation of people who have not been part of this experience with those who have.
We are going to deal with cultural differences, but no one wants to be torn away
from their roots. And there are common grounds here by which consensus can
be built.... Reconciliation means finding a way that brings together the legitimate
concerns of the people in this room, and the apprehensions, call them fear ...
that might exist elsewhere in the country.... Among the things we have to do is to
ensure that not only the stories of abuse as they touch First Nations and Aboriginal people, but also the story of their contribution to Canada, and the values that
are inherent in those communities [are] much better known.[40]

Joe Clark's observations reinforce this Commission's view that learning happens in a different manner when life stories are shared and witnessed in ways that connect knowledge, understanding, and human relationships. He pinpointed a key challenge to reconciliation: how to bridge the divides between those who have been part of the residential school experience and those who have not, and between those who have participated in the Truth and Reconciliation Commission's proceedings and those who have not.

Former minister of Aboriginal affairs and northern development Canada the late Honourable Andy Scott was inducted as an Honorary Witness at the 2012 Atlantic National Event in Halifax. He then served to welcome new inductees to the Honorary Witness Circle at the Saskatchewan National Event, and reflected on his experience. His comments reinforce the Commission's conviction that relationship-based learning and ways of remembering lead to a deeper knowledge and understanding of the links between the Survivors' experiences and community memory, on the one hand, and our collective responsibility and need to re-envision Canada's national history, identity, and future, on the other.

> When I was invited to become an Honorary Witness, I thought I was prepared, having been involved in the Settlement [Agreement] process and having already met and heard from Survivors. I was not. In Halifax, I heard about not knowing what it meant to be loved, not knowing how to love. I heard about simply wanting to be believed that it happened, 'just like I said.' ... We heard about a deliberate effort to disconnect young children from who they are. We heard about a sense of betrayal by authority—government, community, and church. We heard about severe punishment for speaking one's language, living one's spirituality, seeking out one's siblings. We heard about forced feeding, physical and sexual abuse. And we heard about deaths.
>
> We heard about forgiving as a way to move on and we heard from those who felt that they would never be able to forgive. I could not and cannot imagine being taken away to a strange place as a five or a six year old, never knowing why or for how long. Perhaps I remember most poignantly Ruth, who said simply, "I never thought I'd talk about this, and now I don't think I'll ever stop. But Canada is big. I'll need some help."
>
> Reconciliation is about Survivors speaking about their experiences, being heard, and being believed, but it's also about a national shared history. As Canadians, we must be part of reconciling what we have done collectively with who we believe we are. To do that with integrity and to restore our honour, we must all know the history so we can reunite these different Canadas.[41]

The Commission also heard from other Aboriginal and non-Aboriginal witnesses from many walks of life. Some were there on behalf of their institution or organization.

Some had close personal or professional ties to Aboriginal people, and others had none. Many said that the experience opened their eyes and was powerfully transformative. They commented on how much they had learned by listening to Survivors' life stories. This was true for both non-Aboriginal witnesses and Aboriginal witnesses whose own families had been impacted by the schools but who may have had few opportunities to learn more about the residential schools themselves, especially in those many families where no one was yet willing or able to talk about it.

At the 2011 Northern National Event in Inuvik, Therese Boullard, then the director of the Northwest Territories Human Rights Commission, told us,

> We need to have an accurate record of history.... As long as there are some that are in denial of what really happened, as long as we don't have the full picture of what happened, we really can't move forward in that spirit of reconciliation.... I want to acknowledge these stories as gifts, a hand towards reconciliation. I think it's amazing that after all that has passed, after all that you've experienced, that you would be willing to share your pain with the rest of Canada in this spirit of openness and reconciliation and in this faith that the Government of Canada and non-Aboriginal Canadians will receive them in a way that will lead to a better relationship in the future. That you have that faith to share your stories in that spirit is amazing, and it's humbling, and it's inspiring, and I just want to thank Survivors for that.[42]

At the 2010 Manitoba National Event, Ginelle Giacomin, a high school history teacher from Winnipeg who served as a private statement gatherer at the event, said,

> I was talking to a few students before I came this week to do this, and they said, "Well, what do you mean there are Survivors? That was a long time ago. That was hundreds of years ago." To them, this is a page in a history book.... So, I'm so blessed to have spent the past week sitting down one-on-one with Survivors and listening to their stories. And I have heard horrific things and the emotions. It's been very hard to hear. But what every single person I've spoken to has said is that "we are strong." And the strength is one thing that I'll carry with me when I leave. You carry on, and that's something that I want to bring back to my classrooms, is the strength of everyone that I spoke to and their stories. And it is so important for high school students, and all students in Canada, to be talking about this a lot more than they are. I just want to thank everyone involved for doing this, for educating me. I have a history degree in Canadian history. I learned more in the past five days about Canada than I have in three years of that degree.[43]

Whether attitudes and actions were changed and transformed in any sustainable way can be known only in the fullness of time. There are however some early indications that for those who witnessed Survivors' testimonies, the impacts were significant. In one study, interviews were conducted with a small sample of twenty-three non-Indigenous witnesses who had attended TRC events in British Columbia. Reflecting on their experiences in the months following these events, they told the researcher why they had attended and what they had learned in the process. Some of their reflections included the following:

> Having [a] direct connection to stolen land, (grandfather cleared land and financially supported the residential schools) so I felt a personal reason to attend; also a wider more political reason, I wanted to be part of the larger effort. There is clearly a need for reconciliation between Indigenous and non-Indigenous people and non-Indigenous [people] have an important role—to deal with our own stuff and show up. I really wanted to witness.[44]

> It opened my mind and my heart to how deep those impacts could be: it grows in me every time I'm part of a process around residential schools. What I got from the TRC is that it's not just about people doing abusive things: it's the whole experience. Even if everybody had been the best, nicest, kindest white person in the world, it would still have been a completely abusive system. I feel like my learning grows and my understanding grows.[45]

> [S]haring of stories is really important because being in the room with someone talking about intergenerational effects is so human, so poignant, so unsettling and powerful. I can relate to them, I feel compassion for them. Hearing the stories firsthand was the only way it could pierce all that racism; it certainly was transformational.[46]

> My witnessing pushes me to do more than just look on ... Everyone has to be involved to right some of the wrongs and everyone has a responsibility to do whatever they can.[47]

> A responsibility comes with hearing these stories ... It was a real chance to communicate, a chance to connect to humanity for all of us, a chance to be there with an open heart and mind to connect with a thousand people as a human being, in a way to hope for change. It was powerful.[48]

The Commission's seven National Events, by all accounts, provided a respectful space for public dialogue. Over 150,000 Canadians came out to participate in them and in some 300 smaller-scale Community Events. One of the most common words used in describing them was "transformational." It will be up to others to determine their long-term effectiveness, and to judge this model's potential in terms of ongoing public education. However, as Commissioners of the Truth and Reconciliation Commission of Canada, we are both confident and convinced that public dialogue is critical to the reconciliation process.

The arts: Practising resistance, healing, and reconciliation

The reconciliation process is not easy. It asks those who have been harmed to revisit painful memories and those who have harmed others—either directly or indirectly—to be accountable for past wrongs. It asks us to mourn and commemorate a terrible loss of people, cultures, and languages, even as we celebrate their survival and revitalization. It asks us to envision a more just and inclusive future, even as we struggle with the living legacies of injustice.

As the TRC has experienced in every region of the country, creative expression can play a vital role in this national reconciliation, providing alternative voices, vehicles, and venues for expressing historical truths and present hopes. Creative expression supports everyday practices of resistance, healing, and commemoration at individual, community, regional, and national levels.

Across the globe, the arts have provided a creative pathway to breaking silences, transforming conflicts, and mending the damaged relationships of violence, oppression, and exclusion. From war-ravaged countries to local communities struggling with everyday violence, poverty, and racism, the arts are widely used by educators, practitioners, and community leaders to deal with trauma and difficult emotions, and to communicate across cultural divides.[49]

Art is active, and "participation in the arts is a guarantor of other human rights because the first thing that is taken away from vulnerable, unpopular or minority groups is the right to self-expression."[50] The arts help to restore human dignity and identity in the face of injustice. Properly structured, they can also invite people to explore their own worldviews, values, beliefs, and attitudes that may be barriers to healing, justice, and reconciliation.

Even prior to the establishment of the TRC, a growing body of work, including Survivors' memoirs and works of fiction by well-known Indigenous authors, as well as films and plays, had brought the history and legacy of the residential schools to a wider Canadian public, enabling people to learn about the schools through the eyes of Survivors. This body of work includes memoirs such as Isabelle Knockwood's *Out of the Depths: The Experiences of Mi'kmaw Children at the Indian Residential School at Shubenacadie, Nova Scotia* (1992), and more recently, Agnes Grant's *Finding My Talk: How Fourteen Native Women Reclaimed Their Lives after Residential School* (2004), Alice Blondin's *My Heart Shook Like a Drum: What I Learned at the Indian Mission Schools, Northwest Territories* (2009), Theodore Fontaine's *Broken Circle: The Dark Legacy of Indian Residential Schools: A Memoir* (2010), Bev Sellars's *They Called Me Number One: Secrets and Survival at an Indian Residential School* (2013), and Edmund Metatawabin and Alexandra Shimo's *Up Ghost River: A Chief's Journey through the Turbulent Waters of Native History* (2014).

Works of fiction (sometimes drawn from the author's own life experiences), such as Tomson Highway's *Kiss of the Fur Queen* (1998), Robert Alexie's *Porcupines and China Dolls* (2009), and Richard Wagamese's *Indian Horse* (2012), tell stories about abuse, neglect, and loss that are also stories of healing, redemption, and hope. In 2012, the Aboriginal Healing Foundation published *Speaking My Truth: Reflections on Reconciliation and Residential Schools*, and invited book clubs across the country to read and discuss the book. Documentary films such as *Where the Spirit Lives* (1989), *Kuper Island: Return to the Healing Circle* (1997), and *Muffins for Granny* (2008), as well as docu-dramas such as *We Were Children* (2012), all serve to educate Canadians and the wider world about the residential school experience, using the power of sound and images. Intergenerational Survivor Georgina Lightning was the first Indigenous woman in North America to direct a full-length feature film, *Older Than America* (2008). Kevin Loring's stage play, *Where the Blood Mixes*, won the Governor General's Award for literary drama in 2009. It combines drama and humour to tell the stories of three Survivors living in the aftermath of their residential school experiences.

Art can be powerful and provocative. Through their work, Indigenous artists seek to resist and challenge the cultural understandings of settler-dominated versions of Canada's past and its present reality. Sharing intercultural dialogue about history, responsibility, and transformation through the arts is potentially healing and transformative for both Aboriginal and non-Aboriginal peoples.[51] Yet art does not always cross this cultural divide, nor does it have to in order to have a high impact. Acts of resistance sometimes take place in "irreconcilable spaces" where artists choose to keep their residential school experiences private or share them only with other Aboriginal people.[52] This choice is also essential to individual and collective reclaiming of identity, culture, and community memory.

The Commission notes that the use of creative arts in community workshops promotes healing for Survivors, their families, and the whole community through the recovery of cultural traditions. In conducting surveys of 103 community-based healing projects, the Aboriginal Healing Foundation found that 80% of those projects included cultural activities and traditional healing interventions. These components included Elders' teachings, storytelling and traditional knowledge, language programs, land-based activities, feasts, and powwows, as well as learning traditional art forms, harvesting medicines, and drumming, singing, and dancing. The foundation's report observes,

> A notable component of successful healing programs was their diversity—interventions were blended and combined to create holistic programs that met the physical, emotional, cultural, and spiritual needs of participants. Not surprisingly, arts-based interventions were included in many cultural activities (drum making, beading, singing, and drumming) as well as in therapeutic healing (art therapy and psychodrama).[53]

The Aboriginal Healing Foundation's findings make clear that creative art practices are highly effective in reconnecting Survivors and their families to their cultures, languages, and communities. In our view, this report confirms yet again that funding for community-based healing projects is an urgent priority for Aboriginal communities.

Art exhibits have played a particularly powerful role in the process of healing and reconciliation. In 2009, nationally acclaimed Anishinaabe artist Robert Houle, who attended the Sandy Bay Residential School in Manitoba, created a series of twenty-four paintings to be housed permanently in the University of Manitoba's School of Art Gallery. In an interview with CBC News on September 24, 2013, he explained that "during the process memories came back that he had previously suppressed ... [but that] he found the whole experience cathartic. At the end, he felt a sigh of relief, a sigh of liberation."[54]

Over the course of the Commission's mandate, several major art exhibits ran concurrently with its National Events. During the British Columbia National Event in Vancouver, for example, three major exhibits opened featuring well-known Aboriginal artists, some of whom were also Survivors or intergenerational Survivors. A number of non-Aboriginal artists were also featured. Their work explored themes of denial, complicity, apology, and government policy. Two of these exhibits were at the University of British Columbia: *Witnesses: Art and Canada's Indian Residential Schools* at the Morris and Helen Belkin Art Gallery, and the Museum of Anthropology's *Speaking to Memory: Images and Voices from the St. Michael's Residential School*. Both exhibits were collaborative efforts that also engaged Survivors, artists, and curatorial staff in related public education initiatives, including workshops, symposiums, and public dialogues based on the exhibits.[55]

A significant number of the statements gathered by the Commission also came to us in artistic formats. Some Survivors said that although it hurt too much to tell their story in the usual way, they had been able to find their voice instead by writing a poem, a song, or a book. Some made a video or audio recording, offered photographs, or produced a theatre performance piece or a film. Others created traditional blankets, quilts, carvings, or paintings to depict residential school experiences, to celebrate those who survived them, or to commemorate those who did not. Lasting public memory of the schools has therefore been produced not only through oral testimonies but also through this wide range of artistic expressions. The arts have opened up new and critical space for Survivors, artists, curators, and public audiences to explore the complexities of truth, healing, and reconciliation.

The Commission funded or supported several arts-related projects. Early in its mandate, the TRC sponsored the Living Healing Quilt Project, which was organized by Anishinaabe quilter Alice Williams from Curve Lake First Nation in Ontario. Women Survivors and intergenerational Survivors from across the country created individual quilt blocks depicting their memories of residential schools. These were then stitched together into three quilts, *Schools of Shame*, *Child Prisoners*, and *Crimes against Humanity*.

The quilts tell a complex story of trauma, loss, isolation, recovery, healing, and hope through women's eyes. The sewing skills taught to young Aboriginal girls in the residential schools and passed along to their daughters and granddaughters are now used to stitch together a counter-narrative.[56] This project also inspired the Healing Quilt Project, which linked education and art. At the Manitoba National Event, as an expression of reconciliation, the Women's and Gender Studies and the Aboriginal Governance Departments at the University of Winnipeg gave the TRC a quilt created by students and professors as part of their coursework. Through classroom readings, dialogue, and art, they created a space for learning about, and reflecting on, the history and legacy of the residential schools in the context of reconciliation.[57]

The ArtsLink Project, initiated by intergenerational Survivor Carol Greyeyes, is an online, interactive showcase featuring the artwork and cultural practices of ten Aboriginal artists who are also Survivors. Ms. Greyeyes summarizes the purpose of the project.

> The ArtsLink website shares the wisdom, the stories, and insights of residential school survivors from the Western Provinces who have reclaimed their identity and pride through art and culture. Each webpage includes a biography, a short interview with the artist, samples of artwork and documents, innovative arts and learning practices, and community arts projects.
>
> ArtsLink also provides an accessible, safe forum for discussion and expression of the residential school experience....
>
> Art bridges age, language, culture, economics, and promotes understanding by its transformative power. ArtsLink allows artists and website visitors to "link up" in the educative process. Just as the artists have reconnected with their own inner creative selves and transformed their lives, by showcasing their artwork and sharing their amazing stories, other Canadians will be able to connect to the artistic journey and healing process too.[58]

A report commissioned by the TRC, "Practicing Reconciliation: A Collaborative Study of Aboriginal Art, Resistance and Cultural Politics," was based on the findings of a one-year research project. Working with Survivors, artists, and curators, a multi-disciplinary team of researchers examined the general question of how artistic practice contributes to the reconciliation process. The research was done through a series of interviews, workshops, artist residencies, planning sessions, symposia, artistic incubations, publications, and online learning platforms. The report reveals the depth and potential of arts-based approaches to reconciliation.

> We should begin by echoing what many of our interview and artist subjects have repeatedly said: that the act of reconciliation is itself deeply complicated, and that success should not be measured by *achieving* a putative [commonly accepted or supposed] reconciliation, but by *movement* towards these lofty goals. Indeed, it could be proposed that full reconciliation is both mercurial and impossible, and that the efforts of theorists, artists, survivors, and the various publics engaged in this difficult process are best focused on working collaboratively for better understanding our histories, our traumas, and ourselves.[59]

These various projects indicate that the arts and artistic practices may serve to shape public memory in ways that are potentially transformative for individuals, communities, and national history.

Residential school commemoration projects

Commemoration should not put closure to the history and legacy of the residential schools. Rather, it must invite citizens into a dialogue about a contentious past and why this history still matters today. Commemorations and memorials at former school sites and cemeteries are visible reminders of Canada's shame and church complicity. They bear witness to the suffering and loss that generations of Aboriginal peoples have endured and overcome. The process of remembering the past together is an emotional journey of contradictory feelings: loss and resilience, anger and acceptance, denial and remorse, shame and pride, despair and hope.

The Settlement Agreement identified the historic importance and reconciliation potential of such remembering by establishing a special fund for projects that would commemorate the residential school experience, and by assigning a role in the approval of these projects to the Truth and Reconciliation Commission of Canada.

Twenty million dollars was set aside for Aboriginal communities and various partners and organizations to undertake community-based, regional or national projects. The Commission evaluated and made recommendations to Aboriginal Affairs and Northern Development Canada, which was responsible for administering the funding for the commemoration projects.

The Settlement Agreement commemoration policy set out specific project criteria. Commemoration projects were to:

- Assist in honouring and validating the healing and reconciliation of former students and their families through commemoration initiatives that address their residential school experience;

- Provide support towards efforts to improve and enhance Aboriginal relationships and between Aboriginal and non-Aboriginal people;

- Provide an opportunity for former students and their families to support one another and to recognize and take pride in their strengths, courage, resiliency, and achievements;

- Contribute to a sense of identity, unity and belonging;

- Promote Aboriginal languages, cultures, and traditional and spiritual values;

- Ensure that the legacy of residential schools and former students' and their families' experiences and needs are affirmed; and

- Memorialize in a tangible and permanent way the residential school experience.[60]

Unlike more conventional state commemorations, which have tended to reinforce Canada's story as told through colonial eyes, residential school commemorative projects challenged and recast public memory and national history. Many First Nations, Inuit, and Métis communities partnered with regional or national Aboriginal organizations, and involved local churches, governments, and their non-Aboriginal neighbours. The scope, breadth, and creativity of the projects were truly impressive.

Projects included traditional and virtual quilts, monuments and memorials, traditional medicine gardens, totem pole and canoe carving, oral history, community ceremonies and feasts, land-based culture and language camps, cemetery restoration, film and digital storytelling, commemorative walking trails, and theatre or dance productions.[61]

The Commission, advised by the TRC Survivor Committee, identified three elements of the commemoration process that were seen as being essential to supporting long-term reconciliation. First, the projects were to be Survivor-driven; that is, their success was contingent upon the advice, recommendations, and active participation of Survivors. Second, commemoration projects would forge new connections that linked Aboriginal family and community memory to Canada's public memory and national history. Third, incorporating Indigenous oral history and memory practices into commemoration projects would ensure that the processes of remembering places, reclaiming identity, and revitalizing cultures were consistent with the principle of self-determination.

Commemorating the life stories of Survivors strengthens the bonds of family and community memory that have been disrupted but not destroyed. Families grieve for all that was lost and can never be recovered. The act of commemoration remembers and honours those who are no longer living and comforts those for whom a history of injustice and oppression is still very much alive. Commemorations can also symbolize hope, signifying cultural revitalization and the reclaiming of history and identity.

Even as they grieve, families envision a better future for children and youth and for generations yet unborn.

The collective memory of Aboriginal peoples lives in places: in their traditional homelands and in the actual physical locations where residential schools once stood.[62] On March 24, 2014, the Grand Council of Treaty 3 brought together Survivors, Elders, and others in Kenora, Ontario, for a final ceremony to mark commemorations that were held earlier at each site of the five residential schools that were located in the territory. Monuments had been placed at each of the sites. Richard Green, who coordinated the two-year memorial project, said, "This is a commemoration for all the sites together. This meeting is about honouring all the children and is part of remembering the legacy. Lest we forget, as they say. We can probably forgive, but we can never forget our history." He explained that the monuments "have been a big success with plenty of positive feedback. Now we have a physical place where people can go and commemorate."[63]

Bearing witness to the child: Children's art from the Alberni Residential School

The story of a small collection of children's art created at the Alberni Residential School demonstrates how recognizing and respecting Indigenous protocols and practices of ceremony, testimony, and witnessing can breathe life, healing, and transformation into public memory making through dialogue, the arts, and commemoration. The story has deep roots within the family histories of the Survivors and in the oral history and community memory of the Nuu-chah-nulth peoples.

The paintings from the Alberni Residential School are part of a larger collection of Indigenous children's art donated to the University of Victoria in 2009 by the late artist Robert Aller. As a resident of Port Alberni, British Columbia, Aller initially volunteered his time to teach art classes to selected students outside of the regular curriculum at the residential school. He was hired by Indian Affairs to teach art between 1956 and 1987 at the Alberni school, and also at the McKay Residential School in Dauphin, Manitoba, as well as in Aboriginal communities in several other provinces.

There are over 750 paintings in the collection, including 36 paintings from the Alberni Residential School. Aller also donated to the university his private papers, and hundreds of photographs, slides, and archival documents that detail his teaching philosophy and approach to art. Aller did not agree with the philosophy behind the residential schools. He saw art as a way to free students from their everyday environment and as a way for them to express their creativity, either through traditionally inspired works or through paintings that used the theories and ideas of the contemporary art world. The paintings from the Alberni Residential School portray images of landscapes, people, animals, masks, and traditional stories, as well as some images of the school itself. Most of the artists signed their paintings, putting their age next to their name. In this sense, the children stand out; the anonymity that depersonalizes so much of the residential school history is removed.

In 2010, the University of Victoria's Dr. Andrea Walsh, who was in the early stages of a research project on the art collection, met with the Commissioners, and we urged her to begin her research with ceremony. She turned to two Elders from the First Peoples House at the university to guide her in this process: Tousilum (Ron George), who is a residential school Survivor; and Sulsa'meeth (Deb George), his wife. They helped her to reach out to Survivors, Elders, and chiefs in Port Alberni in Nuu-chah-nulth territory when the group travelled there with the paintings. As community members leafed through the paintings drawn by children's hands so many years ago, memories were shared about the artists, the school, and the parents and communities they had left behind.

Working under the direction of these community members, and in collaboration with her colleague Qwul'sih'yah'maht (Dr. Robina Anne Thomas) and TRC staff, Walsh began preparations to bring the artwork to the Learning Place at the TRC's Victoria Regional Event in April 2012. In a powerfully moving ceremony, Nuu-chah-nulth Elders, Survivors, and Hereditary Chiefs drummed, sang, and danced the art into the Learning Place. In this way, each painting, carried with respect and love by a Nuu-chah-nulth woman dressed in button blanket regalia, was brought out to be shared with others.

After being inducted as a TRC Honorary Witness at the Victoria Regional Event, Dr. Walsh spoke about her journey with the children's paintings. She explained that she had come to understand the children's paintings as a living archive and that as witnesses to the marks of the children, we agree to take responsibility for the personal knowledge they contain. From her perspective, we must not simply see the works of art; we must bear witness to the child.

> These paintings done by the children of the Alberni school all tell stories; however, what I witnessed, what I saw, went beyond the Alberni school. These paintings moved Survivors from other schools to share their stories of making art, and the images depicted in the paintings prompted non-art stories, and memories of the schools. I heard stories of horrible trauma, fear, hurt, abuse, addiction, hate, pain, starvation. I watched tears fall in front of the paintings. I saw shoulders shaking from the memories emerging. The paintings are that powerful....
>
> I witnessed something else, though, around the paintings. It was pride, it was strength, it was pleasure, and it was a profound sense of truth. I've come to think of these paintings as direct connections to the children who created them. They

are the children, and as Chief Ed John said, the truth is in the Survivors. And against all odds, these paintings too have survived. They are not small things forgotten. Survivors, Elders, their families, and communities have worked together to bring these paintings to us in a good way. Through their work, they've ensured that the children's art, their stories, their lives lived, will be forever great things remembered.[64]

The community later received commemoration project funding to hold a traditional feast on March 30, 2013, in Port Alberni in order to reunite artists and their families with the paintings. Robert Aller's family members were also invited to attend. They were visibly moved when they heard the stories of the paintings, and said that Aller would have been happy that the paintings were being returned. Paintings were returned to those who wished to have them; the remaining art was loaned to the University of Victoria, where it will be housed, cared for, and exhibited based on agreed-upon protocols with Survivors and their families.[65]

In a media interview, Survivor and Hereditary Chief Lewis George said that the art classes probably saved him from being sexually abused by convicted pedophile Arthur Plint, who had taught at the Alberni Residential School. He remembered the kindness shown to him by Aller as being in stark contrast to the harsh realities of life at the school, and he said, "I want my story kept alive." Wally Samuel, another Survivor of the Alberni school who helped coordinate the project, said everyone reacted differently when told about the paintings. "Some got really quiet and others looked forward to seeing them ... but they all remembered being in art class."[66]

In May 2013, the Alberni Residential School paintings were displayed in a special exhibit, *To Reunite, To Honour, To Witness*, at the Legacy Art Gallery at the University of Victoria. Survivors, Elders, and community members continue to work with Walsh and Qwul'sih'yah'maht in order to document the story of the creation and return of the children's paintings as part of reconnecting individual, family, and community memory, and educating the public about a previously unknown part of the history and legacy of the residential schools.

In September 2013, the paintings returned once again to the Learning Place at the TRC's British Columbia National Event in Vancouver, and the group made an expression of reconciliation by providing copies of the artwork to the Commission's Bentwood Box, where it has become part of the permanent record of the Commission's work.

Canada's public commemoration

The Commission takes note of the federal government's own national commemoration initiative, which was described as an "expression of reconciliation" when it was publicly announced at the Atlantic National Event in 2011. It is a specially commissioned stained-glass window entitled *Giniigaaniimenaaning (Looking Ahead)*, designed by Métis artist Christi Belcourt. Its two-sided imagery depicts the history of the residential schools, the cultural resilience of Aboriginal peoples, and hope for the future.

The window was permanently installed in the Centre Block of the federal Parliament Buildings, and unveiled in a dedication ceremony on November 26, 2012.[67] Putting this window in such a prominent public place helps to make the history and legacy of the residential schools more visible to the Canadian public and the world at large, while also acknowledging the federal government's responsibility in establishing the residential school system.

At the dedication ceremony, artist Christi Belcourt said that her inspiration for the window's design came from Survivors themselves.

> The stories of residential school students were never told in this building, so I'm going to tell you one now.... I asked Lucille [Kelly-Davis] who is a residential school survivor what she wanted to see on the window. I had assisted her through the residential school settlement process, and like so many survivors, her story is horrific.... Despite her childhood, she married, had four children, and now has many grandchildren. She is a pipe carrier, attends traditional ceremonies, and helps younger people learn the traditions. She's a powerful Anishnabeg grandmother who is generous, loving and caring, and gives all she can to her community and her family. She is not a victim, but a survivor. When I asked her what to put on the window, she said, "Tell our side of the story." ... She said, "Make it about hope." ... It's about looking ahead, as the name of the window says, "giniigaaniimenaaning," looking to the future for those yet unborn....

> Because she told me to make it about hope, what I've tried to show in the design is all the positive things I've seen in my life. Despite residential schools, children, adults, and Elders dance in full regalia in celebration of who they are as Indigenous people. We see Métis youth learning fiddling and jigging with pride across the country. We see arenas full of Inuk Elders drum dancing, with little kids running around, speaking Inuktitut. We see whole communities come together in times of joy and in times of great grief. The lodges are growing, the traditional songs are being sung, the ceremonies are being taught, and the ceremonies are still practiced.

> I wish I could show the government that reconciliation has the potential to be so much more. I wish I could convince them that reconciliation is not an unattainable goal, if there's the will and the courage to discard old paternalistic ways of thinking and of behaviour. We need action, and where we need action, don't meet us with silence. Where we need support, don't accuse us of being a burden.... I wish I could speak to the hearts of MPs [members of Parliament],

whether Conservative, or NDP [New Democratic Party], or Liberal, and let them know that renewal and reconciliation can be found between Aboriginal peoples and the rest of Canada through the sustained wellness of generations of Aboriginal people to come.[68]

At Commission hearings, we heard from many Survivors about windows. We heard from those who looked out from the school windows, waiting and hoping to see their parents come for them; those who cried when no one came for them, especially when it was Christmas or another holiday. We heard from those who were told, sometimes while being pulled away from the window by the hair, to "get away from that window," or "your parents are not coming for you anyway." We heard from those who simply looked out into the dark or into the distance, crying because they were so lonesome and homesick. Windows were also a beacon of hope. Survivors told us how they smiled and laughed and could not contain their tears of joy when they looked out the window and saw their parents or grandparents coming to visit them or take them away from the school.[69] The windows of the residential schools evoked both good and bad memories for Survivors. Thus a commemorative window seems a fitting monument to remember and honour the children who went to residential schools.

Commemorations in highly visible public spaces such as the Parliament Buildings create openings for dialogue about what happened, why, and what can be learned from this history. Through dialogue, citizens can strengthen their ability to "accommodate difference, acknowledge injustice, and demonstrate a willingness to share authority over the past."[70] In the context of national reconciliation, ongoing public commemoration has the potential to contribute to human rights education in the broadest sense.

Although Canada's commemorative window was a significant gesture of reconciliation, the Commission believes that the federal government must do more to ensure that national commemoration of the history and legacy of the residential schools becomes an integral part of Canadian heritage and national history. Under the *Historic Sites and Monuments Act* (1985), the minister responsible for Parks Canada has the authority to designate historic sites of national significance and approve commemorative monuments or plaques.[71] The minister is advised by the Historic Sites and Monuments Board of Canada "on the commemoration of nationally significant aspects of Canada's past, including the designation of national historic sites, persons and events."[72] The board reviews and makes recommendations on submissions received from Canadian citizens who make nominations through the National Program of Historical Commemoration.[73]

Heritage sites, monuments, and plaques that celebrate Canada's past are common, but commemorating those aspects of our national history that reveal cultural genocide, human rights violations, racism, and injustice are more problematic.

As we noted earlier, at the international level, the *Joinet-Orentlicher Principles* adopted by the United Nations have established that states have a responsibility to take measures to ensure that collective violence against a targeted group of people does not reoccur. In addition to providing compensation, making apologies, and undertaking educational reform, states also have a duty "to remember." Under Principle 2,

> A people's knowledge of the history of its oppression is part of its heritage and, as such, must be preserved by appropriate measures in fulfillment of the State's duty to remember.... On a collective basis, symbolic measures intended to provide moral reparation, such as formal public recognition by the State of its responsibility, or official declarations aimed at restoring victims' dignity, commemorative ceremonies, naming of public thoroughfares or the erection of monuments, help to discharge the duty of remembrance.[74]

In 2014, the UN Special Rapporteur in the Field of Cultural Rights, Farida Shaheed, issued a report on memorialization processes in countries where victims and their families, working collaboratively with artists and various civic society groups, have commemorated their experiences in unofficial ways that may run counter to state-sanctioned versions of national history.[75] Shaheed observed that the commemorations of Indigenous peoples' experience—both their oppression and their positive contributions to society—that have occurred in many countries, including Canada, have not been state-driven initiatives. Rather, they have been initiated by Indigenous peoples themselves.

> In Canada, a memorial to indigenous veterans from the First World War was built at the request of indigenous peoples, integrating many elements of indigenous cultures. This recognition took place at a later stage in history, however, and in a different venue to the main memorial established for other Canadian soldiers. Commemoration projects are also taking place ... regarding the history of Indian residential schools.[76]

The report concluded that state authorities have a key role to play in the commemoration process. The state is responsible for managing public space and has the capacity to maintain monuments and develop long-term national commemoration policies and strategies.[77]

The Special Rapporteur further concluded that states should ensure that

> memorial policies contribute to, in particular ... providing symbolic reparation and public recognition to the victims in ways that respond to the needs of all victims oppressed in a recent or distant past and contribute to their healing ... the development of reconciliation policies between groups ... [and] promoting civic engagement, critical thinking and stimulating discussions on the representation of the past, as well as contemporary challenges of exclusion and violence.[78]

The report recommended that states and relevant stakeholders

> promote critical thinking on past events by ensuring that memorialisation
> processes are complemented by measures fostering historical awareness and
> support the implementation and outreach of high-quality research projects, cul-
> tural interventions that encourage people's direct engagement and educational
> activities.... States should ensure the availability of public spaces for a diversity of
> narratives conveyed in artistic expressions and multiply opportunities for such
> narratives to engage with each other.... [States must also] take into consideration
> the cultural dimension of memorial processes, including where repression has
> targeted indigenous peoples.[79]

The Commission concurs with these conclusions and recommendations. They are consistent with our own findings on the residential schools commemoration projects. These Survivor-driven, community-based initiatives revealed the importance of integrating Indigenous knowledge and revitalizing Indigenous memory practices in commemorating the history and legacy of the residential schools. They demonstrated the critical role that artists play in healing and commemoration.

The Commission believes that Canada's national heritage network also has a vital role to play in reconciliation. Our views were further confirmed in a study of residential school commemorations in the context of Canada's national heritage and commemoration policy. The research documented the Assembly of First Nations and the Aboriginal Healing Foundation's national commemoration project to create a heritage plaque program in order to place commemorative markers at all residential school sites across the country.[80] Faced with logistical challenges and based on input from Survivors and communities, "the project transformed from what ostensibly had been an IRS [Indian residential school] site heritage plaque program to a community-oriented public monumental art project."[81] The commemorative markers were not placed at residential school sites, many of which are in remote locations or otherwise inaccessible. Instead, they were placed in Aboriginal communities where Survivors and their families could access them more easily, where ceremonies and community events could be held, and where there were opportunities for ongoing healing, commemoration, and education.[82]

The study revealed the fundamental tensions that exist between the goals of Aboriginal peoples and those of Canada with regard to the commemoration of the residential schools. Under the existing policies of the National Program of Historical Commemoration, as overseen by Parks Canada's Historic Sites and Monuments Board of Canada, residential school sites do not meet the program criteria for heritage designation, which is based on the Western heritage values of conservation and preservation.[83]

For Survivors, their families, and their communities, commemorating their residential school experiences does not necessarily involve preserving the school buildings, but is intended instead to contribute to individual and collective healing. For example, a residential school located in Port Alberni, British Columbia, was demolished by Survivors and their families, who burned sage and cedar in ceremonies in order to "cleanse and allow the trapped spirits to finally be freed."[84] Commemoration activities involving the destruction of a residential school structure are in direct conflict with Canadian heritage goals.[85]

Ultimately, reconciliation requires a paradigm shift in Canada's national heritage values, policies, and practices, which focus on conservation and continue to exclude Indigenous history, heritage values, and memory practices, which prioritize healing and the reclaiming of culture in public commemoration.[86] For this shift to happen, Parks Canada's heritage and commemoration policies and programs must change.

By shaping commemoration projects to meet their own needs, Survivors, their families, and their communities have provided a wealth of information and best practices for commemorating the history and legacy of the residential school system. These contributions can inform and enrich the National Program of Historical Commemoration and the work of the Historic Sites and Monuments Board of Canada to ensure that Canada's heritage and commemoration legislation, programs, policies, and practices contribute constructively to the reconciliation process in the years ahead.

Calls to action:

79) We call upon the federal government, in collaboration with Survivors, Aboriginal organizations, and the arts community, to develop a reconciliation framework for Canadian heritage and commemoration. This would include, but not be limited to:

   i. Amending the *Historic Sites and Monuments Act* to include First Nations, Inuit, and Métis representation on the Historic Sites and Monuments Board of Canada and its Secretariat.

   ii. Revising the policies, criteria, and practices of the National Program of Historical Commemoration to integrate Indigenous history, heritage values, and memory practices into Canada's national heritage and history.

   iii. Developing and implementing a national heritage plan and strategy for commemorating residential school sites, the history and legacy of residential schools, and the contributions of Aboriginal peoples to Canada's history.

80) We call upon the federal government, in collaboration with Aboriginal peoples, to establish, as a statutory holiday, a National Day for Truth and Reconciliation to honour Survivors, their families, and communities, and ensure that public commemoration of the history and legacy of residential schools remains a vital component of the reconciliation process.

81) We call upon the federal government, in collaboration with Survivors and their organizations, and other parties to the Settlement Agreement, to commission and install a publicly accessible, highly visible, Residential Schools National Monument in the city of Ottawa to honour Survivors and all the children who were lost to their families and communities.

82) We call upon provincial and territorial governments, in collaboration with Survivors and their organizations, and other parties to the Settlement Agreement, to commission and install a publicly accessible, highly visible, Residential Schools Monument in each capital city to honour Survivors and all the children who were lost to their families and communities.

83) We call upon the Canada Council for the Arts to establish, as a funding priority, a strategy for Indigenous and non-Indigenous artists to undertake collaborative projects and produce works that contribute to the reconciliation process.

CHAPTER 6

We are all Treaty people: Canadian society and reconciliation

Although much of the Truth and Reconciliation Commission's (TRC) report has focused on the federal government and the churches that ran the residential schools, other institutions, sectors, and organizations in Canadian society must also contribute to reconciliation. Public dialogue and action on reconciliation must extend beyond addressing the history and legacy of the residential schools. If Canada is to thrive in the twenty-first century, First Nations, Inuit, and Métis peoples must also thrive. This requires healthy communities and real economic and social change.

Just as government, church, legal, and public education institutions in this country have been shaped by colonial systems, attitudes, and behaviours, so too have the media, sports organizations, and the business sector. Each has a role in supporting reconciliation moving forward. Non-Aboriginal citizens, those whose families settled here generations ago and those who are more recent newcomers, must also be active participants in the reconciliation process. National reconciliation involves building respectful relationships at the community level.

Media and reconciliation

Since Confederation, as historians Mark Anderson and Carmen Robertson point out, "Colonialism has always thrived in Canada's press," and "Canadian newspapers (as well as radio and television] have, over time, played an integral role in shaping the nation's colonial story."[1] The mainstream press has reinforced and been "supportive of the thinking that underwrote and gave rise to [sometimes coerced] treaties and residential schools."[2] The Commission acknowledges that many media outlets and individual journalists have provided news coverage that includes Aboriginal peoples' perspectives on a wide range of issues. Yet more must be done.

In many countries where violence and injustice has occurred on a large scale, the media has had the potential to either fuel conflict or facilitate conflict resolution and peace building.[3] The media play a critical role in educating the public, and through public scrutiny can hold the state accountable for its actions. In the Canadian context, the media can shape public memory and influence societal attitudes towards reconciliation.[4]

In their analysis of media coverage of residential schools and the activities of the TRC at the Québec National Event, scholars Rosemary Nagy and Emily Gillespie found that most of the media stories about truth and reconciliation were narrowly framed to focus on individual Survivor's stories of abuse, forgiveness, and healing. Stories presented by local Kanien'kehaka (Mohawk) people that framed truth and reconciliation more expansively to include the need for societal change and concrete action on Treaties, land rights, and gender equity received far less attention.[5]

The Commission believes that in the coming years, media outlets and journalists will greatly influence whether or not reconciliation ultimately transforms the relationship between Aboriginal and non-Aboriginal peoples. To ensure that the colonial press truly becomes a thing of the past in twenty-first-century Canada, the media must engage in its own acts of reconciliation with Aboriginal peoples.

The media has a role to play in ensuring that public information both for and about Aboriginal peoples reflects their cultural diversity and provides fair and non-discriminatory reporting on Aboriginal issues. This is consistent with Article 16:2 of the *United Nations Declaration on the Rights of Indigenous Peoples*, which says, "States shall take effective measures to ensure that State-owned media duly reflect indigenous cultural diversity." Canada's *Broadcasting Act* (1991) sets out national broadcasting policy for all Canadian broadcasters with regard to Aboriginal peoples. The policy states the need to,

> through its programming and employment opportunities arising out of its operations, serve the needs and interests, and reflect the circumstances and aspirations of Canadian men, women, and children, including equal rights, the linguistic duality and multicultural and multiracial nature of Canadian society, and the special place of aboriginal peoples within that society [S. 3.1.d.iii].

The Act then states a more controversial obligation, that "programming that reflects the aboriginal cultures of Canada should be provided within the Canadian broadcasting system as resources become available for the purpose" (S.3.1.o).[6]

A submission to the federal Task Force on Aboriginal Languages and Cultures in 2004 pointed out deficiencies in the *Broadcasting Act* related to these service provisions for Aboriginal peoples.

> The Act did not enshrine Aboriginal language broadcasting as a priority: instead it noted that ... [S.3.1.d.iii] means that Aboriginal language programming is not recognized nor protected to the same extent as English and French programming ... [and that] the phrase "as resources become available for the purpose" [S.3.1.o] has become a stumbling block for many producers and programmers, linking the availability of Aboriginal language broadcasting to the political process.[7]

The report recommended that the *Broadcasting Act* be revised to address these gaps. As of 2014, these provisions of the Act remain unchanged.

As Canada's national public broadcaster, the Canadian Broadcasting Corporation (CBC/Radio-Canada) is responsible for fulfilling national broadcasting policy. For many years, it has been providing a minimum level of Aboriginal radio and television programming and news in a few specific regions, including some Aboriginal-language programming, especially in northern Canada.

In the Commission's view, the budget cuts to the CBC over the past decade have significantly reduced and further limited its capacity to provide Aboriginal programming and dedicated news coverage of Aboriginal issues, and to increase the number of Aboriginal people in staff and leadership positions. As of March 31, 2014, Aboriginal people made up 1.6% of the CBC workforce, well below the demographic makeup of Aboriginal people, who represent 4.3% of the total Canadian population.[8]

The Aboriginal Peoples Television Network (APTN), an independent, non-profit broadcaster, in part to make up for the programming and scheduling limitations of CBC/Radio-Canada, has taken a leadership role since the 1990s in providing nation-wide programming and news that reflect Aboriginal peoples' perspectives, concerns, and experiences. The APTN has provided an outlet for Aboriginal journalists, producers, directors, writers, artists, and musicians, and it attracts a wide Aboriginal and non-Aboriginal Canadian and international audience.[9] As of 2014, over 75% of APTN employees were Aboriginal, and 28% of its programming was broadcast in various Aboriginal languages.[10] In the Commission's view, the APTN is well positioned to provide media leadership in support of the reconciliation process.

National public and private broadcasters must provide comprehensive and timely information and services to Aboriginal peoples and the Canadian public.

Calls to action:

84) We call upon the federal government to restore and increase funding to the CBC/Radio-Canada, to enable Canada's national public broadcaster to support reconciliation, and be properly reflective of the diverse cultures, languages, and perspectives of Aboriginal peoples, including, but not limited to:

i. Increasing Aboriginal programming, including Aboriginal-language speakers.

ii. Increasing equitable access for Aboriginal peoples to jobs, leadership positions, and professional development opportunities within the organization.

iii. Continuing to provide dedicated news coverage and online public information resources on issues of concern to Aboriginal peoples and all Canadians, including the history and legacy of residential schools and the reconciliation process.

85) We call upon the Aboriginal Peoples Television Network, as an independent non-profit broadcaster with programming by, for, and about Aboriginal peoples, to support reconciliation, including but not limited to:

i. Continuing to provide leadership in programming and organizational culture that reflects the diverse cultures, languages, and perspectives of Aboriginal peoples.

ii. Continuing to develop media initiatives that inform and educate the Canadian public, and connect Aboriginal and non-Aboriginal Canadians.

Educating journalists for reconciliation

In a submission to the Royal Commission on Aboriginal Peoples (RCAP) in 1993, the Canadian Association of Journalists noted, "The country's large newspapers, TV and radio news shows often contain misinformation, sweeping generalizations, and galling stereotypes about Natives and Native affairs.... The result is that most Canadians have little real knowledge of the country's Native peoples, or the issues that affect them."[11] In 1996, the RCAP report noted,

> Public opinion polls in the past few years have consistently shown broad sympathy for Aboriginal issues and concerns, but that support is not very deep. More recent events have brought a hardening of attitudes towards Aboriginal issues in many parts of the country.... This growing hostility can be traced in large part to recent negative publicity over land claims, Aboriginal hunting and fishing rights, and issues of taxation.[12]

More recent studies indicate that this historical pattern persists.[13] Media coverage of Aboriginal issues remains problematic; social media and online commentary are often inflammatory and racist in nature.

In August 2013, Journalists for Human Rights[14] conducted a study of media coverage of Aboriginal issues in Ontario from June 1, 2010, to May 31, 2013. The study found that

1. "the Aboriginal population is widely underrepresented in mainstream media";

2. "when Aboriginal people choose to protest or 'make more noise' the number of stories focused on the community increase[s]"; and

3. "as coverage related to the protests and talks between Aboriginal people and government became more frequent, the proportion of stories with a negative tone correspondingly increased."[15]

Media coverage of residential schools was low. From June 1, 2011, to May 31, 2012, media coverage of Aboriginal issues in Ontario accounted for only 0.23% of all news stories, and, of these, only 3% focused on residential schools. From June 1, 2012, to May 31, 2013, news stories on Aboriginal issues amounted to 0.46% of all news stories, and, of these, 3% focused on deaths in residential schools.[16]

The report included expert opinions on its findings, including those of CBC journalist Duncan McCue, who observed that editorial opinions "are often rooted in century-old stereotypes rather than reality."[17] He pointed out,

> Yes, protests often meet the test of whether a story is 'newsworthy,' because they're unusual, dramatic, or involve conflict. Yes, Aboriginal activists, who understand the media's hunger for drama, also play a role by tailoring protests in ways that guarantee prominent headlines and lead stories. But, does today's front-page news of some traffic disruption in the name of Aboriginal land rights actually have its roots in a much older narrative—of violent and "uncivilized" Indians who represent a threat to 'progress' in Canada? Are attitudes of distrust and fear underlying our decisions to dispatch a crew to the latest Aboriginal blockade? Is there no iconic photo of reconciliation, because no one from the newsrooms believes harmony between Aboriginal peoples and settlers is 'newsworthy'?[18]

Historian J. R. Miller has observed that when conflicts between Aboriginal peoples and the state occurred in places like Oka or Ipperwash Park, for example, "politicians, journalists and ordinary citizens understood neither how nor why the crisis of the moment had arisen, much less how its deep historical roots made it resistant to solutions.... [This] does not bode well for effective public debate or sensible policy-making."[19]

In the Commission's view, the media's role and responsibility in the reconciliation process require journalists to be well informed about the history of Aboriginal peoples and the issues that affect their lives. As we have seen, this is not necessarily the case. Studies of media coverage of conflicts involving Aboriginal peoples have borne this out. In the conflict between some of the descendants of members of the Stony Point Reserve and their supporters and the Ontario Provincial Police in Ipperwash Provincial Park in 1995, which resulted in the death of Dudley George, journalism professor John Miller concludes,

> Much of the opinion—and there was a lot of it—was based not on the facts of the Ipperwash occupation, but on crude generalizations about First Nations people that fit many of the racist stereotypes that ... have [been] identified.... Accurate, comprehensive coverage can promote understanding and resolution, just as inaccurate, incomplete and myopic coverage can exacerbate stereotypes and prolong confrontations.... Reporters are professionally trained to engage in a discipline of

verification, a process that is often mistakenly referred to as "objectivity." But ... research shows that news is not selected randomly or objectively.[20]

Miller discusses nine principles of journalism that journalists themselves have identified as essential to their work. Of those, he says,

> Journalism's first obligation is to the truth.... Journalism does not pursue truth in an absolute or philosophical sense, but it can—and must—pursue it in a practical sense.... Even in a world of expanding voices, accuracy is the foundation upon which everything else is built—context, interpretation, comment, criticism, analysis and debate. The truth, over time, emerges from this forum....

> Its practitioners must be allowed to exercise their personal conscience. Every journalist must have a personal sense of ethics and responsibility—a moral compass. Each of us must be willing, if fairness and accuracy require, to voice differences with our colleagues.... This stimulates the intellectual diversity necessary to understand and accurately cover an increasingly diverse society. It is this diversity of minds and voices, not just numbers, that matters.[21]

With respect to the history and legacy of residential schools, all the major radio and television networks and newspapers covered the events and activities of the Commission. The TRC provided regular information briefings to members of the media who attended the National Events. We discussed earlier how students must not only learn the truth about what happened in the residential schools but also understand the ethical dimensions of this history. So too must journalists.

Many of the reporters who covered the National Events were themselves deeply affected by what they heard from Survivors and their families. Some required the assistance of health-support workers. Some told us in off-the-record conversations that their perspectives on, and understanding of, the impacts of residential schools, and the need for healing and reconciliation, had changed based on their observations and experiences at the National Events.

Call to action:

86) We call upon Canadian journalism programs and media schools to require education for all students on the history of Aboriginal peoples, including the history and legacy of residential schools, the *United Nations Declaration on the Rights of Indigenous Peoples*, Treaties and Aboriginal rights, Indigenous law, and Aboriginal–Crown relations.

Sports: Inspiring lives, healthy communities

The Commission heard from Survivors that the opportunity to play sports at residential school made their lives more bearable and gave them a sense of identity, accomplishment, and pride. At the Alberta National Event, Survivor Theodore (Ted) Fontaine placed a bundle of mementoes into the TRC Bentwood Box as expressions of reconciliation. It included a pair of baseball pants that he had worn at residential school. He said,

> These woollen baseball pants carry a story of their own ... These are the baseball pants that I wore in 1957–58, as a fifteen-year-old incarcerated boy at the Fort Alexander Residential School.... Little did I know that my mom would treasure and keep them as a memento of her youngest boy. When I leave this land, they won't have anywhere else to go, so I hope the Bentwood Box keeps them well....

> When we were little boys at Fort Alexander Residential School, our only chance to play hockey literally did save our lives. A lot of people here will attest to that. As a young man, playing hockey saved me.... And later, playing with the Sagkeeng Old-Timers saved me again.... I came back twenty years later, fifteen years later and started playing with an old-timers hockey team in Fort Alexander.... In 1983, we ended up winning the first World Cup by an Indigenous team, in Munich, Germany.... So I'm including in this bundle a story of the old-timers, a battalion of Anishinaabe hockey players who saved themselves and their friends by winning, not only winning in Munich, Germany, but in three or four other hockey tournaments in Europe.... People ask me, "Why don't you just enjoy life now instead of working so hard on reconciliation and talking about residential schools? What do you expect to achieve?" The answer is "freedom." I am free.[22]

Later that same day, journalist Laura Robinson's expression of reconciliation was a copy of the documentary *FrontRunners*, which she produced for APTN, about some residential school athletes who had made history. She said,

> In 1967, ten teenage First Nations boys, all good students and great runners, ran with the 1967 Pan Am Games torch, from St. Paul, Minnesota, to Winnipeg, a distance of 800 kilometres, which they did successfully.... But the young men who delivered that torch to the stadium were turned away at the door. They were not allowed in to watch those games. They were not allowed to run that last 400 metres. One of them told me that he remembered being turned around, [and] put back on the bus to residential school.... In 1999, Winnipeg hosted the Pan Am Games again and the organizers realized what had happened. They tracked down the original runners, apologized, and thirty-two years later, as men in their fifties, those runners finished that 400 metres and brought the torch in....

Sport is a place that we speak a universal language—a language of shared passion for moving our bodies through time and space, with strength and skill. This summer [2014], Regina will host the North American Indigenous Games.... Let us all hope and commit to reconcile divisiveness, racism, and stereotypes through the world of sport, and support each and every young person attending those games. Because they are the frontrunners of the future.[23]

Such stories are an indication that the rich history of Aboriginal peoples' contributions to sport needs to become part of Canadian sport history.

On November 18, 2014, we attended an event hosted by the Law Society of Upper Canada to celebrate the first time that an Aboriginal community—the Mississaugas of the New Credit First Nation—was to be a host nation for the Pan-Parapan American Games, held in Toronto in July and August 2015. The 1967 torchbearers attended and were honoured in a traditional blanketing ceremony.[24]

Calls to action:

87) We call upon all levels of government, in collaboration with Aboriginal peoples, sports halls of fame, and other relevant organizations, to provide public education that tells the national story of Aboriginal athletes in history.

88) We call upon all levels of government to take action to ensure long-term Aboriginal athlete development and growth, and continued support for the North American Indigenous Games, including funding to host the games and for provincial and territorial team preparation and travel.

Aboriginal youth today face many barriers to leading active, healthy lives in their communities. They lack opportunities to pursue excellence in sports. There is little access to culturally relevant traditional sports activities that strengthen Aboriginal identity and instill a sense of pride and self-confidence. A lack of resources, sports facilities, and equipment limits their ability to play sports. Racism remains an issue. Aboriginal girls face the extra barrier of gender discrimination.[25]

Despite the many achievements of individual Indigenous athletes, too many Aboriginal youth remain excluded from community-based sports activities and the pursuit of excellence in sport. The *Physical Activity and Sport Act* (2003) set out the federal government's sport policy regarding the full and fair participation of all Canadians in sport, and mandated the minister to "facilitate the participation of under-represented groups in the Canadian sport system" (S.5.m). However, the Act made no specific reference to Aboriginal peoples.[26]

Call to action:

89) We call upon the federal government to amend the *Physical Activity and Sport Act* to support reconciliation by ensuring that policies to promote physical activity as a fundamental element of health and well-being, reduce barriers to sports participation, increase the pursuit of excellence in sport, and build capacity in the Canadian sport system, are inclusive of Aboriginal peoples.

In 2005, Sport Canada developed the Aboriginal Peoples' Participation in Sports Policy, which recognized the unique circumstances of Aboriginal peoples and the role of sport as a vehicle for individual and community health and cultural revitalization. It recognized that Aboriginal peoples have their own culturally diverse traditional knowledge and cultural teachings of play, games, and sports.[27] However, no action plan was subsequently developed to implement the policy.[28]

In 2011, in preparation for revising the 2002 Canadian Sport Policy (CSP), Sport Canada conducted a series of consultations across the country, including a roundtable on "Sport and Aboriginal Peoples." The roundtable summary report noted,

> Participants believe that the needs and issues of Aboriginal Peoples were not adequately reflected in the 2002 CSP.... The feeling among the participants was that the previous policy had "no teeth." ... The new CSP should acknowledge the unique identity of Aboriginal Peoples, what Aboriginal Peoples can contribute to Canadian sport ... and make a clear commitment to action. The CSP can support sport for Aboriginal Peoples by reflecting Aboriginal culture and realities, cross-cultural issues between Aboriginal and non-Aboriginal Peoples, and an understanding of the motivation behind the interest of Aboriginal Peoples in sport.... If the new policy doesn't reflect the needs and issues of Aboriginal sport, then it will not be relevant to the Aboriginal population.... It would be important to recognize that the barriers to sport extend beyond a lack of resources and gaps and weaknesses in the sport system. Aboriginal peoples are also affected by issues of identity and historical trauma.[29]

Despite this roundtable report based on the 2011 consultation, the Commission notes that the subsequent Canadian Sport Policy released in 2012 contains no specific references to Aboriginal peoples.[30]

Call to action:

90) We call upon the federal government to ensure that national sports policies, programs, and initiatives are inclusive of Aboriginal peoples, including, but not limited to, establishing:

   i. In collaboration with provincial and territorial governments, stable funding for, and access to, community sports programs that reflect the diverse cultures and traditional sporting activities of Aboriginal peoples.

   ii. An elite athlete development program for Aboriginal athletes.

   iii. Programs for coaches, trainers, and sports officials that are culturally relevant for Aboriginal peoples.

   iv. Anti-racism awareness and training programs.

The 2010 Winter Olympics in Vancouver, British Columbia, were held on the traditional territories of the Squamish, Musqueam, Tsleil-Waututh, and Lil'wat peoples, and they were an integral part of the event. In the spirit of reconciliation, which aligns easily with the spirit of the games themselves, the four Host First Nations and the Vancouver Olympic Committee formed a partnership to ensure that Indigenous peoples were full participants in the decision-making process—a first in Olympic history. At the opening ceremonies and throughout the games, territorial protocols were respected, and the four Host First Nations and other Indigenous peoples from across the province were a highly visible presence at various Olympic venues.

Call to action:

91) We call upon the officials and host countries of international sporting events such as the Olympics, Pan Am, and Commonwealth games to ensure that Indigenous peoples' territorial protocols are respected, and local Indigenous communities are engaged in all aspects of planning and participating in such events.

Corporate sector: Land, sustainability, and economic development

Survivors and their family members told us that their hope for the future lies in reclaiming and regenerating their own cultures, spirituality, laws, and ways of life, which are deeply connected to their homelands. Indigenous nations are already doing this work in their communities, despite the many challenges they face. At the TRC's Traditional Knowledge Keepers Forum, Elder Dave Courchene said,

> As people who have gained this recognition to be Knowledge Keepers for our people, we accept that work in the most humble way.... It's going to be the spirit of our ancestors, the spirit that's going to help us to reclaim our rightful place in our homeland. We do have a lot of work and there's certainly a lot of challenges,

but with the help of the spirit, we will overcome [them].... We've arrived in a time of great change and great opportunity ... We are the true leaders of our homeland and they cannot take that away from us, and they never will because our Creator put us here. This is our homeland and we have a sacred responsibility to teach all those that have come to our homeland how to be proper human beings because we have all been given original instructions on how to be a human being. We have great responsibilities as people to take care of the Earth, to speak on behalf of Mother Earth. That is our responsibility and that's the kind of leadership that we must reflect as a people.[31]

That same day, Chief Ian Campbell of the Squamish Nation said,

I want to acknowledge my grandparents and my mentors for their generosity in teaching us our connections to our lands and our territories. Right now we're preparing back home for a canoe journey, as our young people are training to represent our people on their journey to Bella Bella in a couple of weeks.... A number of families are travelling all up and down the coast to celebrate the resurgence of our identity, of our culture.[32]

In the face of global warming, growing economic inequities, and conflicts over large-scale economic development projects, there is an emerging consensus that the land that sustains all of us must be protected for future generations. In the wake of the Supreme Court of Canada *Tsilhqot'in* decision, Aboriginal peoples, corporations, and governments must find new ways to work together. Speaking to local community leaders at a convention of the Union of British Columbia Municipalities in September 2014, Tsilhqot'in Chief Percy Guichon said,

We do live side-by-side and we need to work on a relationship to create or promote a common understanding among all our constituents ... We need to find the best way forward to consult with each other, regardless of what legal obligations might exist. I mean, that's just neighbourly, right? ... We share a lot of common interests in areas like resource development. We need to find ways to work together, to support one another on these difficult topics.[33]

In 1977, the *Report of the Mackenzie Valley Pipeline Inquiry* recommended that a proposed natural gas pipeline down the Mackenzie Valley in the Northwest Territories not be built before Aboriginal land claims in the region were resolved and environmental concerns were addressed. Justice Thomas Berger, who led the inquiry, identified the potentially devastating consequences that building a pipeline through the North would have for Dene and Inuvialuit peoples and for the fragile ecosystems. His observations, made almost forty years ago, foreshadowed similar controversies and conflicts over proposed pipelines still occurring in various regions of Canada as the TRC prepared this final report.[34]

The political and legal landscape has shifted significantly since Justice Berger issued his report in 1977. As Canada maps its economic future in regions covered by historical Treaties, modern land claims agreements, and unceded Aboriginal title, governments and industry must now recognize that accommodating the rights of Aboriginal peoples is paramount to Canada's long-term economic sustainability. Governments aim to secure the economic stability and growth necessary to ensuring prosperity for all Canadians.

Corporations invest time and resources in developing large-scale projects that create jobs and aim to produce profits for their shareholders. Although the corporate sector is not a direct party to the negotiation of Treaties and land claims agreements, industry and business play an extremely significant role in how the economic, social, and cultural aspects of reconciliation are addressed, including the extent to which opportunities and benefits are truly shared with Indigenous peoples and the environment of traditional homelands is safeguarded.

The 1996 *Report of the Royal Commission on Aboriginal Peoples* noted that, historically, land and resource development activities, such as hydroelectric dams, mines, and agricultural and urban development, have had many adverse impacts on Aboriginal communities. Communities were not consulted before they were relocated from their vast traditional territories to much smaller, more remote, and more crowded reserves to make way for government and industrial land and resource development projects.

Even when they were not relocated, Aboriginal peoples were economically marginalized in their own homelands when irreversible environmental damage was done in the name of 'progress.' All too often, economic development has disrupted Indigenous peoples' cultural, spiritual, and economic ties to the land, resulting in the devastation of traditional economies and self-sufficiency, community trauma, public welfare dependency, and poor health and socio-political outcomes.[35]

In the post-RCAP period, the Supreme Court of Canada has developed a body of law on the federal, provincial, and territorial governments' duty to consult with Aboriginal peoples where land and resource development might infringe on their Aboriginal or Treaty rights.[36] The court has ruled that governments can still infringe on Aboriginal rights if it can demonstrate that it is in the broader public interest to do so. In the *Delgamuukw* case, the court described the nature of that public interest:

> [T]he development of agriculture, forestry, mining and hydroelectric power, the general economic development of the interior of British Columbia, protection of the environment or endangered species, the building of infrastructure and the settlement of foreign populations to support those aims, are the kinds of objectives that are consistent with this purpose and, in principle, can justify the infringement of aboriginal title.[37]

Governments must also demonstrate that any infringement of Aboriginal rights is consistent with the Crown's fiduciary duty towards Aboriginal peoples and upholds the honour of the Crown. To meet these legal obligations, governments in all jurisdictions have developed Aboriginal consultation policies.

Although the court has ruled that the duty to consult rests solely with governments, it has also said that "the Crown may delegate procedural aspects of consultation to industry proponents seeking a particular development."[38] On a practical level, the business risks associated with legal uncertainty created by the duty to consult have motivated industry proponents to negotiate with Aboriginal communities in order to establish a range of mechanisms designed to ensure that Aboriginal peoples benefit directly from economic development projects in their traditional territories. These may include, for example, joint venture business partnerships; impact and benefit agreements; revenue-sharing agreements; and education, training, and job opportunities.[39]

Between 2012 and 2014, several reports highlighted the fact that Canada is once again facing significant challenges and potential opportunities related to land and resource development. Economic reconciliation will require finding common ground that balances the respective rights, legal interests, and needs of Aboriginal peoples, governments, and industry in the face of climate change and competitive global markets. In addition to the concrete remedial measures required, these reports emphasized that so-called soft skills—establishing trust, engaging communities, resolving conflicts, and building mutually beneficial partnerships—are important to advancing reconciliation.

In 2012, Canada's Public Policy Forum, a non-profit organization, held a series of six regional dialogues across the country, bringing together Aboriginal leaders; senior federal, provincial, and territorial government officials; and representatives from industry, business, and financial institutions. The dialogues were used to discuss issues, identify best practices, and make recommendations for action on how to ensure that Aboriginal communities benefit from large-scale resource development projects.

The resulting report, "Building Authentic Partnerships: Aboriginal Participation in Major Resource Development Opportunities," identified five key opportunities for action: (1) developing authentic partnerships among Aboriginal communities, industry, governments, and academic institutions by building trust; (2) developing human capital by removing barriers to education, training, and skills development for Aboriginal entrepreneurs, workers, and leaders; (3) enhancing community control over decision making; (4) promoting entrepreneurship and business development; and (5) increasing financial participation.[40] The report concluded,

> Natural resource companies are recognizing that their operational success relies on strong, authentic community engagement. Private sector initiatives have already demonstrated positive examples in areas such as revenue sharing, skills

training, and business development for Aboriginal communities. Now corporations and governments need to build on these successes to keep up with the rapid pace of development, moving beyond superficial consultations toward genuine engagement. Aboriginal communities must also play a leadership role to help forge these relationships, to develop local and adaptive solutions that will be essential to success.[41]

In November 2013, after eight months of consultations with representatives from Aboriginal communities, industry, and local and provincial governments in British Columbia and Alberta, Douglas Eyford, Canada's special representative on West Coast energy infrastructure, issued his report to the prime minister. Entitled "Forging Partnerships, Building Relationships: Aboriginal Canadians and Energy Development," it focused on Aboriginal–Crown relations in the context of proposed energy infrastructure projects in British Columbia. He noted that although there are many differences among Aboriginal representatives, there was general consensus that development projects must respect constitutionally protected Aboriginal rights, involve Aboriginal communities in decision making and project planning, and mitigate environmental risks.[42]

Eyford made recommendations for taking action in three key areas: building trust, fostering inclusion, and advancing reconciliation. He noted in particular that "Aboriginal communities view natural resource development as linked to a broader reconciliation agenda."[43] This is consistent with the Commission's view that meaningful reconciliation cannot be limited to the residential school legacy, but must become the ongoing framework for resolving conflicts and building constructive partnerships with Aboriginal peoples.

In December 2013, a group of current and former high-profile leaders from Aboriginal communities, business, banking, environment organizations, and federal and provincial governments released a report, "Responsible Energy Resource Development in Canada," which summarizes the results of a year-long dialogue. They concluded that Canada is facing an "energy resource development gridlock." In their view, the potential economic and social benefits derived from the exploitation of Canada's rich natural resources must be weighed against the potential risks to Aboriginal communities and their traditional territories, and must also address broader environmental concerns associated with global warming.[44] They emphasized that there are significant barriers to reconciliation, including conflicting values, lack of trust, and differing views on how the benefits of resource development should be distributed and adverse effects be mitigated.[45]

The report identified four principles for moving forward on responsible energy resource development: (1) forging and nurturing constructive relationships, (2) reducing cumulative social and environmental impacts, (3) ensuring the continuity of cultures and traditions, and (4) sharing the benefits fairly.[46]

Writing about the 2014 Supreme Court of Canada decision in *Tsilhqot'in Nation v. British Columbia*, Kenneth Coates, Canada Research Chair in Regional Innovation at the University of Saskatchewan, and Dwight Newman, law professor and Canada Research Chair in Indigenous Rights in Constitutional and International Law at the University of Saskatchewan, concluded that although many challenges and barriers to reconciliation remain,

> [w]hat the Supreme Court of Canada has highlighted at a fundamental level is that Aboriginal communities have a right to an equitable place at the table in relation to natural resource development in Canada. Their empowerment through *Tsilhqot'in* and earlier decisions has the potential to be immensely exciting as a means of further economic development in Aboriginal communities and prosperity for all.... [T]he time is now for governments, Aboriginal communities, and resource sector companies to work together to build partnerships for the future.... We need to keep building a national consensus that responsible resource development that takes account of sustainability issues and that respects Indigenous communities, contributes positively—very positively—to Canada and its future.[47]

Internationally, there is a growing awareness in the corporate sector that the *United Nations Declaration on the Rights of Indigenous Peoples* is an effective framework for industry and business to establish respectful relationships and work collaboratively with Indigenous peoples. In 2013, the United Nations Global Compact published a business guide that sets out practical actions that corporations and businesses can undertake in compliance with the *Declaration*. It notes,

> Business faces both challenges and opportunities when engaging with indigenous peoples. When businesses collaborate with indigenous peoples, they are often able to achieve sustainable economic growth, for example, by optimizing ecosystem services and harnessing local or traditional knowledge. Positive engagement with indigenous peoples can also contribute to the success of resource development initiatives—from granting and maintaining social licenses to actively participating in business ventures as owners, contractors and employees. Failing to respect the rights of indigenous peoples can put businesses at significant legal, financial and reputational risk.... Continuing dialogue between business and indigenous peoples can potentially strengthen indigenous peoples' confidence in partnering with business and building healthy relationships.[48]

In the Commission's view, sustainable reconciliation on the land involves realizing the economic potential of Indigenous communities in a fair, just, and equitable manner that respects their right to self-determination. Economic reconciliation involves working in partnership with Indigenous peoples to ensure that lands and resources within their traditional territories are developed in culturally respectful ways that fully recognize Treaty and Aboriginal rights and title.

Establishing constructive, mutually beneficial relationships and partnerships with Indigenous communities will contribute to their economic growth, improve community health and well-being, and ensure environmental sustainability, which will ultimately benefit Indigenous peoples and all Canadians. Unlike with the residential schools of the past, where Aboriginal peoples had no say in the design of the system and no ability to protect their children from intrinsic harms, First Nations, Inuit, and Métis peoples today want to manage their own lives. In terms of the economy, this autonomy means participation on their own terms. They want to be part of the decision-making process. They want their communities to benefit if large-scale economic projects come into their territories. They want to establish and develop their own businesses in ways that are compatible with their identity, cultural values, and worldviews as Indigenous peoples. They want opportunities to work for companies that are proactively addressing systemic racism and inequity. Corporations can demonstrate leadership by using the *Declaration* as a reconciliation framework.

Call to action:

92) We call upon the corporate sector in Canada to adopt the *United Nations Declaration on the Rights of Indigenous Peoples* as a reconciliation framework and to apply its principles, norms, and standards to corporate policy and core operational activities involving Indigenous peoples and their lands and resources. This would include, but not be limited to, the following:

    i. Commit to meaningful consultation, building respectful relationships, and obtaining the free, prior, and informed consent of Indigenous peoples before proceeding with economic development projects.

    ii. Ensure that Aboriginal peoples have equitable access to jobs, training, and education opportunities in the corporate sector, and that Aboriginal communities gain long-term sustainable benefits from economic development projects.

    iii. Provide education for management and staff on the history of Aboriginal peoples, including the history and legacy of residential schools, the *United Nations Declaration on the Rights of Indigenous Peoples,* Treaties and Aboriginal rights, Indigenous law, and Aboriginal–Crown relations. This will require skills-based training in intercultural competency, conflict resolution, human rights, and anti-racism.

We are all Treaty people: Communities, alliances, and hope

The Commission believes that reconciliation cannot be left up to governments, the courts, and churches alone. There must also be dialogue and action in communities across the country. Reconciliation must happen across all sectors of Canadian society. Canadians still have much to learn from each other. Past generations of newcomers faced injustices and prejudices similar to those experienced by the residential school students and their families. More recent immigrants have struggled with racism and misconceptions as they come to take their place in the Canadian nation.

Despite the many barriers to reconciliation, this Commission remains cautiously optimistic. At the Alberta National Event in March 2014, TRC Honorary Witness Wab Kinew spoke about the changes that are already happening across this land that give rise to hope. He began by explaining that all day he had been carrying with him

> a ceremonial pipe, a sacred pipe, which when you bind the two sides together—the stem and the bowl—it offers us a model of reconciliation, of two forces coming together to be more powerful than they were otherwise. So it's important for me to come up here before you all and to speak Anishnaabemowin, and a little bit of Lakota, and to carry a pipe because it sends a message. It sends a message to those who designed the residential school system, that you have failed. We were abused. Our languages were assaulted. Our families were harmed, in some cases, irreparably. But we are still here. We are still here. So in honour of my late father, Tobasonakwut, a Survivor of St. Mary's Residential School in Rat Portage, Ontario, I wanted to say that. I so wish that he could have seen this—the final event of the Truth and Reconciliation Commission—so that he could see how this country has changed. How when he was a child, he was told that he was a savage. He was told that he was nothing. He was assaulted, taken away from his family, taken away from his father's trapline. To see the change that has happened, where today in Canada, there are tens of thousands of people from all walks of life gathering together to set that right and to stand up for justice for Indigenous peoples.
>
> The world has changed in another way as well; the old dichotomy of white people versus Indians no longer applies. Look around at Canada today. There are the descendants of Europeans. There are the descendants of Indigenous peoples. But there are also the descendants of Arab nations, of Iran, of the Slavic nations, of Africa, of the Caribbean, Southeast Asian, Chinese, and Japanese peoples. The challenge of reconciliation may have begun between Indigenous peoples and Europeans, but now the project of reconciliation will be undertaken by the children of all those nations that I just mentioned. And though the world has changed, and Canada has changed, we still have a long way to go…. We are all in this together. Let us commit to removing the political, economic, and social barriers that prevent the full realization of that vision [of

reconciliation] on these lands. Let us raise up the residential school Survivors, and their example of courage, grace, and compassion, in whose footsteps we walk towards that brighter day.[49]

At the community level, where contact between Aboriginal and non-Aboriginal peoples is often minimal or marred by distrust and racism, establishing respectful relationships involves learning to be good neighbours. This means being respectful—listening to, and learning from, each other; building understanding; and taking concrete action to improve relationships. At the Victoria Regional Event, intergenerational Survivor Victoria Wells said,

> I'll know that reconciliation is happening in Canadian society when Canadians, wherever they live, are able to say the names of the tribes with which they're neighbours; they're able to pronounce names from the community, or of people that they know, and they're able to say "hello" [and] "goodbye" in the language of their neighbours.... That will show me manners. That will show me that they've invested in finding out the language of the land [on] which they live ... because the language comes from the land ... The language is very organic to where it comes from, and the invitation to you is to learn that, and to be enlightened by that, and to be informed by [our] ways of thinking, and knowing, and seeing, and understanding. So that, to me, is reconciliation.[50]

Former public school teacher Lynne Phillips cautioned that establishing trust will be one of the major challenges of the reconciliation process.

> I really understand the reticence of some First Nations people about wanting to accept offers of friendship and possibilities of interaction. I understand why that is and I hope that in time we will be able to gain trust and some kind ways of interacting with one another that will be mutually beneficial.... I think we're moving.... I think civil society, non-governmental organizations, church organizations, Aboriginal organizations are moving in the direction of openness ... and I think we have a long ways to go.[51]

In July 2013, at the Community Hearing in Maskwacis (formerly Hobbema), Alberta, at the former site of the Ermineskin Residential School, Professor Roger Epp said that over the years his Cree students had helped him to understand

> what it was that a fourth-generation grandson of settler people needed to know in order to live here ... with a sense of memory and care and obligation. For I too have ancestors buried on Treaty 6 land.... I learned from a student from Hobbema that we're all Treaty people here.... A Treaty is a relationship after all, and we live here on the basis of an agreement signed in 1876, 1877—the first time, not very far from where my settler ancestors homesteaded.... While it is good for national leaders to make public apologies, the work of reconciliation is not just for governments. Actually, I don't think they're very good at it. The work of reconciliation is work for neighbours.... I think the words [of the

apology] were sincere, but they were not enough. They did not change relationships, not enough.[52]

We also heard that day from Mayor Bill Elliot, from the nearby city of Wetaskiwin.
He explained that prior to the TRC's Community Hearing, he, along with Grade Ten
students and others from Hobbema and Wetaskiwin, had attended a workshop with
Survivors. Listening to their residential school experiences helped those who attended
to begin to understand how deeply the residential schools had scarred Survivors, their
families, and the whole community.

> I think it helped the people of Wetaskawin come to an understanding of some
> of the trials and tribulations that our neighbours to the south have been going
> through all their lives.... We are working on a healing journey between the City of
> Wetaskiwin and the Cree First Nations.... As you come into Wetaskiwin from the
> south, you will see that our [city] sign is in Cree syllabics as well—that welcomes
> you.... We still have a long way to go. We are taking baby steps in the healing
> process. But we are working together for better communities, to understand and
> respect the differences and similarities in our cultures.[53]

At the Alberta National Event in 2014, Mayor Elliot, who was also inducted as a TRC
Honorary Witness, offered an expression of reconciliation.

> Our community is trying to learn more about the Survivors and the residen-
> tial schools. Our schools, churches, and community have made cupcakes and
> birthday cards for the big birthday party tomorrow. Members of our community
> have been here for the last two days.... They are very, very supportive and they
> want to learn. We are trying to learn more about and understand the effects of
> residential schools and our friends from Maskwacis because we want to be good
> neighbours.[54]

The Cities of Vancouver, Toronto, Edmonton, and Calgary have also issued procla-
mations declaring a year of reconciliation. City officials committed to a variety of initiatives, including educating their own managers and staff about residential schools.
For example, at the Alberta National Event, Edmonton mayor Don Iveson declared
a Year of Reconciliation in the city. He committed to three projects: educating city
staff about residential schools, creating more opportunities for Aboriginal cultural
events, and developing an Aboriginal youth initiative. One year later, the city brought
Aboriginal and non-Aboriginal youth together with city managers to participate in
leadership training on reconciliation together. Mike Chow, the director of Aboriginal
and multicultural relations for the city, said, "We needed something that would jolt
our senior leadership. You can't force reconciliation or take a powerful idea and hope
that a person will change in a year. We're laying the groundwork with this year of reconciliation, so the journey for people will be ongoing."[55]

In 2014, Vancouver went a step further, declaring that it was now a "City of
Reconciliation," and it has established a long-term framework for partnership and
relationship building with the Musqueam, Squamish, and Tsleil-Waututh Nations

and urban Aboriginal people.[56] At the British Columbia National Event, TRC Honorary Witness Mayor Gregor Robertson said,

> We are blessed to have so many different cultures in this place, and all of us who come from afar ... have been incredibly lucky to be able to come to this place. Many of us come from families, from clans, from cultures that were wiped out, that had to leave. We were forced off our territories, and somehow we've managed to make a home here. That's largely because of those First Nations ancestors who welcomed us ... who made it possible for refugees, for people of broken cultures all over the world to settle here, to stay here, even though our predecessors and our ancestors turned it right around and terrible things have happened. I think the strength that is in Aboriginal peoples across Canada is something for the world to learn from, something that we can apply to the big decisions that we have to make in our governments, our communities, our cities.
>
> When I hear the strength in Survivors, when I hear the phrase "brave children," when I think about brave Elders, I think "brave culture"—that bravery and that determination to learn from this past and to make the best decisions about how we look after each other, how we take care of each other, and those that need that help the most.... [It is important] that we lift each other up, that we take care of the land and the sea that we inherited for the generations to come.[57]

Intergenerational youth across cultures

At the British Columbia National Event, the Commission, in partnership with the Inspirit Foundation, hosted a Youth Panel, "Be the Change: Young People Healing the Past and Building the Future." In this cross-cultural dialogue, youth leaders described the intergenerational impacts of human rights violations such as the residential schools, the Holocaust, Canada's internment of Japanese Canadians during World War Two, and the head tax imposed on Chinese immigrants to Canada. They spoke about community and about turning reconciliation into action. Tsilhqot'in intergenerational Survivor Kim Harvey said,

> I encountered many uncomfortable moments trying to explain what happened to my people and why there is so much alcoholism and drug abuse. There is so much focus on all the negative things.... No one talked about the residential schools.... There are so many horrible stereotypes that our young people face every day. I struggle with issues of family, identity, and community every day.... Reconciliation to me comes down to truth, education, and knowledge sharing practices.... Reconciliation is about relationship. To reconcile, I really need to understand what happened to you, who you are, and what, as a community member, I can do to make our community better....

Reconciliation is a shared experience.... The residential schools were done by an outside party ... When people ask "why don't you just get over it?" I find that frustrating because it takes the onus off the shared relationship [as if] somehow this entire country is not involved in the reconciliation process.... That, to me, is a disservice to this nation in terms of reconciliation.... It's everyone's responsibility to educate themselves about what happened.... With relationship comes respect.... What helps young people, Indigenous or not, is to find your role, have adult allies to help you find that role, fulfill your responsibilities within that role, and then be of service to the community.... If we all did that ... to me that would be reconciliation in action.... It's about finding out about your neighbour.[58]

Kevin Takahide Lee, an intergenerational Survivor of the internment of Japanese Canadians during World War Two, said,

I acknowledge that we are on Coast Salish lands. It was also on these very lands here at the PNE [Pacific National Exhibition fairgrounds] that my family was held during the war before being sent to the internment camp. It is my parents and grandparents who are Survivors.... [They] never talked about what happened in the internment camps ... even after the Japanese Canadian redress happened ... [H]earing these stories from our Elders is very rare.... When I was four or five, I came here to the PNE as most families do.... When it came to going inside the barn here, just two doors away, my grandmother would not come in. That's because that livestock building was used to hold her and other women and children during the war for months.... When I was a child, I couldn't comprehend this, but as an adult, I understand.... This is what it means to me, as an intergenerational Survivor. People who I love and admire were wronged, humiliated, and forgotten, and unjustly imprisoned by the country I ... call home.... [The part of the Japanese redress program that worked best] was the investment in communities and culture ... [and the establishment of] the Canadian Race Relations Foundation ... to ensure that this never happened again.... Only when "you" and "me" become "us" and "we" can there be any reconciliation.[59]

Caroline Wong said that as an intergenerational Survivor of the Chinese head tax, which her grandfathers had to pay when they entered Canada from China,

I grew up rejecting the stereotypical [identity] of the Chinese person because I wanted to be as 'white' as possible.... In terms of reconciliation, my grandmother is a warrior ... She's been fighting for head tax redress. In 2006, the federal government offered an apology and compensation for head tax survivors and their spouses, but very few were still living. It was a huge slap in the face for many Survivors like my grandmother and other first-generation Chinese Canadians who suffered the impacts of discrimination.... What is the price you can put on loss of life, loss of land, loss of family, and discrimination and abuse. You can't put a price on these things.... Compensation is only part of the answer.... Reconciliation is not just an apology but a two-way path of apology and forgiveness.... education ... [and] exposing the truth of what happened and making sure it's never forgotten.... Reconciliation starts with youth and building intercultural understanding ... I hope this is the start of many other intercultural dialogues.... We need to understand about residential schools and also what other cultural groups have experienced. I challenge all of you to ask, "What does it mean to be Canadian?" Or, if you're from another place, "What is your role in this community?"[60]

Danny Richmond, an intergenerational Holocaust Survivor, said,

My grandmother and grandfather lived through things in their twenties that I can't even begin to imagine ... For my people, this history is still an open wound ... What can I tell you that will give you understanding of this? ... It's always been part of my life.... Because the Holocaust was at such a widespread global level ... who is the perpetrator? Everyday people were implicated ... and there were systems and nations involved ... so there's no one person I can accept an apology from. The German government has apologized. It's about the reconciliation of trust in humanity that this kind of persecution won't happen again to the Jews or globally.... Reconciliation is about making sure that none of our communities suffer that persecution again ... For me it's about guarding our institutions to make sure they aren't continuing this kind of persecution ... We've had the apology from the government, but how are we checking in to see how we're doing today? ... We need to create a National Day of Reconciliation that deals with these past human rights abuses, and educates [people] about what [what happens when we] dehumanize people. Canada was a safe haven for my family, but it's also a nation with a lot of pain and warts in its background. We shouldn't be afraid to talk about that and to institutionalize the healing process at a national level.[61]

Newcomers to Canada

For new Canadians, many of whom carry their own traumatic memories of colonial violence, racism, and oppression, finding common ground as Treaty people involves learning about the history of Aboriginal peoples and finding ways to build stronger relationships of solidarity with them. The Commission believes there is an urgent need for more dialogue between Aboriginal peoples and new Canadians.

At the forum "From Remembrance to Reconciliation," co-sponsored by the Ontario Human Rights Commission, by Colour of Poverty, Colour of Change, and by the Metro Toronto Chinese and South-East Asian Legal Clinic, and attended by the TRC Commissioners, participants reflected on how their own histories had shaped their understanding of violence, oppression, and racism, the stereotypes they had learned about Aboriginal peoples in Canada, and the challenges and opportunities of building alliances together.

Akua Benjamin, who came from the Caribbean, with its history of slavery, said,

> How is it that our histories ... [have] so many similarities in terms of violence? The violence of slavery is the violence of destruction in Aboriginal communities.... These are societies that are shaped by violence.... My grandmother talked about working in the fields and being beaten ... [and] my mother carried coal on her head as a child ... so we have a lot in common.... How do we reconcile? How do we have those difficult conversations that say that you are implicated in my struggle? You have privilege that I don't. You have an education that I was not privy to.... This is a safe place for us to really have those difficult conversations.[62]

Ali Kazimi said,

> I came [to Canada] from India thirty years ago.... One of the things that became apparent to me right away was that I came [here] with my own baggage of stereotypes [of Aboriginal peoples]. These were defined by what I had seen in Hollywood films and comic books.... I spent a lot of time in Toronto going to soup kitchens, hanging out with people, trying to understand what the current reality is of First Nations people in an urban centre like Toronto. It was an incredible learning experience. It really humbled me. It really opened my eyes.... I remember having those discussions with people who would challenge me, and those challenges were absolutely essential.... That led me to my own question.... How do I fit into this landscape?
>
> Many Canadians feel that Canadian identity and cultural identity is somehow defined by this universal humanism. On the flip side, we have Prime Minister Harper who says Canada has no history of colonialism. They do the same thing. They deny colonialism and racism and [attitudes of] white superiority ... whose legacy we continue to see today.... It's a very toxic legacy.... One of the truths about Canada is that it was created as a white man's country, and this term was used over and over again.... Twenty years ago, I became a Canadian citizen and one of the things that wasn't made clear to me ... was that when we took that oath [of allegiance] we would become party to the Treaties that were signed.... We were given this very uplifting lecture on the rights of Canadian citizenship, but what was excluded was [information] on our responsibility and obligations ... as now being parties to these Treaties.[63]

Winnie Ng said,

> I was born in Hong Kong and came to Canada in 1968.... I landed in Victoria, BC, the oldest Chinatown in the country.... It has been a journey for me as a person of colour, as a person of the non-Indigenous communities ... to learn about the history of this Native land and my own social location and privilege as a member of the newer arrival communities.... From the [Chinese] labour

of the CPR [Canadian Pacific Railway] to the head tax and the *Chinese Exclusion Act*, ... the Chinese, along with Indigenous children, were secluded in the education system for so many years ... There's been a constant narrative of systemic racism, exclusion, and exploitation.... I think [we need to talk about] remembrance, resistance, and reconciliation.[64]

Becoming citizens

In preparing to become Canadian citizens, all immigrants to Canada study a booklet called *Discover Canada*. It explains, "To understand what it means to be Canadian, it is important to know about our three founding peoples—Aboriginal, French and British." It says the following about Aboriginal peoples:

> The ancestors of Aboriginal peoples are believed to have migrated from Asia many thousands of years ago. They were well established here long before explorers from Europe first came to North America. Diverse, vibrant First Nations cultures were rooted in religious beliefs about their relationship to the Creator, the natural environment and each other. Aboriginal and treaty rights are in the Canadian Constitution. Territorial rights were first guaranteed through the Royal Proclamation of 1763 by King George III, and established the basis for negotiating treaties with the newcomers—treaties that were not always fully respected. From the 1800s until the 1980s, the federal government placed many Aboriginal children in residential schools to educate and assimilate them into mainstream Canadian culture. The schools were poorly funded and inflicted hardship on the students; some were physically abused. Aboriginal languages and cultural practices were mostly prohibited. In 2008, Ottawa formally apologized to the former students. In today's Canada, Aboriginal peoples enjoy renewed pride and confidence, and have made significant achievements in agriculture, the environment, business and the arts.[65]

The guide explains the rights and responsibilities of citizenship. In describing Canada's legal system, it states,

> Canadian law has several sources, including laws passed by Parliament and the provincial legislatures, English common law, the civil code of France and the unwritten constitution that we have inherited from Great Britain. Together, these secure for Canadians an 800-year-old tradition of ordered liberty, which dates back to the signing of the Magna Carta in 1215 in England.[66]

Discover Canada ignores Indigenous peoples as being a source of law for Canada, and says that Canada's tradition of an "ordered liberty" is due to England, and not at all to Canada's Aboriginal peoples, who welcomed the European explorers, helped them survive in this climate, guided them throughout the country, and entered into Treaties with them to share their land with the newcomers from Europe.

A new citizenship oath for Canada

The guide includes the Oath of Citizenship to the Queen that all new citizens must currently pledge: "In Canada, we profess our loyalty to a person who represents all Canadians and not to a document such as a constitution, a banner such as a flag, or a geopolitical entity such as a country." The current oath requires new Canadians to pledge as follows: "I swear (or affirm) that I will be faithful and bear true allegiance to Her Majesty Queen Elizabeth II, Queen of Canada, Her Heirs and Successors, and that I will faithfully observe the laws of Canada and fulfill my duties as a Canadian citizen."

Precisely because "we are all Treaty people," Canada's Oath of Citizenship must include a solemn promise to respect Aboriginal and Treaty rights.

Calls to action

93) We call upon the federal government, in collaboration with the national Aboriginal organizations, to revise the information kit for newcomers to Canada and its citizenship test to reflect a more inclusive history of the diverse Aboriginal peoples of Canada, including information about the Treaties and the history of residential schools.

94) We call upon the Government of Canada to replace the Oath of Citizenship with the following:

I swear (or affirm) that I will be faithful and bear true allegiance to Her Majesty Queen Elizabeth II, Queen of Canada, Her Heirs and Successors, and that I will faithfully observe the laws of Canada including Treaties with Indigenous Peoples, and fulfill my duties as a Canadian citizen.

Closing words

On September 22, 2013, the day after the British Columbia National Event, the Commissioners joined 70,000 people gathered in the pouring rain to participate in a Walk for Reconciliation, organized by Reconciliation Canada, a non-profit organization. If one was looking down Georgia Street in downtown Vancouver, a sea of multi-coloured umbrellas was visible as far as the eye could see. Traditional ceremonies and protocols began the walk. Chiefs in regalia, women wrapped in button blankets and cedar capes, and drumming, dancing, and singing accompanied Survivors, their families, and people from multiple faith traditions and all walks of life, who marched together in solidarity. We walked for Survivors and all that they have done to bring the long-hidden story of residential schools to the country's attention. We walked to remember the thousands of children who died in residential schools. We walked to honour all Indigenous peoples as they reclaim and restore their identity, equality, and dignity. We walked to stand up for the transformative social change that is so urgently needed in Canada. And we walked for the uplifting solidarity of being united with tens of thousands of others, all joined together in a new community of common purpose.

Residential school Survivor and Gwawaenuk Elder Chief Dr. Robert Joseph, speaking as Reconciliation Canada's ambassador, has said, "Reconciliation includes anyone with an open heart and an open mind, who is willing to look to the future in a new way. Let us find a way to belong to this time and place together. Our future, and the well-being of all our children, rests with the kind of relationships we build today."[67]

In November 2012, Elders from Indigenous nations and many other cultures gathered for two days in Musqueam territory in Vancouver, British Columbia, to talk about how reconciliation can help Canada move forward. In a statement afterwards, they said,

> As Canadians, we share a responsibility to look after each other and acknowledge the pain and suffering that our diverse societies have endured—a pain that has been handed down to the next generations. We need to right those wrongs, heal together, and create a new future that honours the unique gifts of our children and grandchildren.
>
> How do we do this? Through sharing our personal stories, legends and traditional teachings, we found that we are interconnected through the same mind and spirit. Our traditional teachings speak to acts such as holding one another up, walking together, balance, healing and unity. Our stories show how these teachings can heal their pain and restore dignity. We discovered that in all of our cultural traditions, there are teachings about reconciliation, forgiveness, unity, healing and balance.
>
> We invite you to search in your own traditions and beliefs, and those of your ancestors, to find these core values that create a peaceful harmonious society and a healthy earth.[68]

At the TRC Final Event, held in Ottawa, May 31 to June 3, 2015, there were hopeful signs that Canadians were taking up the responsibility to ensure that reconciliation becomes a reality. A "Declaration of Action" from various charities, foundations, and

philanthropic organizations was offered to the Commission as an expression of reconciliation and placed in the TRC Bentwood Box. Signatories pledged, among other things,

> This is an opportune moment for Canada's philanthropic community to engage
> in and demonstrate leadership on reconciliation. We bring with us our networks,
> our voices, and our resources, along with new ways of thinking and doing our
> work in such areas as: Inclusion, Culture and Language, Health, Housing, Educa-
> tion, Employment, and Environment.

> We are committed to supporting the fulfillment of the vision of Aboriginal
> peoples, to building a fairer and more just country ... We will work, each in our
> own way, and together, towards achieving the goal of reconciliation and, in the
> end, a much stronger, more inclusive Canada....

> We place our Declaration of Action herewith to symbolize that this is concrete
> and will continue. Our signatures are a call to action inviting others to join in
> moving forward in an atmosphere of understanding, dignity, and respect to-
> wards the shared goal of reconciliation.[69]

The TRC Final Event began with another Walk for Reconciliation. Once again, thousands came out to demonstrate their support for and express their commitment to
reconciliation. John Moses, whose father and aunt attended residential school, said
afterward, "It's good to see so many native people from so many different parts of the
country and good to see the non-native supporters and church groups. But I hope it's
not just a come and go. I hope there is some lasting legacy from all this."[70]

Reflecting on his vision for meaningful reconciliation in the coming years, Assembly
of First Nations National Chief Perry Bellegarde writes,

> The issue facing all of us now is our shared future. What is required for real
> reconciliation between First Nations and Canada? I believe that reconciliation
> is about closing the gap—the gap in understanding between First Nations and
> Canadians and the gap in the quality of life between us....

> Our future belongs to the youth and we are the guardians. We must ensure
> that they have access to an education that meets the highest standards and
> provides expertise in modern technologies combined with the wisdom of our
> ancestors so they walk confidently in both worlds. They will learn their lan-
> guages and learn about their rights and the importance of self-determination.
> They will be taught in systems that are fairly funded with the same supports
> that other students enjoy....

> Canadians need education, too. Every citizen should learn our country's true
> shared history, from painful, shameful moments such as the residential schools
> and the Indian Act to uplifting moments such as our original relationship—the
> promises we made to one another to share and live together in mutual respect

and peaceful co-existence. Reconciliation means repairing our relationship by
honouring these original promises.

We must restore that original relationship of respect, partnership and sharing in
the wealth of this land.... We were not meant to be poor in our own homelands....

What will Canada look like if we act on this agenda? We will see justice, respect
and healing for residential school survivors; First Nations thriving and enjoying
the richness of their traditional territories; elders whispering their languages
in the ears of their grandchildren; and the widespread recognition that First
Nations rights are human rights, the rights that Canadians champion around the
world. That is reconciliation.[71]

On June 1, 2015, the day before the TRC released its Summary Report and Calls
to Action, Member of Parliament Romeo Saganash, who is also a Survivor, spoke
in the House of Commons about the importance of seizing the moment to act on
reconciliation.

After the report of the Royal Commission on Aboriginal Peoples almost 20 years
ago, our common history will provide us with yet another moment to restore
harmony among the peoples of this land that we now call Canada. Tomorrow is
that moment. Let us pause for a moment tomorrow and reflect on the way forward. History will have given us yet another occasion. Canadians want change.
Canadians want us to seize the moment. Change and reconciliation go together.

As a survivor, I can appreciate the fundamental importance of the moment we
are about to experience tomorrow. Let us all collectively seize it, and collectively
commit to genuine change in our relations with the first peoples of this country.
Let us set out to do what 148 years of successive governments have not managed
to achieve, and that is reconciliation.

Reconciliation is about healing relationships, building trust, and working out
our differences. It is about redress and respect for the rights of all. Reconciliation
means a meaningful commitment to change, to honesty, and engaging and re-
conceptualizing relationships to create a future of peace, a future of justice, and a
future of renewed hope for all of us. I suggest that it is not possible to conceive of
reconciliation in the absence of justice. Many segments of Canadian society have
been honestly willing to engage in a dialogue to obtain truth, dignity, and above
all, reconciliation....

The adoption of the TRC report, important though it is, would not in itself change
the everyday lives of women, men and children whose experiences it honours
and gives witness to. No. For this, we need the political and constitutional commitment of not only the governments but the support and goodwill of the public,
of all Canadians, to create and implement substantial and meaningful changes

in co-operation, in partnership, with indigenous peoples themselves. We are all in this together.[72]

We, too, believe that Canada is at a critical turning point in the nation's history. The Commission has established guiding principles and a framework for reconciliation. It is now up to Canadians to take action.

The work of the TRC has shown just how difficult the process of truth determination can be. Thousands of Survivors came forward and, in tears and with anger, shared their pain. They showed how humour, perseverance, and resilience got them through the hardest of times, and how life after the schools sometimes just got too hard. They came forward to share their stories, not just to ease their burden but also to try to make things better for their children and their grandchildren.

Reconciliation is going to take hard work. People of all walks of life and at all levels of society will need to be willingly engaged.

Reconciliation calls for personal action. People need to get to know each other. They need to learn how to speak to, and about, each other respectfully. They need to learn how to speak knowledgeably about the history of this country. And they need to ensure that their children learn how to do so as well.

Reconciliation calls for group action. The 2010 Vancouver Olympics Organizing Committee recognized, paid tribute to, and honoured the four Host First Nations at all public events it organized. Clubs, sports teams, artists, musicians, writers, teachers, doctors, lawyers, judges, and politicians need to learn from that example of how to be more inclusive and more respectful, and how to engage more fully in the dialogue about reconciliation.

Reconciliation calls for community action. The City of Vancouver, British Columbia, proclaimed itself the "City of Reconciliation." The City of Halifax, Nova Scotia, holds an annual parade and procession commemorating the 1761 Treaty of Peace and Friendship. Speeches are delivered and everyone who attends is feasted. The City of Wetaskiwin, Alberta, erected a sign at its outskirts with the city's name written in Cree syllabics. Other communities can do similar things.

Reconciliation calls for federal, provincial, and territorial government action.

Reconciliation calls for national action.

The way we govern ourselves must change.

Law must change.

Policies and programs must change.

The way we educate our children and ourselves must change.

The way we do business must change.

Thinking must change.

The way we talk to, and about, each other must change.

All Canadians must make a firm and lasting commitment to reconciliation in order to ensure that Canada is a country where our children and grandchildren can thrive.

Calls to action

In order to redress the legacy of residential schools and advance the process of Canadian reconciliation, the Truth and Reconciliation Commission makes the following Calls to Action.

LEGACY

Child welfare

1) We call upon the federal, provincial, territorial, and Aboriginal governments to commit to reducing the number of Aboriginal children in care by:

    i. Monitoring and assessing neglect investigations.

    ii. Providing adequate resources to enable Aboriginal communities and child-welfare organizations to keep Aboriginal families together where it is safe to do so, and to keep children in culturally appropriate environments, regardless of where they reside.

    iii. Ensuring that social workers and others who conduct child-welfare investigations are properly educated and trained about the history and impacts of residential schools.

    iv. Ensuring that social workers and others who conduct child-welfare investigations are properly educated and trained about the potential for Aboriginal communities and families to provide more appropriate solutions to family healing.

    v. Requiring that all child-welfare decision makers consider the impact of the residential school experience on children and their caregivers.

2) We call upon the federal government, in collaboration with the provinces and territories, to prepare and publish annual reports on the number of Aboriginal children (First Nations, Inuit, and Métis) who are in care, compared with non-Aboriginal children,

as well as the reasons for apprehension, the total spending on preventive and care services by child-welfare agencies, and the effectiveness of various interventions.

3) We call upon all levels of government to fully implement Jordan's Principle.

4) We call upon the federal government to enact Aboriginal child-welfare legislation that establishes national standards for Aboriginal child apprehension and custody cases and includes principles that:

    i. Affirm the right of Aboriginal governments to establish and maintain their own child-welfare agencies.

    ii. Require all child-welfare agencies and courts to take the residential school legacy into account in their decision making.

    iii. Establish, as an important priority, a requirement that placements of Aboriginal children into temporary and permanent care be culturally appropriate.

5) We call upon the federal, provincial, territorial, and Aboriginal governments to develop culturally appropriate parenting programs for Aboriginal families.

Education

6) We call upon the Government of Canada to repeal Section 43 of the *Criminal Code of Canada*.

7) We call upon the federal government to develop with Aboriginal groups a joint strategy to eliminate educational and employment gaps between Aboriginal and non-Aboriginal Canadians.

8) We call upon the federal government to eliminate the discrepancy in federal education funding for First Nations children being educated on reserves and those First Nations children being educated off reserves.

9) We call upon the federal government to prepare and publish annual reports comparing funding for the education of First Nations children on and off reserves, as well as educational and income attainments of Aboriginal peoples in Canada compared with non-Aboriginal people.

10) We call on the federal government to draft new Aboriginal education legislation with the full participation and informed consent of Aboriginal peoples. The new legislation would include a commitment to sufficient funding and would incorporate the following principles:

    i. Providing sufficient funding to close identified educational achievement gaps within one generation.

   ii. Improving education attainment levels and success rates.

   iii. Developing culturally appropriate curricula.

   iv. Protecting the right to Aboriginal languages, including the teaching of Aboriginal languages as credit courses.

   v. Enabling parental and community responsibility, control, and accountability, similar to what parents enjoy in public school systems.

   vi. Enabling parents to fully participate in the education of their children.

   vii. Respecting and honouring Treaty relationships.

11) We call upon the federal government to provide adequate funding to end the backlog of First Nations students seeking a post-secondary education.

12) We call upon the federal, provincial, territorial, and Aboriginal governments to develop culturally appropriate early childhood education programs for Aboriginal families.

Language and culture

13) We call upon the federal government to acknowledge that Aboriginal rights include Aboriginal language rights.

14) We call upon the federal government to enact an Aboriginal Languages Act that incorporates the following principles:

   i. Aboriginal languages are a fundamental and valued element of Canadian culture and society, and there is an urgency to preserve them.

   ii. Aboriginal language rights are reinforced by the Treaties.

   iii. The federal government has a responsibility to provide sufficient funds for Aboriginal-language revitalization and preservation.

   iv. The preservation, revitalization, and strengthening of Aboriginal languages and cultures are best managed by Aboriginal people and communities.

   v. Funding for Aboriginal language initiatives must reflect the diversity of Aboriginal languages.

15) We call upon the federal government to appoint, in consultation with Aboriginal groups, an Aboriginal Languages Commissioner. The commissioner should help promote Aboriginal languages and report on the adequacy of federal funding of Aboriginal-languages initiatives.

16) We call upon post-secondary institutions to create university and college degree and diploma programs in Aboriginal languages.

17) We call upon all levels of government to enable residential school Survivors and their families to reclaim names changed by the residential school system by waiving administrative costs for a period of five years for the name-change process and the revision of official identity documents, such as birth certificates, passports, driver's licenses, health cards, status cards, and social insurance numbers.

Health

18) We call upon the federal, provincial, territorial, and Aboriginal governments to acknowledge that the current state of Aboriginal health in Canada is a direct result of previous Canadian government policies, including residential schools, and to recognize and implement the health-care rights of Aboriginal people as identified in international law, constitutional law, and under the Treaties.

19) We call upon the federal government, in consultation with Aboriginal peoples, to establish measurable goals to identify and close the gaps in health outcomes between Aboriginal and non-Aboriginal communities, and to publish annual progress reports and assess long-term trends. Such efforts would focus on indicators such as: infant mortality, maternal health, suicide, mental health, addictions, life expectancy, birth rates, infant and child health issues, chronic diseases, illness and injury incidence, and the availability of appropriate health services.

20) In order to address the jurisdictional disputes concerning Aboriginal people who do not reside on reserves, we call upon the federal government to recognize, respect, and address the distinct health needs of the Métis, Inuit, and off-reserve Aboriginal peoples.

21) We call upon the federal government to provide sustainable funding for existing and new Aboriginal healing centres to address the physical, mental, emotional, and spiritual harms caused by residential schools, and to ensure that the funding of healing centres in Nunavut and the Northwest Territories is a priority.

22) We call upon those who can effect change within the Canadian health-care system to recognize the value of Aboriginal healing practices and use them in the treatment of Aboriginal patients in collaboration with Aboriginal healers and Elders where requested by Aboriginal patients.

23) We call upon all levels of government to:

    i. Increase the number of Aboriginal professionals working in the health-care field.

ii. Ensure the retention of Aboriginal health-care providers in Aboriginal communities.

iii. Provide cultural competency training for all health-care professionals.

24) We call upon medical and nursing schools in Canada to require all students to take a course dealing with Aboriginal health issues, including the history and legacy of residential schools, the *United Nations Declaration on the Rights of Indigenous Peoples*, Treaties and Aboriginal rights, and Indigenous teachings and practices. This will require skills-based training in intercultural competency, conflict resolution, human rights, and anti-racism.

Justice

25) We call upon the federal government to establish a written policy that reaffirms the independence of the Royal Canadian Mounted Police to investigate crimes in which the government has its own interest as a potential or real party in civil litigation.

26) We call upon the federal, provincial, and territorial governments to review and amend their respective statutes of limitations to ensure that they conform with the principle that governments and other entities cannot rely on limitation defences to defend legal actions of historical abuse brought by Aboriginal people.

27) We call upon the Federation of Law Societies of Canada to ensure that lawyers receive appropriate cultural competency training, which includes the history and legacy of residential schools, the *United Nations Declaration on the Rights of Indigenous Peoples*, Treaties and Aboriginal rights, Indigenous law, and Aboriginal–Crown relations. This will require skills-based training in intercultural competency, conflict resolution, human rights, and anti-racism.

28) We call upon law schools in Canada to require all law students to take a course in Aboriginal people and the law, which includes the history and legacy of residential schools, the *United Nations Declaration on the Rights of Indigenous Peoples*, Treaties and Aboriginal rights, Indigenous law, and Aboriginal–Crown relations. This will require skills-based training in intercultural competency, conflict resolution, human rights, and anti-racism.

29) We call upon the parties and, in particular, the federal government, to work collaboratively with plaintiffs not included in the Indian Residential Schools Settlement Agreement to have disputed legal issues determined expeditiously on an agreed set of facts.

30) We call upon federal, provincial, and territorial governments to commit to eliminating the overrepresentation of Aboriginal people in custody over the next decade, and to issue detailed annual reports that monitor and evaluate progress in doing so.

31) We call upon the federal, provincial, and territorial governments to provide sufficient and stable funding to implement and evaluate community sanctions that will provide realistic alternatives to imprisonment for Aboriginal offenders and respond to the underlying causes of offending.

32) We call upon the federal government to amend the *Criminal Code* to allow trial judges, upon giving reasons, to depart from mandatory minimum sentences and restrictions on the use of conditional sentences.

33) We call upon the federal, provincial, and territorial governments to recognize as a high priority the need to address and prevent Fetal Alcohol Spectrum Disorder (FASD), and to develop, in collaboration with Aboriginal people, FASD preventive programs that can be delivered in a culturally appropriate manner.

34) We call upon the governments of Canada, the provinces, and territories to undertake reforms to the criminal justice system to better address the needs of offenders with Fetal Alcohol Spectrum Disorder (FASD), including:

   i. Providing increased community resources and powers for courts to ensure that FASD is properly diagnosed, and that appropriate community supports are in place for those with FASD.

   ii. Enacting statutory exemptions from mandatory minimum sentences of imprisonment for offenders affected by FASD.

   iii. Providing community, correctional, and parole resources to maximize the ability of people with FASD to live in the community.

   iv. Adopting appropriate evaluation mechanisms to measure the effectiveness of such programs and ensure community safety.

35) We call upon the federal government to eliminate barriers to the creation of additional Aboriginal healing lodges within the federal correctional system.

36) We call upon the federal, provincial, and territorial governments to work with Aboriginal communities to provide culturally relevant services to inmates on issues such as substance abuse, family and domestic violence, and overcoming the experience of having been sexually abused.

37) We call upon the federal government to provide more supports for Aboriginal programming in halfway houses and parole services.

38) We call upon the federal, provincial, territorial, and Aboriginal governments to commit to eliminating the overrepresentation of Aboriginal youth in custody over the next decade.

39) We call upon the federal government to develop a national plan to collect and publish data on the criminal victimization of Aboriginal people, including data related to homicide and family violence victimization.

40) We call on all levels of government, in collaboration with Aboriginal people, to create adequately funded and accessible Aboriginal-specific victim programs and services with appropriate evaluation mechanisms.

41) We call upon the federal government, in consultation with Aboriginal organizations, to appoint a public inquiry into the causes of, and remedies for, the disproportionate victimization of Aboriginal women and girls. The inquiry's mandate would include:

  i. Investigation into missing and murdered Aboriginal women and girls.

  ii. Links to the intergenerational legacy of residential schools.

42) We call upon the federal, provincial, and territorial governments to commit to the recognition and implementation of Aboriginal justice systems in a manner consistent with the Treaty and Aboriginal rights of Aboriginal peoples, the *Constitution Act, 1982*, and the *United Nations Declaration on the Rights of Indigenous Peoples*, endorsed by Canada in November 2012.

RECONCILIATION

Canadian governments and the *United Nations Declaration on the Rights of Indigenous Peoples*

43) We call upon federal, provincial, territorial, and municipal governments to fully adopt and implement the *United Nations Declaration on the Rights of Indigenous Peoples* as the framework for reconciliation.

44) We call upon the Government of Canada to develop a national action plan, strategies, and other concrete measures to achieve the goals of the *United Nations Declaration on the Rights of Indigenous Peoples*.

Royal Proclamation and Covenant of Reconciliation

45) We call upon the Government of Canada, on behalf of all Canadians, to jointly develop with Aboriginal peoples a Royal Proclamation of Reconciliation to be issued by the Crown. The proclamation would build on the Royal Proclamation of 1763 and the Treaty of Niagara of 1764, and reaffirm the nation-to-nation relationship between Aboriginal peoples and the Crown. The proclamation would include, but not be limited to, the following commitments:

    i. Repudiate concepts used to justify European sovereignty over Indigenous lands and peoples such as the Doctrine of Discovery and *terra nullius*.

    ii. Adopt and implement the *United Nations Declaration on the Rights of Indigenous Peoples* as the framework for reconciliation.

    iii. Renew or establish Treaty relationships based on principles of mutual recognition, mutual respect, and shared responsibility for maintaining those relationships into the future.

    iv. Reconcile Aboriginal and Crown constitutional and legal orders to ensure that Aboriginal peoples are full partners in Confederation, including the recognition and integration of Indigenous laws and legal traditions in negotiation and implementation processes involving Treaties, land claims, and other constructive agreements.

46) We call upon the parties to the Indian Residential Schools Settlement Agreement to develop and sign a Covenant of Reconciliation that would identify principles for working collaboratively to advance reconciliation in Canadian society, and that would include, but not be limited to:

    i. Reaffirmation of the parties' commitment to reconciliation.

    ii. Repudiation of concepts used to justify European sovereignty over Indigenous lands and peoples, such as the Doctrine of Discovery and *terra nullius*, and the reformation of laws, governance structures, and policies within their respective institutions that continue to rely on such concepts.

    iii. Full adoption and implementation of the *United Nations Declaration on the Rights of Indigenous Peoples* as the framework for reconciliation.

    iv. Support for the renewal or establishment of Treaty relationships based on principles of mutual recognition, mutual respect, and shared responsibility for maintaining those relationships into the future.

    v. Enabling those excluded from the Settlement Agreement to sign onto the Covenant of Reconciliation.

    vi. Enabling additional parties to sign onto the Covenant of Reconciliation.

47) We call upon federal, provincial, territorial, and municipal governments to repudiate concepts used to justify European sovereignty over Indigenous peoples and lands, such as the Doctrine of Discovery and *terra nullius*, and to reform those laws, government policies, and litigation strategies that continue to rely on such concepts.

Settlement Agreement parties and the *United Nations Declaration on the Rights of Indigenous Peoples*

48) We call upon the church parties to the Settlement Agreement, and all other faith groups and interfaith social justice groups in Canada who have not already done so, to formally adopt and comply with the principles, norms, and standards of the *United Nations Declaration on the Rights of Indigenous Peoples* as a framework for reconciliation. This would include, but not be limited to, the following commitments:

   i. Ensuring that their institutions, policies, programs, and practices comply with the *United Nations Declaration on the Rights of Indigenous Peoples*.

   ii. Respecting Indigenous peoples' right to self-determination in spiritual matters, including the right to practise, develop, and teach their own spiritual and religious traditions, customs, and ceremonies, consistent with Article 12:1 of the *United Nations Declaration on the Rights of Indigenous Peoples*.

   iii. Engaging in ongoing public dialogue and actions to support the *United Nations Declaration on the Rights of Indigenous Peoples*.

   iv. Issuing a statement no later than March 31, 2016, from all religious denominations and faith groups, as to how they will implement the *United Nations Declaration on the Rights of Indigenous Peoples*.

49) We call upon all religious denominations and faith groups who have not already done so to repudiate concepts used to justify European sovereignty over Indigenous lands and peoples, such as the Doctrine of Discovery and *terra nullius*.

Equity for Aboriginal people in the legal system

50) In keeping with the *United Nations Declaration on the Rights of Indigenous Peoples*, we call upon the federal government, in collaboration with Aboriginal organizations, to fund the establishment of Indigenous law institutes for the development, use, and understanding of Indigenous laws and access to justice in accordance with the unique cultures of Aboriginal peoples in Canada.

51) We call upon the Government of Canada, as an obligation of its fiduciary responsibility, to develop a policy of transparency by publishing legal opinions it develops and upon which it acts or intends to act, in regard to the scope and extent of Aboriginal and Treaty rights.

52) We call upon the Government of Canada, provincial and territorial governments, and the courts to adopt the following legal principles:

    i. Aboriginal title claims are accepted once the Aboriginal claimant has established occupation over a particular territory at a particular point in time.

    ii. Once Aboriginal title has been established, the burden of proving any limitation on any rights arising from the existence of that title shifts to the party asserting such a limitation.

National Council for Reconciliation

53) We call upon the Parliament of Canada, in consultation and collaboration with Aboriginal peoples, to enact legislation to establish a National Council for Reconciliation. The legislation would establish the council as an independent, national, oversight body with membership jointly appointed by the Government of Canada and national Aboriginal organizations, and consisting of Aboriginal and non-Aboriginal members. Its mandate would include, but not be limited to, the following:

    i. Monitor, evaluate, and report annually to Parliament and the people of Canada on the Government of Canada's post-apology progress on reconciliation to ensure that government accountability for reconciling the relationship between Aboriginal peoples and the Crown is maintained in the coming years.

    ii. Monitor, evaluate, and report to Parliament and the people of Canada on reconciliation progress across all levels and sectors of Canadian society, including the implementation of the Truth and Reconciliation Commission of Canada's Calls to Action.

    iii. Develop and implement a multi-year National Action Plan for Reconciliation, which includes research and policy development, public education programs, and resources.

    iv. Promote public dialogue, public/private partnerships, and public initiatives for reconciliation.

54) We call upon the Government of Canada to provide multi-year funding for the National Council for Reconciliation to ensure that it has the financial, human, and technical

resources required to conduct its work, including the endowment of a National Reconciliation Trust to advance the cause of reconciliation.

55) We call upon all levels of government to provide annual reports or any current data requested by the National Council for Reconciliation so that it can report on the progress towards reconciliation. The reports or data would include, but not be limited to:

   i. The number of Aboriginal children—including Métis and Inuit children—in care, compared with non-Aboriginal children, the reasons for apprehension, and the total spending on preventive and care services by child-welfare agencies.

   ii. Comparative funding for the education of First Nations children on and off reserves.

   iii. The educational and income attainments of Aboriginal peoples in Canada compared with non-Aboriginal people.

   iv. Progress on closing the gaps between Aboriginal and non-Aboriginal communities in a number of health indicators such as: infant mortality, maternal health, suicide, mental health, addictions, life expectancy, birth rates, infant and child health issues, chronic diseases, illness and injury incidence, and the availability of appropriate health services.

   v. Progress on eliminating the overrepresentation of Aboriginal children in youth custody over the next decade.

   vi. Progress on reducing the rate of criminal victimization of Aboriginal people, including data related to homicide and family violence victimization and other crimes.

   vii. Progress on reducing the overrepresentation of Aboriginal people in the justice and correctional systems.

56) We call upon the prime minister of Canada to formally respond to the report of the National Council for Reconciliation by issuing an annual "State of Aboriginal Peoples" report, which would outline the government's plans for advancing the cause of reconciliation.

Professional development and training for public servants

57) We call upon federal, provincial, territorial, and municipal governments to provide education to public servants on the history of Aboriginal peoples, including the history and legacy of residential schools, the *United Nations Declaration on the Rights of Indigenous Peoples*, Treaties and Aboriginal rights, Indigenous law, and

Aboriginal–Crown relations. This will require skills-based training in intercultural competency, conflict resolution, human rights, and anti-racism.

Church apologies and reconciliation

58) We call upon the Pope to issue an apology to Survivors, their families, and communities for the Roman Catholic Church's role in the spiritual, cultural, emotional, physical, and sexual abuse of First Nations, Inuit, and Métis children in Catholic-run residential schools. We call for that apology to be similar to the 2010 apology issued to Irish victims of abuse and to occur within one year of the issuing of this Report and to be delivered by the Pope in Canada.

59) We call upon church parties to the Settlement Agreement to develop ongoing education strategies to ensure that their respective congregations learn about their church's role in colonization, the history and legacy of residential schools, and why apologies to former residential school students, their families, and communities were necessary.

60) We call upon leaders of the church parties to the Settlement Agreement and all other faiths, in collaboration with Indigenous spiritual leaders, Survivors, schools of theology, seminaries, and other religious training centres, to develop and teach curriculum for all student clergy, and all clergy and staff who work in Aboriginal communities, on the need to respect Indigenous spirituality in its own right, the history and legacy of residential schools and the roles of the church parties in that system, the history and legacy of religious conflict in Aboriginal families and communities, and the responsibility that churches have to mitigate such conflicts and prevent spiritual violence.

61) We call upon church parties to the Settlement Agreement, in collaboration with Survivors and representatives of Aboriginal organizations, to establish permanent funding to Aboriginal people for:

    i. Community-controlled healing and reconciliation projects.

    ii. Community-controlled culture- and language-revitalization projects.

    iii. Community-controlled education and relationship-building projects.

    iv. Regional dialogues for Indigenous spiritual leaders and youth to discuss Indigenous spirituality, self-determination, and reconciliation.

Education for reconciliation

62) We call upon the federal, provincial, and territorial governments, in consultation and collaboration with Survivors, Aboriginal peoples, and educators, to:

    i. Make age-appropriate curriculum on residential schools, Treaties, and Aboriginal peoples' historical and contemporary contributions to Canada a mandatory education requirement for Kindergarten to Grade Twelve students.

    ii. Provide the necessary funding to post-secondary institutions to educate teachers on how to integrate Indigenous knowledge and teaching methods into classrooms.

    iii. Provide the necessary funding to Aboriginal schools to utilize Indigenous knowledge and teaching methods in classrooms.

    iv. Establish senior-level positions in government at the assistant deputy minister level or higher dedicated to Aboriginal content in education.

63) We call upon the Council of Ministers of Education, Canada to maintain an annual commitment to Aboriginal education issues, including:

    i. Developing and implementing Kindergarten to Grade Twelve curriculum and learning resources on Aboriginal peoples in Canadian history, and the history and legacy of residential schools.

    ii. Sharing information and best practices on teaching curriculum related to residential schools and Aboriginal history.

    iii. Building student capacity for intercultural understanding, empathy, and mutual respect.

    iv. Identifying teacher-training needs relating to the above.

64) We call upon all levels of government that provide public funds to denominational schools to require such schools to provide an education on comparative religious studies, which must include a segment on Aboriginal spiritual beliefs and practices developed in collaboration with Aboriginal Elders.

65) We call upon the federal government, through the Social Sciences and Humanities Research Council, and in collaboration with Aboriginal peoples, post-secondary institutions and educators, and the National Centre for Truth and Reconciliation and its partner institutions, to establish a national research program with multi-year funding to advance understanding of reconciliation.

Youth programs

66) We call upon the federal government to establish multi-year funding for community-based youth organizations to deliver programs on reconciliation, and establish a national network to share information and best practices.

Museums and archives

67) We call upon the federal government to provide funding to the Canadian Museums Association to undertake, in collaboration with Aboriginal peoples, a national review of museum policies and best practices to determine the level of compliance with the *United Nations Declaration on the Rights of Indigenous Peoples* and to make recommendations.

68) We call upon the federal government, in collaboration with Aboriginal peoples, and the Canadian Museums Association to mark the 150th anniversary of Canadian Confederation in 2017 by establishing a dedicated national funding program for commemoration projects on the theme of reconciliation.

69) We call upon Library and Archives Canada to:

    i. Fully adopt and implement the *United Nations Declaration on the Rights of Indigenous Peoples* and the *United Nations Joinet-Orentlicher Principles*, as related to Aboriginal peoples' inalienable right to know the truth about what happened and why, with regard to human rights violations committed against them in the residential schools.

    ii. Ensure that its record holdings related to residential schools are accessible to the public.

    iii. Commit more resources to its public education materials and programming on residential schools.

70) We call upon the federal government to provide funding to the Canadian Association of Archivists to undertake, in collaboration with Aboriginal peoples, a national review of archival policies and best practices to:

    i. Determine the level of compliance with the *United Nations Declaration on the Rights of Indigenous Peoples* and the *United Nations Joinet-Orentlicher Principles*, as related to Aboriginal peoples' inalienable right to know the truth about what happened and why, with regard to human rights violations committed against them in the residential schools.

ii. Produce a report with recommendations for full implementation of these international mechanisms as a reconciliation framework for Canadian archives.

Missing children and burial information

71) We call upon all chief coroners and provincial vital statistics agencies that have not provided to the Truth and Reconciliation Commission of Canada their records on the deaths of Aboriginal children in the care of residential school authorities to make these documents available to the National Centre for Truth and Reconciliation.

72) We call upon the federal government to allocate sufficient resources to the National Centre for Truth and Reconciliation to allow it to develop and maintain the National Residential School Student Death Register established by the Truth and Reconciliation Commission of Canada.

73) We call upon the federal government to work with churches, Aboriginal communities, and former residential school students to establish and maintain an online registry of residential school cemeteries, including, where possible, plot maps showing the location of deceased residential school children.

74) We call upon the federal government to work with the churches and Aboriginal community leaders to inform the families of children who died at residential schools of the child's burial location, and to respond to families' wishes for appropriate commemoration ceremonies and markers, and reburial in home communities where requested.

75) We call upon the federal government to work with provincial, territorial, and municipal governments, churches, Aboriginal communities, former residential school students, and current landowners to develop and implement strategies and procedures for the ongoing identification, documentation, maintenance, commemoration, and protection of residential school cemeteries or other sites at which residential school children were buried. This is to include the provision of appropriate memorial ceremonies and commemorative markers to honour the deceased children.

76) We call upon the parties engaged in the work of documenting, maintaining, commemorating, and protecting residential school cemeteries to adopt strategies in accordance with the following principles:

i. The Aboriginal community most affected shall lead the development of such strategies.

ii. Information shall be sought from residential school Survivors and other Knowledge Keepers in the development of such strategies.

   iii. Aboriginal protocols shall be respected before any potentially invasive technical inspection and investigation of a cemetery site.

National Centre for Truth and Reconciliation

77) We call upon provincial, territorial, municipal, and community archives to work collaboratively with the National Centre for Truth and Reconciliation to identify and collect copies of all records relevant to the history and legacy of the residential school system, and to provide these to the National Centre for Truth and Reconciliation.

78) We call upon the Government of Canada to commit to making a funding contribution of $10 million over seven years to the National Centre for Truth and Reconciliation, plus an additional amount to assist communities to research and produce histories of their own residential school experience and their involvement in truth, healing, and reconciliation.

Commemoration

79) We call upon the federal government, in collaboration with Survivors, Aboriginal organizations, and the arts community, to develop a reconciliation framework for Canadian heritage and commemoration. This would include, but not be limited to:

   i. Amending the *Historic Sites and Monuments Act* to include First Nations, Inuit, and Métis representation on the Historic Sites and Monuments Board of Canada and its Secretariat.

   ii. Revising the policies, criteria, and practices of the National Program of Historical Commemoration to integrate Indigenous history, heritage values, and memory practices into Canada's national heritage and history.

   iii. Developing and implementing a national heritage plan and strategy for commemorating residential school sites, the history and legacy of residential schools, and the contributions of Aboriginal peoples to Canada's history.

80) We call upon the federal government, in collaboration with Aboriginal peoples, to establish, as a statutory holiday, a National Day for Truth and Reconciliation to honour Survivors, their families, and communities, and ensure that public commemoration of the history and legacy of residential schools remains a vital component of the reconciliation process.

81) We call upon the federal government, in collaboration with Survivors and their organizations, and other parties to the Settlement Agreement, to commission and install

a publicly accessible, highly visible, Residential Schools National Monument in the city of Ottawa to honour Survivors and all the children who were lost to their families and communities.

82) We call upon provincial and territorial governments, in collaboration with Survivors and their organizations, and other parties to the Settlement Agreement, to commission and install a publicly accessible, highly visible, Residential Schools Monument in each capital city to honour Survivors and all the children who were lost to their families and communities.

83) We call upon the Canada Council for the Arts to establish, as a funding priority, a strategy for Indigenous and non-Indigenous artists to undertake collaborative projects and produce works that contribute to the reconciliation process.

Media and reconciliation

84) We call upon the federal government to restore and increase funding to the CBC/Radio-Canada, to enable Canada's national public broadcaster to support reconciliation, and be properly reflective of the diverse cultures, languages, and perspectives of Aboriginal peoples, including, but not limited to:

   i. Increasing Aboriginal programming, including Aboriginal-language speakers.

   ii. Increasing equitable access for Aboriginal peoples to jobs, leadership positions, and professional development opportunities within the organization.

   iii. Continuing to provide dedicated news coverage and online public information resources on issues of concern to Aboriginal peoples and all Canadians, including the history and legacy of residential schools and the reconciliation process.

85) We call upon the Aboriginal Peoples Television Network, as an independent non-profit broadcaster with programming by, for, and about Aboriginal peoples, to support reconciliation, including but not limited to:

   i. Continuing to provide leadership in programming and organizational culture that reflects the diverse cultures, languages, and perspectives of Aboriginal peoples.

   ii. Continuing to develop media initiatives that inform and educate the Canadian public, and connect Aboriginal and non-Aboriginal Canadians.

86) We call upon Canadian journalism programs and media schools to require education for all students on the history of Aboriginal peoples, including the history and legacy of residential schools, the *United Nations Declaration on the Rights of Indigenous Peoples*, Treaties and Aboriginal rights, Indigenous law, and Aboriginal–Crown relations.

Sports and reconciliation

87) We call upon all levels of government, in collaboration with Aboriginal peoples, sports halls of fame, and other relevant organizations, to provide public education that tells the national story of Aboriginal athletes in history.

88) We call upon all levels of government to take action to ensure long-term Aboriginal athlete development and growth, and continued support for the North American Indigenous Games, including funding to host the games and for provincial and territorial team preparation and travel.

89) We call upon the federal government to amend the *Physical Activity and Sport Act* to support reconciliation by ensuring that policies to promote physical activity as a fundamental element of health and well-being, reduce barriers to sports participation, increase the pursuit of excellence in sport, and build capacity in the Canadian sport system, are inclusive of Aboriginal peoples.

90) We call upon the federal government to ensure that national sports policies, programs, and initiatives are inclusive of Aboriginal peoples, including, but not limited to, establishing:

   i. In collaboration with provincial and territorial governments, stable funding for, and access to, community sports programs that reflect the diverse cultures and traditional sporting activities of Aboriginal peoples.

   ii. An elite athlete development program for Aboriginal athletes.

   iii. Programs for coaches, trainers, and sports officials that are culturally relevant for Aboriginal peoples.

   iv. Anti-racism awareness and training programs.

91) We call upon the officials and host countries of international sporting events such as the Olympics, Pan Am, and Commonwealth games to ensure that Indigenous peoples' territorial protocols are respected, and local Indigenous communities are engaged in all aspects of planning and participating in such events.

Business and reconciliation

92) We call upon the corporate sector in Canada to adopt the *United Nations Declaration on the Rights of Indigenous Peoples* as a reconciliation framework and to apply its principles, norms, and standards to corporate policy and core operational activities involving Indigenous peoples and their lands and resources. This would include, but not be limited to, the following:

i. Commit to meaningful consultation, building respectful relationships, and obtaining the free, prior, and informed consent of Indigenous peoples before proceeding with economic development projects.

ii. Ensure that Aboriginal peoples have equitable access to jobs, training, and education opportunities in the corporate sector, and that Aboriginal communities gain long-term sustainable benefits from economic development projects.

iii. Provide education for management and staff on the history of Aboriginal peoples, including the history and legacy of residential schools, the *United Nations Declaration on the Rights of Indigenous Peoples*, Treaties and Aboriginal rights, Indigenous law, and Aboriginal–Crown relations. This will require skills-based training in intercultural competency, conflict resolution, human rights, and anti-racism.

Newcomers to Canada

93) We call upon the federal government, in collaboration with the national Aboriginal organizations, to revise the information kit for newcomers to Canada and its citizenship test to reflect a more inclusive history of the diverse Aboriginal peoples of Canada, including information about the Treaties and the history of residential schools.

94) We call upon the Government of Canada to replace the Oath of Citizenship with the following:

I swear (or affirm) that I will be faithful and bear true allegiance to Her Majesty Queen Elizabeth II, Queen of Canada, Her Heirs and Successors, and that I will faithfully observe the laws of Canada including Treaties with Indigenous Peoples, and fulfill my duties as a Canadian citizen.

Notes

Introduction

1. TRC, AVS, Alma Mann Scott, Statement to the Truth and Reconciliation Commission of Canada, Winnipeg, Manitoba, 17 June 2010, Statement Number: 02-MB-16JU10-016.
2. Media coverage of the call for an inquiry on missing and murdered Aboriginal women has been extensive. See, for example, CBC News, "Women's Memorial March"; CBC News, "Murdered and Missing"; and Coates, "Aboriginal Women." On economic development issues, see, for example, Lewis, "TransCanada CEO"; Schwartz and Gollom, "NB Fracking Protests"; and MacDonald, "Shale Gas Conflict."
3. On the role of the courts in Aboriginal rights and reconciliation, see Brean, "'Reconciliation' with First Nations." On Aboriginal rights cases, see, for example, CBC News, "6 Landmark Rulings." On day schools litigation, see, for example, CBC News, "Residential School Day Scholars"; and Moore, "Federal Appeal Court." On Sixties Scoop legislation, see, for example, CBC News, "Sixties Scoop Case"; and Mehta, "'Sixties Scoop' Class-Action."
4. Miller, Lethal *Legacy*, vi.
5. TRC, AVS, Mary Deleary, Statement to the Truth and Reconciliation Commission of Canada, Winnipeg, Manitoba, 26 June 2014, Statement Number: SE049.
6. TRC, AVS, Archie Little, Statement to the Truth and Reconciliation Commission of Canada, Victoria, British Columbia, 13 April 2012, Statement Number: SP135.
7. McKay, "Expanding the Dialogue," 107. McKay was the first Aboriginal moderator of the United Church of Canada (1992–1994).
8. TRC, AVS, Jessica Bolduc, Statement to the Truth and Reconciliation Commission of Canada, Edmonton, Alberta, 30 March 2014, Statement Number: ABNE401.
9. Truth and Reconciliation Commission of Canada, *Educating Our Youth*.
10. TRC, AVS, Patsy George, Statement to the Truth and Reconciliation Commission of Canada, Vancouver, British Columbia, 21 September 2013, Statement Number: BCNE404.
11. TRC, AVS, Dave Courchene, Statement to the Truth and Reconciliation Commission of Canada, Winnipeg, Manitoba, 25 June 2014, Statement Number: SE048.
12. For the mandate of the Commission, see Indian Residential Schools Settlement Agreement, "Schedule N." In accordance with the TRC's mandate, the Commission was required to recognize "the significance of Aboriginal oral and legal traditions in its activities," as per Schedule N, 4(d); and to "witness, support, promote and facilitate truth and reconciliation events at both the national and community levels," as per Schedule N, 1(c). The term *witness* "refers to the Aboriginal principle of 'witnessing,'" as per Schedule N, 1(c), n1.

Aboriginal oral history, legal traditions, and the principle of witnessing have deep historical roots and contemporary relevance for reconciliation. Indigenous law was used to resolve family and community conflict, to establish Treaties among various Indigenous nations, and to negotiate nation-to-nation Treaties with the Crown. For a comprehensive history of Aboriginal–Crown Treaty making from contact to the present, see Miller, *Compact, Contract, Covenant*. The Aboriginal principle of witnessing varies among First Nations, Métis, and Inuit peoples. Generally speaking, witnesses are called to be the keepers of history when an event of historic significance occurs. Through witnessing, the event or work that is undertaken is validated and provided legitimacy. The work could not take place without honoured and respected guests to witness it. Witnesses are asked to store and care for the history they witness and to share it with their own people when they return home. For Aboriginal peoples, the act of witnessing these events comes with a great responsibility to remember all the details and be able to recount them accurately as the foundation of oral histories. See Qwul'sih'yah'maht (Thomas), "Honouring the Oral Traditions," 243–244.

13. TRC, AVS, Jim Dumont, Statement to the Truth and Reconciliation Commission of Canada, Winnipeg, Manitoba, 26 June 2014, Statement Number: SE049.

14. TRC, AVS, Wilfred Whitehawk, Statement to the Truth and Reconciliation Commission of Canada, Key First Nation, Saskatchewan, 21 January 2012, Statement Number: SP039.

15. TRC, AVS, Vitaline Elsie Jenner, Statement to the Truth and Reconciliation Commission of Canada, Winnipeg, Manitoba, 16 June 2010, Statement Number: 02-MB-16JU10-131.

16. TRC, AVS, Daniel Elliot, Statement to the Truth and Reconciliation Commission of Canada, Victoria, British Columbia, 13 April 2012, Statement Number: SP135.

17. TRC, AVS, Clement Chartier, Statement to the Truth and Reconciliation Commission of Canada, Saskatoon, Saskatchewan, 22 June 2013, Statement Number: SNE202.

18. TRC, AVS, Steven Point, Statement to the Truth and Reconciliation Commission of Canada, Vancouver, British Columbia, 20 September 2013, Statement Number: BCNE304.

19. TRC, AVS, Merle Nisley, Statement to the Truth and Reconciliation Commission of Canada, Thunder Bay, Ontario, 14 December 2011, Statement Number: 2011-4199.

20. TRC, AVS, Tom Cavanaugh, Statement to the Truth and Reconciliation Commission of Canada, Victoria, British Columbia, 14 April 2012, Statement Number: SP137.

21. TRC, AVS, Ina Seitcher, Statement to the Truth and Reconciliation Commission of Canada, Victoria, British Columbia, 14 April 2012, Statement Number: SP136.

22. TRC, AVS, Evelyn Brockwood, Statement to the Truth and Reconciliation Commission of Canada, Winnipeg, Manitoba, 18 June 2010, Statement Number: SC110.

23. Indian Residential Schools Settlement Agreement, "Schedule N," Principles, 1.

24. Johnston, "Aboriginal Traditions."

25. TRC, AVS, Barney Williams, Statement to the Truth and Reconciliation Commission of Canada, Winnipeg, Manitoba, 26 June 2014, Statement Number: SE049.

26. TRC, AVS, Stephen Augustine, Statement to the Truth and Reconciliation Commission of Canada, Winnipeg, Manitoba, 25 June 2014, Statement Number: SE048.

27. TRC, AVS, Reg Crowshoe, Statement to the Truth and Reconciliation Commission of Canada, Winnipeg, Manitoba, 26 June 2014, Statement Number: SE049.

28. TRC, AVS, Kirby Littletent, Statement to the Truth and Reconciliation Commission of Canada, Regina, Saskatchewan, 16 January 2012, Statement Number: SP035.

29. TRC, AVS, Simone (last name not provided), Statement to Truth and Reconciliation Commission of Canada, Inuvik, Northwest Territories, 1 July 2011, Statement Number: SC092.

30. TRC, AVS, Patrick Etherington, Statement to the Truth and Reconciliation Commission of Canada, Winnipeg, Manitoba, 17 June 2010, Statement Number: SC108.

31. TRC, AVS, Maxine Lacorne, Statement to the Truth and Reconciliation Commission of Canada, Inuvik, Northwest Territories, 29 June 2011, Statement Number: SC090.

32. TRC, AVS, Barney Williams, Statement to the Truth and Reconciliation Commission of Canada, Vancouver, British Columbia, 21 September 2013, Statement Number: BCNE404.

33. TRC, AVS, Honourable Chuck Strahl, Statement to the Truth and Reconciliation Commission of Canada, Winnipeg, Manitoba, 16 June 2010, Statement Number: SC093.

34. TRC, AVS, Archbishop Fred Hiltz, Statement to the Truth and Reconciliation Commission of Canada, Inuvik, Northwest Territories, 1 July 2011, Statement Number: NNE402.

35. TRC, AVS, Anonymous, Statement to the Truth and Reconciliation Commission of Canada, Regina, Saskatchewan, 17 January 2012, Statement Number: SP036.

The challenge of reconciliation

1. TRC, AVS, Ian Campbell, Statement to the Truth and Reconciliation Commission of Canada, Winnipeg, Manitoba, 25 June 2014, Statement Number: SE048.

2. Canada, Debates of the Senate (Hansard), 2nd Session, 40th Parliament, volume 146, issue 45, 11 June 2009.

3. Miller, *Lethal Legacy*, 165.

4. For various perspectives on the events at Oka, see, for example, Alfred, *Heeding the Voices*; Pertusati, *In Defense of Mohawk Land*; Miller, *Lethal Legacy*; and Simpson and Ladner, editors, *This Is an Honour Song*.

5. On the place of media in shaping popular opinion on the role of warriors in conflicts with the state, see Valaskakis, "Rights and Warriors." On warriors and warrior societies in contemporary Indigenous communities, see Alfred and Lowe, "Warrior Societies."

6. Prime Minister Brian Mulroney to Tony Penikett, Government Leader, Government of the Yukon Territory, 15 November 1990, and to Dennis Patterson, Government Leader, Government of the Northwest Territories, 15 November 1990, PCO 2150-1, Identification Number 34788, TRC Document Number TRC3379.

7. Canada, Royal Commission on Aboriginal Peoples, *Report*, volume 5, 2–3, emphasis in original.

8. Canada, Royal Commission on Aboriginal Peoples, *Report*, volume 1, 675–697.

9. Canada, Royal Commission on Aboriginal Peoples, *Report*, volume 1, part 1, chapter 7, 229.

10. Canada, Minister of Indian Affairs and Northern Development, "Gathering Strength."

11. A copy of the "Statement of Reconciliation" is available in Younging, Dewar, and DeGagné, editors, *Response, Responsibility, and Renewal*, 353–355.

12. Assembly of First Nations, "Royal Commission on Aboriginal Peoples at 10 Years," 2.

13. Eyford, "New Direction," 3, 5.

14. Canada, Aboriginal Affairs and Northern Development Canada, "Renewing the Comprehensive Land Claims Policy."

15. Eyford, "New Direction," 29.

16. Eyford, "New Direction," 35.

17. Eyford, "New Direction," 80.

18. United Nations, *Declaration on the Rights of Indigenous Peoples*, Article 43.

19. Anaya, "Right of Indigenous Peoples," 196.

20. Canada, Aboriginal Affairs and Northern Development Canada, "Canada's Statement of Support."

21. Canada, Aboriginal Affairs and Northern Development Canada, "Canada's Statement of Support."

22. United Nations General Assembly, "Outcome Document."

23. Canada, Permanent Mission of Canada to the United Nations, "Canada's Statement on the World Conference."

24. Amnesty International Canada et al., "Canada Uses World Conference."

25. John, "Survival, Dignity, Well-Being," 58. Grand Chief John, an executive member of the First Nations Summit Task Group in British Columbia, participated in the development of the *Declaration*. He is a former co-chair of the North American Indigenous Peoples Caucus and will serve as a North American representative to the United Nations Permanent Forum on Indigenous Issues until 2016. See First Nations Summit, "Grand Chief Edward John."

26. *Tsilhqot'in Nation v. British Columbia*, 2014 SCC 44, para. 73.

27. *Tsilhqot'in Nation v. British Columbia*, 2014 SCC 44, para. 97.

28. Canada, Royal Commission on Aboriginal Peoples, *Report*, volume 1, chapter 16, 695.

29. Canada, Royal Commission on Aboriginal Peoples, *Report*, volume 1, 696, Recommendation 1.16.2.

30. TRC, AVS, Sol Sanderson, Statement to the Truth and Reconciliation Commission of Canada, Winnipeg, Manitoba, 17 June 2010, Statement Number: SC108.

31. Reid, "Roman Catholic Foundations," 5.

32. The Permanent Observer Mission of the Holy See explains its role and function at the United Nations as follows: "The Holy See ... is the central government of the Roman Catholic Church. As such, the Holy See is an institution, which under international law and in practice, has a legal personality that allows it to enter into treaties as the juridical equal of a State.... The Holy See maintains full diplomatic relations with one hundred seventy-seven (177) countries out of the one hundred ninety-three (193) member countries of the UN.... The Holy See enjoys *by its own choice* the status of Permanent Observer at the United Nations, rather than of a full Member. This is due primarily to the desire of the Holy See to obtain absolute neutrality in specific political problems" (emphasis in original). See United Nations Permanent Observer Mission of the Holy See, "Short History."

33. United Nations Permanent Observer Mission of the Holy See, "Statement to Economic and Social Council."

34. For example, in a study of how the doctrine was used to justify colonization, American legal scholar Robert A. Williams Jr. observed that the United States Supreme Court decision issued by Chief Justice John Marshall in 1823 in the case of *Johnson v. McIntosh* 21 US 543 (1823) "represents the most influential legal opinion on indigenous peoples' human rights ever issued by a court of law in the Western world. All the major English-language-speaking settler states adopted Marshall's understanding of the Doctrine of Discovery and its principle that the first European discoverer of lands occupied by non-Christian tribal savages could claim a superior right to those lands under the European Law of Nations. Canada, Australia, and New Zealand all followed Marshall's opinion as a precedent for their domestic law on indigenous peoples' in-ferior rights to property and control over their ancestral lands." Williams, *Savage Anxieties*, 224. See also Williams, *American Indian*; Miller et al., *Discovering Indigenous Lands*; and Newcomb, *Pagans in the Promised Land*.

35. United Nations Permanent Forum on Indigenous Issues, "Study on the Impacts of the Doctrine."

36. Anglican Church of Canada, "Resolution A086 R1."

37. Sison, "Primate's Commission." See also Anglican Church of Canada, "Message to the Church"; and Anglican Church of Canada, "Learning to Call."

38. World Council of Churches, "What Is the World Council of Churches?" Settlement Agreement signatories the Anglican Church of Canada, the Presbyterian Church in Canada, and the United Church of Canada are members of the WCC.

39. World Council of Churches, "Statement on the Doctrine of Discovery."

40. United Church of Canada, Executive of the General Council, "Meeting Summary."

41. Assembly of First Nations et al., "Doctrine of Discovery."

42. United Nations Permanent Forum on Indigenous Issues, "Study on the Impacts," para. 13. For the views of the court on the need for reconciliation, John cited *Haida Nation v. British Columbia (Minister of Forests)*, 2004 SCC 73, para. 20. On the need for courts to take judicial notice of the impacts of colonialism, residential schools, and displacement, John cited *R. v. Ipeelee*, 2012 SCC 13, para. 60.

43. Onondaga Nation, "Oren Lyons Presents." Article 7, paragraph 2, of the *Declaration* affirms that "Indigenous peoples have the collective right to live in freedom, peace and security as distinct peoples and shall not be subjected to any act of genocide or any other act of violence, including forcibly removing children of the group to another group."

44. Miller, *Compact, Contract, Covenant*, 283–284.

45. Kelly, "Confession," 22–23.

46. See, for example, Treaty 7 Tribal Council et al., *True Spirit*; Miller, *Compact, Contract, Covenant*; and Ray, Miller, and Tough, *Bounty and Benevolence*.

47. The Treaty commissions in Ontario, Saskatchewan, and Manitoba have developed public education programs and materials designed to teach Canadians, particularly children and youth, about the Treaties. See, for example, Treaty Relations Commission of Manitoba, "Public Education."

48. Borrows, "Wampum at Niagara," 160–161.

49. Miller, *Compact, Contract, Covenant*, 72.

50. Captain Thomas G. Anderson, "Report on the Affairs of the Indians of Canada, Section III," appendix 95 in Appt. T of the *Journals of the Legislative Assembly of Canada*, volume 6 (1818), cited in Borrows, "Wampum at Niagara," 166.

51. Cited in Borrows, "Wampum at Niagara," 167–168.

52. Johnston, "Symposium in Honour."

53. First Nations Summit, "Royal Proclamation Still Relevant."

54. Cited in Rennie, "Idle No More Protestors." For more on the Idle No More movement, see Kino-nda-niimi Collective, *Winter We Danced*.

55. Legal scholar Robert A. Williams Jr. explains the Gus-Wen-Tah, or Two-Row Wampum, as "a sacred treaty belt ... comprised of a bed of white wampum shell beads symbolizing the sacredness and purity of the treaty agreement between the two sides. Two parallel rows of purple wampum beads that extend down the length of the belt represent the separate paths travelled by the two sides on the same river. Each side travels in its own vessel: the Indians in a birch bark canoe, representing their laws, customs, and ways, and the whites in a ship, representing their laws, customs, and ways." Williams, *Linking Arms Together*, 4.

56. Cited in BasicNews.ca, "Two-Row Wampum."

57. Williams, *Linking Arms Together*, 119.

58. Borrows, *Canada's Indigenous Constitution*, 76.

59. Assembly of First Nations, "Silver Covenant Chain."

60. Williams, *Linking Arms Together*, 5–6.

61. See, for example, Borrows, *Recovering Canada*, 13; Miller, *Compact, Contract, Covenant*, 283–309; and Williams, *Linking Arms Together*, 1–13.

62. Aboriginal Rights Coalition, *New Covenant*.

63. Aboriginal Rights Coalition, *New Covenant*. The signatories to the covenant were the Anglican Church of Canada, Canadian Conference of Catholic Bishops, Council of Christian Reformed Churches in Canada, Evangelical Lutheran Church in Canada, Mennonite Central Committee Canada, Presbyterian Church in Canada, Religious Society of Friends (Quakers) in Canada, Oblate Conference of Canada, and United Church of Canada.

64. Anglican Church of Canada, "Submission by the Anglican Church"; Canadian Conference of Catholic Bishops, "Let Justice Flow"; Aboriginal Rights Coalition, "Recommendations to the Royal Commission."

65. Anglican Church of Canada, "Canadian Churches."

Indigenous law: Truth, reconciliation, and access to justice

1. Borrows, *Canada's Indigenous Constitution*, 11.

2. Borrows, *Canada's Indigenous Constitution*, 129–130.

3. TRC, AVS, Reg Crowshoe, Statement to the Truth and Reconciliation Commission of Canada, Winnipeg, Manitoba, 26 June 2014, Statement Number: SE049.

4. Napoleon, "Thinking about Indigenous Legal Orders," 230.

5. United Nations, *Declaration on the Rights of Indigenous Peoples*, Article 40.

6. United Nations Expert Mechanism on the Rights of Indigenous Peoples, "Access to Justice," 22–24.

7. United Nations Expert Mechanism on the Rights of Indigenous Peoples, "Access to Justice," 6, 8, 22–4.

8. Anaya, "Report of the Special Rapporteur," 13, 20.

9. See, for example, Borrows, *Canada's Indigenous Constitution*.

10. Canada, Royal Commission on Aboriginal Peoples, *Highlights from the Report*.

11. TRC, AVS, Stephen Augustine, Statement to the Truth and Reconciliation Commission of Canada, Winnipeg, Manitoba, 26 June 2014, Statement Number: SE049.

12. Royal Commission on Aboriginal Peoples, *Report*, volume 4, chapter 2.

13. Green, "Balancing Strategies," 153, emphasis in original.

14. See, for example, Gabriel, "Aboriginal Women's Movement"; McKay and Benjamin, "Vision for Fulfilling"; Borrows, "Aboriginal and Treaty Rights."

15. Articles 21 and 22 of the *UN Declaration on the Rights of Indigenous Peoples* also affirm and protect the rights and interests of Elders, children and youth, and persons with disabilities.

16. Borrows, "Aboriginal and Treaty Rights."

17. LaRocque, "Colonization of a Native Woman," 401.

18. Anderson, "Affirmations of an Indigenous Feminist," 88.

19. Snyder, "Gender and Indigenous Law," 19–20. See also Snyder, "Indigenous Feminist Legal Theory."

20. Snyder, "Gender and Indigenous Law," 19–20.

21. The Haudenosaunee, more commonly known as Iroquois or Six Nations, are a confederacy of the Mohawk, Oneida, Onondaga, Cayuga, Seneca, and Tuscarora Nations.

22. Jennings et al., editors, *History and Culture*, 18–21.

23. Foster, "Another Look," 110.

24. Mohawk scholar Taiaiake Alfred writes, "Condolence cannot happen if we are all in grief. The healthy ones, the bright-eyed ones, must accept their responsibility to restore those in grief, temporarily in dysfunction, so to speak, to health, to accept, recognize, restore, ameliorate, admonish, and provide the new mentor, model and inspiration." Alfred, *Wasáse*, 79–80, citing Rarihokwats to Alfred, personal communication, 2003.

25. "Treaty of Peace, between the French, the Iroquois, and Other Nations," reprinted in Jennings et al., *History and Culture*, 137–144.

26. Williams, *Linking Arms Together*, 76.

27. Williams, *Linking Arms Together*, 55–56.

28. Foley, "Iroquois Mourning," 31.

29. Alfred explains that Rotinoshonni are "the people of the longhouse ... referring to the people of what is commonly known as the Six Nations, or Iroquois Confederacy." Alfred, *Wasáse*, 288.

30. Alfred, *Peace, Power, Righteousness*, xii.

31. Monet, "Mohawk Women Integrate."

32. Borrows, *Canada's Indigenous Constitution*, 76.

33. Cardinal and Hildebrandt, *Treaty Elders of Saskatchewan*, 14.

34. Black Elk and Neihardt, *Black Elk Speaks*, 121.

35. Cardinal and Hildebrandt, *Treaty Elders of Saskatchewan*, 15.

36. Cardinal and Hildebrandt, *Treaty Elders of Saskatchewan*, 16; Friedland, "Witeko (Windigo) Legal Principles," 93–96.

37. Muskeg Lake Cree Nation, "Nêhiyaw Wiyasowêwina (Cree Law)."

38. Napoleon et al., *Mikomosis and the Wetiko*.

39. Napoleon et al., *Mikomosis and the Wetiko*, 21.

40. Snyder et al., *Mikomosis and the Wetiko: A Teaching Guide*, 22–24, 81–83.

41. For a discussion of Inuit traditional law aimed at societal safety, see generally Oosten, Laugrand, and Rasing, editors, *Interviewing Inuit Elders*.

42. Bennett and Rowley, editors, *Uqalurait*, 131.

43. For contemporary chronicles of Inuit traditions related to conflict and resolution, see Hunhdorf, "'Atanarjuat, the Fast Runner.'" See also Kreelak, director, *Kikkik E1-472*.

44. The living nature of Inuit tradition is often demonstrated in Nunavut legislation. For example, the preamble of the *Nunavut Family Abuse Intervention Act* SNu 2006, chapter 18, describes Inuit tradition as follows:

> Recognizing that the values and cultures of Nunavummiut and the guiding principles and concepts of Inuit Qaujimajatuqangit reflect the right of every individual in Nunavut to a full and productive life, free from harm and fear of harm;
> Recognizing that family abuse continues to be a serious problem in Nunavut;
> Stressing the importance of inuuqatigiitsiarniq, which means respecting others, relationships and caring for people, and tunnganarniq, which means fostering good spirit by being open, welcoming and inclusive;
> Affirming the commitment of the Government of Nunavut to pijitsirniq, which means serving and providing for families and communities;

Incorporating and encouraging qanuqtuurniq, which means being innovative and resourceful.

45. James Muckpah, Tununirmiut, 1979, cited in Bennett and Rowley, editors, *Uqalurait*, 99.

46. Hubert Amarualik, Amiiturmiut, cited in Bennett and Rowley, editors, *Uqalurait*, 99, 394.

47. Jose Angutingurniq, Arviligjuarmiut, cited in Bennett and Rowley, editors, *Uqalurait*, 99, 100.

48. For a discussion of process pluralism from a feminist perspective, see Menkel-Meadow, "Peace and Justice."

49. Bennett and Rowley, editors, *Uqalurait*, 99.

50. Such a display of emotion by wrongdoers in response to the harm they caused is remarkable given the need among Inuit to attenuate emotional displays in other settings. See Briggs, "Emotions Have Many Faces"; and Pauktuutit Inuit Women of Canada, *Inuit Way*, 38.

51. Bennett and Rowley, editors, *Uqalurait*, 99.

52. Pauktuutit Inuit Women of Canada, *Inuit Way*, 9.

53. Battiste, *Honouring 400 Years Kepmite'tmnej*, 2, 6.

54. Henderson, *Mi'Kmaw Concordat*; Henderson, "Ayukpachi," 264–265.

55. Henderson, "First Nations' Legal Inheritances," 12.

56. Prosper et al., "Returning to Netukulimk," 1.

57. Metallic and Cavanaugh, "Mi'gmewey 'Politics.'"

58. Borrows, Mayer, and Mi'kmaq Legal Services Network, Eskasoni, "Mi'kmaq Legal Traditions Report," 7. See also First Voices, "Mikmaw Community Portal."

59. Borrows, Mayer, and Mi'kmaq Legal Services Network, Eskasoni, "Mi'kmaq Legal Traditions Report," 11–33.

60. Barkwell, Carriere Acco, and Rozyk, "Origins of Metis Customary Law," 12–14. See also Borrows, *Canada's Indigenous Constitution*, 87.

61. Barkwell, Carriere Acco, and Rozyk,, "Origins of Metis Customary Law," 9, 16.

62. Barkwell, Carriere Acco, and Rozyk, "Origins of Metis Customary Law," 17.

63. Barkwell, Carriere Acco, and Rozyk, "Origins of Metis Customary Law," 10.

64. Law Commission of Canada, *Justice Within*, at 2:43–4:20 mins.

65. Métis National Council, "Proceedings from 'Nobody's Children.'" For more on the Métis experience at residential schools, see Chartrand, Logan, and Daniels, *Métis History and Experience*.

66. Métis National Council, "Proceedings from 'Nobody's Children,'" 24.

67. Métis National Council, "Proceedings from 'Nobody's Children,'" 31–32.

68. Métis National Council, "Proceedings from 'Nobody's Children,'" 43.

69. Ghostkeeper, "*Weche* Teachings," 162.

70. Ghostkeeper, "*Weche* Teachings," 165.

71. Teslin Tlingit Council, "Constitution."

72. For the *Peacemaker Court and Justice Council Act* (2011) and other important Tlingit legislation, see Teslin Tlingit Council, "Legislation."

73. For clan information, see Teslin Tlingit Council, "Our Clans"; Teslin Tlingit Council, "Clan Based Governance"; and Teslin Tlingit Council, "Government Organization Chart."

74. *Peacemaker Court and Justice Council Act* (2011).

75. Johnston, "Aboriginal Traditions."

76. Benton-Benai, *Mishomis Book*; Simpson and Manitowabi, "Theorizing Resurgence"; Edna Manitowabi, "Grandmother Teachings," cited in Simpson, *Dancing on Our Turtle's Back*, 35–44.

77. Johnston, *Ojibway Ceremonies*.

78. Borrows, "Seven Generations, Seven Teachings," 11.
79. Miller, *Compact, Contract, Covenant*, 33–65; Borrows, "Wampum at Niagara," 155.
80. Johnston, *Ojibwe Ceremonies*. On the use of tobacco in ceremonies, see Native Women's Centre, *Traditional Teachings Handbook*.
81. Johnston, *Ojibway Ceremonies*, 44.
82. Johnston, *Honour Earth Mother*, 51–52.
83. Cardinal and Hildebrandt, *Treaty Elders of Saskatchewan*; Office of the Treaty Commissioner, *Treaty Implementation*; Ray, Miller, and Tough, *Bounty and Benevolence*.
84. This account of the event is based on Borrows, "Residential Schools, Respect and Responsibilities," 502–504. "In 2009, as president of the Canadian Conference of Catholic Bishops, Weisgerber asked Pope Benedict XVI to meet with a delegation of school survivors to acknowledge their pain and suffering. Kinew and Phil Fontaine were part of the group that travelled to the Vatican to hear the Pope address the Catholic Church's involvement in the residential school system and offer his personal apology." James Buchok, "Anishinaabe Elders Adopt Archbishop Weisgerber," *Catholic Register*, 17 April 2012, cited in Borrows, "Residential Schools, Respect and Responsibilities," 503.
85. Cited in Martin, "Fontaine Regrets."
86. Cited in Buchok, "Anishinaabe Elders."
87. Cited in Buchok, "Anishinaabe Elders." See also Martin, "Fontaine Regrets."
88. "The Hul'q'umi'num people are a sub-group of the Coast Salish people of the south-east coast of Vancouver Island, the Lower Mainland and the northern coast of Washington state. The Coast Salish people are a group of people that share a common culture and similar language dialects in British Columbia and Washington State." Paige, "In the Voices," 1.
89. Paige, "In the Voices," 1.
90. Cited in Paige, "In the Voices," 11n59.
91. Paige, "In the Voices," 42.
92. Paige, "In the Voices," 64.
93. Mansfield, "Balance and Harmony," 342.
94. Mansfield, "Balance and Harmony," 345–346.
95. Mansfield, "Balance and Harmony," 346.
96. Cited in Miller, *Problem of Justice*, 146.
97. McMullin, "Bringing the Good Feelings Back," 29.
98. Cited in McMullin, "Bringing the Good Feelings Back," 29.
99. Cited in McMullin, "Bringing the Good Feelings Back," 29.
100. Mansfield, "Balance and Harmony," 347.
101. Charelson and Tsleil-Waututh Nation, "Coast Salish Legal Traditions," 33–35.
102. Borrows, *Recovering Canada*, 79–80.
103. McCue, "Treaty-Making," 238.
104. Napoleon, "Who Gets to Say?" 188–189. See also Napoleon, "Ayook."
105. Regan, *Unsettling the Settler Within*, 198.
106. Regan, *Unsettling the Settler Within*, 203.
107. Regan, *Unsettling the Settler Within*, 200.
108. Regan, *Unsettling the Settler Within*, 201.
109. Regan, *Unsettling the Settler Within*, 209.
110. Regan, *Unsettling the Settler Within*, 210–211.
111. Friedland, "Accessing Justice and Reconciliation," 2.

112. For a comprehensive summary of the AJR project, see Friedland, "Accessing Justice and Reconciliation." The AJR project website is at http://indigenousbar.ca/indigenouslaw.

113. For community reports and other materials, see the AJR project website at http://indigenousbar.ca/indigenouslaw.

114. Friedland, "Accessing Justice and Reconciliation," 3.

115. Friedland, "Accessing Justice and Reconciliation," 18, citing Chief Doug S. White III, Snuneymuxw First Nation, 16 November 2012.

116. Cited in McGrady, "'Cedar as Sister,'" 3.

117. Borrows, *Canada's Indigenous Constitution*, 6–22.

118. Borrows, "(Ab)Originalism and Canada's Constitution," 351, 396–397.

119. Napoleon, "Ayook," 15.

120. See generally Borrows, *Canada's Indigenous Constitution*.

From apology to action: Canada and the churches

1. Kinew, "It's the Same Great Spirit."

2. Minow, *Between Vengeance and Forgiveness*, 116.

3. de Greiff, "Role of Apologies," 128, 131. See also Tavuchis, *Mea Culpa*.

4. Nobles, *Politics of Official Apologies*, 29.

5. Nobles, *Politics of Official Apologies*, 2.

6. Gibney et al., editors, *Age of Apology*.

7. Corntassel and Holder, "Who's Sorry Now?" 467.

8. Marrus, "Official Apologies," 7.

9. James, "Wrestling with the Past," 139.

10. Regan, *Unsettling the Settler Within*, 182–183. See also Chapter Two of the present volume.

11. TRC, AVS, Shawn A-in-chut Atleo, Statement to the Truth and Reconciliation Commission of Canada, Saskatoon, Saskatchewan, 22 June 2012, Statement Number: SNE202.

12. On the importance of recognizing that victims of violence are also holders of rights, see de Greiff, "Report of the Special Rapporteur," 9 August 2012, 10, para. 29.

13. Simpson, *Dancing on Our Turtle's Back*, 22.

14. TRC, AVS, Honourable Steven Point, Statement to the Truth and Reconciliation Commission of Canada, Vancouver, British Columbia, 20 September 2013, Statement Number: BCNE304.

15. Stanton, "Canada's Truth and Reconciliation Commission," 4.

16. Castellano, Archibald, and DeGagné, "Introduction," 2–3.

17. de Greiff, "Report of the Special Rapporteur," 9 August 2012, 10–12.

18. Canada, Royal Commission on Aboriginal Peoples, *Report*, volume 1, 38.

19. *R. v. Sparrow* (1990) 1 SCR 1075. See also *Guerin v. R.* (1984) 2 SCR 335; *Delgamuukw v. British Columbia* (1997) 3 SCR 1010; and *Haida Nation v. British Columbia (Minister of Forests)*, 2004 SCC 73.

20. *Manitoba Métis Federation v. Canada (Attorney General)*, 2013 SCC 14, Appellants Factum, para. 94, citing Manitoba Court of Appeal ruling in *Manitoba Métis Federation v. Canada (Attorney General) et al.*, 2010 MBCA 71, paras. 533, 534.

21. For the "Solicitor's Opinions" on Native American issues, see United States Department of the Interior, Office of the Solicitor, "Solicitor's Opinions."

22. On the unfair burden of proof placed on Aboriginal peoples and the need to shift the onus onto the Crown, see, for example, Borrows, *Recovering Canada*, 101.

23. Canada, Royal Commission on Aboriginal Peoples, *Report*, volume 1, 8. The Commission adopts the definition of *civic trust* put forward by justice scholar Pablo de Greiff as it relates to the role of apologies in reconciliation processes: "Trust involves an expectation of ... commitment to the norms and values we share ... not the thick form of trust characteristic of relations between intimates, but rather 'civic' trust ... that can develop among citizens who are strangers to one another, but who are members of the same political community.... Trusting an institution, then, amounts to knowing that its constitutive rules, values, and norms are shared by participants and that they regard them as binding.... Reconciliation, minimally, is the condition under which citizens can trust one another as citizens again (or anew).... It presupposes that both institutions and persons can become *trustworthy*, and this is not something that is merely granted but *earned*." de Greiff, "Role of Apologies," 125–127, emphasis in original.

24. TRC, AVS, Eugene Arcand, Statement to the Truth and Reconciliation Commission of Canada, Saskatoon, Saskatchewan, 22 June 2012, Statement Number: SNE202.

25. TRC, AVS, Allan Sutherland, Statement to the Truth and Reconciliation Commission of Canada, Winnipeg, Manitoba, 16 June 2010, Statement Number: 02-MB-16JU10-067.

26. TRC, AVS, Lisa Scott, Statement to the Truth and Reconciliation Commission of Canada, Victoria, British Columbia, 13 April 2012, Statement Number: 2011-3978.

27. TRC, AVS, Ron McHugh, Statement to the Truth and Reconciliation Commission of Canada, Batoche, Saskatchewan, 21 July 2010, Statement Number: 01-SK-18-25JY10-011.

28. On the role of official apologies in reparations and reconciliation, see, for example, Barkan and Karn, editors, *Taking Wrongs Seriously*; de Greiff, "Role of Apologies"; James, "Wrestling with the Past"; Nobles, *Politics of Official Apologies*; and Tavuchis, *Mea Culpa*.

29. Canada, Debates of the Senate (Hansard), 2nd Session, 40th Parliament, volume 146, issue 45, 11 June 2009. Other speakers included Inuit Tapiriit Kanatami national president Mary Simon, Métis National Council president Clément Chartier, and Congress of Aboriginal Peoples interim National Chief Kevin Daniels.

30. TRC, AVS, Theodore Fontaine, Statement to the Truth and Reconciliation Commission of Canada, Edmonton, Alberta, 28 March 2014, Statement Number: SP203.

31. TRC, AVS, Noel Starblanket, Statement to the Truth and Reconciliation Commission of Canada, Regina, Saskatchewan, 16 January 2012, Statement Number: SP035.

32. TRC, AVS, Geraldine Bob, Statement to the Truth and Reconciliation Commission of Canada, Fort Simpson, Northwest Territories, 23 November 2011, Statement Number: 2011-2685.

33. TRC, AVS, Stephen Kakfwi, Statement to the Truth and Reconciliation Commission of Canada, Inuvik, Northwest Territories, 30 June 2011, Statement Number: 2011.06.30 NNE.

34. TRC, AVS, Robert Keesick, Statement to the Truth and Reconciliation Commission of Canada, Winnipeg, Manitoba, 16 June 2010, Statement Number: 02-MB-16JU10-038.

35. TRC, AVS, Elaine Durocher, Statement to the Truth and Reconciliation Commission of Canada, Winnipeg, Manitoba, 16 June 2010, Statement Number: 02-MB-16JU10-059.

36. TRC, AVS, Ava Bear, Statement to the Truth and Reconciliation Commission of Canada, Saskatoon, Saskatchewan, 23 June 2012, Statement Number: 2011-4497.

37. TRC, AVS, Iris Nicholas, Statement to the Truth and Reconciliation Commission of Canada, Halifax, Nova Scotia, 27 October 2011, Statement Number: 2011.10.26-29 ANE.

38. Vatican, "Communiqué of the Holy See."

39. Cited in CBC News, "Pope Expresses 'Sorrow.'"

40. Vatican, "Pastoral Letter."

41. Vatican, "Pastoral Letter."

42. TRC, AVS, Commissioner Wilton Littlechild, speaking at Oblates of St. Mary Immaculate gathering in St. Albert, Alberta, 2 May 2011, Statement Number: SC012.

43. The Learning Places at National Events included information posters about the schools in the region, a Legacy of Hope Foundation exhibit, an information booth on the Missing Children Project, interactive maps, and a writing wall where people could offer their personal reflections. At each event in or near the Learning Place, the Settlement Agreement churches also organized a Churches Listening Area. The intent was to provide an opportunity for those Survivors who wished to do so to speak personally with a church representative about their residential school experience. When requested, church representatives also offered apologies to Survivors.

44. TRC, AVS, Alvin Dixon, Statement to the Truth and Reconciliation Commission of Canada, Inuvik, Northwest Territories, 30 June 2011, Statement Number: NNE302.

45. TRC, AVS, Anonymous, Statement to the Truth and Reconciliation Commission of Canada, Winnipeg, Manitoba, 18 June 2010, Statement Number: 02-MB-18JU10-055.

46. Kelly, "Confession," 20–21, 39.

47. TRC, AVS, Jennie Blackbird, Statement to the Truth and Reconciliation Commission of Canada, Muncey, Ontario, 16 September 2011, Statement Number: 2011-4188.

48. TRC, AVS, Martina Therese Fisher, Statement to the Truth and Reconciliation Commission of Canada, Bloodvein, Manitoba, 26 January 2012, Statement Number: 2011-2564.

49. The right of Indigenous peoples to observe traditional spiritual practices is upheld by the United Nations. Article 12:1 of the *United Nations Declaration on the Rights of Indigenous Peoples* says, "Indigenous peoples have the right to manifest, practice, develop and teach their spiritual and religious traditions, customs and ceremonies; the right to maintain, protect, and have access in privacy to their religious and cultural sites; the right to use and control of their ceremonial objects; and the right to the repatriation of their human remains." United Nations, *Declaration on the Rights of Indigenous Peoples.*

50. One example is a Christian Cree community that passed a resolution denying some of its community members the right to construct a sweat lodge and to teach youth about Cree spirituality. See *APTN National News*, "Cree Community"; and Taliman, "Christian Crees."

51. TRC, AVS, Jim Dumont, Statement to the Truth and Reconciliation Commission of Canada, Winnipeg, Manitoba, 26 June 2014, Statement Number: SE049.

52. Dumont and Hutchinson, "United Church Mission Goals," 226–227.

53. Mullin (Thundering Eagle Woman), "We Are One," 29.

54. Presbyterian Church in Canada, "Aboriginal Spirituality," 2, 6, emphasis in original.

55. Anglican Church of Canada, "New Agape."

56. United Church of Canada, "Living Faithfully," 2.

57. United Church of Canada, "Reviewing Partnership," 26.

58. United Church of Canada, Executive of the General Council, "Addendum H."

59. Presbyterian Church in Canada, "Presbyterian Statement."

60. United Church of Canada, "Affirming Other Spiritual Paths."

61. Canadian Conference of Catholic Bishops, "Let Justice Flow," 24–25.

62. Canadian Conference of Catholic Bishops, "Canadian Catholic Aboriginal Council."

63. TRC, AVS, Dr. Alan L. Hayes, Statement to the Truth and Reconciliation Commission of Canada, Toronto, Ontario, 2 June 2012, Statement Number: SE020.

64. MacKenzie, "For Everything," 89.

65. Toronto Urban Native Ministry, cited in Bush, "How Have the Churches?" 16.

66. Presbyterian Church in Canada, *Acts and Proceedings*, 368.

67. Healing Fund, Anglican Church, 2008, cited in Bush, "How Have the Churches?" 24–25.

68. Healing Fund, Anglican Church, 2008, cited in Bush, "How Have the Churches?" 24–25.

69. Healing Fund, Anglican Church, 2000, cited in Bush, "How Have the Churches?" 19.

70. Bush, "How Have the Churches?" 18.

71. The Aboriginal Healing Foundation was mandated to provide funding and support for Aboriginal community-based healing projects. For more on its history and the circumstances surrounding its closure, see Spear, *Full Circle*.

72. TRC, AVS, Bruce Adema, Christian Reformed Church of North America, Statement to the Truth and Reconciliation Commission of Canada, Regina, Saskatchewan, 22 June 2012, Statement Number: 2012.06.22 SNE.

73. TRC, AVS, Claire Ewert Fisher, Mennonite Central Committee, Statement to the Truth and Reconciliation Commission of Canada, Regina, Saskatchewan, 24 June 2012, Statement Number: 2012.06.24 SNE.

74. TRC, AVS, Jonathan Infeld, Statement to the Truth and Reconciliation Commission of Canada, Vancouver, British Columbia, 18 September 2013, Statement Number: 2013.09.18 BCNE.

75. TRC, AVS, Deloria Bighorn,, Bahá'í Community of Canada, Statement to the Truth and Reconciliation Commission of Canada, Vancouver, British Columbia, 20 September 2013, Statement Number: 2013.09.20 BCNE. See also Bahá'í Community of Canada, "Submission of the Bahá'í Community."

76. TRC, AVS, World Sikh Organization of Canada and Sikh Gurdwaras, Statement to the Truth and Reconciliation Commission of Canada, Vancouver, British Columbia, 21 September 2013, Statement Number: 2013.09.21 BCNE.

77. TRC, AVS, Canadian Council of Churches, Statement to the Truth and Reconciliation Commission of Canada, Edmonton, Alberta, 28 March 2014, Statement Number: ABNE 202.

78. TRC, AVS, Anonymous, Honour Walkers, Statement to the Truth and Reconciliation Commission of Canada, Edmonton, Alberta, 28 March 2014, Statement Number: ABNE 202.

Education for reconciliation

1. TRC, AVS, Allan Sutherland, Statement to the Truth and Reconciliation Commission of Canada, Winnipeg, Manitoba, 16 June 2010, Statement Number: 02-MB-16JU10-067.

2. TRC, AVS, Esther Lachinette-Diabo, Statement to the Truth and Reconciliation Commission of Canada, Thunder Bay, Ontario, 24 November 2010, Statement Number: 01-ON-24Nov10-020.

3. TRC, AVS, Charlotte Marten, Statement to the Truth and Reconciliation Commission of Canada, Lethbridge, Alberta, 9 October 2013, Statement Number: SP127.

4. Education scholar Penney Clark's study identifies how Aboriginal peoples have been portrayed in Canadian history textbooks and how gaps in the history impact students. Clark, "Representations of Aboriginal People," 96–98, 103–111.

5. Council of Ministers of Education, Canada, "Developments on Indian Residential Schools by Jurisdiction," July 2014, email correspondence from Christy Bressette, Coordinator, Aboriginal Education, Council of Ministers of Education, Canada, to Truth and Reconciliation Commission of Canada, 18 July 2014, TRC Document Number TRC3353.

6. Legacy of Hope Foundation, "NWT and NU Curriculum."

7. Council of Ministers of Education, Canada, "Education Ministers Signal Transformation."

8. Freedom of conscience and religion is protected under Section 2 of the Canadian Charter of Rights and Freedoms, and Section 3 of Québec's Charter of Human Rights and Freedoms.

9. *S. L. v. Commission scolaire des Chênes*, 2012 SCC 7, 237.

10. Educator and scholar Marie Battiste's work on decolonizing and transforming the education system has informed the Commission's thinking on this issue. Battiste, *Decolonizing Education*, 175–191.

11. Education scholars Megan Boler and Michalinas Zembylas describe this way of teaching as a "pedagogy of discomfort" that requires both educators and students to "move outside their comfort zones" in constructive ways that can "radically alter their worldviews." Boler and Zembylas, "Discomforting Truths," 111. See also Sheppard, "Creating a Caring Classroom."

12. See, for example, Immordino-Yang and Domasio, "We Feel, Therefore We Learn"; and Schonert-Reichl and Hymel, "Educating the Heart." See also Mary Gordon's initiative Roots of Empathy, "an evidence-based classroom program that has shown significant effect in reducing levels of aggression among school children while raising social/emotional competence and increasing empathy," at http://www.rootsofempathy.org; and Gordon, *Roots of Empathy*.

13. More information on Project of Heart is available at http://projectofheart.ca.

14. Sylvia Smith on Project of Heart, 2011, at http://projectofheart.ca/history.

15. TRC, AVS, Samantha Crowe, Statement to the Truth and Reconciliation Commission of Canada, Edmonton, Alberta, 30 March 2014, Statement Number: ABNE401. For more information on the project, see Ontario Provincial Advocate for Children and Youth, "Feathers of Hope."

16. Cultural theorist Roger Simon makes this point in an essay on the pedagogical practice of public history in the context of the Commission's public education mandate. Simon, "Towards a Hopeful Practice," 135–136.

17. The 2013 annual report of the Historical Thinking Project makes a similar point, arguing that the education system must produce historically literate citizens. Seixas and Colyer, "Report on the National Meeting," 3. The purpose of the Historical Thinking Project was to provide teachers with history education resources for training students to think critically and effectively about history. Seixas and Colver, "Report on the National Meeting," 2.

18. Centre for Youth and Society, University of Victoria, "Residential Schools Resistance Narratives," report. To view the project videos, see Centre for Youth and Society, University of Victoria, "Residential Schools Resistance Narratives," video collection.

19. Prairie Women's Health Centre of Excellence, "Nitâpwewininân," 3–7.

20. Prairie Women's Health Centre of Excellence, "Nitâpwewininân," 14–16.

21. Turpel-Lafond, "Aboriginal Children," iii.

22. Turpel-Lafond, "Aboriginal Children," 15, 17.

23. Turpel-Lafond, "Aboriginal Children," 44.

24. See, for example, Magill and Hamber, "If They Don't Start."

25. Parmar et al., editors, *Children and Transitional Justice*.

26. TRC, AVS, Brooklyn Rae, Saskatchewan National Event Education Day, Saskatoon, Saskatchewan, 23 June 2013, video, Statement Number: SNE502, https://vimeo.com/48143907.

27. TRC, AVS, Barney Williams, Saskatchewan National Event Education Day, Saskatoon, Saskatchewan, 23 June 2013, video, Statement Number: SNE502, https://vimeo.com/48143907.

28. International Center for Transitional Justice, "ICTJ/Canada TRC Youth Retreat."

29. International Center for Transitional Justice, "ICTJ/Canada TRC Youth Retreat."

30. International Center for Transitional Justice, "ICTJ Program Report."

31. International Center for Transitional Justice, "Youth Reporters."

32. International Center for Transitional Justice, "Our Legacy, Our Hope," press release; International Center for Transitional Justice, *Our Legacy, Our Hope*, video.

33. International Center for Transitional Justice, "ICTJ Program Report."

34. TRC, AVS, Rory Shade, Statement to the Truth and Reconciliation Commission of Canada, Vancouver, British Columbia, 19 September 2013, Statement Number: 2013.09.19 BCNE.

35. TRC, AVS, Centre for Global Citizenship Education and Research, Statement to the Truth and Reconciliation Commission of Canada, Edmonton, Alberta, 27 March 2014, Statement Number: ABNE102.

36. More information on the Canadian Roots Exchange is available at http://canadianroots.ca.

37. Reconciliation Canada, "New Youth Program."

38. Bolton, "Museums Taken to Task," 146–147.

39. Buchanan, "Decolonizing the Archives," 44.

40. Morse, "Indigenous Human Rights," 2, 10.

41. The decisions state that "the laws of evidence must be adapted in order that this type of evidence be accommodated and placed on an equal footing with the types of historic evidence that courts are familiar with, which largely consists of historical documents." Reasons for Decision, *Delgamuukw v. British Columbia* (1997) 3 SCR 1010, para. 87. On the honour of the Crown, see, for example, *R. v. Sparrow* (1990) 1 SCR 1075; *Haida Nation v. British Columbia (Minister of Forests)*, 2004 SCC 73; and *Delgamuukw v. British Columbia* (1997) 3 SCR 1010.

42. Legal scholar Bradford W. Morse makes this point. Morse, "Indigenous Human Rights," 12, 26.

43. Canada, Royal Commission on Aboriginal Peoples, *Report*, volume 5, 232–233.

44. They have done so in accordance with their legislated mandate. Canada's *Museums Act* SC 1990, chapter 3, section 3, provides the legislative framework for museums. The Act was amended in 2008 to include the Canadian Museum for Human Rights.

45. Bolton, "Museums Taken to Task," 151.

46. On December 12, 2013, Bill C-7, *An Act to Amend the Museums Act in Order to Establish the Canadian Museum of History*, received royal assent, thus officially establishing the legislative authority to "rebrand" the Canadian Museum of Civilization. Neither the original *Museums Act* nor the amendment made specific reference to Aboriginal peoples. See CBC News, "Civilization Museum."

47. House of Commons Standing Committee on Canadian Heritage, 1st Session, 41st Parliament, 5 June 2013.

48. Canadian Museum of Civilization and Canadian War Museum, "Research Strategy," 7.

49. Canadian Museum of Civilization and Canadian War Museum, "Research Strategy," 8–9.

50. Canadian Museum of Civilization and Canadian War Museum, "Research Strategy," 10.

51. Canadian Museum for Human Rights, "About the Museum."

52. Canadian Museum for Human Rights, "Speech Delivered by President."

53. Edmiston, "'Indian Residential Schools'?"

54. Canadian Museum for Human Rights, "Statement from the President."

55. Canadian Museum for Human Rights, "Speech Delivered by CMHR President."

56. Library and Archives Canada, "Collection Development Framework," 7–8.

57. Library and Archives Canada, "Aboriginal Heritage."

58. Library and Archives Canada, "Native Residential Schools."

59. Wilson, "Peace, Order and Good Government," 239.

60. Library and Archives Canada, "New Exhibition." See also Legacy of Hope Foundation, *Where Are the Children?*; and Legacy of Hope Foundation, *"We were so far away."*

61. Library and Archives Canada, "Legacy of the Residential School."

62. Library and Archives Canada, "Conducting Research."

63. Indian Residential Schools Settlement Agreement, "Schedule N," 11.

64. *Fontaine v. Canada (Attorney General)*, 2013 ONSC 684.

65. Canada, Office of the Auditor General of Canada, "Documentary Heritage," 3.

66. Canada, Office of the Auditor General of Canada, "Documentary Heritage," 7.

67. Professor Terry Cook, University of Manitoba, long-time archivist at the National Archives, a Fellow of the Association of Canadian Archivists, and a Fellow of the Royal Society of Canada, makes this point. Cook, "Evidence, Memory, Identity," 111.

68. United Nations Commission on Human Rights, Subcommission on the Prevention of Discrimination and Protection of Minorities, *The Administration of Justice and the Human Rights of Detainees: Question of the Impunity of Perpetrators of Human Rights Violations (Civil and Political)*, revised final report prepared by Mr. Joinet to the subcommission decision 1996/199, UN Doc. E/CN.4/Sub,2/1997/20/Rev.1, 1997-10-02, updated by UN Doc. E/CN.4/2005/102 (18 February 2005) and UN Doc E/CN.4/2005/102/Add.1 (8 February 2005), cited in University of Manitoba, "Written Argument," 14n35.

69. de Greiff, "Report of the Special Rapporteur," 28 August 2013, 22.

70. de Greiff, "Report of the Special Rapporteur," 28 August 2013, 23.

71. de Greiff, "Report of the Special Rapporteur," 28 August 2013, 29.

72. Several prominent archivists have noted this trend. See, for example, Cook, "Evidence, Memory, Identity"; Wilson, "Peace, Order and Good Government"; Harris, "Archival Sliver"; and Jimerson, "Archives for All."

73. TRC, AVS, Peter Cunningham, Statement to the Truth and Reconciliation Commission of Canada, Edmonton, Alberta, 28 March 2014, Statement Number: ABNE201.

74. Rev. Fausak is also General Council Liaison Minister, Indigenous Justice and Residential Schools, United Church of Canada.

75. TRC, AVS, Remembering the Children Society, Statement to the Truth and Reconciliation Commission of Canada, Edmonton, Alberta, 29 March 2014, Statement Number: ABNE302. Based on their experience, United Church of Canada staff, in collaboration with the Remembering the Children Society, developed an educational resource with guidelines for other communities wishing to develop their own commemoration projects for residential school cemeteries and unmarked burials. See United Church of Canada, "Residential Schools Update."

76. The United Church of Canada's online resources are available at http://thechildrenremembered.ca. The Anglican Church's online resources and school histories are available at http://www.anglican.ca/relationships/trc. The Presbyterian Church in Canada's online resources are available at http://www.presbyterianarchives.ca/RS%20-%20Home%20Page.html.

77. United Church of Canada, Residential School Archive Project, "The Children Remembered."

78. Ian Wilson makes this point. Wilson, "Peace, Order and Good Government," 238.

79. This is based on the concept and philosophy of "sites of conscience," as described by the International Coalition of Sites of Conscience, which is "a global network of historic sites, museums and memory initiatives connecting past struggles to today's movements for human rights and social justice." International Coalition of Sites of Conscience, http://www.sitesof-conscience.org.

80. Truth and Reconciliation Commission of Canada, *Sharing Truth*. Videos of the forum can be viewed at http://www.trc.ca/websites/trcinstitution/index.php?p=513.

81. Georges Erasmus, in Truth and Reconciliation Commission of Canada, *Sharing Truth*, 2 March 2011, https://vimeo.com/album/1744451/video/20788339.

82. Charlene Belleau, in Truth and Reconciliation Commission of Canada, *Sharing Truth*, 3 March 2011, https://vimeo.com/album/1750974/video/20696021.

83. James Scott, in Truth and Reconciliation Commission of Canada, *Sharing Truth*, 3 March 2011, https://vimeo.com/album/1750974/video/20694696.

84. Truth and Reconciliation Commission of Canada and University of Manitoba, "Centre for Truth and Reconciliation Administrative Agreement," Clauses 9 (c), 9 (d), 11 (a), 11 (e).

85. As of April 2015, existing partners included the National Association of Friendship Centres, Legacy of Hope Foundation, Canadian Museum for Human Rights, University of British Columbia, Lakehead University, University College of the North, University of Winnipeg, Red River College, Archives of Manitoba, Université de Saint-Boniface, St. John's College, St. Paul's College, Manitoba Museum, Centre for Indigenous Environmental Resources, and Sandy-Saulteaux Spiritual Centre. It is anticipated that more partners will be added as the centre develops. See National Centre for Truth and Reconciliation, "Our Partners."

86. University of Manitoba, "Written Argument," 6–7.

87. Sue McKemmish, Shannon Faulkhead, and Lynette Russell, "Distrust in the Archive: Reconciling Records," *Archival Science* 11, nos. 3–4 (2011): 212, cited in University of Manitoba, "Written Argument," 11.

88. University of Manitoba, "Written Argument," 11–12.

89. University of Manitoba, "Written Argument," 12–13.

90. University of Manitoba, "Statement of Apology."

91. University of Manitoba, "Statement of Apology."

92. University of Manitoba, "Historic Agreement Signed."

93. Such access will be "subject to privacy law and culturally appropriate protocols." Truth and Reconciliation Commission of Canada and University of Manitoba, "Centre for Truth and Reconciliation Trust Deed," 3–4.

94. National Centre for Truth and Reconciliation, "Reconciliation." See also Truth and Reconciliation Commission of Canada and University of Manitoba, "Centre for Truth and Reconciliation Administrative Agreement."

Public memory: Dialogue, the arts, and commemoration

1. Campbell, *Our Faithfulness*, 153.

2. TRC, AVS, Jennifer Adese, Truth and Reconciliation Commission of Canada, "Reconciliation and Collective Memory in a Divided Society," panel, Edmonton, Alberta, 29 March 2014, Statement Number: ABNE305.

3. Anderson, *Life Stages*, 4–5.

4. Cited in Anderson, *Life Stages*, 3, emphasis in original.

5. TRC, AVS, Sharon Jinkerson-Brass, Truth and Reconciliation Commission of Canada, "Honouring Women's Wisdom: Pathways of Truth, Resilience and Reconciliation," panel, 21 September 2013, Statement Number: 2013.09.21.

6. Anderson and Robertson, *Seeing Red*, 192–218.

7. Cited in Anderson and Robertson, *Seeing Red*, 200.

8. The Commission's definition of *public memory* is based on the work of historians who study public memory. For example, James Opp and John C. Walsh define "public memory" as "memories that are made, experienced, and circulated in public spaces and that are intended to be communicated and shared." Opp and Walsh, *Placing Memory*, 9. John Bodnar says that "public memory" is "a body of beliefs and ideas about the past that help[s] a public or society understand both its past, [and] present, and by implication, its future." Bodnar, *Remaking America*, 15.

9. Historian W. James Booth makes this important point in his study of how communities of memory are established, maintained, or disrupted through everyday habits and practices. Booth, *Communities of Memory*, 45.

10. In its report "Strengthening Indigenous Rights through Truth Commissions: A Practitioner's Resource," the International Center for Transitional Justice identifies four thematic areas where commissions must rethink widely held assumptions in the field of transitional justice in order to become more responsive to Indigenous rights. These include: moving beyond a state-centric approach; moving beyond an individualistic form of analysis; moving beyond a focus only on recent violations; and moving beyond an overreliance on archival and written sources. International Centre for Transitional Justice, "Strengthening Indigenous Rights," 3–5.

11. Chamberlin, *If This Is Your Land*, 238–239.

12. Schirch, *Ritual and Symbol*, 1–2.

13. Truth and Reconciliation Commission of Canada, "Atlantic National Event," 4.

14. TRC, AVS, Ms. Lussier, Statement to the Truth and Reconciliation Commission of Canada, Winnipeg, Manitoba, 19 June 2010, Statement Number: 2010.06.19 WNE.

15. TRC, AVS, Ms. Kenny, Statement to the Truth and Reconciliation Commission of Canada, Winnipeg, Manitoba, 19 June 2010, Statement Number: 2010.06.19 WNE.

16. In 2015, the Bentwood Box was on temporary loan to the Canadian Museum for Human Rights, where it was part of a public exhibit.

17. Campbell, "Remembering for the Future," 30. See also Campbell, *Our Faithfulness*, 154.

18. Qwul'sih'yah'maht (Thomas), "Honouring the Oral Traditions," 253.

19. TRC, AVS, Charles Cardinal, Statement to the Truth and Reconciliation Commission of Canada, St. Paul, Alberta, 7 January 2011, Statement Number: 01-AB-06JA11-005.

20. TRC, AVS, Laurie McDonald, Statement to the Truth and Reconciliation Commission of Canada, Beausejour, Manitoba, 4 September 2010, Statement Number: 01-MB-3-6SE10-005.

21. TRC, AVS, Victoria Grant-Boucher, Statement to the Truth and Reconciliation Commission of Canada, Ottawa, Ontario, 25 February 2011, Statement Number: 01-ON-05-FE11-004.

22. TRC, AVS, Desarae Eashappie, Statement to the Truth and Reconciliation Commission of Canada, Winnipeg, Manitoba, 19 June 2010, Statement Number: SC112.

23. Regan, *Unsettling the Settler Within*, 13.

24. TRC, AVS, Anonymous, Statement to the Truth and Reconciliation Commission of Canada, St. Albert, Alberta, 2–3 May 2011, Statement Number: 2011.05.02-03.

25. TRC, AVS, Anonymous, Statement to the Truth and Reconciliation Commission of Canada, St. Albert, Alberta, 2–3 May 2011, Statement Number: 2011.05.02-03.

26. TRC, AVS, Agnes Moses, Statement to the Truth and Reconciliation Commission of Canada, Inuvik, Northwest Territories, 29 June 2011, Statement Number: 2011.06.29 NNE.

27. TRC, AVS, Samuel Tapiatic, Statement to the Truth and Reconciliation Commission of Canada, Chisasabi, Québec, 19 March 2013, Statement Number: 2011-0056.

28. TRC, AVS, Florence Kaefer, Statement to Truth and Reconciliation Commission of Canada, Winnipeg, Manitoba, 18 June 2010, Statement Number: SC111.

29. CBC News, "Teachers Seek Healing."

30. TRC, AVS, Jack Lee, Statement to the Truth and Reconciliation Commission of Canada, Winnipeg, Manitoba, 18 June 2010, Statement Number: SC111.

31. TRC, AVS, Mark DeWolf, Statement to the Truth and Reconciliation Commission of Canada, Halifax, Nova Scotia, 28 October 2011, Statement Number: SC075.

32. TRC, AVS, Rev. Dr. John Vissers, Statement to the Truth and Reconciliation Commission of Canada, Saskatoon, Saskatchewan, 22 June 2012, Statement Number: 2012.06.22 SNE.

33. TRC AVS, Bishop Don Bolen, Statement to the Truth and Reconciliation Commission of Canada, Saskatoon, Saskatchewan, 22 June 2013, Statement Number: 2012.06.22 SNE.

34. TRC, AVS, Ian Gray, Statement to the Truth and Reconciliation Commission of Canada, Halifax, Nova Scotia, 27 October 2011, Statement Number: 2011.10.26-29 ANE.

35. TRC, AVS, Resolution Managers, Resolution West, Resolution and Individual Affairs, Aboriginal Affairs and Northern Development Canada, Statement to the Truth and Reconciliation Commission of Canada, Vancouver, British Columbia, 19 September 2013, Statement Number: BCNE205b.

36. Cited in Threlfall, "Her Next Chapter," 24.

37. Cited in Joseph, "Shelagh Rogers."

38. TRC, AVS, Tina Keeper, Statement to the Truth and Reconciliation Commission of Canada, Saskatoon, Saskatchewan, 24 June 2013, Statement Number: SNE403.

39. TRC, AVS, the Right Honourable Paul Martin, Statement to the Truth and Reconciliation Commission of Canada, Montreal, Québec, 26 April 2013, Statement Number: QNE303.

40. TRC, AVS, the Right Honourable Joe Clark, Statement to Truth and Reconciliation Commission of Canada, Saskatoon, Saskatchewan, 23 June 2012, Statement Number: SNE301.

41. TRC, AVS, Andy Scott, Statement to the Truth and Reconciliation Commission of Canada, Saskatoon, Saskatchewan, 22 June 2012, Statement Number: SNE203.

42. TRC, AVS, Therese Boullard, Statement to the Truth and Reconciliation Commission of Canada, Inuvik, Northwest Territories, 28 June 2011, Statement Number: NNE103.

43. TRC, AVS, Ginelle Giacomin, Statement to the Truth and Reconciliation Commission of Canada, Winnipeg, Manitoba, 19 June 2010, Statement Number: SC112.

44. O'Connor, "Role of the Non-Indigenous Witness," 50.

45. O'Connor, "Role of the Non-Indigenous Witness," 53.

46. O'Connor, "Role of the Non-Indigenous Witness," 56.

47. O'Connor, "Role of the Non-Indigenous Witness," 55.

48. O'Connor, "Role of the Non-Indigenous Witness," 69.

49. See, for example, Cohen, Varea, and Walker, editors, *Acting Together*.

50. Francois Matarraso in correspondence with Eugene van Erven, 19 March 2008, cited in van Erven and Gardner, "Performing Cross-Cultural Conversations," 41.

51. David Garneau, artist, writer, curator, and professor of visual arts, makes this critical point. Garneau, "Imaginary Spaces," 38.

52. Garneau, "Imaginary Spaces," 33–34.

53. Archibald et al., *Dancing, Singing, Painting*, 18.

54. Ratuski, "Residential School Art Series."

55. Morris and Helen Belkin Art Gallery, *Witnesses*; University of British Columbia Museum of Anthropology, *Speaking to Memory*.

56. Robertson, "Threads of Hope," 87, 99–101.

57. University of Winnipeg, "UWinnipeg Healing Quilt."

58. ArtsLink: Residential School Artists, "About ArtsLink."

59. Dewar et al., "Practicing Reconciliation," 5–6, emphasis in original.

60. Indian Residential Schools Settlement Agreement, "Schedule J."

61. For full descriptions of the projects, see Aboriginal Affairs and Northern Development Canada, "Commemoration 2011–2012"; and Aboriginal Affairs and Northern Development Canada, "Commemoration 2012–2013."

62. Cliff Hague refers to place as "a geographic space that is defined by meanings, sentiments and stories rather than by a set of co-ordinates." Cliff Hague, "Planning and Place Identity," in *Place Identity, Participation and Planning*, edited by Cliff Hague and Paul Jenkins (New York: Routledge, 2005), 3, cited in Opp and Walsh, *Placing Memory*, 5.

63. Hale, "Treaty 3 Holds Commemoration."

64. TRC, AVS, Andrea Walsh, Statement to the Truth and Reconciliation Commission of Canada, Victoria, British Columbia, 14 April 2012, Statement Number: 2013.04.14 VRE.

65. Steel, "Alberni Indian Residential Students."

66. Lavoie, "Paintings Bear Witness."

67. Canada, Aboriginal Affairs and Northern Development Canada, "Remembering the Past."

68. For Christi Belcourt's speech at the dedication ceremony for the stained-glass window on Parliament Hill on November 26, 2012, see Belcourt, "Stained Glass Window." For a detailed description of the window, see Canada, Aboriginal Affairs and Northern Development Canada, "Christi Belcourt Describes 'Giniigaaniimenaaning.'"

69. Commissioner Wilton Littlechild speaking at the dedication ceremony for the stained-glass window on Parliament Hill on November 26, 2012, see Littlechild, "Stained Glass Window."

70. Opp and Walsh, *Placing Memory*, 15–16.

71. *Historic Sites and Monuments Act* RSC 1985, chapter H-4.

72. Canada, Parks Canada, Historic Sites and Monuments Board of Canada, "Info Source."

73. Canada, Parks Canada, Historic Sites and Monuments Board of Canada, "National Program of Historical Commemoration."

74. *Joinet-Orentlicher Principles*, cited in Shaheed, "Report of the Special Rapporteur," 8.

75. Shaheed, "Report of the Special Rapporteur," 14.

76. Shaheed, "Report of the Special Rapporteur," 19. The Special Rapporteur is referencing the commemoration projects undertaken as part of the Settlement Agreement.

77. Shaheed, "Report of the Special Rapporteur," 20–21.

78. Shaheed, "Report of the Special Rapporteur," 21–22.

79. Shaheed, "Report of the Special Rapporteur," 22.

80. The study was based on research conducted by Trina Cooper-Bolam and incorporated her experiences as the Legacy of Hope's former executive director, her work with the Aboriginal Healing Foundation, and her role as a project leader for the Assembly of First Nations and

the Aboriginal Healing Foundation's national commemoration project. See Cooper-Bolam, "Healing Heritage," 8–9, 106–107.

81. Cooper-Bolam, "Healing Heritage," 108–109.
82. Cooper-Bolam, "Healing Heritage," 109.
83. Cooper-Bolam, "Healing Heritage," 61–63.
84. Jeff Corntassel, Chaw-win-is, and T'lakwadzi, "Indigenous Storytelling, Truth-Telling and Community Approaches to Reconciliation," *ESC: English Studies in Canada* 35, no. 1 (2009): 143, cited in Cooper-Bolam, "Healing Heritage," 98.
85. Cooper-Bolam, "Healing Heritage," 97–99.
86. Cooper-Bolam, "Healing Heritage," ii.

We are all Treaty people: Canadian society and reconciliation

1. Anderson and Robertson, *Seeing Red*, 3, 276.
2. Anderson and Robertson, *Seeing Red*, 6.
3. Ramirez-Barat, "Transitional Justice," 38–39.
4. Nagy and Gillespie, "Representing Reconciliation," 6–7.
5. Nagy and Gillespie, "Representing Reconciliation," 34–35.
6. *Broadcasting Act* SC 1991, chapter 11.
7. David, "Aboriginal Languages Broadcasting," 14.
8. CBC/Radio-Canada, "Going the Distance," 48. The annual report also provides information on the CBC's Aboriginal-languages programming and news coverage. In 2013, Statistics Canada published these data as part of the National Household Survey conducted in 2011. See Canada, Statistics Canada, "Aboriginal Peoples in Canada," 4.
9. Aboriginal Peoples Television Network, "Annual Report, 2013."
10. Aboriginal Peoples Television Network, "Factsheet."
11. Cited in Canada, Royal Commission on Aboriginal Peoples, *Report*, volume 5, 103–104.
12. Canada, Royal Commission on Aboriginal Peoples, *Report*, volume 2, 614.
13. See, for example, Anderson and Robertson, *Seeing Red*.
14. Journalists for Human Rights is a media development organization that provides education and resources to "help journalists build their capacity to report ethically and effectively on human rights and governance issues in their communities." Canada, Government of Canada, "Journalists for Human Rights (JHR)." See also Journalists for Human Rights, "About."
15. Journalists for Human Rights, "Buried Voices," 18–19.
16. Journalists for Human Rights, "Buried Voices," 5–6.
17. Journalists for Human Rights, "Buried Voices," 16.
18. Journalists for Human Rights, "Buried Voices," 19.
19. Miller, *Lethal Legacy*, vi.
20. Miller, "Ipperwash and the Media," 11, 14.
21. Miller, "Ipperwash and the Media," 19–20, 22–23.
22. TRC, AVS, Theodore Fontaine, Statement to the Truth and Reconciliation Commission of Canada, Edmonton, Alberta, 28 March 2014, Statement Number: AB202.
23. TRC, AVS, Laura Robinson, Statement to the Truth and Reconciliation Commission of Canada, Edmonton, Alberta, 28 March 2014, Statement Number: ABNE202.

24. *Gazette: Law Society of Upper Canada*, "Law Society Throws Support."

25. Mason and Koehli, "Barriers to Physical Activity," 103–105.

26. *Physical Activity and Sport Act* SC 2003, chapter 2.

27. IndigenACTION, "Phase One: Roundtable Report," appendix 2, 18–19.

28. Te Hiwi, "What Is the Spirit?" 3.

29. Sport Canada, Canadian Sport Policy Renewal, Roundtable on Sport and Aboriginal Peoples, "Summary Report," 4.

30. Sport Canada, "Canadian Sport Policy."

31. TRC, AVS, David Courchene Jr., Statement to the Truth and Reconciliation Commission of Canada, Winnipeg, Manitoba, 25 June 2014, Statement Number: SE048.

32. TRC, AVS, Ian Campbell, Statement to the Truth and Reconciliation Commission of Canada, Winnipeg, Manitoba, 25 June 2014, Statement Number: SE048.

33. Lee, "Tsilhqot'in Nation," A6.

34. Canada, *Northern Frontier, Northern Homeland*, volume 1, 1, 82–83. Beginning in the 1980s, several land claims agreements were signed across the North, including the Inuvialuit Final Agreement (1984), the Gwich'in Comprehensive Land Claim Agreement (1992), the Sahtu Dene and Métis Comprehensive Land Claim Agreement (1994), and the Tlicho Agreement (2005) in the Northwest Territories.

    Although there have been attempts to revitalize the Mackenzie Valley pipeline project with the participation of a coalition of Aboriginal partners, as of 2014 it remained unclear whether the project would proceed. See Jang, "Gas Exports from B.C."; and Lewis, "Northwest Territories Eyes Revival."

35. Canada, Royal Commission on Aboriginal Peoples, *Report*, volume 1, 466–504.

36. See, for example, *Delgamuukw v. British Columbia* (1997) 3 SCR 1010; *Haida Nation v. British Columbia (Minister of Forests)*, 2004 SCC 73; *Mikisew Cree First Nation v. Canada (Minister of Canadian Heritage)* [2005] 3 SCR 388, 2005 SCC 69; *Rio Tinto Alcan Inc. v. Carrier Sekani Tribal Council*, 2010 SCC 43, [2010] 2 SCR 650; *Tsilhqot'in Nation v. British Columbia*, 2014 SCC 44; and *Grassy Narrows First Nation v. Ontario (Natural Resources)*, 2014 SCC 48.

37. *Delgamuukw v. British Columbia* (1997) 3 SCR 1010, para. 165.

38. *Haida Nation v. British Columbia (Minister of Forests)*, 2004 SCC 73, para. 53, cited in Newman, "Rule and Role of Law," 10.

39. Newman, "Rule and Role of Law," 13.

40. Public Policy Forum, "Building Authentic Partnerships," 7.

41. Public Policy Forum, "Building Authentic Partnerships," 6.

42. Eyford, "Forging Partnerships," 3, 7.

43. Letter of transmission from Douglas R. Eyford to Prime Minister, 29 November 2013, in Eyford, "Forging Partnerships," 1.

44. The Charrette on Energy, Environment and Aboriginal Issues, "Responsible Energy Resource Development," 2.

45. The Charrette on Energy, Environment and Aboriginal Issues, "Responsible Energy Resource Development."

46. The Charrette on Energy, Environment and Aboriginal Issues, "Responsible Energy Resource Development," 8–14.

47. Coates and Newman, "End Is Not Nigh," 21.

48. United Nations Global Compact, *Business Reference Guide*.

49. TRC, AVS, Wab Kinew, Statement to the Truth and Reconciliation Commission of Canada, Edmonton, Alberta, 28 March 2014, Statement Number: ABNE202.
50. TRC, AVS, Victoria Wells, Statement to the Truth and Reconciliation Commission of Canada, Victoria, British Columbia, 13 April 2012, Statement Number: SP016.
51. TRC, AVS, Lynne Phillips, Statement to the Truth and Reconciliation Commission of Canada, Victoria, British Columbia, 5 December 2010, Statement Number: 01-BC-03DE10-007.
52. TRC, AVS, Roger Epp, Statement to the Truth and Reconciliation Commission of Canada, Hobbema, Alberta, 25 July 2013, Statement Number: SP125.
53. TRC, AVS, Bill Elliot, Statement to the Truth and Reconciliation Commission of Canada, Hobbema, Alberta, 25 July 2013, Statement Number: SP125.
54. TRC, AVS, Bill Elliot, Statement to the Truth and Reconciliation Commission of Canada, Edmonton, Alberta, 29 March 2014, Statement Number: ABNE301.
55. Cited in Zabjek, "Youths Picked."
56. Reconciliation Canada, "City of Vancouver Council." See also City Manager, "Framework for City of Reconciliation."
57. TRC, AVS, Gregor Robertson, Statement to the Truth and Reconciliation Commission of Canada, Vancouver, British Columbia, 18 September 2013, Statement Number: BCNE102.
58. TRC, AVS, Kim Harvey, "Be the Change: Young People Healing the Past and Building the Future," Vancouver, British Columbia, 18 September 2013, Statement Number: BCNE105, https://vimeo.com/78638476.
59. TRC, AVS, Kevin Takahide Lee, "Be the Change: Young People Healing the Past and Building the Future," Vancouver, British Columbia, 18 September 2013, Statement Number: BCNE105, https://vimeo.com/78638476.
60. TRC, AVS, Caroline Wong, "Be the Change: Young People Healing the Past and Building the Future," Vancouver, British Columbia, 18 September 2013, Statement Number: BCNE105, https://vimeo.com/78638476.
61. TRC, AVS, Danny Richmond, "Be the Change: Young People Healing the Past and Building the Future," Vancouver, British Columbia, 18 September 2013, Statement Number: BCNE105, https://vimeo.com/78638476.
62. TRC, AVS, Akua Benjamin, Statement to the Truth and Reconciliation Commission of Canada, Toronto, Ontario, 12 November 2013, Statement Number: SE036B.
63. TRC, AVS, Ali Kazimi, Statement to the Truth and Reconciliation Commission of Canada, Toronto, Ontario, 12 November 2013, Statement Number: SE036B.
64. TRC, AVS, Winnie Ng, Statement to the Truth and Reconciliation Commission of Canada, Toronto, Ontario, 12 November 2013, Statement Number: SE036B.
65. Canada, Minister of Citizenship and Immigration Canada, *Discover Canada*.
66. Canada, Minister of Citizenship and Immigration Canada, *Discover Canada*.
67. Reconciliation Canada, "Chief Joseph Shares."
68. Reconciliation Canada, "Shared Tomorrow."
69. The Philanthropist, "Philanthropic Community's Declaration."
70. Cobb, "More than 3,000."
71. Bellegarde, "Truth and Reconciliation."
72. Canada, Debates of the House of Commons (Hansard), 2nd Session, 41st Parliament, volume 221, 1 June 2015, 1515.

Bibliography

Primary Sources

1. Truth and Reconciliation Commission Databases

Audio/Video Statement (AVS) Database

2. Legislation

Act to Amend the Museums Act in Order to Establish the Canadian Museum of History 2013. http://www.parl.gc.ca/LegisInfo/BillDetails.aspx?Language=E&Mode=1&bill-Id=6263562&View=3.

Broadcasting Act SC 1991, chapter 11. http://laws-lois.justice.gc.ca/PDF/B-9.01.pdf.

Historic Sites and Monuments Act RSC 1985, chapter H-4. http://laws-lois.justice.gc.ca/PDF/H-4.pdf.

Museums Act SC 1990, chapter 3, section 3. http://laws-lois.justice.gc.ca/PDF/M-13.4.pdf.

Nunavut Family Abuse Intervention Act SNu 2006, chapter 18. http://canlii.ca/t/kkdz.

Peacemaker Court and Justice Council Act 2011. http://www.ttc-teslin.com/legislation-guiding-principles.html.

Physical Activity and Sport Act SC 2003, chapter 2. http://laws-lois.justice.gc.ca/eng/acts/P-13.4/page-1.html?texthighlight=under-represented#s-5.

3. Legal Cases

Delgamuukw v. British Columbia (1997) 3 SCR 1010.

Fontaine v. Canada (Attorney General), 2013 ONSC 684.

Grassy Narrows First Nation v. Ontario (Natural Resources), 2014 SCC 48.

Guerin v. R. (1984) 2 SCR 335.

Haida Nation v. British Columbia (Minister of Forests), 2004 SCC 73.

Manitoba Métis Federation v. Canada (Attorney General), 2013 SCC 14.

Mikisew Cree First Nation v. Canada (Minister of Canadian Heritage) [2005] 3 SCR 388, 2005 SCC 69.

R. v. Ipeelee, 2012 SCC 13.

R. v. Sparrow (1990) 1 SCR 1075.

Rio Tinto Alcan Inc. v. Carrier Sekani Tribal Council, 2010 SCC 43, [2010] 2 SCR 650.

S. L. v. Commission scolaire des Chênes, 2012 SCC 7. http://scc-csc.lexum.com/scc-csc/scc-csc/en/item/7992/index.do.

Tsilhqot'in Nation v. British Columbia, 2014 SCC 44.

4. Legal Documents

Indian Residential Schools Settlement Agreement. "Schedule J: Commemoration Policy Directive." n.d. http://www.residentialschoolsettlement.ca/Schedule_J-CommemorationPolicyDirective.PDF.

Indian Residential Schools Settlement Agreement. "Schedule N: Mandate for the Truth and Reconciliation Commission." n.d. http://www.residentialschoolsettlement.ca/SCHEDULE_N.pdf.

Truth and Reconciliation Commission of Canada and University of Manitoba. "Centre for Truth and Reconciliation Administrative Agreement." n.d. http://chrr.info/images/stories/Centre_For_Truth_and_Reconciliation_Administrative_Agreement.pdf.

Truth and Reconciliation Commission of Canada and University of Manitoba. "Centre for Truth and Reconciliation Trust Deed." 21 June 2013. http://umanitoba.ca/admin/indigenous_connect/media/IND-00-013-NRCAS-TrustDeed.pdf.

United Nations. *Declaration on the Rights of Indigenous Peoples*. March 2008. http://www.un.org/esa/socdev/unpfii/documents/DRIPS_en.pdf.

University of Manitoba. "Written Argument." 13 December 2012. In *Fontaine v. Canada (Attorney General)*, 2013 ONSC 684. http://chrr.info/images/stories/Materials_filed_by_UM_2_.pdf.

Secondary Sources

1. Books

Alfred, Gerald R. (Taiaiake). *Heeding the Voices of Our Ancestors: Kannawake Mohawk Politics and the Rise of Native Nationalism*. Toronto: Oxford University Press, 1995.

Alfred, Taiaiake. *Peace, Power, Righteousness: An indigenous Manifesto*. Don Mills, Ontario: Oxford University Press, 1999.

Alfred, Taiaiake. *Wasáse: Indigenous Pathways of Action and Freedom*. Peterborough, Ontario: Broadview, 2005.

Anderson, Kim. *Life Stages and Native Women: Memory, Teachings and Story Medicine*. Winnipeg: University of Manitoba Press, 2011.

Anderson, Mark Cronlund, and Carmen L. Robertson. *Seeing Red: A History of Natives in Canadian Newspapers*. Winnipeg: University of Manitoba Press, 2011.

Archibald, Linda, with Jonathan Dewar, Carrie Reid, and Vanessa Stevens. *Dancing, Singing, Painting, and Speaking the Healing Story: Healing through Creative Arts*. Ottawa: Aboriginal Healing Foundation, 2012.

Barkan, Elazar, and Alexander Karn, editors. *Taking Wrongs Seriously: Apologies and Reconciliation*. Stanford, California: Stanford University Press, 2006.

Battiste, Jaime. *Honouring 400 Years Kepmite'tmnej*. Eskasoni, Nova Scotia: Mi'kmaq Grand Council, 2010. Available in part at http://www.mawiomi.com/files/WebBook.pdf.

Battiste, Marie. *Decolonizing Education: Nourishing the Learning Spirit*. Saskatoon: Purich, 2013.

Bennett, John, and Susan Rowley, editors. *Uqalurait: An Oral History of Nunavut*. Montreal and Kingston: McGill-Queen's University Press, 2004.

Benton-Benai, Eddie. *The Mishomis Book*. Saint Paul, Minnesota: Red School House, 1988.

Black Elk and John G. Neihardt. *Black Elk Speaks: The Complete Edition*. Lincoln: University of Nebraska Press, 2014.

Bodnar, John. *Remaking America: Public Memory, Commemoration and Patriotism in the Twentieth Century*. Princeton, New Jersey: Princeton University Press, 1992.

Booth, W. James. *Communities of Memory: On Witness, Identity, and Justice*. Ithaca, New York: Cornell University Press, 2006.

Borrows, John. *Canada's Indigenous Constitution*. Toronto: University of Toronto Press, 2010.

Borrows, John. *Recovering Canada: The Resurgence of Indigenous Law*. Toronto: University of Toronto Press, 2002.

Briggs, Jean. *Inuit Morality Play: The Emotional Education of a Three-Year-Old*. St. John's, Newfoundland: Institute of Social and Economic Research, 1998.

Campbell, Sue. *Our Faithfulness to the Past: The Ethics and Politics of Memory*. Edited by Christine M. Koggel and Rockney Jacobsen. New York: Oxford University Press, 2014.

Cardinal, Harold, and Walter Hildebrandt. *Treaty Elders of Saskatchewan: Our Dream Is That Our Peoples Will One Day Be Clearly Recognized as Nations*. Calgary: University of Calgary Press, 2000.

Chamberlin, J. Edward. *If This Is Your Land, Where Are Your Stories? Finding Common Ground*. Toronto: Alfred A. Knopf, 2003.

Chartrand, Larry N., Tricia E. Logan, and Judy D. Daniels. *Métis History and Experience and Residential Schools in Canada*. Ottawa: Aboriginal Healing Foundation, 2006.

Cohen, Cynthia E., Roberto Gutiérrez Varea, and Polly O. Walker, editors. *Acting Together: Performance and the Creative Transformation of Conflict*. Volumes 1 and 2. Oakland, California: New Village, 2011.

Gibney, Mark, Rhoda E. Howard-Hassmann, Jean-Marc Coicaud, and Niklaus Steiner, editors. *The Age of Apology: Facing Up to the Past*. Philadelphia: University of Pennsylvania Press, 2008.

Gordon, Mary. *Roots of Empathy: Changing the World Child by Child*. New York: The Experiment, 2009.

Henderson, Sákéj. *The Mi'Kmaw Concordat*. Halifax: Fernwood, 1997.

Jennings, Francis, William N. Fenton, Mary A. Druke, and David R. Miller, editors. *The History and Culture of Iroquois Diplomacy: An Interdisciplinary Guide to the Treaties of the Six Nations and Their League*. Syracuse, New York: Syracuse University Press, 1995.

Johnston, Basil. *Honour Earth Mother*. Cape Croker Reserve, Neyaashiinigmiing, Ontario: Kegedonce, 2003.

Johnston, Basil. *Ojibway Ceremonies*. Toronto: McClelland and Stewart, 1982.

Kino-nda-niimi Collective. *The Winter We Danced: Voices from the Past, the Future, and the Idle No More Movement*. Winnipeg: Arbeiter Ring, 2014.

Miller, Bruce. *The Problem of Justice: Tradition and law in the Coast Salish World*. Lincoln: University of Nebraska Press, 2001.

Miller, J. R. *Compact, Contract, Covenant: Aboriginal Treaty-Making in Canada*. Toronto: University of Toronto Press, 2009.

Miller, J. R. *Lethal Legacy: Current Native Controversies in Canada*. Toronto: McClelland and Stewart, 2004.

Miller, Robert J., Jacinta Ruru, Larissa Behrendt, and Tracey Lindberg. *Discovering Indigenous Lands: The Doctrine of Discovery in the English Colonies*. New York: Oxford University Press, 2012.

Minow, Martha. *Between Vengeance and Forgiveness: Facing History after Genocide and Mass Violence*. Boston: Beacon, 1998.

Napoleon, Val, Hadley Friedland, Jim Henshaw, Ken Steacy, Janine Johnston, and Simon Roy. *Mikomosis and the Wetiko*. Victoria: Indigenous Law Research Unit, Faculty of Law, University of Victoria, 2013. http://www.indigenousbar.ca/indigenouslaw/wp-content/uploads/2013/04/Mikomosis-and-the-Wetiko-Teaching-Guide-Web.pdf.

Native Women's Centre. *Traditional Teachings Handbook*. 2008. http://www.nativewomenscentre.com/files/Traditional_Teachings_Booklet.pdf.

Newcomb, Steven T. *Pagans in the Promised Land: Decoding the Doctrine of Christian Discovery*. Golden, Colorado: Fulcrum, 2008.

Nobles, Melissa. *The Politics of Official Apologies*. Cambridge: Cambridge University Press, 2008.

Oosten, Jarich, Frédéric Laugrand, and Wim Rasing, editors. *Interviewing Inuit Elders*, volume 2, *Perspectives on Traditional Law*. Iqaluit: Nunavut Arctic College, 1999. http://tradition-orale.ca/english/pdf/Perspectives-On-Traditional-Law-E.pdf.

Opp, James, and John C. Walsh. *Placing Memory and Remembering Place in Canada*. Vancouver: UBC Press, 2010.

Parmar, Sharanjeet, Mindy Jane Roseman, Saudamini Siegrist, and Theo Sowa, editors. *Children and Transitional Justice: Truth-Telling, Accountability and Reconciliation*. Florence, Italy: UNICEF Innocenti Research Centre; and Cambridge, Massachusetts: Human Rights Program, Harvard University Law School, 2010.

Pauktuutit Inuit Women of Canada. *The Inuit Way: A Guide to Inuit Culture*. 2006. http://www.uqar.ca/files/boreas/inuitway_e.pdf.

Pertusati, Linda. *In Defense of Mohawk Land: Ethnopolitical Conflict in Native North America*. Albany, New York: SUNY Press, 1997.

Ray, Arthur J., Jim Miller, and Frank Tough. *Bounty and Benevolence: A History of Saskatchewan Treaties*. Montreal and Kingston: McGill-Queens University Press, 2000.

Regan, Paulette. *Unsettling the Settler Within: Indian Residential Schools, Truth Telling and Reconciliation in Canada*. Vancouver: UBC Press, 2010.

Schirch, Lisa. *Ritual and Symbol in Peacebuilding*. Bloomfield, Connecticut: Kumarian, 2005.

Simpson, Leanne, and Kiera L. Ladner, editors. *This Is an Honour Song: Twenty Years since the Blockades, an Anthology of Writing on the Oka Crisis*. Winnipeg: Arbeiter Ring, 2010.

Simpson, Leanne. *Dancing on Our Turtle's Back: Stories of Nishnaabeg Re-creation, Resurgence and a New Emergence*. Winnipeg: Arbeiter Ring, 2011.

Snyder, Emily, Lindsay Borrows, and Val Napoleon, with Hadley Friedland. *Mikomosis and the Wetiko: A Teaching Guide for Youth, Community, and Post-secondary Educators*. Victoria: Indigenous Law Research Unit, Faculty of Law, University of Victoria, 2014.

http://www.indigenousbar.ca/indigenouslaw/wp-content/uploads/2013/04/Mikomo-sis-and-the-Wetiko-Teaching-Guide-Web.pdf.

Spear, Wayne K. *Full Circle: The Aboriginal Healing Foundation and the Unfinished Work of Hope, Healing and Reconciliation.* Ottawa: Aboriginal Healing Foundation, 2014. http://www.ahf.ca/downloads/full-circle-2.pdf.

Tavuchis, Nicholas. *Mea Culpa: A Sociology of Apology and Reconciliation.* Stanford, California: Stanford University Press, 1991.

Treaty 7 Tribal Council, Walter Hildebrandt, Sarah Carter, and Dorothy First Rider. *The True Spirit and Original Intent of Treaty 7.* Montreal and Kingston: McGill-Queens University Press, 1996.

United Nations Global Compact. *A Business Reference Guide: United Nations Declaration on the Rights of Indigenous Peoples.* 2013. https://www.unglobalcompact.org/docs/issues_doc/human_rights/IndigenousPeoples/BusinessGuide.pdf.

Williams, Robert A., Jr. *The American Indian in Western Legal Thought: The Discourses of Conquest.* New York: Oxford University Press, 1990.

Williams, Robert A., Jr. *Linking Arms Together: American Indian Treaty Visions of Law and Peace, 1600–1800.* New York: Oxford University Press, 1997.

Williams, Robert A., Jr. *Savage Anxieties: The Invention of Western Civilization.* New York: Palgrave MacMillan, 2012.

Younging, Gregory, Jonathan Dewar, and Mike DeGagné, editors. *Response, Responsibility, and Renewal: Canada's Truth and Reconciliation Journey.* Ottawa: Aboriginal Healing Foundation, 2009.

2. Book Chapters, Journal Articles, and Papers

Anaya, S. James. "The Right of Indigenous Peoples to Self-Determination in the Post-Declaration Era." In *Making the Declaration Work: The United Nations Declaration on the Rights of Indigenous Peoples*, edited by Claire Charters and Rodolfo Stavenhagen, 184–198. Copenhagen: International Work Group for Indigenous Affairs, 2009.

Anderson, Kim. "Affirmations of an Indigenous Feminist." In *Indigenous Women and Feminism: Politics, Activism, Culture*, edited by Cheryl Suzack, Shari M. Huhndorf, Jeanne Perreault, and Jean Barman, 81–91. Vancouver: UBC Press, 2010.

Barkwell, Lawrence J., Anne Carriere Acco, and Amanda Rozyk. "The Origins of Metis Customary Law with a Discussion of Métis Legal Traditions." Unpublished paper, n.d. http://www.metismuseum.ca/media/db/07232.

Boler, Megan, and Michalinos Zembylas. "Discomforting Truths: The Emotional Terrain of Understanding Difference." In *Pedagogies of Difference: Rethinking Education for Social Change*, edited by Peter Pericles Trifonas, 110–136. New York: Routledge Falmer, 2003.

Bolton, Stephanie. "Museums Taken to Task: Representing First Peoples at the McCord Museum of Canadian History." In *First Nations, First Thoughts: The Impact of Indigenous Thought in Canada*, edited by Annis May Timpson, 145–169. Vancouver: UBC Press, 2009.

Borrows, John. "Aboriginal and Treaty Rights and Violence against Women." *Osgoode Hall Law Journal* 50, no. 3 (2013): 699–736. http://digitalcommons.osgoode.yorku.ca/cgi/viewcontent.cgi?article=1021&context=ohlj.

Borrows, John. "(Ab)Originalism and Canada's Constitution." *Supreme Court Law Review* 58, no. 2d (2012): 351–398.

Borrows, John. "Residential Schools, Respect and Responsibilities for Past Harms." *University of Toronto Law Journal* 64, no. 4 (2014): 486–504.

Borrows, John. "Wampum at Niagara: The Royal Proclamation, Canadian Legal History, and Self-Government." In *Aboriginal and Treaty Rights in Canada: Essays on Law, Equality and Respect for Difference*, edited by Michael Asch, 155–172. Vancouver: UBC Press, 1997.

Briggs, Jean. "Emotions Have Many Faces: Inuit Lessons." *Anthropologica: Reflections on Anthropology in Canada* 42, no. 2 (2000): 157–164.

Buchanan, Rachel. "Decolonizing the Archives: The Work of New Zealand's Waitangi Tribunal." *Public History Review* 14 (2007): 44–63.

Castellano, Marlene Brant, Linda Archibald, and Mike DeGagné. "Introduction: Aboriginal Truths in the Narrative of Canada." In *From Truth to Reconciliation: Transforming the Legacy of Residential Schools*, edited by Marlene Brant Castellano, Linda Archibald, and Mike DeGagne, 1–8. Ottawa: Aboriginal Healing Foundation, 2008.

Clark, Penney. "Representations of Aboriginal People in English Canadian History Textbooks: Toward Reconciliation." In *Teaching the Violent Past: History Education and Reconciliation*, edited by Elizabeth A. Cole, 81–120. Lanham, Maryland: Rowman and Littlefield, 2007.

Cook, Terry. "Evidence, Memory, Identity, and Community: Four Shifting Archival Paradigms." *Archival Science: International Journal on Recorded Information* 13, nos. 2–3 (2013): 95–120.

Corntassel, Jeff, and Cindy Holder. "Who's Sorry Now? Government Apologies, Truth Commissions, and Indigenous Self-Determination in Australia, Canada, Guatemala, and Peru." *Human Rights Review* 9, no. 4 (2008): 465–489.

Corntassel, Jeff, Chaw-win-is, and T'lakwadzi. "Indigenous Storytelling, Truth-Telling and Community Approaches to Reconciliation." *ESC: English Studies in Canada* 35, no. 1 (2009): 137–159.

de Greiff, Pablo. "The Role of Apologies in National Reconciliation Processes: On Making Trustworthy Institutions Trustworthy." In *The Age of Apology: Facing Up to the Past*, edited by Mark Gibney, Rhoda E. Howard-Hassmann, Jean-Marc Coicaud, and Niklaus Steiner, 120–136. Philadelphia: University of Pennsylvania Press, 2008.

Dumont, Alf, and Roger Hutchinson. "United Church Mission Goals and First Nations Peoples." In *The United Church of Canada: A History*, edited by Don Schweitzer, 221–238. Waterloo, Ontario: Wilfrid Laurier University Press, 2011.

Foley, Denis. "Iroquois Mourning and Condolence Installation Rituals: A Pattern of Social Integration and Continuity." In *Preserving Tradition and Understanding the Past: Papers from the Conference on Iroquois Research, 2001–2005*, edited by Christine Sternberg Patrick, 25–34. Albany, New York: State Education Department, University of the State of New York, 2010. http://www.nysm.nysed.gov/publications/record/vol_01/pdfs/CH03Foley.pdf.

Foster, Michael K. "Another Look at the Function of Wampum in Iroquois-White Councils." In *The History and Culture of Iroquois Diplomacy*, edited by Francis Jennings, William N. Fenton, Mary A. Druke, and David R. Miller, 99–114. Syracuse, New York: Syracuse University Press, 1995.

Friedland, Hadley. "Reflective Frameworks: Methods for Accessing, Understanding and Applying Indigenous Laws." *Indigenous Law Journal* 11, no. 1 (2012): 1–40. http://ilj.law.utoronto.ca/sites/ilj.law.utoronto.ca/files/media/ILJ%20vol%2011%20to%20post%20b.7-46.pdf.

Gabriel, Ellen. "Commentary: Aboriginal Women's Movement: A Quest for Self-Determination." *Aboriginal Policy Studies* 1, no. 1 (2011): 183–188.

Garneau, David. "Imaginary Spaces of Conciliation and Reconciliation." In *Reconcile This!* Issue of *West Coast Line 74* 46, no. 2 (2012): 28–38.

Ghostkeeper, Elmer. "*Weche* Teachings: Aboriginal Wisdom and Dispute Resolution." In *Intercultural Dispute Resolution in Aboriginal Contex*ts, edited by Catherine Bell and David Kahane, 161–175. Vancouver: UBC Press, 2004.

Green, Joyce. "Balancing Strategies: Aboriginal Women and Constitutional Rights in Canada." In *Making Space for Indigenous Feminism*, edited by Joyce Green, 140–159. Black Point, Nova Scotia: Fernwood, 2007.

Harris, Verne. "The Archival Sliver: Power, Memory, and Archives in South Africa." *Archival Science* 2 (2002): 63–86.

Henderson, Sakej. "Ayukpachi: Empowering Aboriginal Thought." In *Reclaiming Indigenous Voice and Vision*, edited by Marie Battiste, 248–278. Vancouver: UBC Press, 2000.

Henderson, Sakej. "First Nations' Legal Inheritances in Canada: The Mikmaq Model." *Manitoba Law Journal* 23, nos. 1–2 (1996): 1–31.

Hunhdorf, Shari. "'Atanarjuat, the Fast Runner': Culture, History, and Politics in Inuit Media." *American Anthropologist* 105, no. 4 (2003): 822–826.

Immordino-Yang, M. H., and Antonio Damasio. "We Feel, Therefore We Learn: The Relevance of Affective and Social Neuroscience to Education." *Mind, Brain, and Education* 1, no. 1 (2007): 3–10.

James, Matt. "Wrestling with the Past: Apologies, Quasi-apologies, and Non-apologies in Canada." In *The Age of Apology: Facing Up to the Past*, edited by Mark Gibney, Rhoda E. Howard-Hassmann, Jean-Marc Coicaud, and Niklaus Steiner, 137–153. Philadelphia: University of Pennsylvania Press, 2008.

Jimerson, Randall C. "Archives for All: Professional Responsibility and Social Justice." *American Archivist* 70, no. 2 (2007): 252–281.

John, Edward. "Survival, Dignity, Well-Being: Implementing the Declaration in British Columbia." In *Realizing the UN Declaration on the Rights of Indigenous Peoples: Triumph, Hope and Action*, edited by Jackie Hartley, Paul Joffee, and Jennifer Preston, 47–58. Saskatoon: Purich, 2010.

Johnston, Darlene. "Aboriginal Traditions of Tolerance and Reparation: Introducing Canadian Colonialism." In *Le Devoir de Memoire et les Politiques du Pardon*, edited by Micheline Labelle, Rachad Antoinius, and Georges Leroux, 141–159. Québec: Presses de l'Universite de Québec, 2005. http://ssrn.com/abstract=1879396.

Kelly, Fred. "Confession of a Born Again Pagan." In *From Truth to Reconciliation: Transforming the Legacy of Residential Schools*, edited by Marlene Brant Castellano, Linda Archibald, and Mike DeGagne, 13–40. Ottawa: Aboriginal Healing Foundation, 2008.

LaRoque, Emma. "The Colonization of a Native Woman Scholar." In *In the Days of Our Grandmothers: A Reader in Aboriginal Women's History in Canada*, edited by Mary-Ellen Kelm and Lorna Townsend, 397–406. Toronto: University of Toronto Press, 2006.

MacKenzie, Ian. "For Everything There Is a Season." In *Response, Responsibility, and Renewal: Canada's Truth and Reconciliation Journey*, edited by Gregory Younging, Jonathan Dewar, and Mike DeGagne, 87–96. Ottawa: Aboriginal Healing Foundation, 2009.

Magill, Clare, and Brandon Hamber. "If They Don't Start Listening to Us, the Future Is Going to Look the Same as the Past: Young People and Reconciliation in Northern Ireland, and Bosnia and Herzegovina." *Youth and Society* 43, no. 2 (2011): 509–527.

Mansfield, Emily. "Balance and Harmony: Peacemaking in Coast Salish Tribes of the Pacific Northwest." *Mediation Quarterly* 10, no. 4 (1993): 339–353.

Mason, Courtney, and Joshua Koehli. "Barriers to Physical Activity for Aboriginal Youth: Implications for Community Health, Policy and Culture." *Pimatisiwin: A Journal of Aboriginal and Indigenous Community Health* 10, no. 1 (2012): 97–107.

Marrus, Michael R. "Official Apologies and the Quest for Historical Justice." Occasional Paper III. Munk Centre for International Studies, University of Toronto, 2006.

McKay, M. Celeste, and Craig Benjamin. "A Vision for Fulfilling the Indivisible Rights of Indigenous Women." In *Realizing the UN Declaration on the Rights of Indigenous Peoples: Triumph, Hope and Action*, edited by Jackie Hartley, Paul Joffe, and Jennifer Preston, 156–168. Saskatoon: Purich, 2010.

McKay, Stan. "Expanding the Dialogue on Truth and Reconciliation – in a Good Way." In *From Truth to Reconciliation: Transforming the Legacy of Residential Schools*, edited by Marlene Brant Castellano, Linda Archibald, and Mike DeGagne, 103–115. Ottawa: Aboriginal Healing Foundation, 2008.

Menkel-Meadow, Carrie. "Peace and Justice: Notes on the Evolution and Purposes of Legal Processes." *Georgetown Law Journal* 94 (2006): 553–580.

Metallic, Alfred, and Robin Cavanaugh. "Mi'gmewey 'Politics': Mi'gmaq Political Traditions." 1 May 2002. http://www.migmawei.ca/documents/MigmeweyPoliticsMigmaqPoliticalTraditions_final.pdf.

Morse, Bradford W. "Indigenous Human Rights and Knowledge in Archives, Museums and Libraries: Some International Perspectives with specific Reference to New Zealand and Canada." n.d., 1–39. http://researchcommons.waikato.ac.nz/handle/10289/6350?show=full. Published in *Archival Science* 12, no. 2 (2012): 113–140.

Mullin, Margaret, Rev. (Thundering Eagle Woman). "We Are One in the Spirit: A Sermon on Healing and Reconciliation." In *We Are One in the Spirit: Liturgical Resources*, edited by Presbyterian Church in Canada, 27–29. http://presbyterian.ca/healing.

Nagy, Rosemary, and Emily Gillespie. "Representing Reconciliation: A News Frame Analysis of Print Media Coverage of Indian Residential Schools." *Transitional Justice Review* 1, no. 3 (2015): 3–41.

Napoleon, Val. "Thinking about Indigenous Legal Orders." In *Dialogues on Human Rights and Legal Pluralism*, edited by René Provost and Colleen Sheppard, 229–245. Dordrecht, Germany: Springer, 2013.

Napoleon, Val. "Who Gets to Say What Happened? Reconciliation Issues for the Gitxsan." In *Intercultural Dispute Resolution in Aboriginal Contexts*, edited by Catherine Bell and David Kahane, 176–195. Vancouver: UBC Press, 2004.

Prosper, Kerry, L. Jane McMillan, Anthony A. Davis, and Morgan Moffit. "Returning to Netukulimk: Mi'kmaq Cultural and Spiritual Connections with Resource Stewardship and Self-Governance." *International Indigenous Policy Journal* 2, no. 4 (2011): 1–17. http://ir.lib.uwo.ca/cgi/viewcontent.cgi?article=1037&context=iipj.

Qwul'sih'yah'maht (Robina Anne Thomas). "Honouring the Oral Traditions of My Ancestors through Storytelling." In *Research as Resistance: Critical, Indigenous, and Anti-oppressive*

Approaches, edited by Leslie Brown and Susan Strega, 237–254. Toronto: Canadian Scholars' Press and Women's Press, 2005.

Ramirez-Barat, Clara. "Transitional Justice and the Public Sphere." In *Transitional Justice, Culture and Society: Beyond Outreach*, edited by Clara Ramirez-Barat, 27–45. New York: International Centre for Transitional Justice and Social Science Research Council, 2014. https://s3.amazonaws.com/ssrc-cdn1/crmuploads/new_publication_3/%7B222A3D-3D-C177-E311-A360-001CC477EC84%7D.pdf.

Reid, Jennifer. "The Roman Catholic Foundations of Land Claims in Canada." In *Historical Papers 2009: Canadian Society of Church History* (2009): 5–19.

Robertson, Kirsty. "Threads of Hope: The Living Healing Quilt Project." *ESC: English Studies in Canada* 35, no. 1 (2009): 85–107.

Schonert-Reichl, K. A., and S. Hymel. "Educating the Heart as well as the Mind: Social and Emotional Learning for School and Life Success." *Education Canada* 47, no. 2 (2007): 20–25.

Sheppard, Maia G. "Creating a Caring Classroom in Which to Teach Difficult Histories." *History Teacher* 43, no. 3 (2010): 411–426.

Simon, Roger. "Towards a Hopeful Practice of Worrying: The Problematics of Listening and the Educative Responsibilities of Canada's Truth and Reconciliation Commission." In *Reconciling Canada: Critical Perspectives on the Culture of Redress*, edited by Jennifer Henderson and Pauline Wakeham, 129–142. Toronto: University of Toronto Press, 2013.

Simpson, Leanne Betasamosake, with Edna Manitowabi. "Theorizing Resurgence from within Nishnaabeg Thought." In *Centering Anishinaabeg Studies: Understanding the World through Stories*, edited by Niiganwewidam James Sinclair, Jill Doerfler, and Heidi Kiiwetinepinesiik Stark, 279–296. Winnipeg: University of Manitoba Press, 2013.

Snyder, Emily. "Indigenous Feminist Legal Theory." *Canadian Journal of Women and the Law* 26, no. 2 (2014): 365–401.

Stanton, Kim. "Canada's Truth and Reconciliation Commission: Settling the Past?" *International Indigenous Policy Journal* 2, no. 3 (2011): 1–18. http://ir.lib.uwo.ca/cgi/viewcontent.cgi?article=1034&context=iipj.

Te Hiwi, Braden P. "'What Is the Spirit of This Gathering?' Indigenous Sport Policy-Makers and Self-Determination in Canada." *International Indigenous Policy Journal* 5, no. 4 (2014): 1–16.

Valaskakis, Gail Guthrie. "Rights and Warriors: Media Memories and Oka." In *Indian Country: Essays on Contemporary Native Culture*, 35–66. Waterloo, Ontario: Wilfrid Laurier University Press, 2005.

van Erven, Eugene, and Kate Gardner. "Performing Cross-Cultural Conversations: Creating New Kinships through Community Theatre." In *Acting Together: Performance and the Creative Transformation of Conflict*, volume 2, *Building Just and Inclusive Communities*, edited by Cynthia E. Cohen, Roberto Gutierrez Varea, and Polly O. Walker, 9–41. Oakland, California: New Village, 2011.

Wilson, Ian E. "Peace, Order and Good Government: Archives in Society." *Archival Science: International Journal on Recorded Information* 12, no. 2 (2012): 235–244.

3. Theses

Cooper-Bolam, Trina. "Healing Heritage: New Approaches to Commemorating Canada's Indian Residential School System." MA thesis, Carleton University, 2014.

Friedland, Hadley. "The Wetiko (Windigo) Legal Principles: Responding to Harmful People in Cree, Anishinabek and Saulteaux Societies – Past, Present and Future Uses, with a Focus on Contemporary Violence and Child Victimization Concerns." LLM thesis, University of Alberta, 2009.

McCue, Lorna June. "Treaty-Making from an Indigenous Perspective: A Ned'u'ten-Canadian Treaty Model." LLM thesis, University of British Columbia, 1998.

McMullen, Cindy Leanne. "Bringing the Good Feelings Back: Imagining Stó:lo Justice." MA thesis, University of British Columbia, 1998. https://circle.ubc.ca/bitstream/id/20874/ubc_1998-0543.pdf.

Napoleon, Val. "Ayook: Gitksan Legal Order, Law, and Legal Theory." PhD dissertation, University of Victoria, 2009. http://dspace.library.uvic.ca/bitstream/handle/1828/1392/napoleon%20dissertation%20April%2026-09.pdf?sequence=1&isAllowed=y.

O'Connor, Oonagh. "The Role of the Non-Indigenous Witness in Canada's Truth and Reconciliation Commission." MA thesis, Royal Roads University, 2013.

Paige, S. Marlo. "In the Voices of the Sul-hween/Elders, on the Snuw'uyulh Teachings of Respect: Their Greatest Concerns Regarding Snuw'uyulh Today in the Coast Salish Hul'q'umi'num' Treaty Group Territory." MA thesis, University of Victoria, 2004.

4. Newspapers and News Reports

Amnesty International Canada, Assembly of First Nations, Canadian Friends Service Committee, Chiefs of Ontario, Federation of Saskatchewan Indian Nations, First Nations Summit, Grand Council of the Crees (Eeyou Istchee), Indigenous World Association, KAIROS: Canadian Ecumenical Justice Initiatives, Native Women's Association of Canada, Union of British Columbia Indian Chiefs. "Canada Uses World Conference to Continue Indefensible Attack on *UN Declaration on the Rights of Indigenous Peoples*." 24 September 2014. http://www.fns.bc.ca/pdf/Joint_Public_Statement_re_Canada_attack_on_UNDRIP_Sept_24_2014.pdf.

Anglican Church of Canada. "Canadian Churches to Formally Renew Covenant of Solidarity with Indigenous People." 19 June 2007. http://www.anglican.ca/news/canadian-churches-to-formally-renew-covenant-of-solidarity-with-indigenous-people/3006100.

APTN National News. "Cree Community Bans FNs Spirituality." 17 January 2011. http://aptn.ca/news/2011/01/17/crees-ban-sweat-lodges-fns-spirituality-from-community.

Assembly of First Nations. "The Silver Covenant Chain of Peace and Friendship Belt." 24 January 2012. http://www.afn.ca/uploads/files/cfng/sccpfb.pdf.

BasicNews.ca "Two-Row Wampum Centers Idle No More Toronto Rally, Not the Royal Proclamation." 9 October 2013. http://basicsnews.ca/two-row-wampum-centers-idle-no-more-toronto-rally-not-the-royal-proclamation.

Bellegarde, Perry. "Truth and Reconciliation: This Is Just the Beginning." *Globe and Mail*, 1 June 2015. http://www.theglobeandmail.com/globe-debate/truth-and-reconciliation-this-is-just-the-beginning/article24705066.

Brean, Joseph. "'Reconciliation' with First Nations, Not the Charter of Rights and Freedoms, Will Define the Supreme Court in Coming Years, Chief Justice Says." *National Post*, 13 March 2014. http://news.nationalpost.com/2014/03/13/reconciliation-with-first-nations-not-the-charter-of-rights-freedoms-will-define-the-supreme-court-in-coming-years-chief-justice-says.

Buchok, James. "Anishinaabe Elders Adopt Archbishop Weisgerber." *Catholic Register*, 17 April 2012. http://www.catholicregister.org/item/14277-anishinaabe-elders-adopt-weisgerber.

CBC News. "Civilization Museum Now the Canadian Museum of History." 12 December 2013. http://www.cbc.ca/news/canada/ottawa/civilization-museum-now-the-canadian-museum-of-history-1.2461738.

CBC News. "Murdered and Missing Aboriginal Women Deserve Inquiry, Rights Group Says." 12 January 2015. http://www.cbc.ca/news/politics/murdered-and-missing-aboriginal-women-deserve-inquiry-rights-group-says-1.2897707.

CBC News. "Pope Expresses 'Sorrow' for Abuse at Residential Schools." 29 April 2009. http://www.cbc.ca/news/world/pope-expresses-sorrow-for-abuse-at-residential-schools-1.778019.

CBC News. "Residential School Day Scholars Launch Class-Action Lawsuit." 16 August 2012. http://www.cbc.ca/news/canada/british-columbia/residential-school-day-scholars-launch-class-action-lawsuit-1.1146607.

CBC News. "6 Landmark Rulings on Native Rights." 8 January 2013. http://www.cbc.ca/news/canada/6-landmark-rulings-on-native-rights-1.1316961.

CBC News. "Sixties Scoop Case Moves Forward as Class-Action Lawsuit." 3 December 2014. http://www.cbc.ca/news/canada/thunder-bay/sixties-scoop-case-moves-forward-as-class-action-lawsuit-1.2859332.

CBC News. "Teachers Seek Healing through Truth Commission." 18 June 2010. http://www.cbc.ca/news/canada/manitoba/story/2010/06/18/mb-truth-reconciliation-healing-teachers-winnipeg.html.

CBC News. "Women's Memorial March in Vancouver Attracts Hundreds." 14 February 2015. http://www.cbc.ca/news/canada/british-columbia/womens-memorial-march-in-vancouver-attracts-hundreds-1.2957930.

Coates, Ken S. "Aboriginal Women Deserve Much More Than an Inquiry." *National Post*, 16 February 2015. http://news.nationalpost.com/2015/02/16/ken-s-coates-aboriginal-women-deserve-much-more-than-an-inquiry.

Cobb, Chris. "More than 3,000 Make the Reconciliation March from Gatineau to Ottawa City Hall." *Ottawa Citizen*, 31 May 2015. http://ottawacitizen.com/news/local-news/more-than-3000-make-the-reconciliation-march-from-gatineau-to-ottawa-city-hall.

Council of Ministers of Education, Canada. "Education Ministers Signal Transformation Key to the Future." 9 July 2014. http://cmec.ca/278/Press-Releases/Education-Ministers-Signal-Transformation-Key-to-the-Future.html?id_article=826.

Edmiston, Jake. "'Indian Residential Schools' or 'Settler Colonial Genocide'? Native Group Slams Human Rights Museum over Exhibit Wording." *National Post*, 8 June 2013. http://news.nationalpost.com/news/canada/indian-residential-schools-or-settler-colonial-genocide.

Gazette: Law Society of Upper Canada. "Law Society Throws Support Behind Reconciliation Initiatives." 11 December 2014. http://www.lawsocietygazette.ca/news/law-society-throws-support-behind-reconciliation-initiatives.

Hale, Alan S. "Treaty 3 Holds Commemoration Ceremony for Survivors of District Residential School System." *Kenora Daily Miner and News*, 25 March 2014. http://www.kenoradailyminerandnews.com/2014/03/25/treaty-3-holds-commemoration-ceremony-for-survivors-of-district-residential-school-system.

International Center for Transitional Justice. "Youth Reporters Tell the Story of Residential Schools." 18 November 2011. http://ictj.org/news/youth-reporters-tell-story-residential-schools.

International Center for Transitional Justice. "Our Legacy, Our Hope." 20 June 2012. https://www.ictj.org/news/our-legacy-our-hope.

Jang, Brent. "Gas Exports from B.C. Seen as Key to Reviving Pipeline." *Globe and Mail*, 2 February 2014. http://www.theglobeandmail.com/report-on-business/industry-news/energy-and-resources/gas-exports-from-bc-said-key-to-reviving-pipeline/article16657138.

Kinew, Wab. "It's the Same Great Spirit." *Winnipeg Free Press*, 22 October 2012. http://www.winnipegfreepress.com/local/its-the-same--great-spirit-175193351.html.

Lavoie, Judith. "Paintings Bear Witness to Residential Schools' Harsh Life." *Victoria Times-Colonist*, 31 March 2013. http://www.timescolonist.com/news/local/paintings-bear-witness-to-b-c-residential-schools-harsh-life-1.101179.

Lee, Jeff. "Tsilhqot'in Nation Strikes Conciliatory Note with Municipalities." *Vancouver Sun*, 24 September 2014, A6.

Legacy of Hope Foundation. "NWT and NU Curriculum on Residential Schools Unveiled." 3 October 2012. http://www.legacyofhope.ca/projects/nwt-nu-curriculum.

Lewis, Jeff. "Northwest Territories Eyes Revival of Mackenzie Valley Pipeline Project." *Financial Post*, 11 June 2013. http://business.financialpost.com/2013/06/11/northwest-territories-eyes-revival-of-mackenzie-valley-pipeline-project/?__lsa=c5d4-608a.

Lewis, Jeff. "TransCanada CEO Says Canada Needs to Resolve Conflicts over Pipelines." *Globe and Mail*, 4 February 2015. http://www.theglobeandmail.com/report-on-business/economy/transcanada-ceo-says-canada-needs-to-resolve-conflicts-over-pipelines/article22798276.

Library and Archives Canada. "New Exhibition Reflecting the Uniqueness of the Inuit Experience of Residential Schools Launched at Library and Archives Canada." 4 March 2009. http://www.collectionscanada.gc.ca/013/013-380-e.html.

MacDonald, Michael. "Shale Gas Conflict in New Brunswick Underscores Historical Grievances, Rights of First Nations." *Toronto Star*, 25 December 2013. http://www.thestar.com/news/canada/2013/12/25/shale_gas_conflict_in_new_brunswick_underscores_historic_grievances_rights_of_first_nations.html.

Martin, Nick. "Fontaine Regrets Blaming All Catholics for His School Trauma." *Winnipeg Free Press*, 15 April 2012. http://www.winnipegfreepress.com/breakingnews/Fontaine-regrets-blaming-all-Catholics-for-his-school-trauma-147494005.html.

Mehta, Diana. "'Sixties Scoop' Class-Action Lawsuit to Proceed." *Canadian Press*, 4 December 2014. http://www.ctvnews.ca/canada/60s-scoop-class-action-lawsuit-to-proceed-1.2132317.

Monet, Jenni. "Mohawk Women Integrate the Condolence Ceremony into Modern Systems." *Indian Country Today*, 21 March 2012. http://indiancountrytodaymedianetwork.com/2012/03/21/mohawk-women-integrate-condolence-ceremony-modern-systems-103853.

Moore, Dene. "Federal Appeal Court Gives OK on Hearing First Nations' Day-School Suit." *Canadian Press*, 4 March 2014. http://www.ctvnews.ca/canada/federal-appeal-court-gives-ok-on-hearing-first-nations-day-school-suit-1.1713809.

Onondaga Nation. "Oren Lyons Presents at U.N. 5/15/14." 15 May 2014. http://www.onondaganation.org/news/2014/oren-lyons-presents-at-u-n-51514.

Ratuski, Andrea. "Residential School Art Series Awarded to U of M." CBC News, 24 September 2013. http://www.cbc.ca/news/canada/manitoba/scene/residential-school-art-series-awarded-to-u-of-m-1.1865994.

Reconciliation Canada. "City of Vancouver Council Unanimously Support City of Reconciliation Framework." 29 October 2014. http://reconciliationcanada.ca/city-of-vancouver-council-unanimously-support-city-of-reconciliation-framework.

Reconciliation Canada. "New Youth Program: Through Our Eyes: Changing the Canadian Lens." 9 January 2014. http://reconciliationcanada.ca/new-youth-program-through-our-eyes-changing-the-canadian-lens.

Rennie, Steve. "Idle No More Protestors Mark 25th Anniversary of Royal Proclamation." *Canadian Press*, 7 October 2013. http://www.thestar.com/news/canada/2013/10/07/idle_no_more_protesters_mark_250th_anniversary_of_royal_proclamation.html.

Schwartz, Daniel, and Mark Gollom. "NB Fracking Protests and the Fight for Aboriginal Rights." CBC News, 19 October 2013, http://www.cbc.ca/news/canada/n-b-fracking-protests-and-the-fight-for-aboriginal-rights-1.2126515.

Sison, Marites N. "Primate's Commission Begins Work." *Anglican Journal*, 2 May 2014. http://www.anglicanjournal.com/articles/primate-s-commission-begins-work.

Steel, Debora. "Alberni Indian Residential Students Reunited with Childhood Art." *Ha-Shilth-Sa*, 3 April 2013. http://www.hashilthsa.com/news/2013-04-03/alberni-indian-residential-students-reunited-childhood-art.

Taliman, Valerie. "Christian Crees Tear Down Sweat Lodge." *Indian Country Today*, 7 February 2011. http://indiancountrytodaymedianetwork.com/2011/02/07/christian-crees-tear-down-sweat-lodge-15500.

Threlfall, John. "Her Next Chapter." *UVic Torch*, Spring 2015, 24. http://issuu.com/uvic_torch_alumni_magazine/docs/2015_spring.

University of Manitoba. "Historic Agreement Signed on National Aboriginal Day." 21 June 2013. http://umanitoba.ca/news/blogs/blog/2013/06/21/historic-agreement-signed-on-national-aboriginal-day.

University of Winnipeg. "UWinnipeg Healing Quilt Gifted to TRC Commissioners." 17 June 2010. http://www.uwinnipeg.ca/index/uw-news-action/story.364/title.uwinnipeg-healing-quilt-gifted-to-trc-commissioner.

Vancouver Province. "Historic Children's Paintings on Display at the BC National Event Learning Centre." 15 September 2013. http://www.theprovince.com/entertainment/Historic+children+paintings/8914210/story.html.

Zabjek, Alexandra. "Youths Picked to 'Jolt' City Managers about Legacy of Residential Schools." *Edmonton Journal*, 26 March 2015. http://www.pressreader.com/canada/edmonton-journal/20150326/281509339682927/TextView.

5. Government Records and Publications

Canada, Debates of the House of Commons (Hansard). 2nd Session, 41st Parliament, volume 221, 1 June 2015. http://www.parl.gc.ca/HousePublications/Publication.aspx?Language=E-&Mode=1&Parl=41&Ses=2&DocId=8015455.

Canada, Debates of the Senate (Hansard). 2nd Session, 40th Parliament, volume 146, issue 45, 11 June 2009. http://www.parl.gc.ca/Content/Sen/Chamber/402/Debates/045d-b_2009-06-11-e.htm#3.

Canada, House of Commons Standing Committee on Canadian Heritage. 1st Session, 41st Parliament, 5 June 2013. http://www.parl.gc.ca/HousePublications/Publication.aspx?DocId=6209352&Language=E&Mode=1&Parl=41&Ses=1.

Canada, Minister of Citizenship and Immigration Canada. *Discover Canada: The Rights and Responsibilities of Citizenship*. 2012. http://www.cic.gc.ca/english/resources/publications/discover/index.asp.

Library and Archives Canada. "Collection Development Framework." 30 March 2005. http://www.collectionscanada.gc.ca/obj/003024/f2/003024-e.pdf.

Library and Archives Canada. "Conducting Research on Residential Schools: A Guide to the Records of the Indian and Inuit Affairs Program and Related Resources at Library and Archives Canada." 2010. http://www.collectionscanada.gc.ca/obj/020008/f2/020008-2000-e.pdf.

Library and Archives Canada. "The Legacy of the Residential School System in Canada: A Selective Bibliography." 2009. http://www.bac-lac.gc.ca/eng/archives/archives-en/aboriginal-heritage/Pages/residential-schools-bibliography-2009.aspx.

Library and Archives Canada. "Native Residential Schools in Canada: A Selective Bibliography." 2002. http://www.collectionscanada.gc.ca/native-residential/index-e.html.

Sport Canada. "Canadian Sport Policy." 27 June 2012. http://canadiansporttourism.com/sites/default/files/docs/csp2012_en_lr.pdf.

6. Reports, statements, and speeches

Aboriginal Peoples Television Network. "Annual Report, 2013." n.d. http://aptn.ca/corporate/PDFs/APTN_2013_AnnualReport_ENG.pdf.

Aboriginal Rights Coalition. *A New Covenant: Towards the Constitutional Recognition and Protection of Aboriginal Self-Government in Canada: A Pastoral Statement by the Leaders of the Christian Churches on Aboriginal Rights and the Canadian Constitution*. 5 February 1987. http://home.istar.ca/~arc/english/new_cov_e.html.

Aboriginal Rights Coalition. "Recommendations to the Royal Commission on Aboriginal Peoples." 1 June 1993. http://home.istar.ca/~arc/english/RCAP.html.

Alfred, Taiaiake, and Lana Lowe. "Warrior Societies in Contemporary Indigenous Communities." Research paper for the Ipperwash Inquiry, 2007. http://www.attorneygeneral.jus.gov.on.ca/inquiries/ipperwash/policy_part/research/pdf/Alfred_and_Lowe.pdf.

Anaya, S. James. "Report of the Special Rapporteur on the Rights of Indigenous Peoples: The Situation of Indigenous Peoples in Canada." United Nations General Assembly, Human Rights Council, A/HRC/27/52/Add.2, 4 July 2014. http://unsr.jamesanaya.org/docs/countries/2014-report-canada-a-hrc-27-52-add-2-en.pdf.

Anglican Church of Canada. "Learning to Call One Another Friends: The Primate's Commission on Discovery, Reconciliation and Justice." June 2014. http://www.anglican.ca/primate/files/2014/06/PCDRJ_June2014_Update.pdf.

Anglican Church of Canada. "A Message to the Church Concerning the Primate's Commission on Discovery, Reconciliation and Justice." 10 June 2014. http://www.anglican.ca/primate/communications/2014archive/commission-on-discovery-reconciliation-justice.

Anglican Church of Canada. "A New Agape: Plan of Anglican Work in Support of a New Partnership between Indigenous and non-Indigenous Anglicans." n.d. http://www.anglican.ca/about/ccc/acip/a-new-agape.

Anglican Church of Canada. "Resolution A086 R1: Repudiate the Doctrine of Discovery." 2010. http://archive.anglican.ca/gs2010/resolutions/a086.

Anglican Church of Canada. "A Submission by the Anglican Church of Canada to the Royal Commission on Aboriginal Peoples." November 1993. http://www.anglican.ca/relationships/newsarchive/rcap_summary.

Assembly of First Nations. "Royal Commission on Aboriginal Peoples at 10 Years: A Report Card." 2006. http://www.turtleisland.org/resources/afnrcap2006.pdf.

Assembly of First Nations, Chiefs of Ontario, Grand Council of the Crees (Eeyou Istchee), Amnesty International, Canadian Friends Service Committee (Quakers), and KAIROS: Canadian Ecumenical Justice Initiatives. "The Doctrine of Discovery: Its Enduring Impact on Indigenous Peoples and the Right to Redress for Past Conquests (Article 28 and 37 of the United Nations Declaration on the Rights of Indigenous Peoples)." Joint statement to the Permanent Forum on Indigenous Issues, 11th Session, New York, 7-18 May 2012. http://www.afn.ca/uploads/files/pfii_2012_-_doctrine_of_discovery_-_joint_statement_fe.pdf.

Bahá'í Community of Canada. "Submission of the Bahá'í Community of Canada to the Truth and Reconciliation Commission." 20 September 2013. http://www.ca.bahai.org/sites/default/files/file_attach/1.%202013%20-%20Submission%20to%20the%20Truth%20and%20Reconciliation%20Commission.pdf.

Belcourt, Christie. "Stained Glass Window Dedication Ceremony -- Christi Belcourt, Artist." Speech on Parliament Hill, 26 November 2012. https://www.aadnc-aandc.gc.ca/eng/1370613921985/1370613942308.

Borrows, John. "Seven Generations, Seven Teachings: Ending the Indian Act." Research paper for the National Centre for First Nations Governance, May 2008. http://fngovernance.org/resources_docs/7_Generations_7_Teachings.pdf.

Borrows, Lindsay, Laura Mayer, and Mi'kmaq Legal Services Network, Eskasoni. "Mi'kmaq Legal Traditions Report." Accessing Justice and Reconciliation Project, Indigenous Law Research Unit, University of Victoria, 2013.

Bush, Peter. "How Have the Churches Lived Out Their Apologies?" Research report prepared for the Truth and Reconciliation Commission of Canada, 2012.

Campbell, Sue. "Remembering for the Future: Memory as a Lens on the Indian Residential School Truth and Reconciliation Commission." Discussion paper prepared for the Truth and Reconciliation Commission of Canada, April 2008.

Canada, Aboriginal Affairs and Northern Development Canada. "Canada's Statement of Support on the United Nations Declaration on the Rights of Indigenous Peoples." 12 November 2010. http://www.aadnc-aandc.gc.ca/eng/1309374239861/1309374546142.

Canada, Aboriginal Affairs and Northern Development Canada. "Renewing the Comprehensive Land Claims Policy: Towards a Framework for Addressing Section 35 Aboriginal Rights." 2014. https://www.aadnc-aandc.gc.ca/DAM/DAM-INTER-HQ-LDC/STAGING/texte-text/ldc_ccl_renewing_land_claims_policy_2014_1408643594856_eng.pdf.

Canada, Minister of Indian Affairs and Northern Development. "Gathering Strength: Canada's Aboriginal Action Plan: A Progress Report." 2000. http://publications.gc.ca/collections/Collection/R32-192-2000E.pdf.

Canada. *Northern Frontier, Northern Homeland: The Report of the Mackenzie Valley Pipeline Inquiry.* Volume 1. Ottawa: Supply and Services Canada, 1977.

Canada, Office of the Auditor General of Canada. "Documentary Heritage of the Government of Canada: Library and Archives Canada." 2014. http://www.oag-bvg.gc.ca/internet/docs/parl_oag_201411_07_e.pdf.

Canada, Permanent Mission of Canada to the United Nations. "Canada's Statement on the World Conference on Indigenous Peoples Outcome Document." 22 September 2014. http://www.canadainternational.gc.ca/prmny-mponu/canada_un-canada_onu/statements-declarations/other-autres/2014-09-22_WCIPD-PADD.aspx?lang=eng.

Canada, Royal Commission on Aboriginal Peoples. *Highlights from the Report of the Royal Commission on Aboriginal Peoples: People to People, Nation to Nation.* Ottawa: Minister of Supply and Services Canada, 1996. http://www.aadnc-aandc.gc.ca/eng/1100100014597/1100100014637.

Canada, Royal Commission on Aboriginal Peoples. *Report of the Royal Commission on Aboriginal Peoples.* 5 volumes. Ottawa: Minister of Supply and Services Canada, 1996. http://www.collectionscanada.gc.ca/webarchives/20071115053257/http://www.ainc-inac.gc.ca/ch/rcap/sg/sgmm_e.html.

Canada, Statistics Canada. "Aboriginal Peoples in Canada: First Nations People, Métis and Inuit: National Household Survey, 2011." http://www12.statcan.gc.ca/nhs-enm/2011/as-sa/99-011-x/99-011-x2011001-eng.pdf.

Canadian Conference of Catholic Bishops. "Let Justice Flow Like a Mighty River: Brief to the Royal Commission on Aboriginal Peoples." 1995. http://www.cccb.ca/site/images/stories/pdf/let_justice_flow_like_a_mighty_river.pdf.

Canadian Museum for Human Rights. "Speech Delivered by CMHR President and CEO Stuart Murray at 2017 Starts Now|Débute maintenant in Winnipeg." 3 May 2013. https://human-rights.ca/about-museum/news/speech-delivered-cmhr-president-and-ceo-stuart-murray-2017-starts-nowdebute.

Canadian Museum for Human Rights. "Speech Delivered by President and CEO Stuart Murray to the Truth and Reconciliation Commission National Research Centre Forum." 3 March 2011. https://humanrights.ca/about-museum/news/speech-delivered-president-and-ceo-stuart-murray-truth-and-reconciliation.

Canadian Museum for Human Rights. "Statement from the President and CEO: Use of 'Genocide' in Relation to Treatment of Indigenous Peoples in Canada." 26 July 2013. http://museumforhumanrights.ca/about-museum/news/statement-president-and-ceo-use-genocide-relation-treatment-indigenous-peoples.

Canadian Museum of Civilization and Canadian War Museum. "Research Strategy." 15 July 2013. http://www.civilization.ca/research-and-collections/files/2013/07/research-strategy.pdf.

CBC/Radio-Canada. "Going the Distance: Annual Report 2013-2014." n.d. http://www.cbc.radio-canada.ca/_files/cbcrc/documents/annual-report/2013-2014/cbc-radio-canada-annual-report-2013-2014.pdf.

Centre for Youth and Society, University of Victoria. "Residential Schools Resistance Narratives: Significance and Strategies for Indigenous Youth." Research report prepared for the Truth and Reconciliation Commission of Canada, 27 March 2012.

Charelson, Estella, and Tsleil-Waututh Nation. "Coast Salish Legal Traditions Report." Accessing Justice and Reconciliation Project, Indigenous Law Research Unit, University of Victoria, 2013.

The Charrette on Energy, Environment and Aboriginal Issues. "Responsible Energy Resource Development in Canada: Summary of the Dialogue of the Charrette on Energy, Environment and Aboriginal Issues." December 2013.

City Manager. "Framework for City of Reconciliation." Report to Vancouver City Council, 18 September 2014. http://former.vancouver.ca/ctyclerk/cclerk/20141028/documents/rr1.pdf.

Coates, Kenneth, and Dwight Newman. "The End Is Not Nigh: Reason over Alarmism in Analysing the *Tsilhqot'in* Decision." MacDonald-Laurier Institute, September 2014. http://www.macdonaldlaurier.ca/files/pdf/MLITheEndIsNotNigh.pdf.

David, Jennifer. "Aboriginal Languages Broadcasting in Canada: An Overview and Recommendations to the Task Force on Aboriginal Languages and Cultures, 2004." Report prepared for Aboriginal Peoples Television Network, 26 November 2004. http://aptn.ca/corporate/PDFs/Aboriginal_Language_and_Broadcasting_2004.pdf.

Eyford, Douglas R. "Forging Partnerships, Building Relationships: Aboriginal Canadians and Energy Development." Report to the Prime Minister, November 2013. https://www.nrcan.gc.ca/sites/www.nrcan.gc.ca/files/www/pdf/publications/ForgPart-Online-e.pdf.

Eyford, Douglas R. "A New Direction: Advancing Aboriginal and Treaty Rights." Report to Minister of Aboriginal Affairs and Northern Development Canada, the Honourable Bernard Valcourt, February 2015. https://www.aadnc-aandc.gc.ca/DAM/DAM-INTER-HQ-LDC/STAGING/texte-text/eyford_newDirection-report_april2015_1427810490332_eng.pdf.

de Greiff, Pablo. "Report of the Special Rapporteur on the Promotion of Truth, Justice, Reparations and Guarantees on Non-recurrence." UN General Assembly, Human Rights Council, A/HRC/21/46, 9 August 2012. http://www.ohchr.org/Documents/HRBodies/HRCouncil/RegularSession/Session21/A-HRC-21-46_en.pdf.

de Greiff, Pablo. "Report of the Special Rapporteur on the Promotion of Truth, Justice, Reparations and Guarantees on Non-recurrence." UN General Assembly, Human Rights Council, A/HRC/24/42, 28 August 2013. http://www.ohchr.org/EN/HRBodies/HRC/RegularSessions/Session24/Pages/ListReports.aspx.

Dewar, Jonathan, David Gaertner, Ayumi Goto, Ashok Mathur, and Sophie McCall. "Practicing Reconciliation: A Collaborative Study of Aboriginal Art, Resistance and Cultural Politics." Research report prepared for the Truth and Reconciliation Commission of Canada, 2013.

First Nations Summit. "Royal Proclamation Still Relevant on 250th Anniversary." n.d. http://www.fns.bc.ca/pdf/FNS_Op-ed_re_250th_anniver_of_Royal_Proclamation_10_07_13.pdf.

Friedland, Hadley. "Accessing Justice and Reconciliation." Final report of the IBA Accessing Justice and Reconciliation Project, 4 February 2014. http://indigenousbar.ca/indigenous-law/wp-content/uploads/2013/04/iba_ajr_final_report.pdf.

IndigenACTION. "Phase One: Roundtable Report." 2012. http://www.afn.ca/uploads/files/indigenaction/indigenactionroundtablereport.pdf.

International Centre for Transitional Justice. "ICTJ Program Report: Children and Youth." 9 August 2013. http://www.ictj.org/news/ictj-program-report-children-and-youth.

International Centre for Transitional Justice. "Strengthening Indigenous Rights through Truth Commissions: A Practitioner's Resource." 2012. https://www.ictj.org/sites/default/files/ICTJ-Truth-Seeking-Indigenous-Rights-2012-English.pdf.

Johnston, David. "Symposium in Honour of the 250th Anniversary of the Royal Proclamation." Speech, Gatineau, Québec, 7 October 2013. http://www.gg.ca/document.aspx?id-=15345&lan=eng.

Journalists for Human Rights. "Buried Voices: Media Coverage of Aboriginal Issues in Ontario -- Media Monitoring Report, 2010-2013." August 2013. http://www.documentcloud.org/documents/784473-media-coverage-of-aboriginal-issues.html#document/p1.

Littlechild, Wilton. "Stained Glass Window Dedication Ceremony: Wilton Littlechild, Commissioner of the Truth and Reconciliation Commission." Speech on Parliament Hill, 26 November 2012. https://www.aadnc-aandc.gc.ca/eng/1370615213241/1370615618980.

McGrady, Leo. "'Cedar as Sister': Indigenous Law and the Common Law of Protests." Report prepared for the Canadian Union of Public Employees British Columbia, 28 February 2013. http://www.cupe.bc.ca/sites/default/files/Guide%20to%20the%20Law%20of%20Protests%20in%20BC%20February%2028%20%202013.pdf.

Métis National Council. "Proceedings from 'Nobody's Children': A Métis Nation Residential School Dialogue." 28-29 March 2012. http://www.metisnation.ca/wp-content/uploads/2012/03/Minutesfinal-Metis-Nation-Residential-School-Dialogue-Proceedings-Mar-28-29-2012.pdf.

Miller, John. "Ipperwash and the Media: A Critical Analysis of How the Story Was Covered." Report prepared for Aboriginal Legal Services of Toronto, October 2005. http://www.attorneygeneral.jus.gov.on.ca/inquiries/ipperwash/policy_part/projects/pdf/ALST_Ipperwash_and_media.pdf.

Newman, Dwight. "The Rule and Role of Law: The Duty to Consult, Aboriginal Communities, and the Canadian Natural Resource Sector." MacDonald-Laurier Institute, May 2014. http://www.macdonaldlaurier.ca/files/pdf/DutyToConsult-Final.pdf.

Office of the Treaty Commissioner. *Treaty Implementation: Fulfilling the Covenant.* Saskatoon: Office of the Treaty Commissioner, 2007.

Ontario Provincial Advocate for Children and Youth. "Feathers of Hope: A First Nations Youth Action Plan." n.d. http://cwrp.ca/sites/default/files/publications/en/Feathers_of_Hope.pdf.

The Philanthropist. "The Philanthropic Community's Declaration of Action." 15 June 2015. http://thephilanthropist.ca/2015/06/the-philanthropic-communitys-declaration-of-action.

Prairie Women's Health Centre of Excellence. "Nitâpwewininân: Ongoing Effects of Residential Schools on Aboriginal Women -- Towards Inter-generational Reconciliation." Final report to the Truth and Reconciliation Commission of Canada, March 2012.

Presbyterian Church in Canada. "Aboriginal Spirituality: A Theological Framework For." 2013. http://presbyterian.ca/gao/2013referrals.

Presbyterian Church in Canada. "Acts and Proceedings of the 137th General Assembly of the Presbyterian Church in Canada." 2011. http://presbyterian.ca/acts-and-proceedings.

Presbyterian Church in Canada. "Presbyterian Statement on Aboriginal Spiritual Practices." 29 January 2015. https://ecumenism.net/2015/01/presbyterian-statement-on-aboriginal-spiritual-practices.htm.

Public Policy Forum. "Building Authentic Partnerships: Aboriginal Participation in Major Resource Development Opportunities." 2012. http://www.ppforum.ca/sites/default/files/Aboriginal%20Participation%20in%20Major%20Resource%20Development_ENG_3.pdf.

Reconciliation Canada. "A Shared Tomorrow." Elders' statement. n.d. http://reconciliation-canada.ca/explore/elders-statement.

Seixas, Peter, and Jill Colyer. "A Report on the National Meeting of the Historical Thinking Project." 15–17 January 2013. http://historicalthinking.ca/sites/default/files/files/docs/HT-P2013Report.pdf.

Shaheed, Farida. "Report of the Special Rapporteur in the Field of Cultural Rights: Memorialization Processes." United Nations General Assembly, Human Rights Council, A/HRC/25/49, 23 January 2014. http://www.ohchr.org/EN/HRBodies/HRC/RegularSessions/Session25/Pages/ListReports.aspx.

Sport Canada, Canadian Sport Policy Renewal, Roundtable on Sport and Aboriginal Peoples. "Summary Report." 15 July 2011. https://sirc.ca/sites/default/files/content/docs/pdf/aboriginal.pdf.

Snyder, Emily. "Gender and Indigenous Law." Report for the University of Victoria Indigenous Law Unit, the Indigenous Bar Association, and the Truth and Reconciliation Commission of Canada, 31 March 2013. http://indigenousbar.ca/indigenouslaw/wp-content/uploads/2013/04/Gender-and-Indigenous-Law-report-March-31-2013-ESnyder1.pdf.

Truth and Reconciliation Commission of Canada. "Atlantic National Event Concept Paper." 26-29 October 2011. http://www.myrobust.com/websites/atlantic/File/Concept%20Paper%20atlantic%20august%2010%20km_cp%20_3_.pdf.

Turpel-Lafond, Mary Ellen. "Aboriginal Children: Human Rights as a Lens to Break the Intergenerational Legacy of Residential Schools." Report submitted by the Office of the British Columbia Representative for Children and Youth, Victoria, British Columbia, to the Truth and Reconciliation Commission of Canada, July 2012. http://www.llbc.leg.bc.ca/public/pubdocs/bcdocs2012_2/522248/rcy-aboriginalchildren-final.pdf.

United Church of Canada. "Affirming Other Spiritual Paths." 18 February 2015. http://www.united-church.ca/files/aboriginal/schools/affirming-other-spiritual-paths.pdf.

United Church of Canada. "Living Faithfully in the Midst of Empire: Report to the 39th General Council 2006." 2007. http://www.united-church.ca/files/economic/globalization/report.pdf.

United Church of Canada. "Residential Schools Update." January 2012. http://develop.united-church.ca/files/communications/newsletters/residential-schools-update_120101.pdf.

United Church of Canada. "Reviewing Partnership in the Context of Empire." 2009. http://www.gc41.ca/sites/default/files/pcpmm_empire.pdf.

United Church of Canada, Executive of the General Council. "Addendum H: Covenanting for Life." 24–26 March 2012. http://www.united-church.ca/files/general-council/gc40/addenda_2012-03-2426_executive.pdf.

United Church of Canada, Executive of the General Council. "Meeting Summary." 24-26 March 2012. http://www.united-church.ca/files/general-council/gc40/gce_1203_highlights.pdf.

United Nations Expert Mechanism on the Rights of Indigenous Peoples. "Access to Justice in the Promotion and Protection of the Rights of Indigenous Peoples." United Nations General Assembly, Human Rights Council, A/HRC/EMRIP/2013/2, 29 April 2013. http://www.ohchr.org/Documents/Issues/IPeoples/EMRIP/Session6/A-HRC-EMRIP-2013-2_en.pdf.

United Nations General Assembly. "Outcome Document of the High-Level Plenary Meeting of the General Assembly Known as the World Conference on Indigenous Peoples." A/RES/69/2, 25 September 2014. http://www.un.org/en/ga/search/view_doc.asp?symbol=A/RES/69/2.

United Nations Permanent Forum on Indigenous Issues. "A Study on the Impacts of the Doctrine of Discovery on Indigenous Peoples, Including Mechanisms, Processes, and Instruments of Redress." E/C.19/2014/3, 12-23 May 2014. http://undesadspd.org/Indigenous-Peoples/UNPFIISessions/Thirteenth/Documents.aspx.

United Nations Permanent Observer Mission of the Holy See. "Statement to Economic and Social Council, 9th Session of the Permanent Forum on Indigenous Issues, on Agenda Item 7: Discussion on the Reports 'Impact on Indigenous Peoples of the International Legal Construct Known as the Doctrine of Discovery, which Has Served as the Foundation of the Violation of Their Human Rights' and 'Indigenous Peoples and Boarding Schools: A Comparative Study." 27 April 2010. http://www.ailanyc.org/wp-content/uploads/2010/09/Holy-See.pdf.

United States Department of the Interior, Office of the Solicitor. "Solicitor's Opinions." n.d. http://www.doi.gov/solicitor/opinions.html.

University of Manitoba. "Statement of Apology and Reconciliation to Indian Residential School Survivors." 27 October 2011. http://umanitoba.ca/about/media/StatementOfApology.pdf.

Vatican. "Communiqué of the Holy See Press Office." 29 April 2009. http://www.vatican.va/resources/resources_canada-first-nations-apr2009_en.html.

Vatican. "Pastoral Letter of His Holiness Pope Benedict XVI to the Catholics of Ireland." 19 March 2010. http://www.vatican.va/holy_father/benedict_xvi/letters/2010/documents/hf_ben-xvi_let_20100319_church-ireland_en.html.

World Council of Churches. "Statement on the Doctrine of Discovery and Its Enduring Impact on Indigenous Peoples." 17 February 2012. http://www.oikoumene.org/en/resources/documents/executive-committee/bossey-february-2012/statement-on-the-doctrine-of-discovery-and-its-enduring-impact-on-indigenous-peoples.

7. Websites and Multimedia

Aboriginal Peoples Television Network. "Factsheet." September 2005. http://aptn.ca/corporate/facts.php.

Accessing Justice and Reconciliation Project. http://indigenousbar.ca/indigenouslaw.

Anglican Church of Canada, Mission and Justice Relationships. "Truth and Reconciliation." n.d. http://www.anglican.ca/relationships/trc.

ArtsLink: Residential School Artists. "About ArtsLink." n.d. https://www.edonline.sk.ca/bbcs-webdav/library/materials/ArtsLink/main_pages/about-us.html.

Canada, Aboriginal Affairs and Northern Development Canada. "Christi Belcourt Describes 'Giniigaaniimenaaning.'" n.d. https://www.aadnc-aandc.gc.ca/eng/1353338933878/1353338974873.

Canada, Aboriginal Affairs and Northern Development Canada. "Commemoration 2011-2012: Project Descriptions." n.d. http://www.aadnc-aandc.gc.ca/eng/1370974213551/1370974338097.

Canada, Aboriginal Affairs and Northern Development Canada. "Commemoration 2012-2013: Project Descriptions." n.d. http://www.aadnc-aandc.gc.ca/eng/1370974253896/1370974471675.

Canada, Aboriginal Affairs and Northern Development Canada. "Remembering the Past: A Window to the Future." n.d. http://www.aadnc-aandc.gc.ca/eng/1332859355145/13328594 33503.

Canada, Government of Canada. "Journalists for Human Rights (JHR)." n.d. http://www.canadainternational.gc.ca/libya-libye/highlights-faits/2015/human_rights-droits_personne. aspx?lang=en.

Canada, Parks Canada, Historic Sites and Monuments Board of Canada. "Info Source: Sources of Federal Government and Employee Information." 2013. http://www.pc.gc.ca/clmhc-hsmbc/comm-board/Transparence-Transparency.aspx.

Canada, Parks Canada, Historic Sites and Monuments Board of Canada. "National Program of Historical Commemoration." n.d. http://www.pc.gc.ca/clmhc-hsmbc/ncp-pcn.aspx.

Canadian Conference of Catholic Bishops. "Canadian Catholic Aboriginal Council." n.d. http://www.cccb.ca/site/eng/commissions-committees-and-aboriginal-council/aboriginal-council/canadian-catholic-aboriginal-council.

Canadian Museum for Human Rights. "About the Museum." n.d. https://humanrights.ca/about.

Canadian Roots Exchange. http://canadianroots.ca.

Centre for Youth and Society, University of Victoria. "Residential Schools Resistance Narratives: Significance and Strategies for Indigenous Youth." Video collection, n.d. http://youth. society.uvic.ca/TRC.

First Nations Summit. "Grand Chief Edward John (Akile Ch'oh): Biography." n.d. http://www. fns.bc.ca/about/e_john.htm.

First Voices. "Mikmaw Community Portal." n.d. http://www.firstvoices.com/en/Mikmaw.

Institute for Women's and Gender Studies, University of Winnipeg. "TRC Quilting Project: Education and Art." 2010. http://archive-ca.com/ca/i/iwgs.ca/2012-12-07_875494-titles_7/Fort_Garry_Women_s_Resource_Centre.

International Center for Transitional Justice. "ICTJ/Canada TRC Youth Retreat." Video, 2010. http://vimeo.com/26397248.

International Center for Transitional Justice. *Our Legacy, Our Hope.* Video, 23 May 2012. http://www.youtube.com/watch?v=Xz2SUV0vFCI.

International Coalition of Sites of Conscience. http://www.sitesofconscience.org.

Joseph, Bob. "Shelagh Rogers Her Journey from Her Head to Her Heart as Hon. Witness." Interview, 17 September 2013. http://www.ictinc.ca/blog/shelagh-rogers-journey-head-heart-honorary-witness-trc.

Journalists for Human Rights. "About." n.d. http://www.jhr.ca/en/about.

Kreelak, Martin, director. *Kikkik E1-472.* Film, second version. Inuit Broadcasting Corporation, n.d. http://www.isuma.tv/hi/en/imaginenative/kikkik-e1-472.

Law Commission of Canada. *Justice Within: Indigenous Legal Traditions.* DVD. 2006.

Legacy of Hope Foundation. *"We were so far away": The Inuit Experience of Residential Schools.* Exhibition, 2009. http://weweresofaraway.ca.

Legacy of Hope Foundation. *Where Are the Children? Healing the Legacy of the Residential Schools.* Exhibition, 2009. http://wherearethechildren.ca/en.

Library and Archives Canada. "Aboriginal Heritage." n.d. http://www.bac-lac.gc.ca/eng/discover/aboriginal-heritage/Pages/introduction.aspx#d.

Morris and Helen Belkin Art Gallery. *Witnesses: Art and Canada's Indian Residential Schools.* Exhibition, 6 September to 1 December 2013. http://www.belkin.ubc.ca/past/witnesses.

Muskeg Lake Cree Nation. "Nêhiyaw Wiyasowêwina (Cree Law)." n.d. http://www.muskeg-lake.com/services/community-justice/cree-law.

National Centre for Truth and Reconciliation. "Our Partners." n.d. http://umanitoba.ca/centres/nctr/partners.html.

National Centre for Truth and Reconciliation. "Reconciliation." n.d. http://umanitoba.ca/centres/nctr/reconciliation.html.

Presbyterian Church in Canada, Indian Residential Schools. "Photographs from the Presbyterian Church in Canada Archives." n.d. http://www.presbyterianarchives.ca/RS%20-%20Home%20Page.html.

Project of Heart. http://projectofheart.ca.

Reconciliation Canada. "Chief Joseph Shares His Perspective on Our Partners." Video, 13 September 2013. http://reconciliationcanada.ca/2013/09.

Roots of Empathy. http://www.rootsofempathy.org.

Teslin Tlingit Council. "Clan Based Governance." n.d. http://www.ttc-teslin.com/clan-based-governance.html.

Teslin Tlingit Council. "Constitution." March 2013. http://www.ttc-teslin.com/constitution.html.

Teslin Tlingit Council. "Government Organization Chart." n.d. http://www.ttc-teslin.com/government-organization-chart.html.

Teslin Tlingit Council. "Legislation." n.d.. http://www.ttc-teslin.com/legislation-guiding-principles.html.

Teslin Tlingit Council. "Our Clans." n.d.. http://www.ttc-teslin.com/our-clans.html.

Treaty Relations Commission of Manitoba. "Public Education: Learning Centre." n.d. http://www.trcm.ca/public-education/learning-centre.

Truth and Reconciliation Commission of Canada. *Educating Our Youth.* Video, 19 September 2013. http://www.trc.ca/websites/trcinstitution/index.php?p=3.

Truth and Reconciliation Commission of Canada. *Sharing Truth: Creating a National Research Centre on Residential Schools.* Videos of TRC forum, Vancouver, British Columbia, 1–4 March 2011. http://www.trc.ca/websites/trcinstitution/index.php?p=513.

United Church of Canada, Residential School Archive Project. "The Children Remembered." n.d. http://thechildrenremembered.ca.

United Nations Permanent Observer Mission of the Holy See. "A Short History of the Diplomacy of the Holy See." n.d. http://www.holyseemission.org/about/history-of-diplomacy-of-the-holy-see.aspx.

University of British Columbia Museum of Anthropology. *Speaking to Memory: Images and Voices from the St. Michael's Residential School.* Exhibition, 18 September 2013 to 11 May 2014. http://moa.ubc.ca/portfolio_page/speaking-to-memory.

World Council of Churches. "What Is the World Council of Churches?" n.d. http://www.oikoumene.org/en/about-us.

Index

Page numbers in italics refer to graphs, illustrations, or tables.
Residential schools are indexed under their geographic location, as listed in the Truth and
Reconciliation Report, volume 4, Canada's Residential Schools: Missing Children and Unmarked
Burials, Appendix 1.1 and 1.2, 141–151.
Variations on similar names of people have in some cases been grouped together under one heading.
When this has been done, all variations are represented in the heading.